D0821154

DATE DUE			

HIDDEN POWER

HIDDEN POWER

THE PALACE EUNUCHS
OF IMPERIAL CHINA

MARY M. ANDERSON

PROMETHEUS BOOKS

BUFFALO, NEW YORK

Library of Congress Cataloging-in-Publication Data

Anderson, Mary M.
    Hidden power : the palace eunuchs of imperial China / by Mary M. Anderson.
        p.   cm.
    Includes bibliographical references.
    ISBN 0-87975-574-1
    1. Eunuchs—China—History. 2. China—Court and courtiers.
3. China—Politics and government. I. Title.
DS727.A74   1990
951—dc20
                                                                80-70053
                                                                CIP

To my grandson
Stephen William Howell

Table of Contents

Preface

That emperors of Imperial China kept castrated males as palace servitors and harem chamberlains—often numbering in the thousands—is a well-known fact. Less familiar is the decided influence these eunuchs had in shaping China's 2,000-year history of absolute, autocratic rule. Eunuchs became so powerful that they dominated emperors, gained control of state affairs, and caused the fall of some of China's greatest dynasties. Yet the story of Chinese palace eunuchs has never been thoroughly and systematically traced from their origins in antiquity to their abrupt termination with the fall of the last dynasty in 1911. This book attempts to fill that void.

Who were the untold multitudes down through the ages who lost their manhood to serve the monarchs of China? Why and how were they emasculated? What were the original functions of the eunuchs, and how did their role change over time? Why was this seemingly cruel system of wholesale mutilation accepted as a normal part of Chinese court life? What opportunities allowed this despised class to rise to power in a vast, highly cultured society? Why, with an immense officialdom of sophisticated, educated mandarins, did emperors repeatedly turn to eunuchs as their most trusted agents? As the story of Chinese eunuchs unfolds in the Introduction and following chapters, these and related questions will be addressed.

Aspects of China's culture and long history are presented as a background for eunuch activity during the various dynasties. Individual emperors, empresses, and concubines are introduced as intimate associates of the palace eunuchs. Other personalities famous in Chinese history will appear as they relate to our subject.

This work may be viewed as a window on Imperial China as seen through the eyes of the eunuchs. Their story is important because—as the Chinese themselves believe—if we are ever to understand a people, we must first become familiar with all aspects of their past.

To avoid confusion for the reader, Chinese names wherever possible are rendered in the spelling most familiar to the West, and references and footnotes within the text are kept to a minimum. Writings and records consulted in research are listed in the bibliography.

My special thanks go to typist Betty Nozer, and to Jack Foran, whose careful editing of the manuscript greatly improved it.

Introduction

Eunuchs, males who have been rendered sexually impotent by mutilation or removal of the external genitals, served as palace menials, harem watch-dogs, and spies for rulers in most of the ancient world—kingdoms stretching from Rome, Greece, and North Africa, through the biblical lands, and on across the Asian continent. Nor were *castrati* unknown in modern times. They were idolized in eigtheenth-century opera houses of Europe, having been emasculated as children to preserve their male soprano voices. The practice of using eunuchs for Vatican choirs was banned only in 1878. Castrated aides attended the Great Moghul emperors of India, and the maharajas of Indian princely states under British rule well into the twentieth century. Nowhere, however, were eunuchs of such great and long-continuing historical significance as in the palaces of Imperial China.

Down through the centuries of China's dynastic rule, officials repeatedly memorialized the Dragon Throne, pleading that eunuch interference in state affairs be curbed. However, almost none recommended that the ancient eunuch system be abolished. This is but one indication of how deeply ingrained in Chinese thinking was the custom that allowed only sexless males to serve the Imperial Presence, the ladies of his royal family, and his thousands of concubines, all amassed together in the "Great Within" behind forbidden palace doors.

It should be pointed out that Chinese dynastic histories were all written by mandarins, the educated elite who, as a class, despised the palace eunuchs.

Mandarins alone were eligible to hold office in the bureaucracy, the "Great Without." Men qualified for coveted bureaucratic positions by passing grueling official examinations that required years of arduous study. The examinations were based on the philosophy of Confucius, the Great Sage, whose teachings became the backbone of Chinese culture. Records indicate that Confucius himself, some 500 years before Christ, gave his stamp of disapproval to eunuch assumption of power, thereby lending authority for centuries of Confucianists to defame all palace eunuchs. Some researchers suggest that the scholar-officials hated the eunuchs because, as personal attendants to the sovereign, the eunuchs always had his ear, and so were in a better position than even the most powerful minister to curry favor, exercise influence, and accumulate wealth. Thus, when considering old Chinese accounts of eunuch treachery, allowance must be made for prejudice or exaggeration. Nonetheless, the bulk of evidence weighs so heavily against the eunuchs that few can doubt the harm they did the nation.

The use of eunuchs in Chinese courts was based in very old tradition, and no society clung more tenaciously to long-established custom than the Chinese. Court chronicles reveal that Chinese kings as early as the eighth century B.C., and no doubt long before that, kept castrated servitors. Confucianism exalted all that was ancient, and admonished monarchs of every dynasty to meticulously follow precedents set not only by saintly historical kings of old, but also by god-kings glorified in China's legendary past.

Since remotest times, and especially after the advent of Confucianism, Chinese males, including rulers, demanded strict moral purity in their womenfolk. Hordes of sexually impotent men were needed to guard the chastity of imperial ladies languishing in the teeming women's quarters. The emperor kept the largest harem in the land not only to support his image as paramount personage of the realm, but also to ensure many heirs to the throne in a time of high infant mortality. If the emperor's queens failed to bear a living heir, sons of the highest ranking concubines could succeed to the throne. The presence of numerous ever-watchful eunuchs lurking in the recesses of the sprawling palace guaranteed that each child born therein was sired by the monarch. Non-eunuch males, even relatives of the ruler or of his consorts, were barred from the vicinity of the women's apartments on penalty of death.

Irrefutable royal paternity was essential to Chinese rulers, for the hoary cult of ancestor worship decreed that each emperor must perform the official sacrifices made to his deceased forebears as far back as the dynasty's near-deified founder. Each emperor, as Heaven's representative on earth, had to conduct the vital state religious rites necessary to maintain the harmonious balance between Heaven and the Chinese nation.

Eunuchs were also required to preserve the aura of sacredness and secrecy that surrounded the Imperial Presence. The emperor of China was exalted as the recipient of the mystical Mandate of Heaven that sanctified his right to rule. Since it was believed that this Heaven-sent mandate could be rescinded if the emperor misgoverned or conducted himself unvirtuously, the personal life of the Son of Heaven was carefully shielded from ordinary mortals lest they observe any human failings. Only the "effeminate, cringing eunuchs," slavishly dependent upon the emperor for their very lives, were considered cowed enough to be silent witnesses to his private foibles and weaknesses.

During imperial audiences officials kept their eyes decorously lowered, for to look upon the royal countenance was strictly forbidden. When the emperor proceeded through the capital city carried in the royal sedan chair by eunuchs, bamboo curtains were erected across the side streets to shield him from the vulgar view. All audience-seekers, including envoys from vassal states and courts, had to kowtow before the Chinese emperor by sinking to their knees and knocking their heads nine times on the floor to demonstrate total obeisance.

Much speculation exists as to why most monarchs of China so trusted their eunuchs—one emperor praised them as "creatures docile and loyal as gelded animals"—when bodily mutilation was universally abhorred in orthodox Chinese culture. Loss of limb or castration rendered a man unfit to worship before the carved wooden spirit tablets to which the ancestral souls descended during memorial services. More deplorable still, a eunuch, since he was incapable of siring sons, had no one to perform the obligatory sacrificial rites for his own soul after death. Thus, one who suffered this most shameful of deformities was deemed outside the pale of Chinese society.

The belief was prevalent that a *castrato,* since he would always be childless, would not covet political power and position to pass on to sons, according to the Chinese tradition. Similarly, he would have no need to accumulate riches by selling inside palace information or stealing the treasure and tribute that flowed to the imperial coffers. Yet history repeatedly proved this faith in eunuch passivity and loyalty unfounded. Official records, perhaps unfairly, cite few instances where palace eunuchs displayed genuine fidelity or civic concern.

In Chinese thinking, all forces—indeed, all things—proceed in naturally recurring cycles of *yin* and *yang,* reaching a peak (*yang*) and then inexorably receding to opposite depths (*yin*). (Maleness, strength, and virtue were under the influence of *yang;* while females, eunuchs, and evil were ruled by the forces of *yin.*) The *yin-yang* theory seemed to be borne out in the waxing and waning of eunuch power. What were some of the factors which led to the recurring, disastrous excesses of eunuch influence in the imperial courts?

Male infants sired by the emperor were reared in the profound seclusion of the palace, nourished by wet nurses till weaned. Thereafter, the young princes were placed almost exclusively in the hands of eunuchs who cherished the hope of remaining forever near the seat of power. Toward this end, many eunuchs went to exhaustive lengths to win and hold a future emperor's favor. Unscrupulous, power-hungry eunuchs could—and often did—mold a young heir apparent's character to suit their own ambitions.

Many a prince became emperor while still a child. By the time he had reached his majority, his eunuchs had introduced him to enervating extremes of promiscuity and other debilitating habits. Once corrupted morally and physically, the new sovereign was a weak-willed tool in the hands of his caretakers—easily convinced that enemies and traitors lurked everywhere in the Great Without. In this way, his faith in legitimate government advisors was destroyed. His only recourse was to depend on his eunuchs for information, counsel, and support.

Sometimes eunuchs played upon the fierce female rivalries, jealousies, and raw ambitions prevalent in the harem. There, several thousand ladies competed for the attention of the emperor—their only road to wealth and power for themselves, their clans, and their hoped-for princely sons. More than one eunuch joined forces with a scheming empress or concubine in dark plots to do away with the heir apparent and place her own son or favorite in line for succession. If the intrigue was successful, the conspiring eunuch was in a position to usurp enormous authority.

Often a young ruler found himself completely beholden to eunuchs who had usurped such power that they were able to put him on the throne over a rival candidate. In such cases, the eunuchs were almost impossible to dislodge from power, for they kept control in their own hands from one short reign to the next. In some instances, the emperor actually feared his eunuch "benefactors."

It must be acknowledged that certain Chinese emperors, had it not been for the backing of their eunuchs, would have been powerless in the face of organized factions of officials or mighty consort clans seeking control of the throne. Moreover, though many of the emperors were dominated by their eunuchs, many others throughout China's imperial past were forceful and self-determined, and led their nation to a greatness and level of culture more advanced than those of contemporary civilizations in the West.

All countries large and small suffer one defect in common: the surrounding of the ruler with unworthy personnel. . . . Those who would control rulers first discover their secret fears and wishes.

—Han Fei Tzu, revered Chinese minister of state and man of letters who died 233 B.C.

I

How Ancient Was the Chinese Eunuch System?

SHANG DYNASTY (c. 1766-1122 B.C.)

The very earliest mention of palace eunuchs in China's recorded history is found in Chou Dynasty annals of the eighth century B.C., and sinologists have long assumed that the eunuch system in Chinese courts originated at that time. Now this assumption is being questioned. Indications are that kings of earlier times were already using castrated servitors.

When the Chou Dynasty founder overthrew the House of Shang in 1050 B.C., in setting up Chou rule, he is known to have deliberately continued the Shang Dynasty's institutions and customs. With growing archeological knowledge of these two ancient dynasties, modern scholars are no longer reluctant to project almost all the features of the Chou ruling system—including palace eunuchs—backwards into the Shang era. Moreover, the earliest-mentioned Chou Dynasty eunuchs are alluded to so casually and briefly that the institution appears to be commonplace and completely accepted, as if inherited from older times.

For these reasons, to give a picture of the times and life in the palaces in which the earliest of Chinese eunuchs lived and served, we begin their story with the Shang Dynasty.

Much of our authenticated knowledge of the Shang Dynasty comes from inscriptions in archaic Chinese pictographs on thousands of "oracle bones" unearthed in North Central China during the early decades of the twentieth century. These flat shoulder blade bones of cattle, along with turtle shells, were used by shaman mediums to record the Shang kings' questions—and the answers received—seeking advice or approval from the gods and royal ancestors in matters vital to the ruling family and the nation. Understandably, there would be no reference in these all-important divinations to lowly, castrated palace servants.

However, deciphered oracle-bone inscriptions from the Shang era do tell us of great numbers of war captives taken from defeated enemy tribes, thousands of whom became human sacrifices offered up to the gods and spirits in the kings' religious rites. Conquered warriors of the Chiang sheep-herding tribes, often as many as 200 at a time, were especially favored as victims in these ceremonies.

Prisoners of war also became slaves to Shang rulers. Many of them ended up buried alive with their deceased royal master to serve him in the Afterworld, as heaps of skeletal remains in Shang royal tombs attest. There is little doubt that some of the captured or surrendered enemy were also subdued by castration to become eunuchs for Shang palace service, as was the practice in the following Chou Dynasty.

Writings on both oracle bones and excavated ceremonial vessels confirm, almost exactly, the list of Shang kings handed down through the Chinese generations—a genealogy Western sinologists had heretofore considered purely myth or legend. These ancient pictographs, which are still being deciphered today, give considerable insight into the Shang Dynasty social order, depicting a brilliant, if barbaric, civilization.

The House of Shang ruled China from about 1766 to 1122 B.C., building impressive palaces, temples, and pleasure pavilions in gardens and parks in the capitals. They located their last capital near modern An Yang, in Honan province. Here in the basin of the Yellow River—"the cradle of Chinese civilization"—extensive archeological diggings tell how Shang kings extended China's borders by overcoming neighboring tribes and aborigine peoples. As these new lands were opened up to farming, the supreme Chinese ruler sent out entire family-clans to build and occupy mud-walled, planned villages, overlordship of which was granted to Shang princes, royal ladies, or worthy officials.

Countless inscriptions and artifacts from the crypt of one influential Shang queen reveal that she was bequeathed her own rural town, gathered a peasant militia, and even performed official religious rituals. She was repeatedly the subject of the sovereign's oracle-bone questions regarding her illnesses, childbirths, and general well-being.

Prosperous vassal lords governing outlying city-states organized their palaces and courts as smaller replicas of the Shang king's in the capital. They recruited and led great peasant armies to fight their ruler's many wars of conquest, riding in cumbersome, two-wheeled horse-drawn chariots, several of which have now been excavated. Vassal lords were duty-bound to pay scheduled ceremonial visits to the capital for audiences before the king. There they presented him with tribute—jades, precious stones and artifacts, bones and shells for divinations, as well as stores of grain and local produce to feed the populous central court.

Many skeletons found in tombs of Shang kings are those of palace ladies and attendants who were buried alive with their ruler to pleasure him in the Next World. Also sacrificed were horses and hunting dogs used in great, royal war-like hunts to which all the nobility were invited. Engraved funerary and sacrificial vessels, along with bejewelled ceremonial battle-axes, bells, and weapons, exhibit a level of excellence in bronze metal-working never equalled in later dynasties. Many Shang bronzes are beautifully incised with stylized dragons—that hoary Chinese bringer-of-rain, the emblem sacred to Chinese emperors through all eras of imperial rule. Pictographs on these priceless Shang relics show that writing had already been practiced for a long time, possibly for centuries.

All evidence seems to confirm assertions of ancient Chinese historians that extravagance and wholesale corruption in the last Shang palaces—and a series of weak kings whose reigns were short—led this once strong house into irreversible decline.

The last Shang ruler, King Chou Hsin, is depicted historically as a heartless, greedy, immoral tyrant, the product of a luxurious, dissipated court life. Records show that he once had a concubine ground into mince-meat when she showed disinterest in his lustful demands. For daring to object to his disgraceful excesses, Chou Hsin had a senior lord killed and his flesh prepared as dried meat. When his own uncle rebuked him for gross misrule, King Chou Hsin retorted, "Men say you are a sage, and that the heart of a sage has seven openings,"[1] and he cut his uncle open and tore out his heart to see.

Chou Hsin met his match when he captured the beautiful Ta Chi in a raid on a northern tribe, for she proved to be as wanton and cruel as he was. He made her a concubine in his harem and soon became so utterly enamored of her charms that her every request and most diabolical whims were granted.

Ta Chi successfully plotted to depose the rightful Shang queen. She saw to it that all who opposed her met with horrible death. Some of her victims were tied to metal pillars that were then heated from within by fires which roasted the victims alive. She organized scandalous palace entertainments with voluptuous dancing and lewd songs that greatly amused her, while sober-minded courtiers recoiled in shock.

The most notorious affair devised by the infamous royal couple took place in a forested palace park, the pond therein having been filled with intoxicating liquor on Ta Chi's order. In this "lake of wine," male and female guests cavorted naked, frolicking and gorging themselves among trees hung with shanks of roasted meat—a drunken, erotic orgy destined to remain forever in Chinese memory.

Eventually, in 1050 B.C., the vassal lord governing the city-state of Chou became so outraged at King Chou Hsin's debaucheries and insatiable demands for tribute that he formed an alliance with neighboring tribes and led his armies in open revolt. In the ensuing combat near the capital, royal Shang forces were annihilated. The histories say that blood flowed from the battlefield like a river.

After this humiliating defeat, the Shang king fled back to the court, donned his regal pearl-and-jade ornaments, climbed a high terrace, and hurled himself into the flames of his razed and burning palace. Some say the concubine Ta Chi hung herself, but was disgraced in death when the Chou conqueror decapitated her corpse. Other records maintain that when she was taken captive, her beauty was such that none could bear to kill her, until finally an aged Chou state councilor covered his eyes and put her to death with one blow of his sword.

The Chou victor destroyed the entire Shang capital, but magnanimously allowed the remaining royal relatives to continue their family line out in one of the smaller states—family having always been more important to the Chinese than country.

Thus it is written, "The Shang Dynasty's sacrifices were cut off," meaning that their kings could no longer perform the vital state religious rites of a legitimate ruler. Heaven had withdrawn its mandate from the corrupt House of Shang and bestowed the right to rule upon the "triumphant, virtuous" new king from the Chou state. The Chou Dynasty was to preside over China for nearly the next 900 years.

Many writers now wonder if the wickedness of the last Shang king and his consort was perhaps exaggerated by Chou Dynasty scribes to justify their leader's "unfilial and treasonable act" of rebelling against his king. Others conjecture that the Mandate of Heaven theory may have been invented at this long-ago time to give sanction to the Chou victor's take-over.

It is certain, at least, that concubine Ta Chi's depraved example bolstered the universal Chinese conviction that neither palace women nor eunuchs should ever be allowed to corrupt or influence the sovereign. Given the long memory of the Chinese—and their addiction to their own history—some sinologists even speculate that this age-old conviction played a part in bringing the politically powerful wife of Chairman Mao Tse-Tung to such a fateful end in our own times.

Note

1. C. P. Fitzgerald, *China: A Short Cultural History.*

2

Early Eunuchs in Palace Intrigue
CHOU DYNASTY (1122-250 B.C.)

Over a thousand years before Christ, the first Chou Dynasty kings ordered their lords to organize their courts following precedents set by the preceding Shang Dynasty. From these early beginnings there developed a sprawling, complex, bureaucratic administration that was to characterize imperial Chinese rule for the next 3,000 years.

The earliest Chou Dynasty sovereigns are hallowed as ideal rulers, credited in the histories with having put the empire in order; inspired the people to be unflagging in their work; and by their wisdom and diligence established firm rule. However, the dynasty founders, following old tradition, bequeathed innumerable fiefdoms to members of the Chou royal family and military aides, who became very powerful. This heralded a long "Age of Feudalism" that later was to prove so dangerous to the Chou ruling house and the entire federation of Chinese city-states.

The proud vassal lords, some of whose ancestors had held the same fiefdoms for centuries, considered the peasants who tilled their lands just one rung below themselves in the social order. At the bottom, looked upon with utter disdain, were merchants, artisans, and slaves. Palace eunuchs were not considered a part of the social order or even humanity.

Chou kings and their landed lords were polished, wealthy aristocrats who revered learning, drawing to their courts sages, philosophers, astrologers, diviners, and men of medicine. Official scribes kept careful records of state affairs and the ruler's pronouncements, parts of which are still preserved in old chronicles.

Chou monarchs traced their ancestry directly back to legendary god-kings of remote antiquity. They called their little confederacy "The Middle Kingdom," meaning the center of the civilized world. Men of Chou China were masters of "All Under Heaven," while their tribal and aborigine neighbors were "barbarians" or "dog and reptile people." As Chou borders gradually expanded with continued subjugation of these outsiders, the conquered were considered true Chinese only when they had learned to speak the Chinese language, had adopted Chinese culture, and accepted the Chou Son of Heaven as supreme ruler. Even then, these sinicized subjects were never deemed quite on a par with those whose ancestors had been born in the Yellow River plains—the "original Chinese."

Chou rulers called themselves kings, not emperors. As representatives of Heaven on earth, their most important function was to perform official religious rites at the four seasons, as Shang kings had done before them. At these costly, elaborate ceremonies, wines, grains, and domestic animals were sacrificed to Heaven, the royal ancestors, and deities. It is said that the gods and the shades of the ancestors actually governed Chou China, for rarely did a king make a move or decision, in war or peace, without seeking their approval by means of shaman oracles.

The few incidental and brief references to eunuchs in Chou records indicate that they were already implicated in intrigues among the palace inmates, but their influence had not yet extended into vital affairs of state, as it would in dynasties to follow.

In early Chou centuries, court eunuchs did not even serve their royal master's meals; this was the duty of an official food-taster. A grand chamberlain had management of the palace, with command over the eunuchs and domestics. Apparently, the prime duty of Chou eunuchs was to act as personal lackeys to the king, and to guard and serve his royal consorts and harem concubines. Eunuchs performed these same duties in palaces of princes and lords out in the countryside.

One of the earliest recorded incidents involving eunuchs indicates that by 720 B.C. they had already learned to pander to the man who showed greatest potential for success. One of the princely state rulers was holding court when a powerful minister dared to murder a rival official under the very eyes of the prince and his courtiers. Thunderstruck at this affront, a group of ministers devised a plan to kill the offender next day at court. Their scheme went awry, however, when a eunuch named Ch'in-yen secretly warned the minister who had committed the murder of the conspiracy against his life. The following morning, the minister strode into court leading 800 armed soldiers and slaughtered not only his fellow ministers but the ruling prince as well. Eunuch Ch'in-yen went down tersely in history for his treacherous interference in the affair.

Annals from 650 B.C. reveal that palace eunuchs were frequently used to carry out their king's private punishments and executions. The monarch at that time, Chin Hsien-kung, at the instigation of his favorite concubine, ordered a eunuch named Kuo-chi to slay his son, the prince who was second in line to the throne. Secretly informed of this plot, the prince narrowly escaped by scaling the palace walls. He was so closely pursued that the eunuch managed to cut off a sleeve of his robe with a swipe of his knife. This piece of cloth was all the evidence Kuo-chi had to prove to his master that he had done his utmost to carry out the royal will.

Another episode from about this same time attests that eunuchs were already manipulating inner-palace affairs to suit their own ends. It also brings to mind the old saying that nothing was sweeter to the Chinese soul than revenge. The feudal ruler of Ch'i city-state had a favorite eunuch named I-li who bore an intense hatred toward the ruler's heir apparent for having kicked him as a punishment for insolent insubordination. I-li seethed with resentment, but kept the matter from the ruler, knowing that an investigation would expose his own misconduct. Instead, he bided his time until he could convince the ruler's most beloved concubine that the crown prince was vilifying her name by spreading rumors casting doubt on her chastity. This misinformation so inflamed the concubine that she determined to have the prince done away with. Scratching her own face until the blood ran, and disheveling her hair and robes, she ran to her royal master, claiming that his son had attempted to take liberties with her virtue, a crime against the throne. Enraged, the ruler ordered I-li to behead his son at once.

Having been secretly forewarned—as so often happened in these stories—the prince managed to escape by night from the palace. He was apprehended by authorities for being abroad, taken to a censor for judgment, and his royal identity soon came to light. The sympathetic censor concealed the heir apparent in his own residence, while the eunuch and palace soldiers scoured the area. When they searched the censor's home, the prince, disguised as a female family member, again eluded them. Eventually, the prince fled his home state altogether, but in later years, on learning of his father's death, he returned to the palace and chopped off the head of his old enemy, eunuch I-li.

Little information is available to reveal who or what the Chou eunuchs were before their mutilation, but indications are that most were neighboring tribals captured in the kings' wars of expansion. Some were Chinese subjects who suffered castration in penalty for crimes against the throne.

Unequivocal records exist of Chou Dynasty modes of punishment. These included: cutting off the nose, ears, hands, or feet, piercing an eye, tattooing or branding the face, imprisonment in shackles, or loss of manhood by castration. A common sentence was exile of the offender to distant frontiers, and permanent banishment of his female family members outside the capital to tend the royal cemeteries.

Condemned noblemen and high ministers were generally exempt from mutilations. Instead, they were allowed—indeed expected—to save themselves, their families, and their ancestors from eternal disgrace by committing ritual suicide.

Capital punishment often included extermination of the criminal and his extended family down to the last child. Decapitation was common; the severed head was mounted on a pole in the market place. In extreme cases, the penalty was the slow, excruciating "death of a thousand cuts"—the terrible "slicing and mincing process." Many criminals temporarily survived being chopped in half at the waist. The upper body was displayed publicly on a platform until it toppled in death.

Those condemned to castration were more fortunate. The Chinese term for castration, *kung-hsing,* meant palace punishment. One official who had offended the throne and suffered emasculation referred to himself as *hsing-chen,* meaning palace servant, leaving no doubt that some castrated wrongdoers served in Chou palaces as eunuchs.

As the luxury of court life and the size of the harems increased, with a consequent increase in the demand for eunuch attendants, destitute Chinese subjects had themselves or their sons castrated for service in the palace. In later dynasties, the corps of imperial eunuchs would come almost entirely from impoverished Chinese homes.

After some three centuries of strong central rule, a disaster struck the House of Chou from which it never completely recovered. Here again, as in the Shang Dynasty, trouble started with a concubine's hold over the monarch. This time it was Chou Dynasty's King Yu, who ruled in 771 B.C. Concubine Pao Szu came to his harem as a peace offering from a neighboring ruler, and King Yu soon fell completely under the spell of her somber beauty. Though Pao Szu docilely accepted the infatuated king's attentions, he failed to make her happy, for she was never known to smile or laugh. The story has it that she had the morbid habit of tearing vast quantities of silk into bits each day. Even the grandest palace amusements featuring performing bears, jugglers, and whirling dancers failed to relieve her chronic melancholia.

At last, the frustrated king hit upon a solution. One night he had all the beacon fires ignited in the surrounding hills—flares which normally signaled to outlying vassal lords and their troops that the capital was under attack. When Pao Szu saw the hilltops outlined in a glow which lit up the night sky and clouds, she was delighted. And when the lords and knights came galloping into the capital, bristling with bows and arrows, clanging bronze-bladed halberds about in a fruitless search for invaders, Pao Szu turned to her royal master and burst into peals of laughter.

Happy to have found a way to make Pao Szu happy, King Yu performed this ruse for his favorite again and again. But he "cried wolf" once too often. When barbarian nomadic horsemen from the west staged a ferocious surprise attack and the beacon signals were lit in earnest, the military lords ignored the call, sure they were being tricked once more. The barbarians pillaged the capital, overran the palace, and killed King Yu. The members of the royal family who survived the onslaught beat an ignoble retreat to the east, leaving troops from their vassal state of Ch'in to drive off the marauders. The House of Chou was forced to reestablish its capital and dynastic line at Loyang in present-day Honan province.

Although the Chou Dynasty held nominal rule from its new capital for some 500 years longer, it never regained its former position of respect and authority over the feudal states. As Chou dominion weakened, the petty princes and landed lords ruled their realms like independent kings, all but ignoring the Son of Heaven. Their primary interest seemed to be waging chivalrous warfare against one another at the slightest provocation.

For a long time the provincial lords remained faithful to hallowed tradition and journeyed to Loyang for the required audiences and official religious sacrifices. The Chou Son of Heaven still sat on the Dragon Throne, decked in rich ceremonial robes of state, surrounded by courtiers and enunchs. Yet in reality, some twenty "Great Families" commanded the armies and controlled political matters from their outlying feudal courts. Rarely was the Chou king called upon to arbitrate their frequent disputes.

During these centuries of feudal anarchy and dwindling dynastic control, some of China's greatest philosophers flourished. These men pondered the nature of good government and of virtue in rulers, and the means of saving the nation. Among these schools of philosophers were the Legalists, who believed in strict controls and harsh punishments, and the Taoists, who taught that the less government interference in the lives of the people the better.

The most famous of all the philosophers, however, was the Great Sage, Confucius, who lived from 551 to 479 B.C. He moved from state court to state court, preaching a return to the golden past when wise and kindly kings of legend presided as "father and mother to all." He advocated ancient ritual, rigid moral codes, and fixed rules of official and social conduct, according to the decrees of Heaven.

In his own time Confucius was not without opposition. One opponent sneered, "He eats without tilling the soil and clothes himself without weaving. Wagging his lips and clacking his tongue, he presumes to be a source of Right and Wrong in order to delude rulers of All Under Heaven."[1] Although Confucius failed utterly to bring about change while he lived, generations of his adherents preserved and promulgated his teachings. Some centuries after his death, his high-minded ideals would catch hold, and Confucianism eventually became synonymous with the term "Chinese culture." Confucius' thoughts gradually came to pervade every area of Chinese life.

Though Confucianists have always maintained that the Great Sage himself abhorred the palace eunuch system—or at least condemned eunuch acquisition of power—there is little in the old records to bolster this belief. It is written, however, that during his wanderings, Confucius quit one petty state entirely, indignant that the ruling noble had lowered himself to ride in the same chariot with one of his eunuchs. According to this story, Confucius seems to have believed that eunuchs should be kept in their place as palace menials.

We know also that Confucius revered the ancient literature preserved in the Book of Odes, and included it in his own teachings. One of these poems opines: "These two can neither be taught nor controlled—palace women and eunuchs."[2] If Confucius himself held this view, as his disciples maintained, he may well have been among the earliest of those who protested against the eunuch institution.

The philosophers proved unable to halt the collapse of the Chou central governing power. By the fifth century B.C., the unruly kingdoms were embroiled in bloody civil wars that were to last for the next 200 years, called the era of Warring States. China was decimated. All traces of old Chou chivalry disappeared, and the feudal kingdoms fell upon one another in vicious, ruthless contests for supremacy or survival. Some feudal lords even assumed the imperial title of king, completely repudiating Chou rule. Greed, deceit, and disloyalty became watchwords, as incessant surprise attacks and sudden raids wiped out whole city-state populations.

The histories say that hordes of peasant soldiers, forced into constant battle, "had to wear their armor day and night until their bodies were covered with lice."[3] The powerful accumulated great wealth, while the masses "could not even get enough dregs and chaff to fill their bellies."[4]

After one victory alone, the old Chou fiefdom of Ch'in buried 400,000 soldiers alive. Ch'in, in the northwest fringes of the Middle Kingdom, was the state whose armies, centuries before, had rescued the Chou royal family from barbarian attack and moved them east to Loyang. In payment for their loyalty, Ch'in state rulers had been bequeathed the Chou Dynasty's old ancestral homelands in Shensi. By the third century B.C., the state of Ch'in had become so powerful militarily that it was single-handedly conquering neighboring principalities "like a silkworm devouring mulberry leaves."[5]

Heady with power, the leaders of Ch'in would continue to pile up victories until they had subdued all China. Little could they know that a palace eunuch would be instrumental in bringing down their own ruling house.

Notes

1. E. H. Schafer, *Ancient China.*
2. H. G. Creel, *The Birth of China.*
3. Isu-ma Chien, *Shih Chi,* in B. Watson, *Records of the Grand Historian of China.*
4. Ibid.
5. Louis Heren, *China's Three Thousand Years.*

3

One Eunuch Fells a Dynasty
CH'IN DYNASTY (221-207 B.C.)

The proud Chou Dynasty fiefdoms had always regarded the feudal state of Ch'in as semibarbarous, for its people, and evidently its overlords, were rude hill men, descended from an uncertain mixture of Chinese, Tibetan, and Mongolian stock. They were not quite "pure Chinese." One Chou nobleman sniffed that before the Ch'in state adopted the refined court music of its more civilized neighbors, their palace orchestra "pounded earthenware pots and jars, and rubbed bones together while intoning the discordant cry of 'Hu! Hu! Hu!' "[1] Another groused that the inhabitants of Ch'in were greedy, miserly, contrary, and cunning, and would even betray their own family members.

Strategically located in the "land within the pass," its capital near modern Sian, the state of Ch'in was looked upon with great fear during the Warring States period, for it had embarked with terrifying success on the goal of "gobbling up all China." State after state had been ruthlessly overrun by Ch'in's formidable armies, which left decapitated bodies by the thousands strewn over the countryside. By 256 B.C., Ch'in had overcome the capital at Loyang, putting an end to Chou Dynasty rule, but the whole of China was still far from subdued.

"The Great Beast of Ch'in," as the state was called, owed much of its success to a court minister, Lord Shang. He had set up a powerful governing organization following the philosophy of the Legalists, many aspects of which would remain forever a part of imperial rule. Lord Shang had no time for pious Confucian abstractions like humility, honor of tradition, and noble example. He put his faith in luck, cunning, and absolute tyranny, and made the Ch'in state invincible by instituting severe laws, merciless punishments, and compulsory military recruitment for all subjects.

So unbending was Lord Shang that when the Ch'in state crown prince broke one of his regulations, he had the prince's tutor severely punished for failing to teach his pupil the law. At the Ch'in ruler's death, Lord Shang, fearing execution at the hands of the former prince and now the new ruler, who hated him, undertook to overthrow the state. When his forces were defeated and Lord Shang himself fell in battle, the new ruler had him tied between four war chariots and pulled to pieces.

Another advisor at the Ch'in court, a roving scholar, foolishly preached Confucian ideals of virtue in rulers and morality in governance. Incensed, the ruler had him punished by castration, saying: "Were I to abide by this prig's pratings, we would be completely annihilated by the other warring kingdoms."[2] The offender served as a eunuch in the palace, while the ruler forged ahead with the business of "rolling up China like a mat."

In 246 B.C. a thirteen-year-old prince of questionable paternity became ducal ruler of Ch'in. He continued the conquests of his predecessors with such savagery that by 221 B.C. he had subdued all China and had the feudal kingdoms begging for mercy. It is written that from beginning to end the Ch'in conquest cost a million and a half Chinese lives.

When the mighty Ch'in victor set himself up on the Dragon Throne of the Middle Kingdom as Son of Heaven, he assumed the grandiose title *Ch'in Shih Huang Ti,* First August Emperor of the Ch'in Dynasty, a near-sacred honorific, heretofore accorded only to holy kings of antiquity.

Chinese historians have always characterized the First Emperor as a despot and egomaniac, and in his own time he was bitterly despised nationwide. Records describe him as a man with a prominent nose, large piercing eyes, chest of a bird of prey, voice of a jackal, and heart of a wolf, a man "entirely without beneficence." A portrait painted after his death depicts an imposing giant of a man with forward-jutting bearded jaw, bearing a huge sheathed sword on his ample chest. The histories say his energy was such that he could read through 120 pounds of official bamboo-strip court records each day. (This was a few centuries before a Chinese court eunuch discovered the making of paper.)

One of the First Emperor's earliest reforms was to abolish the old feudal system by refusing to grant any Chinese soil as fiefs to his relatives and aides. He forced 120,000 old noble families to relocate from their vassal states to his new capital near modern Sian, to populate the capital and

to keep them under his thumb. His own loyal officials and generals administered the city-states and garrisoned commanderies.

To prevent insurrection, the First Emperor decreed that all metal lances,
arrowheads, knives, and utensils be confiscated nationwide and sent to the
capital. There he had them melted down and cast into twelve gigantic statues
of warriors to "guard" the imperial palace. For the same reason, he razed
all provincial fortifications, defense works, and even mud-walls of farm
villages. These moves were very unpopular, but helped put an abrupt end
to the old feudal wars. However, with the end of the feudal wars, hordes
of peasant soldiers were left idle to roam the roads, and the humiliated
aristocracy smoldered with rage and bided their time.

In 214 B.C., determined to wipe out all opposition and egged on by
his Legalist chief minister Li Ssu, the First Emperor committed the infamous
crime known as the "Burning of the Books." Ancient court records and
histories were burned, and the beloved classics—except books on sorcery,
divination, medicine, and horticulture—and especially the teachings of Confucius, were ordered to be burned. Refusal to comply was subject to the
penalty of death.

The Burning of the Books earned the First Emperor the hatred of
Confucian intellectuals for all time. Much learning went up in flames. Some
460 scholars who tried to conceal their manuscripts were executed and
thrown into pits, or as other sources say, castrated and buried alive. For
generations the Chinese expressed their anger at this literary conflagration
by befouling the First Emperor's grave. (Within two centuries most of the
works would be recompiled from copies discovered in the imperial archives,
private editions secreted away in walls or other hiding places, or from the
memories and imaginations of generations of devout Confucian disciples.)

Expert armies of the Ch'in emperor vastly expanded China's territory,
conquering and sinicizing aborigines as far south as the Yangtze River.
To the north, marauding barbarian horsemen were driven back onto the
Mongolian steppes. To keep them there, the First Emperor sent his strongest
general, Meng Tien, with thousands upon thousands of conscripted laborers,
slaves, war captives, and castrated criminals to build the Great Wall.

This stupendous undertaking was accomplished by connecting small
fortifications which already guarded northern valley passes, and extending
the fortification to the eastern sea. Topped by a highway studded with
lookout towers, in just ten years' time, this mammoth defensive barrier
had snaked its 2,000 mile way across the face of China to the far northwest.
Though it became a wonder of the world, the Chinese have ever regarded
the Great Wall as a great sorrow, saying that a million laborers perished,
for every stone cost a human life.

There is little doubt that the First Emperor was one of the ancient world's great builders. Under his rule, peasants were conscripted to serve one month each year in the local militia, another month far from home in imperial armies, and yet another month on far-flung construction projects. Parts of the First Emperor's canal and irrigation systems, especially the famous works in the Szechuan hills, have been maintained for use to this day. His three-lane imperial highways radiated out from the capital "tree-lined and fifty paces wide." These roads, waterways, and horse-relay post stations greatly improved communications, facilitating the movement of troops as well as produce and treasure demanded under his grueling tribute-tax system. They also eased the way for rebels swarming toward the capital when the great revolts arose.

Some 700,000 conscripted laborers built the First Emperor's magnificent palace complex with its protecting walls extending for miles out into the countryside. Landscaped parks and gardens surrounded the main palace, of which the audience hall would hold 10,000 men. Scores of residential and pleasure pavilions were connected by enclosed overhead walkways and underground passages, so that none but a handful of eunuchs would know the First Emperor's whereabouts. He had already barely escaped three assassination attempts. Revelation of his nightly change of sleeping quarters was punished with certain death.

The First Emperor pleasured himself in his expansive gardens, choosing company from among his 3,000 concubines. When he found the grounds could not be maintained by female laborers alone, he selected vast numbers of youths for the purpose, having first had them castrated to protect the harem ladies' chastity. This is one of the first recorded instances where Chinese males were made eunuchs for reasons other than punishment.

While his palace was still being built, court geomancers and diviners selected a scenic spot in the city suburbs as the most propitious location for the emperor's tomb. Here, they assured him, he would find eternal rest where the unseen natural forces—*feng-shui,* meaning wind and water—could not disturb him. His grand, underground mausoleum was modeled after his main palace, with all the heavenly constellations depicted across the ceiling and a map of his earthly domain etched into the bronze-plated floor. Aboveground rose a man-made tumulus of rock and soil planted with trees so it would pass as a natural mountain. Ingenious mechanical devices were erected across the vault entrance to bring instant death to grave robbers who might seek the priceless treasures that were to accompany the First Emperor to the Afterworld. Builders, workmen, and artisans who knew the secrets of the tomb were buried alive nearby.

Chinese archeologists first excavated some of this vast, 2,000-year-old cemetery in 1974, and its contents astounded the world. A short distance from the First Emperor's still-to-be-explored mausoleum, a mammoth vault contained 7,000 brightly painted, life-size pottery soldiers and horses. Each man's figure is precisely cast to show an individual ethnic facial type. Another crypt yielded several half-size replicas of horses pulling two-wheeled war chariots, all cast in solid bronze. Thus was the First Emperor determined to be protected by a mighty army, even in death.

The First Emperor whipped his nation into shape by standardizing laws, customs, weights and measures, coinage—even the length of axles on carriages and dray carts. Without doubt, his most long-lasting reform was the standardization throughout the land of written Chinese characters so they were legible to subjects who spoke entirely different dialects. Still today, Chinese people of different tongues can easily make themselves mutually understood by tracing out the characters with a forefinger on an open palm.

Despite his genius, the First Emperor was as susceptible to gross superstition and belief in magic as his contemporaries nationwide. Morbidly afraid of death, he surrounded himself with shaman diviners, sorcerers, alchemists, and charlatans who encouraged in him the hope of discovering the magic potion which—Taoists claimed—would bring him everlasting life. The elixir of immortality could be found, they convinced him, on three mythical islands off the Shantung coast, where dwelt the Immortal Spirits themselves.

One palace magician claimed that he had personally visited these magic isles and learned that the Immortals would divulge the elixir recipe only after receiving countless "virgin youths and maidens of good family" in prepayment. These the emperor immediately dispatched, loaded in several ships. The huge party was never heard from again. Some say they were swallowed up by a monstrous fish—or capsized in a fierce windstorm. Others are convinced they became the inhabitants of a Japanese island, and were afraid to return to face the wrath of an emperor who had been deceived by sorcerers.

On his frequent long inspection trips around the empire, always accompanied by many members of the court, the First Emperor loved most to gaze out across the eastern sea, hoping the Immortals might appear before his August Presence. He called himself Lord of Ten-thousand Years, expecting that he and his descendants would rule forever. But during a sojourn to the coast in 210 B.C.—after barely a dozen years as Son of Heaven—he made religious sacrifices on the holy mountain of Tai Shan, and then suddenly sickened and died.

His accompanying top minister Li Ssu and chief eunuch Chao Kao hurriedly connived to conceal the news from the rest of the entourage, fearing an attempt to seize the throne before they could consolidate power in their own hands. Toward this end, as the long procession made its slow way back to the capital, they had the imperial chariot followed by a cart of reeking, rotting fish, which successfully overpowered the telltale odor of a decomposing corpse. During the journey back to the capital, the two conspirators laid plans for a vicious palace coup.

Unbeknownst to the court, the First Emperor, in one of his last decrees, had designated his eldest son as his successor to the Ch'in Dynasty throne. This prince was now at the northern frontier with General Meng Tien and his armies, undergoing light punishment for his objection to the Burning of the Books. Minister Li Ssu and eunuch Chao Kao promptly destroyed the dead ruler's decree and forged a false imperial edict which condemned both the general and crown prince to death. When this decree reached the general and the prince by imperial messenger, the Ch'in heir apparent dutifully committed suicide.

Before taking his own life by swallowing poison, the proud General Meng Tien told the envoy, "For three generations my family has served the House of Ch'in. Now in command of 300,000 troops, I have the power to stage a rebellion, but I prefer death, for I am unwilling to disgrace my ancestors, and reluctant to forget the honors which the First Emperor bestowed upon me."[3] In later centuries, as scholarly Chinese gentlemen reread this famous statement of highest loyalty in the old records, they were often literally moved to tears.

Once the deceased emperor was safely laid in his sarcophagus, surrounded by all palace ladies who had not borne him a child, the great burial vault was sealed. Quickly minister Li Ssu and eunuch Chao Kao contrived to put on the throne a younger Ch'in prince as Second Emperor of the Dynasty. Eunuch Chao Kao had long been insinuating himself into this prince's favor with extravagant flattery and by catering to his every wish, while keeping him entirely ignorant of government affairs. As a result, the prince came to the Chinese throne an inexperienced, uninformed incompetent, completely under the sway of the scheming eunuch.

It has always been said that eunuch Chao Kao and the Second Emperor had all the remaining children of the imperial family murdered and buried in a crypt near their famous father, thereby removing any possibility of inner-palace designs on the throne. Archeologists recently have found a tomb near the First Emperor's tumulus containing a group of small skeletons believed to be those of the Second Emperor's young brothers and sisters.

If histories from this ancient era are to be believed, eunuch Chao Kao went to absurd extremes to usurp control at court. One story tells how, before completely taking over, he tested the docility of the palace courtiers.

He presented a live deer as a gift to the Second Emperor, saying: "This is a horse, Your Majesty." When the emperor turned to attending officials for their reaction, most of them remained determinedly silent. Others, with fearful glances at the eunuch, readily kowtowed and agreed that the animal was indeed a horse. Chao Kao soon sorted out the silent objectors and had them executed, considering them enemies who would one day oppose his will.

During the first year of the Second Ch'in Emperor's reign, a revolt broke out, instigated by a common soldier and the men in his unit. Rather than be executed for unavoidably failing to reach their camp on time— as was Ch'in policy—they had decided it was wiser to risk death as rebels. "Carrying only sticks and garden poles as weapons," this small band sparked a flame of revolution that was to ignite all China. Homeless peasants and soldiers wandering the countryside, many of whom had turned to banditry, rallied to the rebels' cry. Soon old noble lords, scholars, and "the whole populace rose up like a great wind" against the oppression of Ch'in rule. At first, the imperial armies were able to hold the rebel hordes in check, but within months the united revolutionaries were gaining the upper hand.

Eunuch Chao Kao, having secluded the Second Emperor in the palace, isolated from all other advisors, easily cajoled him into believing his repeated assurances that all was well.

When one imperial army was forced to retreat before the onslaught of strong rebel troops, an envoy was sent from the Ch'in court to seek out the general in command. Knowing that failure in battle entailed a death sentence for the leader, the distraught general hastily dispatched an aide to the palace to plead his case. Upon arrival, the aide was accosted and threatened by Chao Kao, and forcibly denied audience with the emperor.

After assessing the frightening situation at court, the aide barely escaped with his life to report back to his general: "Eunuch Chao Kao is in complete control of the palace, and the officials are entirely powerless. Even if we again win a battle, the eunuch, through jealous spite, will only discredit us further. And should we suffer another setback by the revolutionaries, we will never escape the death penalty at the eunuch's hands."[4] The general and his armies defected to the rebels, soon to be followed by other imperial forces. Thus, the records say, "The empire slipped from the House of Ch'in like a fleeing deer, and the whole world joined in its pursuit."[5]

Finally, in 208 B.C., Prime Minister Li Ssu—after watching with trepidation Chao Kao's single-handed assumption of control—unwisely advised the eunuch to be less bold in taking over. He further dared to suggest that greater attention be paid the desperate military situation. For this, the eunuch had him thrown into prison, where he "suffered all five mutilations" and was finally "sawn asunder"—cut in two at the waist.

The great rebel armies, led by the common soldier who instigated the revolt, who was now supreme commander, continued to pile up victories. Eunuch Chao Kao feared for his own life, should the emperor learn how he had been deceived. In a desperate decision to make the first move, Chao Kao had the ruler dethroned, assassinated, and replaced by the son of the original Ch'in crown prince. Though this unfortunate third ruler of the Ch'in Dynasty was to sit as a puppet on the Dragon Throne for only forty-three days, when Chao Kao's crimes became evident, he succeeded in having the eunuch put to death.

The Ch'in capital fell to the rebel commander, who set up headquarters at the outskirts of the city. The third ruler of Ch'in, a rope tied about his neck, indicating abject surrender, rode out from the palace to the rebel encampment in a common carriage drawn by a single white horse, the color of mourning. As he handed over the imperial seal and insignia, rebel officers demanded his execution, but their victorious commander told them: "To kill a man who has already surrendered would bring bad luck."[6] He turned the degraded monarch over to the care of his generals. Eventually this last Ch'in ruler fell under the control of another rebel leader, who murdered him, set fire to the great Ch'in palace, razed the capital to the ground, and carried off all the imperial women and royal treasures.

Official scribes who compiled the history of the Ch'in Dynasty fulminated against eunuch Chao Kao, who dared usurp control of the Chinese throne and precipitated the fall of an imperial ruling house. Forever afterwards, his despised name would be held up to Chinese emperors as a dire warning against allowing eunuchs any influence over them.

Also bitterly reviled through the whole time of imperial rule was the First Emperor of the Ch'in Dynasty, the "infamous tyrant" who tried to destroy Confucian ideals and "heartlessly disregarded the welfare of his subjects."[7] All emperors from then on would assiduously avoid any act which might result in comparison with the First Emperor.

However, in 1973, it was reported in a Taiwan newspaper, the aging Chairman Mao Tse-tung, who then controlled Communist China, contemptuously announced to his enemies at home and abroad: "You have berated me by comparison to the First Emperor, who was a dictator. I have constantly admitted that I am just that. Who was this great First Emperor? All he did was bury alive 460 Confucian scholars at the Burning of the Books, while I have buried 46,000! You berate me as another First Emperor, but you are wrong—I have outdone him a hundred times." This was the Chairman's response to criticism of the utter chaos caused by his Cultural Revolution of the 1960s and 1970s, wherein Mao, like the First

Emperor 2,000 years before him, sought to eradicate what he considered corrupt and outmoded thinking.

Founded by the victorious rebel commander, the new House of Han would rule for the next 400 years as one of China's most revered dynasties. The Han Dynasty was the first of the long-lasting regimes to be fatally undermined by organized eunuch power.

Notes

1. J. Gernet, *Ancient China.*
2. D. Bloodworth, *The Chinese Looking Glass.*
3. J. Li Dun, *The Civilization of China.*
4. B. Watson, *Records of the Grand Historian of China.*
5. Ibid.
6. Ibid.
7. Ibid.

4

A Court Beset by Consorts and Eunuchs

EARLY HAN DYNASTY (207-141 B.C.)

There were two Han dynasties, the first spanning the two centuries before Christ, and the second the two centuries after. This 400-year era was so highly regarded that the people of China have ever since preferred to be called the Sons of Han or Men of Han. Even today, citizens of "pure" Chinese blood are known as "Han Chinese," while aborigines, tribals, Mongolians, Tibetans, Muslims—the millions of Chinese subjects of non-Chinese extraction—are known as "the minority races."

During the four centuries of Han Dynasty rule, China became the leading power of Asia, rivaling in strength the distant Roman Empire, which was her contemporary. Aggressive Han armies expanded China's domain almost to her present vast proportions. The Han centuries are especially revered in Chinese annals as the era when Confucianism was revived, reworked, and promoted to become the guiding doctrine of imperial rule for the next 2,000 years.

The founder of Han Dynasty, the crude, jovial farmer and village headman who led the great revolt against Ch'in Dynasty rule, was one of the few Chinese emperors born of the common people. Shrewd in the ways of his countrymen, Emperor Kao Tsu attracted droves of loyal adherents. By 206 B.C. this self-made general had dethroned the last Ch'in ruler, but then had to spend the next four years fighting off, or trying to outwit, rival Chinese strongmen contending for supreme power. When finally, more through guile and deceit than prowess in battle, Kao Tsu overcame his most aristocratic and dangerous adversary, he allowed himself to be declared emperor, naming his new dynasty the Han, after the petty state where he had been military governor during his climb to the top.

Emperor Kao Tsu located his new capital at Chang An, a few miles from modern Sian—just across the Wei River from the razed Ch'in Dynasty capital. He used an outlying Ch'in hunting park lodge as one of his early palaces.

Kao Tsu found himself ruler of a nation so exhausted and impoverished from years of civil strife that he could not locate, in all the land, four like-colored horses to draw his imperial carriage. Even his top officials had to ride in ox-drawn carts, like common folk. Suspecting that the widespread food shortages and exorbitant prices were caused by hoarding and speculating by greedy merchants, Kao Tsu barred this despised class from holding office, from wearing silk, or riding in carts, and saddled them with heavy taxation.

To rule his unruly empire, Kao Tsu wisely retained the strict laws of the preceding dynasty, but contrary to the practice in the preceding dynasty, administered justice with a measure of patience, tact, and leniency. He appointed generals and officials from among his comrades-in-arms who had long supported him, and made other loyal followers palace stewards, chamberlains, secretaries, and intermediaries between the inner and outer courts. When some of his rough-and-ready generals fell to quarreling over his appointments and largess, Kao Tsu did not hesitate to have most of them beheaded, perhaps fearing rivalry from former warriors who had once been his equals.

Fully aware of the damage done by one eunuch in the Ch'in Dynasty, Kao Tsu kept these palace servitors under tight control. Eunuchs are seldom mentioned in the histories of his reign. It has been observed that Chinese historians through the whole period of imperial rule largely ignored palace eunuchs and the peasantry—until either of these two classes rose up to become a menace to the Confucian state.

Although Kao Tsu had no patience with the pompous pretentions of Confucian intellectuals—he had once seized one of their distinctive tall scholar hats and urinated in it—he now had the good sense to invite them into his government. He needed them to bring a semblance of dignity and proper ritual to a court where his hard-drinking cohorts had been raising such havoc. Only to a few of his sons and younger brothers did the emperor grant principalities, and he distributed these kingdoms in such a way that they "interlocked like the teeth of a dog" to protect the House of Han. Thus, Kao Tsu gradually developed a functioning bureaucracy, and allowed the nation time to relax and recover from the rebellions that overthrew Ch'in rule.

Across the Mongolian steppes to the north, tribes of fierce nomadic horsemen who for decades had been marauding into North China, by this time had become federated under a single strong chieftain. These 200,000-some expert mounted archers were now posing a formidable threat to China. In 198 B.C., after they had penetrated the Great Wall and raided areas south of the wall for several days straight, Kao Tsu decided it wisest to sue for peace. In the peace pact he agreed to send the barbarian chieftain an annual subsidy of foodstuffs, wines, grains, silks, as well as one of his own concubines to wed. The khan of the nomads dispatched his own court eunuchs south to escort the new Chinese bride to his encampment in the wild northern grasslands. Chinese poets have ever lamented the fate of this "princess"—the "sad little Chinese partridge who was sacrificed to the savage bird of the north." This policy of pacifying the barbarians with gifts and brides was long continued under Kao Tsu's successors.

Though the earthy Emperor Kao Tsu was a known bisexual, a womanizer, and heavy drinker, his capable, strong-willed village wife stayed by his side through all the vicissitudes of his rise to power. Her astute advice and her instigation of reprisals against his enemies on every side had contributed greatly to his successes. Now that he was emperor, she held the title Empress Lu and could look forward to the day when their son, Hui Ti, would inherit the throne, and she would be mother of an emperor as regent and dowager empress. However, as Emperor Kao Tsu aged, he longed to please a beloved younger concubine, Lady Chi, by making their son Chao the heir. Kao Tsu genuinely loved this lively boy who was so much like himself. In the end, though, the better judgment of court sages prevailed, and the emperor was forced to bow to the dictates of tradition: his son by his original wife, Empress Lu, remained the legitimate heir. Empress Lu never forgot nor forgave Lady Chi, who came so close to replacing her.

After only twelve years on the throne, Kao Tsu fell ill of complications from an old battle wound. He refused all medical aid, holding court physicians in the same contempt that he bore towards intellectuals in general. As a result, this robust peasant ruler died in the Palace of Lasting Joy at fifty-two years of age.

His meek, sensitive son Hui Ti was enthroned as emperor, while Empress Lu—now dowager empress—came into her own as his regent. To fortify her position, she ruthlessly had her husband's imperial family members executed, and banished to distant regions influential ministers who might oppose her, replacing them with her own clansmen. She and her relatives would be only the first of the consort families that would make a bid for the throne of China, though all such attempts would end in disaster.

Young Emperor Hui Ti sat on the throne "with folded hands and unruffled garments" while his mother ran the government. She held to the custom which denied uncastrated men close contact with imperial women. Thus, it was her eunuchs who brought state memorials from the ministers, delivered her imperial decrees, and admitted or denied entrance to her presence. During daily audiences with officials, she stayed discreetly concealed behind a screen or curtain. Her favorite eunuch, chief of the eunuch staff, had a great influence on her imperial decisions. It is written that she even endowed most of her eunuchs with the title of marquis and generous land grants that included tax revenues, the first instance recorded of eunuchs being ennobled.

It is written that the only palace ladies who escaped harm at her hands were those who had never had sex with her husband. Once firmly established in a position of control, the Empress Dowager Lu wreaked a terrible vengeance on her former rival, concubine Lady Chi, and Lady Chi's son, Chao. Her motive was more than vengeance, however, for the dowager still festered with the belief that Chao and his mother coveted the throne. First, she had Lady Chi confined to apartments behind the palace; then she turned on Chao, who had previously been made overlord of an outlying fiefdom. The dowager demanded that Prince Chao journey in to the capital for an audience. He came to the capital, though with great trepidation. Even the dowager's son, Emperor Hui Ti, was skeptical of his mother's motives, and tried to protect his half-brother Chao by keeping the prince constantly by his side. However, one morning in the predawn hours when Hui Ti had slipped from the palace for a bit of hunting, his absence was reported to the dowager, no doubt by the eunuchs, and she promptly had Chao put to death with poison.

And no doubt it was the empress dowager's eunuchs, traditionally in charge of punishments in the women's quarters, who carried out her next order. Lady Chi's hands and feet were chopped off, her eyes gouged out, and her voice and hearing destroyed with acid, whereupon she was thrown, still alive, into an open-pit palace latrine where the hogs rooted. Then, for some further diabolical reason, the dowager summoned Hui Ti and demanded that he view "this human pig" in the latrine. The gruesome sight sickened and shocked the young emperor into near madness. From then on he took to his bed, refusing to rule the nation or face a world where such cruelties could occur.

Emperor Hui Ti did not live long thereafter. He became a debauched alcoholic whose bedchamber was constantly attended by pretty young boys who powdered and rouged their faces and wore gold pheasant feather caps and gem-studded girdles in the manner of officials. In 188 B.C., Hui Ti died at twenty-three years of age. Gossip soon spread that his mother had deliberately caused Hui Ti's death. It is recorded that during his funeral, Empress Dowager Lu wailed aloud, but did not shed a tear.

Immediately after the funeral of Hui Ti, the dowager put on the throne an infant born to one of Hui Ti's minor concubines, had the infant's mother murdered, and claimed the child was the legitimate son of Hui Ti's empress, who had been childless. Later, when this boy-emperor learned the truth and vowed to avenge his real mother's death, the dowager kept him confined in the palace as a virtual prisoner. Eventually, she had him killed, and enthroned another child ruler who was not even of imperial Han blood.

Despite Dowager Lu's unsavory reputation, historians grudgingly admit that during her years in control of China, the populace prospered, crime and brigandry decreased, and the land was at peace, all of which paved the way to the future greatness of the House of Han. Yet she was widely hated by Confucian officials, who considered feminine rule an abomination against the Mandate of Heaven.

At the dowager's death in 180 B.C., a consortium of Han ruling princes and powerful ministers had her entire family-clan executed, down to the last child. They then did away with the infant emperor and prevailed upon deceased Emperor Kao Tsu's eldest living son by a concubine to come in to the capital from his kingdom to become the new Han Emperor Wen Ti. According to custom, Wen Ti accepted most reluctantly, and then only after procuring the approval of his mother and learning that shaman diviners had foretold the future in his favor. One of his first acts was to dispatch a special imperial carriage to his former fiefdom to bring his mother to the Chang An palace as empress dowager. (This action illustrates the prestige accorded the eldest ranking woman in the Chinese imperial palace as well as in private households, where several generations usually lived together. Even into modern times, in tradition-minded extended Chinese families, in a ritual of filial respect, each member was duty-bound to pay the matriarch a daily morning visit.)

Emperor Wen Ti went down in history as the great Han Dynasty patriarch, a paragon of simplicity, kindness, and modesty. All his edicts commenced with self-deprecatory phrases such as, "I, who am without wisdom or virtue, hereby decree. . . ." Such euphemistic phrases would be used by all future Chinese emperors, though often with less sincerity.

Noted for his extreme thriftiness, Wen Ti himself wore common garments of coarse black silk rather than the luxuriously embroidered fine
silken robes appropriate to a Son of Heaven. To avoid wastage of cloth,
he ordered his favorite concubine to set a fashion whereby palace women's
skirts should no longer trail on the floor. He not only forbade the building of a new pleasure pavilion once he learned its cost, but also allowed
no additions or improvements whatever to the palace and grounds. He
further ordained that petty state rulers living at ease and luxury in the
capital should move back to their principalities and work hand-in-hand
with their people.

Under Wen Ti's fatherly rule, civil servants in the provinces and officials in the capital cooperated closely in administrating the empire, which
helped consolidate imperial power and wealth. Cultivation of fresh lands
brought increased agricultural yields. The standard of living rose, especially among the landed gentry, who accrued more riches and slaves and
turned their attention to scholarship, which this emperor avidly promoted.
Imperial treasuries soon held such bounty, it is claimed, that Wen Ti abolished all taxation for a time. Imperial granaries so overflowed that stores
spoiled before they could be completely utilized. By this time, there was
such a glut of horses nationwide that it was considered ill-bred to ride
a mare. Thus, the records say that "the entire world" within the four seas
enjoyed wealth and plenty, and the people devoted themselves to propriety
and duty.

Wen Ti did his best to make the laws of punishment more humane.
He decreed that cutting off limbs and carving the skin and flesh, leaving the victim maimed for life, was intolerable. He abolished mutilations
entirely, evidently including castration. He substituted flogging for bodily
mutilations, but this rule had to be mitigated because of resultant deaths.
He also tried to abolish the execution or enslavement of families of criminals sentenced to death. Most of his humanitarian reforms were soon to
be ignored, however, as influential officials insisted that such leniency would
bring about an increase in crime. Castration as punishment for crimes—
if it was ever outlawed—was soon to be reinstated.

A scholar himself, Wen Ti restored freedom of speech and writing.
No longer could a man who criticized the government be convicted of
high treason and chopped in two at the waist. Under his patronage, scholars
labored in the imperial library, collecting, piecing together, and reworking
what was left of the ancient classics which escaped the Burning of the
Books. This was the beginning of a meticulous and lasting tradition of
scholarship among the Chinese. A deep reverence for learning and the written word prompted careful preservation of all that was ancient, no matter

its political or philosophical tenor. It was this lasting devotion to Confucian literature which would give birth to a truly national Chinese culture—and cement together a nation able to withstand future upheavals.

When in 158 B.C. the northern barbarian nomads again invaded China with great force, Wen Ti journeyed to the frontier encampments to encourage his fighting men. He abandoned his desire to personally lead the troops into battle only when his mother put her foot down. When, in the face of great Han border armies, the enemy horsemen fled back to their pastures, Wen Ti decided against pursuing them into the steppes "lest it prove too great a hardship on my subjects." Instead, he concluded a peace pact guaranteeing the Mongolian khan two embroidered robes, a coat from his own imperial wardrobe, an ornamented gold girdle, thirty rolls of brocade, and eighty rolls of heavy silk. When that khan died and his son became supreme ruler of the northern nomad tribes, Wen Ti sent him a princess bride of imperial Han blood. Wen Ti designated a palace eunuch named Chung-hsing Shou to accompany her north and remain in her entourage as protector and tutor after they reached the khan's encampment. As it turned out, the choice of this particular eunuch was soon to be regretted.

Eunuch Chung-hsing Shou strongly objected, considering it a great indignity to be sent to a lifetime among the Tartars in the northern wilds. Officials who forced the eunuch on his way heard him bitterly vow revenge. When the entourage reached the nomad chief, the eunuch immediately renounced his Chinese nationality and swore loyalty to the Mongolians. He then diligently instructed his new masters in how to outwit the Chinese both militarily and politically, and was amply rewarded when the Mongolian chieftain made him his confidante and showered him with favors and privileges.

Eunuch Chung-hsing Shou convinced the nomads that rolls of silk, which they coveted and which the Chinese had long used to bargain for peace, were useless to rough-riding horsemen who needed only their own sturdy felt and leather clothing. "Throw away the fancy Chinese foodstuffs," he also admonished them, "and stick to your traditional nourishing *kumiss*" —the smelly fermented mare's milk that the Chinese abhorred. When Chinese envoys, who came to bring tribute, scoffed at the barbarians because they did not till the soil, but moved their tents about following their herds, the eunuch sneered that the Chinese custom of building permanent houses with village walls and fortifications only exhausted the strength and resources of the people. He boldly addressed the envoys: "You Chinese and your mud huts! All you do is mouth and blabber. What good are your elegant official hats and girdles and tiresome court rituals?" Then he sent the envoys packing, with the threat that if forthcoming tribute gifts were insufficient, or of less than finest quality, the Mongolian hordes would gallop down with their horses and trample the harvest crops all across North China.[1]

The eunuch instructed the Mongolian chieftain in ways to increase his wealth by keeping an itemized tally of all his subjects and herd animals. He also divulged valuable intelligence regarding the Chinese armies that guarded the border. In 166 B.C., the nomads again swept down into China, pillaging, killing and burning, stealing domestic animals, and carrying away captured Chinese as slaves. The khan even sent his scouts within sight of the Chang An capital. Emperor Wen Ti, at great expense to the nation, pitted 1,000 war chariots and 100,000 troops against the marauders, but when the imperial force attacked, the fleet northern horsemen simply melted back into their vast homelands where cumbersome Chinese armies could not follow. More peace alliances were agreed upon, but as long as the renegade Chinese eunuch acted as their advisor, the barbarians continued their attacks. China's only means to avoid major invasion was to vastly expand her armies, and to continue pacifying the chieftains with ever more valuable tribute and Chinese brides. Thus, eunuch Chung-hsing Shou is remembered in history as an arch traitor.

The histories of Wen Ti's reign also vilify another man, the handsome young commoner and boatman, named Teng Tung, with whom the emperor became completely enamored after having dreamed that just such a lad had ferried him up to Heaven. Wen Ti took the oarsman into the palace and made him his inseparable companion, and even lowered himself to seek amusement in Teng Tung's humble home. Soon—contrary to his reputation for parsimony—the love-sick emperor was showering the catamite and his relatives with titles, wealth, and extensive properties. When a palace fortune-teller predicted that Teng Tung would one day starve to death, the distraught emperor bequeathed his paramour rich copper mines from which the boatman could mint all the money he wanted.

The annals say their relationship was so intimate that Teng Tung once sucked the infection from a tumor on the emperor's body. Pleased, the emperor then insisted that his son, the crown prince, perform the same unsavory task to prove himself equally devoted. The prince did as he was told, but forever after bore a deep hatred towards Teng Tung. When Wen Ti died and the prince became Han Emperor Ching Ti, he confiscated all of Teng Tung's vast holdings and incredible wealth, leaving him, as foretold, a pauper, without even a hairpin to hold his cap on.

Emperor Wen Ti's funeral rites were unaccustomarily frugal, for he had previously decreed that the traditional several-year period of public mourning at a sovereign's death, as well as the construction of lavish imperial tombs, "exhausts the people's wealth and health," and that such wastage was strictly forbidden. His final edicts also provided that all his palace ladies, from the highest ranking concubine down to minor maidservants, were released and returned to their homes. "Ah," say the histories, "was not Wen Ti benevolent, indeed!"

Early in the reign of Wen Ti's son Ching Ti (156–140 B.C.) a serious revolt of seven kingdoms broke out. The revolt was led by a provincial king whose son had accidentally been killed by Ching Ti when they were boys. The accident happened during a quarrel over a game of chess, when Ching Ti smashed the chess board over his opponent's head. The father plotted vengeance, and now that Ching Ti was emperor, goaded other ruling lords to join his rebellion by convincing them that this emperor planned to take away their lands.

Many of the provincial rulers were becoming dangerously powerful, wealthy, and arrogant. Thus, following the advice of a dedicated chief minister, Ching Ti decreed that from now on landed lords must bequeath their holdings equally amongst their sons rather than to just the eldest. The minister's intention was to eventually reduce princely families to unimportance by breaking up their holdings. In one of several sincere attempts to placate the consortium of rebelling kings, Ching Ti even ordered the death of the minister who had promulgated the decree. Yet the seven kingdoms fought on until they were finally overcome by imperial forces, which suffered great losses of men and monies.

The following anecdote concerning Ching Ti's reign seems to have been included in the histories to bolster the general Confucian conviction that it was folly to give eunuchs responsibilities beyond palace servitude. When the Mongolians were once again harassing the borderlands, Ching Ti sent out a favorite palace eunuch to help train troops and assist in frontier defense. One day as the eunuch and some two dozen riders were casually scouting the countryside near their headquarters, they encountered three lone enemy nomadic horsemen and provoked them to a skirmish. When the nomads began their well-known tactic of riding in circles around their combatants and expertly shooting arrows as they rode, the eunuch was wounded and most of his men were killed. The eunuch narrowly escaped and reached camp with his story. Indignant, the Chinese commander galloped forth and overcame the three Mongolians without difficulty, and discovered they had simply been out hunting eagles.

During Ching Ti's time, the production of iron and manufacture of iron tools became so commonplace that metal plowshares and farm implements brought pronounced economic advancement to agrarian China; as a result, the population mushroomed. Ching Ti is admired for decreeing that his imperial treasuries were so amply filled that taxes on cultivated fields should be cut in half.

Before the end of Ching Ti's rule, the proliferation of iron weaponry made China's armaments superior to those of the northern enemy tribes. Now that all men over twenty-one years of age had to register for military service, China's armies were overwhelming the Mongolians. Two barbarian chieftains even brought their mounted troops south and surrendered to the superior Chinese forces. Emperor Ching Ti incorporated these barbarian forces into his military, firmly cementing their loyalty to China by rewarding both leaders with Chinese titles of nobility, a practice that would continue for centuries. The resultant infusion of Mongolian blood with "pure Chinese" blood is still evident today in the faces of the northern Chinese.

During this era ruling lords and gentry enjoyed such luxury that their sophisticated, leisurely way of life rivaled that of the imperial family. Learned scholars of the "Great Families" considered themselves the only "true gentlemen," and emerged as the educated ruling class from which most imperial officials would be drawn henceforth. Their basic Confucian principles were often seasoned with Taoist beliefs advocating quietude and inaction—"let nature take its course."

No matter what their philosophy, all Chinese shared persistent beliefs in the hoary cults of witchcraft, sorcery, and the casting of evil spells. All believed in the power of Heaven to send down natural catastrophes—floods, earthquakes, or unusual, unexplainable occurrences such as bright lights in the sky—as warnings from above against the Son of Heaven's misrule, as well as auspicious omens to signify Heaven's approval of the emperor's actions.

However, while the nation at large prospered, Ching Ti's imperial womenfolk were disrupting life in the palace. His conniving sister caused an uproar by spitefully accusing a high-ranking concubine of hiring female attendants to cast malignant spells and "spit behind the backs" of ladies who spent more nights in the emperor's bed than did the concubine. Frightened at the mere suggestion of witchcraft within the palace, Ching Ti—as his sister had planned—turned against the once-favored concubine and her clansmen.

Next an ambitious, ruthless concubine, Madam Wang, so successfully maligned the empress that Ching Ti deposed his consort, who died of grief when Madam Wang was promoted to replace her. Though Ching Ti sired fourteen sons by various consorts, and made thirteen of them rulers of principalities, it was his son born to Empress Wang who would become the next emperor and bring Han China to its ultimate glory.

Before he died, in 141 B.C., Emperor Ching Ti granted clemency to the thousands of convicts who had labored for years to build his elaborate tomb. In like manner, he decreed that ladies of the harem should not only be returned to their homes, but should also be exempted from taxes for life. Most palace eunuchs, on the other hand, retained their court positions from one reign to the next—a policy which would allow them to become powerful enough to completely undermine the House of Han.

Note

1. All quotes in this paragraph are excerpted from B. Watson's *Records of the Grand Historian of China.*

5

Greatest Han Ruler and His Eunuchs
REIGN OF EMPEROR WU TI (141-87 B.C.)

In 141 B.C. there succeeded to the throne a sixteen-year-old Han prince who proved to be one of the most dynamic monarchs in all Chinese history. This emperor, Wu Ti, brought the Han Dynasty to its peak of power, prestige, and morale.

During the first years of his reign, Wu Ti's empress dowager mother and her male relatives ran the government, and his grandmother, an ardent Taoist, dominated him until her death in 135 B.C. Thereafter, Wu Ti asserted himself, used educated men of integrity as advisors and officials, and firmly established Confucianism as official state doctrine—though more often than not the strong-willed Wu Ti determined his own policies.

Emperor Wu Ti embarked China upon an unprecedented burst of expansion, aggression, and conquest, succeeding during his fifty-year reign in vastly extending Chinese borders. His armies set up a domain in Korea, brought the rebellious leaders of the southern coastal regions under firm control, pushed down into Vietnam, and subdued the wild mountain tribes in the southwest, bordering Burma and Tibet. The conquered peoples became Chinese subjects, vassals who brought tribute, or slaves in great numbers for the state and the Chinese nobility.

Wu Ti's explorers scouted the scarcely known lands in Central Asia, some 3,000 miles to the west, nearly to the borders of Russia. They were followed by Chinese generals and envoys who won considerable concessions from Turkish-Mongolian rulers, many of whom sent tribute to the Great Emperor of Han China. "Silk Roads" were developed leading westward towards the great deserts and garrisoned by Chinese troops to make the route safe for huge government-sponsored trading caravans, often ten in a year, each including several hundred men. These caravans transported Chinese artifacts and rolls of precious silk, which were now in great demand as far away as Rome.

In return, from the Central Asian countries Wu Ti received a much-coveted superior breed of horses, alfalfa seeds for fodder for his expanding cavalry, exotic fruit seeds, raw jade, and luxuries for his imperial palace. After subduing one Tartar nation just north of the Takla Makan Desert, according to the terms of a formal exchange agreement, Wu Ti received 1,000 horses and sent in return a Chinese princess for the alien leader to wed. The bride departed for the far-away land with a rich dowry and a full retinue of personal maidservants and eunuchs.

Despite all the successes abroad, Wu Ti's era was not without troubles at home. China continued to be plagued by almost constant raids of fierce Mongolian nomads from the north. Time and again, these bands of expert riders were able to strike and vanish unscathed, carrying away plunder and captives.

Contemporary historians recorded that "the northern barbarians move on fleet war horses, and in their breasts beat the hearts of beasts. They migrate from place to place with their herds and felt tents, wearing crude clothing of hides and fur, neither building permanent homes nor tilling the soil. They know nothing of propriety and righteousness, nor the elegance of official hats, girdles, and proper rituals of a civilized court. Since most ancient times, they have never been regarded as part of humanity."[1]

Actually, the nomad tribes were well organized under a central khan who, like the Chinese emperor, kept court in elegant tents with harem girls and eunuchs, and hired Chinese bookkeepers to maintain records, for the nomads had no written language. At specified times, chieftains of his numerous tribes gathered at the great khan's luxurious encampment to pay him obeisance. His title, Shen Yu, meant Son of Heaven in the Mongolian language.

Wu Ti's armies won few victories over these hardy Mongolian warriors. His only recourse was to try to hold them at bay beyond the Great Wall by means of a costly border defense, seldom-kept alliances of peace, and exchange treaties wherein the khan sent horses and furs, and received Chinese foodstuffs, grains, silk, and as often as not, a Han princess for his harem. Around 120 B.C., for a few years the nomads were driven far to the north, but in accomplishing this, Wu Ti lost 30,000 men and more than 100,000 horses.

Like many a Chinese sovereign before and after, Wu Ti was a devout believer in occult doctrines propounded since time immemorial by shamans, wizards, and sorcerers. All searched for the magic elixir which would allow one to live forever as a free spirit. During his reign, Wu Ti made several journeys with long imperial entourages to the east coast, where magicians assured him he would meet the Immortals themselves. In Chang An, he had huge copper vessels raised on high pillars to collect the dew—a supposed ingredient of the magic drug.

Wu Ti firmly believed that one of China's most ancient deities, the Queen Mother of the West, descended to him in person and presented several of her special peaches—a magic fruit which also produced everlasting life. Several centuries later it was declared that the actual out-sized peach seeds were found when Wu Ti"s private treasure trove was opened. Even today in China the gift of peaches, or a painting or artifact depicting peaches, is symbolic of the wish for the recipient's long life.

In 118 B.C., when Wu Ti was grieving over the death of a favorite concubine and longing to see her face once more, he ordered a Taoist sorcerer to call back her ghost. By some unknown trickery, this charlatan conjured up her shadowy specter, which floated briefly before the emperor, while he broke down and wept. Next, this magician declared he could summon the Immortal Spirits to divulge the secrets of their elixir of immortality. When he failed after several attempts, he resorted to a scheme in which, unbeknownst to Wu Ti, he wrote magic characters on a scrap of silk cloth and had it swallowed by an .ox Then he prophesied that the emperor would find a message of portent in the animal's stomach. But when Wu Ti had the ox slaughtered and found the cloth, he recognized the charlatan's handwriting and had him slaughtered as well.

By far the most bizarre of all Wu Ti's sorcerers was a tall, handsome eunuch named Luan Ta, who came to the capital after serving in the palace of a Han ruling prince. He had studied magic, divination, and communion with the spirits under the same Taoist teacher as many other imperial court magicians. Eunuch Luan Ta openly declared that he himself had often visited the Immortals on the Isles of the Blest in the eastern ocean, but they had refused to divulge the recipe for their elixir to a mere citizen without rank.

Wu Ti readily succumbed to this thinly veiled suggestion to elevate Luan Ta in rank, conferring upon him such unprecedented honors and prestige that the "whole nation trembled with awe." He made Luan Ta a landed marquis with the right to collect taxes from hundreds of households, and presented him with a palace, a fine carriage, and countless slaves.

Incredibly, Wu Ti then gave the eunuch his own daughter, an imperial princess, as a bride, with a dowry of 10,000 gold pieces, and with great pomp and ceremony, presented him an official jade seal and the title "General of the Heavenly Way." The emperor himself paid visits to the eunuch's abode. He was quickly followed by sycophantic officials and imperial family members who invited Luan Ta to dine and showered him with costly gifts. Surely now, Wu Ti believed, with such exalted standing, Luan Ta's demands at the Isles of the Immortals would be granted.

When next eunuch Luan Ta journeyed forth on his mission, Wu Ti—who had been duped before—secretly sent observers to watch his progress. These spies reported back that when the eunuch reached the eastern seacoast, he failed to embark, but instead made sacrifices on the sacred mountain of Tai Shan and claimed to have met the Immortals there. Bitterly disappointed, Wu Ti had eunuch Luan Ta executed for daring to delude the Son of Heaven.

Emperor Wu Ti and many in his bureaucracy believed in lavish expenditures to display the strength, wealth, and dignity of the Han throne. Subdued alien rulers and their envoys who came to bring tribute and kowtow before the emperor of China were entertained with extravagant banquets and impressive theatricals and outdoor tournaments. No doubt they were further impressed by Wu Ti's gem-studded imperial palaces, expansive parks with gorgeous pleasure pavilions, man-made lakes and ornamental waterways, all of which must have been built and maintained at incredible expense. Han nobility, the wealthy, and imperial officials who governed in the territories made every attempt to echo the same lavish, sophisticated lifestyle, reflecting the pride and glory of the Han empire.

To promote his imperial image at home, Emperor Wu Ti instigated new, and embellished the old, official religious sacrifices, where the essences of wines, cooking meats, and other foods, as well as incense, invited the gods and spirits above to descend and bless his great successes. In one grand offering, light brown calves, a bull, a pig, and a sheep were ritually slaughtered, cooked in ceremonial vessels, and portions of the meat buried at each of five altars built on a mound in the middle of a palace lake. These dignified state ceremonies, often officiated by Emperor Wu Ti himself, together with the solemn music and ritual state dances performed by officials, must have convinced participating grandees—clad as they always were in ornate, new ceremonial robes—that Wu Ti was indeed the true representative of Heaven on earth.

Yet there were a few old die-hard Confucian conservatives, who were always opposed to change, who dared suggest that Wu Ti's military adventures and extravagant show of might and riches would end in dire reversals. "The strength and resources of the people will become exhausted," they warned. But when Wu Ti found the national treasuries near depletion, he called in the despised merchant magnates to straighten out the economy. They saved the nation from financial collapse by instituting government monopolies of natural resources. Imperial titles were sold outright to the wealthy for donations of money, horses, and grain to maintain Han armies. Most petty states ruled by princes were made over into military commanderies under central control. But by this time the impetus of Wu Ti's leadership was on the wane.

In 99 B.C. a series of incidents that resulted in a castration were recorded by the victim, Ssu-ma Chien, who had been the official Director of Records at the court of Wu Ti. It happened that one of Wu Ti's military men, a loyal general of proven worth and bravery, suffered an overwhelming defeat at the hands of vastly superior nomad forces far north of the Great Wall. The general and the handful of men left of his depleted army were compelled to retreat, and finally, when completely encircled, to surrender. Knowing that the emperor would consider this a disgraceful, personal loss of face, and that he himself would be executed should he return to Chang An, the general willingly defected to the northern enemy.

Apoplectic at the news of the defection, Wu Ti turned the matter over to his officials, including Ssu-ma Chien, who remonstrated in the general's behalf, praising the man's past victories and pointing up the unavoidable circumstances of his surrender. Shaken with rage at one who dared support a "traitor," Wu Ti clapped Ssu-ma Chien into prison and had him castrated. Then he proceeded to put to death all the defected general's immediate family members. Rather than commit suicide, as was expected of a scholarly gentleman, Ssu-ma Chien chose to live on as a palace eunuch to complete his histories as he had promised his historian father he would do.

Preserved in Ssu-ma's own words is his explanation of this sad affair: "There is no defilement so great as castration. One who has undergone this punishment nowhere counts as a man. This is not just a modern attitude; it has always been so. Even an ordinary fellow is offended when he has to do business with a eunuch—how much more so, then, a gentleman! Would it not be an insult to the court and my former colleagues if now I, a menial who sweeps floors, a mutilated wretch, should raise my head and stretch my eyebrows to argue right and wrong?"[2]

Of the condemned general, Ssu-ma wrote: "The losses he had formerly inflicted on the enemy were such that his renown had filled the Empire! After his disgrace, I was ordered to give my opinion. I extolled his merits, hoping the Emperor would take a wider view, but despite all my heartfelt sincerity, I was unable to justify myself. In the end it was decided that I was guilty of trying to mislead the Emperor.

"I had not the funds to pay a fine in lieu of punishment, and my colleagues and associates spoke not a word in my behalf. Had I chosen suicide, no one would have credited me with dying for a principle. Rather, they would have thought the severity of my offense allowed no other way out. It was my obligation to my father to finish his historical works which made me submit to the knife without showing the rage I felt. If I had done otherwise, how could I ever have the face again to visit the graves of my parents? This is what makes my bowels burn within me nine times a day. Whenever I think of my shame, the sweat drenches the clothes on my back. I am fit only to be a slave guarding the palace women's apartments. I can hope for justification only after my death, when my histories become known to the world."[3]

Ssu-ma Chien finished his chronicles before he died, around 86 B.C., not knowing that he would one day be acclaimed the "Grand Historian of China." His invaluable works have preserved for posterity all that was known in his time of Chinese civilization from antiquity down through the reign of Han Emperor Wu Ti.

There is little indication that during Wu Ti's era alien prisoners of war were still being castrated to serve in the palace. His extensive eunuch corps evidently was made up mostly of Chinese subjects charged with crimes, together with the poor who voluntarily submitted to become eunuchs. So many educated officials and influential men were castrated in punishment for offenses that the eunuch staff contained a sizable number of men of various capabilities. As a result, many eunuchs were appointed official "Masters of Writing" in Wu Ti's palace secretariat, and eunuchs began to form cliques that became formidable forces in the government. It is believed that another factor that encouraged eunuch participation in state affairs was that Wu Ti spent much of his time in the harem, where only castrated males were allowed, and conducted much of his official business there.

In his middle years, Wu Ti took into the palace an attractive eunuch named Li, an accomplished musician and composer who had been castrated on a charge of immorality. During a palace entertainment, eunuch Li introduced his younger sister, a talented dancer, who became one of Wu Ti's most beloved concubines. She was given the title Lady Li. After Lady Li bore the emperor a son, eunuch Li was promoted to the rank of a high official and basked in the great favor and affection of the emperor. An older Li brother was made a general, though the man had no military experience. After the utter failure of his first Central Asian campaign, General Li would have faced execution had not Lady Li convinced the emperor to send him vast and costly reinforcements. This time, when General Li was victorious, he was awarded a nobility and remained a powerful court figure—until he defected to the enemy after having been accused of plotting to put Lady Li's son on the throne.

When Lady Li died, at an early age, Wu Ti was inconsolable. In her memory he composed this famous poem: "The rustle of her silken skirt has stopped. Dust grows on the marble floors of her cold and empty rooms. Fallen leaves pile against her door. Longing for that lovely lady, how can I bring my aching heart to rest?"[4]

After Lady Li was gone, Wu Ti's affection for eunuch Li cooled. When a third Li brother was caught in an affair with a palace girl, which embroiled him with the eunuchs, Wu Ti had this brother and eunuch Li both put to death.

In these times fear of witchcraft pervaded all levels of Chinese society. After a military defeat by the Mongolians in 90 B.C., Wu Ti issued an edict in which he explained that when the nomad leaders heard of the approach of Han Chinese forces, they had their sorcerers bury sheep and cattle by the roadsides and at watering places in order to bring a curse upon the Chinese armies; and when the nomad leader sent tribute of horses and fur garments to the Chinese Son of Heaven, he regularly had his sorcerers lay a spell upon them to cause harm. Records also show that, before campaigns, Wu Ti had his own sorcerers direct hexes at the northern enemy.

Around 100 B.C. the first of a series of notorious "witchcraft scandals" in the imperial palace shook the capital and had far-reaching consequences. Invariably these scandals arose in the harem, where sexual and political rivalries flared as each consort or concubine vied, with the help of her eunuchs, to make her own son or favorite the heir.

Wu Ti's first consort, Empress Chen, was barren, causing her to be consumed with jealousy of concubine Wei, a one-time singing girl whom Wu Ti favored because she bore him children. Finally Empress Chen resorted to black magic, employing a shaman witch to stage arcane rites of sacrifice and cast evil spells directed against her female rivals and reportedly against the emperor himself. Deeply frightened at these doings, and having but little love for the empress, Wu Ti dethroned her and executed 300 others thought to be implicated. Then he installed concubine Wei as his empress, gave her male kinfolk influential military and government posts, and made his son by her the heir.

Some years later a son of a chancellor, the highest-ranking officer in the land and a brother-in-law of Empress Wei, was found guilty of embezzling military funds and of having illicit sexual relations with his cousin, the princess daughter of Emperor Wu Ti and Empress Wei. Moreover, he was accused of burying devil dolls along the road to the summer palace that Wu Ti frequently traveled, and of having shaman magicians utter curses against the emperor, a most serious crime. Both the chancellor and his son were arrested and died in prison, and several hundred persons thought to be involved were executed. Soon afterwards, the princess involved in the affair was also put to death for employing sorcerers against her enemies.

Within a few months Emperor Wu Ti fell ill at the summer palace just outside the capital. His attending official, a bitter enemy of Empress Wei and her now grown son, succeeded in convincing the aging emperor that he was suffering from a fatal hex which had been cast on him. Filled with anxiety, Wu Ti ordered the official to head up a thorough investigation. Soon the entire capital was gripped by hysteria, as the investigator and his shaman and eunuch accomplices claimed to have dug up evidence of witchcraft everywhere. People accused each other of sorcery, confessions were extracted under torture with hot irons, mass trials were held, and thousands of suspects were executed.

Next, the investigator convinced Wu Ti that there were black magic emanations from the imperial palace itself. His search there left the ladies of the harem hysterical with fear, for a eunuch by the name of Su Wen had found wooden devil doll images in the crown prince's palace. The crown prince and his mother, Empress Wei, who were well aware that anyone accused was rarely acquitted, quickly took matters in their own hands. In the absence of the emperor, who was still away at his summer palace, they arrested the investigator and his cohorts. One of them, a eunuch, escaped wounded and fled to the emperor's summer palace with the misinformation that the crown prince was staging a revolt. On learning the eunuch's treachery, the empress and crown prince, now thoroughly terrified, doled out arms to the palace militia, and had the emperor's investigator publicly executed and his shaman cohorts burned to death.

At this usurpation of imperial power, the enraged emperor issued forth from the summer palace and called out his metropolitan army. There was bloody fighting in the streets between the troops of the emperor and those of his son, leaving tens of thousands dead. But after five days, the crown prince's followers were overrun, Empress Wei's imperial insignia were seized, and both mother and son committed suicide. Immediately, all members of the Empress Wei's family were executed except one infant, a grandson of the crown prince. (This child was imprisoned, but would be secretly rescued from prison and would live to make his own mark in history.) When Emperor Wu Ti later learned that the devil dolls and all the evidence of witchcraft had been planted by his own chief investigator, he mourned his son's death with tears and had the inspector's entire family exterminated, as well as his accomplice, eunuch Su Wen, who was burned alive.

Between 90 and 85 B.C. some sixteen cases of witchcraft within the palace were recorded in which the accused were forced to commit suicide or were decapitated and their heads impaled on stakes and exhibited in the marketplace. These frightening black magic scandals and resulting forced suicides or executions considerably weakened Wu Ti's hold over the nation, sowing suspicion and instability throughout the government, and leaving the populace prey to bewilderment and insecurity

By this time the peasantry across the land, overburdened by high rents, taxation, and long service in the military due to imperial expansion, or as laborers for government projects, were becoming impoverished. Some were forced to indenture themselves for life in conditions of near slavery.

Highways, mountain passes, and cities, especially in the populous east, became unsafe as droves of destitute peasants turned to banditry. When rounded up and captured by a corps of Wu Ti's armed "circuit inspectors," the bandit hordes became prison laborers for the state. Tens of thousands were used to build Wu Ti's mausoleum, nearby which have now been excavated row upon row of shallow pits containing countless skeletons of those who died on the project, many still wearing iron shackles.

Wu Ti's mausoleum has yet to be explored, but excavations of Han Dynasty tombs reveal that the rich and powerful were buried in many-roomed underground vaults built to duplicate their private mansions. The walls were painted with scenes of the good life; the inner sanctums contained vast stores of grains, domestic animals, wines, and costly artifacts for their use in the Afterworld. Only corpses of the highest and mightiest were interred completely encased in "jade suits"—thousands of tiny pieces of precious "life-preserving" green jade laced together with gold or copper wire.

In his last years, Wu Ti favored a Miss Chao and raised her to highest ranking concubine, even though her father had been castrated for a political offense and now served as an influential palace eunuch. Miss Chao bore Wu Ti a son who was destined to become the next emperor. After making her child his heir in 87 B.C., Wu Ti had Miss Chao put to death, as he explained, to avoid a recurrence of the catastrophes caused by ambitious imperial mothers such as Han Empress Lu a century before. Within two days, Wu Ti himself died, after imbibing one of the elixirs for immortality concocted by his endless succession of Taoist court magicians, alchemists, and sorcerers, it has always been suspected.

One of Wu Ti's last acts had been to appoint a powerful official, Huo Kuang, nephew of the dead Empress Wei, to head up a regency to guide the young heir, who would be known as Emperor Chao Ti.

Though the descendants of the House of Han ruled on for over 200 years more—with one short interruption—never again would the dynasty produce an emperor of Wu Ti's dynamic character and strong qualities of leadership.

Notes

1. B. Watson, *Records of the Grand Historian of China.*
2. Excerpted from C. Birch and D. Keene's *Anthology of Chinese Literature.*
3. Ibid.
4. R. H. van Gulik, *Sexual Life in Ancient China.*

6

Ruling House Overcome by Eunuchs and Consorts
LAST COURTS OF THE FIRST HAN DYNASTY (86-6 B.C.)

For the next twenty years the reins of the government of Han China were firmly held by regent Huo Kuang, a shrewd, powerful statesman who had carefully maneuvered his way into a position of authority starting back in Wu Ti's long reign. The new Emperor Chao Ti was only eight years old when placed on the throne, and by the time he was twelve, regent Huo Kuang had arranged his marriage to Huo Kuang's granddaughter, which made a six-year-old girl the empress of China. (Child marriages to cement alliances between families were common at this time, and still occur in parts of Asia.)

Even after Emperor Chao Ti attained his majority, he delegated all authority to regent Huo Kuang. Historians praise Huo Kuang for championing policies aimed to prohibit the extravagances and military expansionism of former reigns. Regent Huo Kuang also successfully quashed conspiracies instigated by jealous princely sons of Wu Ti's concubines—rulers of outlying petty kingdoms who tried to dethrone the boy-emperor and oust Huo Kuang from control. One such petty king, in league with certain officials, submitted a memorial to the throne accusing Huo Kuang of appointing his relatives and friends to office in order to strengthen his own position, and of exceeding his authority by acting as a virtual dictator. The young Emperor Chao

Ti angrily rejected this memorial and threatened dire punishment for any who dared again raise the subject, astonishing the entire court with a four-teen-year-old's determination. Another intrigue against Huo Kuang failed when it came to light that an imperial princess, an older sister of the boy-emperor, was plotting to have Huo Kuang murdered at a banquet. Both she and her conspiring half-brother were forced to commit suicide.

In 74 B.C., after only thirteen years as emperor, Chao Ti suddenly died, leaving no offspring. There were many who claimed his untimely death was caused by the curses of a female shaman employed by the princely son of another of former Emperor Wu Ti's concubines. Huo Kuang lost no time in putting a nineteen-year-old grandson of the former Lady Li on the throne. At the same time, he took the precaution of raising the status of his own granddaughter (Chao Ti's fifteen-year-old widow) to dowager empress, a position of considerable authority.

After only twenty-seven days on the throne, this new emperor's immoral behavior so enraged Huo Kuang and the court that he had him brought before the young dowager empress and an assemblage of armed guards and senior officials to hear a memorial signed by thirty-six ranking statesmen. This document deplored the newly enthroned emperor's complete lack of judgment, charging that he had failed to adhere to conventional proprieties of mourning Emperor Chao Ti's death. Even before the funeral, they pointed out, he had misused the imperial seals (ink stamps of authority) for his own gain, and had held wanton musicals and drunken parties in the palace in the company of his personal retainers, attendants, and slaves. Furthermore, while the imperial coffin was still in state, he had usurped the empress dowager's carriage for pleasure jaunts, held orgies with the dead emperor's harem girls, and taken valuables from palace stores for gifts to his fellow revelers. In all, over a thousand charges of gross impropriety were listed.

Predictably, the young empress dowager gave regent Huo Kuang, her grandfather, authority to have the new emperor deposed and to execute the 200 persons who had encouraged and shared his shocking indulgences. Professing deep regret, Huo Kuang himself removed the imperial insignia from the person of the deposed "Twenty-seven-day Emperor," as he is known, and mercifully allowed him to return to his home state—which was now reduced to a military commandery under control of the throne.

At Huo Kuang's instigation, a commission of officials now journeyed forth to summon and escort to the capital the eighteen-year-old great-grandson of former Emperor Wu Ti and Empress Wei, who would be known as Emperor Hsuan Ti. This Han emperor had had a most unusual past: he had been abandoned as an infant in a Chang An jail, the sole survivor of the Wei family bloodbath following the witchcraft scandals.

Through the kindness of the director of imperial prisons, he was rescued and secretly moved to better quarters in the prison where two female inmates saw to his care. A year later, a soothsayer frightened old Emperor Wu Ti by prophesying that a future emperor was now residing in an imperial jail. Wu Ti immediately sent a eunuch with orders to have every prisoner in the jail slaughtered that very night, but the prison director refused to comply with the order or even to open the gates to the eunuch. Fearing that this unprecedented insubordination on the part of the prison director was an omen of warning from Above, Wu Ti quickly rescinded his order. But taking no further chances, the prison director located the child's maternal grandmother and sent him to her with money for his support. There the future Emperor Hsuan Ti flourished, was well-educated, and was given the daughter of an imperial eunuch as a concubine. (This concubine's father, Hsu Ping-chun by name, had served as a courtier to one of the provincial kings before his emasculation. When he was dispatched to attend Emperor Wu Ti on an imperial tour of the summer palace and religious shrines, he made the unwitting mistake of saddling his horse with another courtier's saddle. For this offense he was brought up on charges of theft and carelessness, and sentenced to death. His sentence was reduced to castration when Emperor Wu Ti, in an "act of mercy," interceded. It was while he served as a eunuch in the imperial palace that influential eunuchs made arrangements for his daughter to be given in marriage to the Wei family "orphan.")

After the "Twenty-seven-day-Emperor" was disgraced and deposed, the former prison director, who was now a court official, confided to the all-powerful regent Huo Kuang that the Wei family "orphan" was alive and now grown into a responsible young man. Delighted at this news, Huo Kuang "received approval" from his granddaughter, the empress dowager, to raise Hsuan Ti from the status of commoner to a titled noble, preparatory to making him emperor.

Hsuan Ti was made emperor. But since he was young and inexperienced in court affairs, Huo Kuang remained in control of government. His position was publicly reaffirmed when the throne increased his nobility with tax rights from 20,000 households and lavish gifts that included 7,000 catties of gold, 60 million taels in cash, 30,000 rolls of silk, 170 slaves, 2,000 horses, and a new residential mansion. His close relatives, who had held influential positions in the inner and outer courts, where they acted as his supporters, were reconfirmed in these positions.

Shortly after Emperor Hsuan Ti's accession, the daughter of eunuch Hsu Ping-chun bore him a son. Thereupon, she became the ranking consort, known to history as Empress Hsu. However, since Huo Kuang and his ambitious wife, together with several high ministers, had planned that Huo's own daughter would fill this position, Huo Kuang protested the elevation of Empress Hsu, pointing out that her father was a eunuch, and so she was not fit to be related by marriage to the Son of Heaven. Emperor Hsuan Ti promptly rectified the matter by giving his eunuch father-in-law an imperial title and official position in the palace. Then he proceeded to restore the honor of his disgraced Wei family name. He had his relatives who were massacred in the witchcraft scandals reburied in the style of nobility and their graves tended by retainers, and appropriated sufficient government monies to ensure that proper ancestral services were regularly held in their honor.

The nation continued to prosper under Huo Kuang's leadership. In 73 B.C. five great Chinese armies collaborated to shatter the forces of the northern Mongolian tribes, who at this time were divided and weakened by internal dissension. One chieftain came to Chang An to "knock his head on the ground in surrender" to Emperor Hsuan Ti, who made him a vassal. Another chieftain and his tribe retreated deep into Central Asia, where China still exercised considerable authority at strategic points as far west as Yarkand. This renegade would harass and endanger Chinese envoys and caravans for many years, until he was finally killed by a young Chinese officer.

Huo Kuang's wife, a vain, grasping woman, continued to harbor deep resentment that their daughter was not chosen as empress. She was equally fearful that Empress Hsu's clan would in time usurp the Huo family's power monopoly. When she learned in 71 B.C. that the empress was expecting a second child, she realized that if it should be another boy, all hope for the Huo family to produce an heir would be lost. Without revealing her plans to a soul, she had the empress poisoned immediately after she gave birth. Empress Hsu died in extreme agony of mysterious "unknown causes." Inside a year, Huo Kuang succeeded in convincing Emperor Hsuan Ti to declare his daughter the new empress. To celebrate this marriage, Hsuan Ti gave gifts of gold, coins, and silks to all officials, and granted a general amnesty to prisoners throughout the empire.

However, Huo Kuang's wife lived in mortal fear that her guilt in the poisoning would come to light. The doctors who attended the empress's death had been thrown in prison and were still alive. At last, in desperation she revealed the truth to her husband. In deep shock and despair, Huo Kuang agonized long over what steps to take, and finally decided that his only recourse was to remain silent to protect the Huo family name. He kept his wife's dark secret.

Not long afterwards, Huo Kuang fell gravely ill. The emperor honored him by visiting his sickbed, and when Huo Kuang died, in 68 B.C., both the emperor and Huo's daughter, the empress, attended his funeral. The lavishness of his burial was unprecedented except for emperors. Emperor Hsuan Ti's gifts to be buried with him included gold, money, silks, jades, and pearls, together with a "jade suit" to encase the entire corpse. By imperial decree, a community of 300 families were resettled to maintain Huo Kuang's mausoleum grounds and periodically perform the necessary sacrificial rites for the dead. Hsuan Ti also granted exemption from state service and taxes to all Huo Kuang's descendants for all time.

Now Hsuan Ti came into his own as ruler. In 67 B.C., when word came to him of the suspicion that his former empress had been murdered by Huo Kuang's wife, he named the former empress's eight-year-old son as heir, and made the former prison director who had rescued him from prison the senior tutor of the eight-year-old, an exalted position from which the man was eventually promoted to premier. The emperor also demoted many Huo family members from their high positions and sent others into virtual exile to distant posts, and made members of his former empress's clan his chief advisors.

Huo Kuang's widow, now beside herself with worry, finally confessed her guilt to prominent Huo family males, who bitterly reviled her for having kept them in ignorance. They now realized that their only chance of survival lay in a complete take-over of the government, and proceeded with a plot to poison the new heir apparent and replace Emperor Hsuan Ti with one of their own family members. Their plans leaked, however, and the emperor had almost the entire Huo clan put to death. All Huo relatives in high office were executed. The man they had planned to put on the throne was chopped in two at the waist, and other relations hastily committed suicide or were imprisoned. Huo Kuang's widow and daughters were put to disgraceful public death. Huo Kuang's daughter, the empress, was deposed and banished to seclusion in a house on the summer palace grounds. In desperation, she finally took her own life.

In running the government, Emperor Hsuan Ti paid little heed to Confucian principles. He favored strict laws and a harsh penal system. To perform the business of government he relied for assistance on his personal palace secretariat, in which trusted eunuchs had a strong hand. Though Confucianists frantically pointed out the dangers of eunuch participation in government, the emperor used them extensively. One senior minister remonstrated that the inner-palace secretariat was so vital to the conduct of state affairs that it should be made up of men of intellect, worth, and experience. He declared that to use eunuchs in influential positions was not in accord with ancient practice, violating the age-old principle that a ruler should not be associated with men who had been castrated for crimes. Others dared point out that Hsuan Ti was emulating Emperor Wu Ti's ruinous extravagances by embarking on military ventures. One also complained that Hsuan Ti's imperial buildings, carriages, and robes of state were far more sumptuous than those of any former emperor.

To all these charges, the clear-headed Hsuan Ti replied: "The Han have their own code: the code of conquerors. We are no longer living in Chou Dynasty times, when government was run by the virtuous and the educated. The literati speak always of the virtues of antiquity and the evils of the present age, failing to understand changing times, filling the ears of the simple-minded with lofty but empty phrases. How can one possibly give responsible positions to men living in a utopian world of the past, devoid of all practical common sense?"[1]

When, after twenty-five years on the throne, the emperor fell fatally ill, he selected several ranking ministers, including the tutor of the crown prince, to assist the young heir in governing. At his death in 49 B.C., Hsuan Ti's son, who was the grandson of an official who had been castrated, became the next Han emperor. His name was Yuan Ti.

Yuan Ti came to the throne at age twenty-seven, a mild-mannered, vacillating man, whose mother had been poisoned just after his birth. His own father had experienced doubt about his ability to rule when Yuan Ti, as a prince, suggested that, rather than relying on excessively harsh punishments to control the nation, a ruler could do better by appointing officials with scholastic training.

Unfortunately, Emperor Yuan Ti inherited from his father's court two powerful eunuchs, Hung Kung and Shih Hsien, who headed up the palace secretariat. Both were highly practiced in applying the law and in handling imperial documents, and had long been accustomed to deciding even the most secret and crucial affairs of state. From the inner palace they accomplished their aims by working in close cooperation with a high minister in the outer court. Now they urged the new emperor, often with complete success, to adopt their own proposals, and to return to the revered institutions of the distant past.

Though eunuchs Hung Kung and Shih Hsien intimidated and were able to impose their will on most court officials, from the chancellor downwards, some ministers did not fear their authority. They remonstrated vehemently against the two eunuchs with almost obsessive persistence, calling for the removal of "castrated criminals" from such important positions as internal secretaries, and objecting adamantly to "mere palace menials" being given special governing powers.

One minister, Yuan Ti's former tutor, who enjoyed great favor with the ruler—the relationship between teacher and pupil having always been one of the most sacred and binding in China—also advocated that the palace secretariat be staffed with orthodox officials, arousing the strong enmity of eunuchs Hung Kung and Shih Hsien. The two eunuchs arranged for one of their cohorts to submit charges against this minister, alleging that he was attempting to drive men out of office and was also alienating the emperor from his own imperial family members. When the eunuchs urged that the minister be turned over to the justice department, the emperor meekly complied, not realizing that his revered former tutor could be thrown into prison. When he learned that this had occurred, the emperor berated the two eunuchs so soundly that they knocked their heads on the floor and offered profuse apologies. But when the emperor ordered that the minister be released and restored to his former position, the two eunuchs persisted, explaining that, having already subjected the man to investigation and prison, now the only acceptable action was to pardon his crime and deny him office. Reluctantly, the emperor again concurred and removed his old tutor's titles, reducing him to a commoner.

Inside a few months, the contrite and wavering ruler retracted this decree, saying that if the empire was to flourish, it was vital that respect and honor be given to teachers everywhere. He further decreed that, because the minister had been his tutor for eight years, guiding him in the study of the classics, he should now be titled a marquis, with revenues from 600 households. Further, as steward of the palace, the minister should now attend all imperial audiences and occupy an honored seat next to the military generals.

Once again, however, the clever eunuchs accused the minister, claiming he had instructed his own son to submit a letter to the throne charging the emperor with wrongdoing. For "the sacred court to treat the sovereign with kindness and mercy," the eunuchs insisted, the former tutor would have to suffer a certain amount of disgrace by imprisonment. Distraught by the accusations against his old tutor and the eunuchs' badgering, Emperor Yuan Ti acquiesced and approved an edict sending the minister back to prison. To the great satisfaction of the two eunuchs, when the minister was handed the edict, he withdrew and took his own life by drinking poison.

When this suicide was reported to the emperor, he wrung his hands and cried out through tears, "I suspected all along that he would be too proud to stoop to imprisonment. So now they have finally killed my worthy tutor!"[2] He refused his food and wept so bitterly that those around him were filled with pity. When he finally ordered the conspiring eunuchs and their accomplices to appear before him, he berated them at such length that they "removed their caps" and crawled on the floor for mercy. That ended the affair, but ever afterwards Emperor Yuan Ti wept for his betrayed tutor. Each year at appropriate times he sent envoys to perform sacrifices at the minister's grave. By way of posthumous compensation, he put three of his old tutor's sons in high office.

By this time there were indications of the need for retrenchment from the extravagance of former Han reigns. With the enormous proliferation of spending and effort to promote the state cult of worship of Han Dynasty imperial ancestors, some 167 shrines had been established in the provinces, along with 176 temples in the capital. At each shrine, four meals of food were offered up daily to the spirits of deceased Han rulers, and in the temples, live domestic animals were sacrificed twenty-five times a year, and services were performed in small side-chapels at each of the four seasons. In all, a total of almost 25,000 meals were offered up each year. In addition, the temple sites were guarded by 45,000 men, and required 12,000 attending priests, cooks, and musicians, to say nothing of the men engaged to tend the sacrificial animals.

In the face of official complaints against this great outlay, Emperor Yuan Ti ordered a discussion of the entire subject. Drastic reductions were recommended and put into effect, and by 40 B.C. many of the shrines had been taken out of service. But a few years later, when Yuan Ti lay ill, he dreamed that spiritual beings had appeared and warned him that dire consequences would result from the abolishment of these shrines. Fearing that his illness had been inflicted on him by angry ghosts of his ancestors, he immediately reinstated the sacrifices at most of the discontinued sites, and restored all the ancestral shrines in the capital. However, his chronic poor health persisted.

During Yuan Ti's reign, Confucian scholars worked arduously interpreting, copying, and embellishing the ancient classics, histories, and records. Now worship of Heaven as the highest deity received official sanction, displacing the cult of the Supreme Power Above, called Shang Ti. Reliance on the theory of yin and yang increased as well. Confucianists blamed the gradual decline in the nation's resources on the absence of social consciousness in government, harking back nostalgically to the "harmonious days of ancient god-kings when yin and yang rested in perfect balance."

Many of Yuan Ti's edicts concerned omens of impending disaster in the form of strange natural phenomena—unusual movements of stars and planets, strange cloud formations, unexplained lights in the night sky—that were seen as warnings of Heaven's displeasure at misgovernment on earth. Belief in omens now became a lasting part of the Confucian creed, despite the fact that the Great Sage 500 years before had advised paying slight heed to "heavenly spirits whom no one has ever seen."

One day while daydreaming in the palace garden, Emperor Yuan Ti beheld coming toward him a young maid of ethereal beauty, a vision which haunted him ever after. One of his closest ministers—the court portrait artist—offered to conduct a search throughout the empire for just such an enchanting girl. Families everywhere, bedazzled by the prospect of court influence and riches, eagerly presented their girls, many paying bribes to the painter-minister if he accepted their daughters as candidates. One scholarly official in Hupeh province, however, had a daughter who had been born in his old age and was now a seventeen-year-old so lovely and devoted that he dreaded lest the search party see her and take her from him. She had been carefully trained in the arts, educated in the principles of Confucius, and was most skillful in singing and playing the lute. When the minister discovered her and ordered that she become a recruit, the helpless father paid him a large bribe, only asking that his daughter be shown kindness and consideration.

When the search was over, the minister had rounded up such numbers of beauties that the emperor bade him paint a portrait of each, that he might study their faces at leisure for a likeness of the girl in his dream. This allowed the crafty painter to garner another fortune in bribes from the contestants who paid him to embellish their pictures to enhance their beauty. Because the girl from Hupeh refused to pay a bribe, he portrayed her with unattractive facial blemishes. From these pictures, the emperor chose many of the loveliest for his harem, but he left the girl shown with the blemished face to spend three lonely years in the Cold Palace, where unwanted ladies were relegated.

Just at this time, the khan of the northern Mongolian tribes demanded that a peace alliance with China be sealed with a gift of a Chinese princess. Yuan Ti, remembering the ugly portrait of the girl from Hupeh, conferred on her the title of lady, and designated her, sight unseen, the "princess" to be given to the barbarian chieftain. As she entered the huge, lavish audience hall to be presented to the khan, Emperor Yuan Ti was dumfounded by her grace and loveliness, and fell instantly in love with her. However, since the emperor was unable to renege on his agreement with the khan, the girl had to depart in the nomad's entourage, leaving Yuan Ti to mourn his loss. She was instrumental in maintaining peace between the Mongols and China through the reigns of five successive khans. But the sixth khan assassinated her beloved son and she died of grief. North of the Great Wall, legend says, amid the dry windswept reaches of desert loess, the tumulus of her grave stays forever green, even in winter.

From 38 to 34 B.C., Emperor Yuan Ti's health degenerated until he was unable to take any part in state affairs. During his illness he indulged his love of music to the full, as well as his addiction to a game whereby he and a favorite son by a concubine by the name of Fu "played the drums" by dropping bronze pellets onto drums from a high balcony, hoping to score a bull's eye. It seems the emperor so favored this son—the only player of this game who could rival his own skill—that he longed to make him heir in place of the legitimate crown prince by Empress Wang. When he voiced admiration for the favorite son's "great talent," he provoked the scorn of a favorite courtier, Shih Tan. As a distant relative of the imperial family, Shih Tan did not hesitate to point out that talent meant intelligence, love of learning, familiarity with precedents set in the past, and an understanding of present times. He noted that the legitimate heir was blest with all these attributes, but said that if the emperor valued people for their performance in playing the drums, he may as well choose a mere musician as future head of the nation. Reluctantly, Yuan Ti acquiesced in keeping the legitimate heir.

However, in 33 B.C., during the emperor's last illness, the courtier Shih Tan again had to intervene on behalf of the legitimate heir. Both the heir and his mother, Empress Wang, had been all but excluded from Yuan Ti's sickroom, while concubine Fu and her drum-playing son were in constant attendance. Courtier Shin Tan insisted to the emperor that since the real heir already commanded the loyal support of the populace, ministers would refuse, even if they were threatened with execution, an edict ordering a change in imperial succession. Shih Tan further declared that in such an event he himself would first seek permission to die (it was the custom to ask the emperor's permission to commit suicide). At last the ailing emperor acknowledged that it was best to let the legitimate heir remain. Before he died, at age forty-three, Yuan Ti asked Shih Tan to assist and guide the rightful heir in his task as next Han ruler, Emperor Cheng Ti.

Though he ascended the throne at age nineteen, Cheng Ti soon made an unfavorable reputation for himself as a playboy and a bounder. It is said that, solely in an attempt to compensate the Hsu family for the poisoning of Empress Hsu back in 71 B.C., his father had arranged Cheng Ti's possibly unhappy marriage as an early teenager to a descendant of his grandmother Hsu.

As emperor, Cheng Ti's tastes ran toward gaming and frivolity, leaving government in the hands of his mother's clan. He spent many nights roaming the capital in disguise, accompanied by his personal eunuchs—thus, to the consternation of high officials, risking attack on his exalted person and the possibility of being recognized. He is the first emperor known to play football, a field game using a leather ball stuffed with hair that contestants buffeted with hands and feet.

Cheng Ti's mother, Empress Dowager Wang, had a strong influence over her young son and saw that her male kin were the dominating element in both the inner and outer courts. Her brother, as marshal of state, controlled imperial business through management of the palace secretariat. This position was to be filled five times in succession by Wang family males. Empress Dowager Wang had great influence in the selection of imperial successors for the next several decades, engaging in fierce competition with her old rival Empress Dowager Fu as well as concubine Ting, who was destined to mother the next emperor.

Confucian officials strongly disapproved of contemporary popular music and songs, promoting instead the heavy, soporific music of antiquity "which brought to light what had been abandoned, and held fast the threads of continuity with the past." Yet modern music was very popular in Cheng Ti's palace. Harem women virtuosos regularly presented musicals, while the Office of Palace Music held performances at the summer palace, both using popular songs of the day. Conservative minds called these theatricals shocking, licentious, and extravagant. Legend has it that Emperor Cheng Ti once became so excited by "lewd music" that he made disgraceful advances toward some of the entertainers.

Shortly after the commencement of Cheng Ti's reign, Shih Hsien, the chief of palace writers who had long imposed his will in imperial decisions, was brought to his knees. Ministers frustrated by his dominance banded together and submitted to the throne an itemized list of the eunuch's misdeeds. Shih Hsien was convicted of usurping power and exceeding his authority, but because he had used his influence to put Cheng Ti on the throne, he was only dismissed in disgrace to his native state. It is recorded that en route he died of starvation and grief.

Historians believe that changes made in the religious sacrifices during Cheng Ti's reign marked the official adoption of the state worship of Heaven. Ministers convinced the ruler to move the great imperial sacrifices into the capital city where worship of Heaven could be properly conducted at the southern boundaries where the force of *yang* is strongest (*yang* being associated with the south, Heaven, and the emperor). Every effort was then made to see that hymns and ritual dances for the sacrifices emulated those of ancient times—"those which were proper for awaiting the arrival of the spirit of Heaven." Sincerity in worship was stressed, as well as simplicity. Calves were now the only sacrificial victims, and the elegant bronze cooking vessels were replaced by common earthenware. Numerous state religious services performed by officials in the provinces were eliminated. A few objectors warned that these shocking changes were a slight to the ghosts of past Han emperors, "to whom the spirit of Heaven had appeared countless times," and that calamities would befall a regime which abused the spirits by changing the sacred rites.

Catastrophes did indeed come within a year. Thirty days of rain brought floods to nineteen provinces, leaving 4,000 dead and 83,000 homes and other buildings in ruins. Panic spread to the capital, where flood waters had begun to accumulate in outlying sections. Many of the 80,000 inhabitants trampled each other in an effort to reach higher ground. In great consternation, Emperor Cheng Ti called a conference of ministers, who excitedly insisted that the dowagers, empress, and palace ladies should be placed in boats. Officials and civilians were advised to climb on top of the city's wide mud walls to avoid the expected high waters. As it happened, the flood never reached the center of the capital. Calm was restored only when Wang Mang, a sensible, powerful minister of Empress Wang's family, succeeded in reassuring the emperor.

Some observers associated the floods with the rising power of Empress Wang's family, which was thought to be causing the *yin* force (controlling dampness, evil, and the female) to become excessive. Eunuchs, too, were considered to be under the influence of *yin* (maleness and strength were controlled by *yang*). Amidst this widespread uneasiness, the people began recollecting unexplained phenomena like the 32 B.C. fire in a Han Dynasty ancestral shrine, and the uncontrollable, mysterious gushing of a spring inside Cheng Ti's palace. These happenings, too, were interpreted as due to the unprecedented rise of *yin* as a result of the predominance of female and eunuch influence in the palace.

Panic again spread in 29 B.C. when the Yellow River burst its embankments, inundating four prefectures, in some places to a depth of thirty feet. The imperial counselor in charge of river control was blamed for failing to take effective precautionary measures and was forced to commit suicide. Five hundred boats were needed to evacuate the 97,000 flood victims, while hordes of conscript laborers worked for thirty-six days to build stronger dikes. This catastrophe, too, was seen as a warning from Heaven that *yin* had overbalanced *yang*.

Meanwhile, Cheng Ti's failure to sire a son was also causing uneasiness and constant dissension. Though he did his best by repeatedly bestowing his sexual favors on Empress Hsu, concubine Pan, and others, imperial princes were not forthcoming. Even when all imperial state religious rites were restored at the discontinued temples in hopes of pleasing the powers above, no legitimate male heir was born.

In 18 B.C. news spread amongst wealthy and prominent males of Chang An that a young dancing girl of exquisite grace and beauty was performing in one of the public pleasure houses. Her family name was Chao. The emperor, in his eagerness to see her, disguised himself as a servant and had his eunuchs escort him to her place of business. Spellbound, he watched the willowy girl's slender body twirling and dipping, causing her long sleeves and silken scarves to float and swoop through the air, which earned her the nickname of "Flying Swallow." Immediately, the emperor had her brought into the imperial harem, where he soon lost all interest in other consorts and concubines.

Before long, Empress Hsu and concubine Pan were deposed and banished outside the palace for reportedly having put a curse on the emperor, the accusation having been made by the beautiful Flying Swallow, who became empress. Whereupon, she brought her teenage sister into the harem, an especially attractive girl, to help her retain the emperor's favor. This younger girl was given the exalted title of "Shining Deportment," and soon replaced Flying Swallow in Cheng Ti's affections. But after ten years, neither of the Chao sisters had born him an heir. It was said, however, that in 11 B.C. Cheng Ti, by his own hand, killed two infant sons by low-class palace women to placate the younger Chao sister, who still hoped to bear an heir.

Thus, after twenty-five years on the throne, Cheng Ti had produced no legitimate heir. Rival dowager empresses and their supporters among the officials put great pressure on him to nominate one of two young princes as heir—the first, a son of the emperor's half-brother, who was rejected but lived to rule at a later date. The other candidate was Cheng Ti's half-nephew, grandson of Dowager Empress Fu. She canvassed and bribed so successfully in his behalf, even securing support from ranking concubine Chao, that he was duly appointed heir in 8 B.C.

One night a year later, reportedly while in the arms of concubine Chao, Cheng Ti suddenly collapsed and died, at the age of only forty-five. In just three weeks, Dowager Empress Fu's grandson became the new Han emperor, known as Ai Ti. The Chao sisters were allowed to remain on in Ai Ti's court for the next five years, until the powerful chancellor Wang Mang and his equally powerful aunt, Empress Dowager Wang, had both Chao sisters degraded to the status of commoners and exiled from the palace. On the day this decree was issued, Flying Swallow committed suicide. Memory of her as a celebrated beauty lives on today in the standard Chinese phrase complimenting a lady's figure, "as slender as the Flying Swallow."

The eighteen-year-old Emperor Ai Ti was also to suffer recurring illnesses during his short reign, possibly as a result of the Han bloodline having been weakened by interfamily marriages. Yet Ai Ti made every attempt to take a personal part in government. Expressing disapproval of his predecessor's penchant for gaming and wanton entertainments and a generally extravagant style of palace administration, Ai Ti and his ministers introduced measures for retrenchment. One edict abolished the huge government agencies which furnished luxury textiles for the wardrobes of thousands of palace inmates. All females in the harem below thirty years of age were released, and palace slaves over fifty were freed. No longer would whole communities be forced to relocate to construct and care for imperial tombs of empress mothers. Also, senior officials could no longer nominate their sons and brothers for office. Considerably reduced were the oppressive controls—often employing cruel methods—maintained by regional officials over the local populace. Ai Ti abolished the Office of Music, calling it a source of corruption because of the extravagance of the performances it sponsored and its endorsement of modern music, which, it was considered, would result in national economic poverty and a general depravity of Chinese life.

This emperor also did his best to mitigate the increasingly bitter successional rivalries between dowagers and consorts, backed by their various eunuchs and political allies. Having observed with disapproval his predecessor's indolence in allowing Empress Dowager Wang and her male relatives to grasp political control, he reduced Wang family influence by the bestowal of titles of the highest honor on his mother, Empress Dowager Ting, and his strong-willed grandmother, Empress Dowager Fu. Empress Dowager Fu had reared Ai Ti from infancy and thus had a special hold on his loyalties. When Ai Ti's scholarly marshal of state (a fourteenth-generation, direct descendant of Confucius) opposed the granting of these titles, he was removed from office and replaced by a brother of Empress Dowager Ting. Granting the two dowagers titles on a par with that of Empress Dowager Wang undermined the political influence of both Dowager Wang and her nephew Wang Mang—though only temporarily.

Prodded by Empress Dowager Fu's resentment at being housed in one of the Chang An lodges provided for kings visiting from principalities, and by her envy of Empress Dowager Wang's imposing palace, Ai Ti moved his grandmother to the elegant North Palace, which gave her direct and private access to his own quarters. There she successfully protected and promoted the interests of her clan and Empress Dowager Ting's, arousing the disapproval of conservatives who could not tolerate female intervention in palace affairs.

Soon the palace was beset by strange occurrences of ill omen. When documents were being ceremonially presented to induct two men into high positions—men known to be in league with Dowagers Fu and Ting—a sudden loud ringing of bells was heard, the origin of which could never be explained. Frightened, Ai Ti called in official interpreters, who declared that the mysterious noise was Heaven's warning to the throne of the danger of domination of palace women, and of appointing ministers who catered to the dowagers' demands. One master diviner even predicted that, according to the signs, the Han Dynasty had reached the end of its allotted span and now stood in danger of replacement. He also said that Ai Ti's continuing illnesses and inability to sire an heir were omens of Heaven's displeasure, and advised Ai Ti to adopt a new reign title and start a new calendar era. When these measures brought no abatement to Ai Ti's poor health, and no imperial heir, either, the diviner was put to death for "disobeying moral principles, misleading mankind, and behaving treacherously."

When, at the beginning of his reign, Ai Ti had replaced Wang Mang as marshal of state with his own childhood tutor, the former tutor introduced reforms to curb the growth of large landed estates and decreased their allowable number of slaves. Ai Ti's edict to this effect, however, could never be implemented due to the objections of Dowagers Fu and Ting, who stood to lose heavily if it were implemented. Another who vehemently objected to these reforms was the court official, Tung Hsien, who had gained wealth and notoriety as the sexual companion and beloved favorite of Emperor Ai Ti.

Historians despised Tung Hsien for his homosexuality as well as his untoward influence over the emperor. However, at this time catamites were not uncommon in Chinese courts. Tung Hsien was two years younger than the emperor, and such was his allure that Ai Ti presented him with priceless gifts from the imperial treasuries and granted him authority to keep arms and to use the royal carriages. He ennobled the man's wife and daughters and invited them to live in the palace as personal attendants. He also ennobled Tung Hsien's father; his younger brother was castrated as eunuch keeper-of-the-palace; and his father-in-law became the palace contractor supervising the building of a luxurious mansion and mausoleum for the Tung family. Ai Ti appointed Tung Hsien a marquis with high military rank, and in the year 1 B.C. made him marshal of state. Ai Ti loved this favorite so much that he abandoned all reliance on his own male relatives, and once even proposed—perhaps under the influence of drink—to abdicate and turn the throne over to his beloved paramour. A member of Empress Dowager Wang's family ultimately was able to shame Ai Ti into abandoning this preposterous idea.

Catamite Hung Tsien's great good fortune suddenly collapsed in 1 B.C. when the twenty-three-year-old Ai Ti's chronic illness culminated in his death after only five years on the throne. Since both Dowagers Fu and Ting were by this time dead and buried in splendid imperial mausoleums, Dowager Empress Wang and her nephew Wang Mang found themselves without opposition for control of national affairs, except for the marshal of state, the catamite Tung Hsien. Empress Wang summoned Tung into her presence purportedly to discuss imperial funeral arrangements, and after that audience imperiously announced to the court that Tung Hsien was such an utter incompetent that she felt justified in having him impeached. The very next day she made her nephew Wang Mang the new chancellor of the outer court, with added powers to supervise the palace secretariat. Unable to stomach this bitter disgrace, both Tung Hsien and his wife committed suicide.

Tung Hsien will always be remembered, however, from an oft-repeated episode that occurred one day when he and Emperor Ai Ti were enjoying an afternoon nap. The emperor was awakened by a eunuch delivering a message summoning him to urgent state business. However, to his consternation, Ai Ti found that his sleeping lover's head was resting on the long, flowing sleeve of his robe. Unable to bring himself to disturb Tung Hsien's rest, the emperor cut off his sleeve with an ornamental sword. Ever after, the phrase "cutting the sleeve" has been used by the Chinese as a euphemism for homosexuality.

Within a month after Ai Ti's death, Empress Dowager Wang and her nephew Wang Mang placed Ping Ti on the throne, an eight-year-old Han prince, the son of former Emperor Cheng Ti's half-brother, who had been bypassed as heir five years before. Now Chancellor Wang Mang, acting as regent over the new child emperor, took the first step toward reinstating the Wang family's former position of power. First, he degraded the deceased Empress Dowagers Fu and Ting by having their graves opened, their imperial insignia removed from their corpses, and their remains reburied in graves of commoners. A few years later, Wang Mang further cemented his own power by arranging the marriage of his daughter to the emperor, who was eleven years of age at the time.

Three years later Ping Ti died, reportedly of poison administered on the instructions of Wang Mang, who then put on the throne a one-year-old baby in whose name he continued to rule; whereupon he secretly did away with this last Han infant and made himself emperor. Though the truth about the deaths of these two child-emperors may never be known for sure, imperial palace secrets ever had a way of leaking out to become common knowledge, usually due to tattling palace eunuchs.

Thus, Wang Mang is branded by Confucian historians as an arch usurper who committed two murders in order to seize the throne from the esteemed Han Dynasty. He is also remembered by the Confucians as a man whose hated social reforms tore the nation asunder. Modern historians are more likely to see Wang Mang as a capable, dedicated, farsighted statesman who had the misfortune of living at the wrong time in history, for Han China at the time of Christ was far from ready to accept Wang Mang's enlightened legislation.

His enemies lost no time in defaming Wang Mang, who, as high minister back in Emperor Wu Ti's reign, had had his own son put to death. This son, then superintendent of the palace guards, had dared question the validity of the emperor's final decree appointing the powerful Huo Kuang as regent for the chosen heir. By so doing, Wang's son had become suspect in a plot to reinstate the Wei family, which had been discredited due to the witchcraft scandal. For this affront to the Han throne, Wang Mang dutifully had his son executed. His enemies also referred to the strong suspicions that Wang Mang had had the boy-emperor Ping Ti poisoned and then did away with the one-year-old baby emperor.

Despite these accusations, Wang Mang had been respected by many as a talented, devoted minister, adept at attracting loyal adherents. His devotion to scholarship and the teachings of antiquity had made him particularly esteemed by Confucian intellectuals. Though rich, he lived modestly and gave generously of his wealth to friends and the poor, which made him the epitome of a Confucian gentleman. The preceeding farcical reigns of the several sickly child emperors had convinced many, including some Han royalty, that Heaven had withdrawn its mandate from the Han Dynasty—an idea which Wang Mang took considerable pains to foster. He accepted the throne, he claimed, because of popular demand, and only after he had repeatedly protested his unworthiness in an age-old ritual of proper Confucian humility.

Under Wang Mang's "New Dynasty"—as he titled his regime—the dispossessed Han imperial family became a house divided against itself. Wang ousted all members of the Han family who did not support him, reducing them to commoners. In his first year as emperor, he crushed three Han family plots against him, after which no less than thirty-two members of the Han family still pledged support in his favor.

To convince the nation that Heaven had discredited the failing Han Dynasty and bestowed the mandate to rule upon his own person, Wang Mang took full advantage of the universal belief that strange phenomena were omens. He had it reported that unusual rocks bearing inscriptions praising his name had rained down from above, and his adherents sent reports from all over the country of good luck signs and auguries in Wang Mang's favor. Some 30,000 poems were mysteriously received at court exalting Wang Mang's virtues and notable achievements. Even a member of the Han royal family reported having had a strange dream predicting that Wang Mang would be the next representative of Heaven on earth.

Wang Mang convinced himself and many others that his family was directly descended from a revered god-king of Chinese mythology, and set about replacing the Han Dynasty's ancestral shrines in the capital with new ones where official sacrifices to his own forebears would lend legitimacy to his reign.

As emperor, Wang Mang longed to emulate the divine rulers of the hoary past, each of whom was exalted in Confucian literature as a kindly "mother and father to all." He surrounded himself with men trained in letters and philosophy, and worked far into the night to devise schemes to make the nation a land of contentment and plenty. "One sees the fields of the rich stretching in the hundreds and thousands, while the poor have not land enough to plant a needle," he wrote, and "slave markets have been established where men are sold like horses and cattle, a thing manifestly contrary to the wishes of Heaven and Earth who gave man a nature nobler than that of animals."[3]

He forbade the buying and selling of land in the hope of halting the concentration of wealth in the hands of great landowners, who had gradually taken over the fields of debt-ridden, destitute farmers. Wang Mang granted small plots to each peasant family of eight, and forbade all traffic in slaves— except for government use.

These and other reforms, in which he tried in vain to stabilize prices, control avaricious moneylenders, and fix equitable taxes, only proved that Wang Mang was more a theorist than a judge of human nature. He was bewildered and heartbroken when his innovations only caused widespread anger and alienation of all classes, especially those whose greed for gain he was trying to thwart. State monopoly of gold ruined the nobility, state control of timber and fisheries hurt the peasantry, and Wang Mang's several experiments with coinage all but destroyed commerce and the merchant class. Thus his reforms failed utterly—indeed, could never be implemented— making it necessary for him to rescind them all within three years.

Everything seemed to conspire against Wang Mang, even nature. Successive years of drought and poor harvest alternated with floods. The Yellow River, known as China's Sorrow, broke its dikes in A.D. 11 and completely inundated vast areas in the east. Uncounted thousands drowned, while more became homeless refugees beset by famine, epidemics, and pestilence. Wandering hordes roamed the land, men sold their starving wives and children, and some were even reduced to cannibalism.

Under these deplorable conditions, droves of destitute were easily enticed to join secret societies, sometimes led by Taoist mystics, sometimes by bandit chiefs, who promised a decent living and better days to come. The most notorious of these peasant sects were the Red Eyebrows, the devotees of which invoked Taoist deities, swore to restore the Han Dynasty, and as a sign of membership in the sect and loyalty to one another dyed their eyebrows scarlet. The spiritual leader of the Red Eyebrows spoke through a Taoist medium, organized peasant hordes into disciplined administrative and military units, and turned them loose to plunder the rich and kill government officials and representatives wherever they could be found.

Emperor Wang Mang sent imperial armies to quell these insurgents, only to see the armies beaten back as soldiers defected to the Red Eyebrows and started looting and plundering themselves. So extensive was the slaughter of troops that replacements for them could not be found, and the army soon disintegrated. Encouraged and supported by the disgruntled populace, and now even the landed gentry—including some kin of the Han family—by A.D. 18 the Red Eyebrow legions were masters of the eastern provinces and had their sights set on Chang An.

Men of the nearly defunct House of Han finally united their forces to storm and take the capital. Wang Mang, deserted by his followers but believing himself protected by the divine sanctity of the Son of Heaven, merely sat on the throne reciting Confucian teachings, shedding tears toward the south. Eventually, he took refuge in a high tower in the middle of an imperial park lake. There soldiers found him holding in one hand an ornamental knife claimed to have been inherited from his god-king forebears, while in the other he clutched an emblem used by Taoist sorcerers in magic rituals. The soldiers cut off Wang Mang's head and carried it back to the Han princes, who kept the skull as a trophy in the imperial Han treasury for the next 200 years.

Meanwhile, a Han prince who had declared himself ruler in the capital proved to be an utter mediocrity. Interested solely in ridiculous pleasures, he even made his cook a high official. Soon the Red Eyebrows swarmed over Chang An, capturing the city with little effort, then indulging in an orgy of killing and looting. The would-be Han emperor fled in terror, but was captured by insurgents and strangled.

In A.D. 25, another Han prince, Kuang Wu Ti, an accomplished soldier and popular leader, set up headquarters at Loyang, the secondary Han capital, some sixty miles east of Chang An. There he was proclaimed emperor of the Second Han Dynasty. Red Eyebrow peasant mobs, possibly sated with pillaging after devastating Chang An, ebbed back toward the east, where they were surrounded by the new emperor's troops and massacred by the thousands. Those that were not killed were made prisoners—in all, some 80,000 bandits and their trollop camp followers. Other rebels were not to be brought completely under control until ten years later.

Thus ended Wang Mang's disastrous thirteen-year reign. Yet his aborted social and economic reforms were never to be forgotten: they would be attempted off and on during later dynasties, as other emperors tried to eradicate widespread inequities.

Historians have ever mourned the fall of the First Han Dynasty to the machinations of scheming, greedy palace females. Even more so would they mourn the collapse of the Second Han Dynasty under the evil and ruinous influence of palace eunuchs, who would become the most powerful faction in government.

Notes

1. R. Grousset, *The Rise and Splendour of the Chinese Empire.*
2. B. Watson, *Courtier and Commoner in Ancient China.*
3. R. Grousset, *The Rise and Splendour of the Chinese Empire.*

7

First Great Rise of Organized Eunuch Power

SECOND HAN DYNASTY (A.D. 25-220)

Fortunately for the war-torn nation, Kuang Wu Ti, founder of the Second Han Dynasty, proved to be an earnest, energetic realist who succeeded in leading China back towards recovery. He devoted most of his thirty-three-year reign towards restoring internal order. By great exertion, he managed to bring the hordes of Red Eyebrow insurgents under control. By A.D. 44 imperial Han armies had quashed revolting aborigine subjects in Szechuan, the Red River basin, and the north Vietnam coast, bringing these peoples firmly under Chinese yoke, after which they became completely sinicized. Most of the independent-minded generals—who could have posed problems with their "private" armies—were peaceably enticed into retirement with liberal allowances from the throne.

To his immediate successors Kuang Wu Ti had to leave the task of restoring Chinese prestige in Turkestan, where vassal Tartar states—watching China's disintegration—had felt it safe to discontinue sending tribute. Several of China's trade routes to Central Asia had also been severed. Humiliating as this rebuff was to China's international prestige, the new Han emperor wisely chose to direct all efforts toward national repair.

Since the Chang An capital had been all but demolished in recent civil strife, Kuang Wu Ti used as his first residence a wing of the South

Palace at Loyang, the former Han auxiliary capital. In time, copying the layout of Chang An, he built a broad three-lane avenue leading up to the Loyang palace gate; the central lane was used solely by the Son of Heaven, while pedestrians were relegated to the two side lanes, one to enter, the other to exit the palace. He also rebuilt the protecting city walls of compressed yellow earth, in some places thirty feet thick, and expanded the area of the capital to over ten miles in circumference.

Well-educated himself, Kuang Wu Ti promoted scholarship, carrying on the tradition which would make the two Han dynasties renowned as a 400-year period when literature flourished, especially historiography. Though the imperial library at Chang An had been reduced to ashes by pillagers, Kuang Wu Ti now rescued and transported to Loyang over 2,000 oxcart-loads of written records. Duplicates of a large number of destroyed manuscripts, owned by private scholars and intellectuals, were collected and reproduced. By A.D. 32 Kuang Wu Ti had completed the archives as well as an imperial academy that at times enrolled over 30,000 students.

Kuang Wu Ti relied heavily for support on the increasingly powerful social class that had carried him to power—the land-owning gentry. Many of the gentry families had been predominant for generations in the Loyang area, and the recent turmoil had resulted in a great influx of uprooted peasants and workers to the area, vastly increasing Loyang's labor force, to the benefit of the gentry. Thus, the landholders were soon able to reestablish their luxurious, cultured living style, as all classes gradually settled back into long-established social patterns.

To his relatives and supporters Kuang Wu Ti granted only 365 estates, equal to the days in the year, and decreed that there would be no more kings ruling in the principalities: from now on these rulers would be titled simply duke or marquis. Kuang Wu Ti also initiated the policy of keeping the empress's family members entirely removed from government affairs, a lesson learned after former Empress Wang's nephew Wang Mang seized the Han throne. This policy would be continued under Kuang Wu Ti's immediate successors.

Kuang Wu Ti's early edicts completely separated the corps of palace eunuchs from that of government officials in the hope of preventing the reemergence of power cliques involving these two factions. However, in his leniency, he reduced the death sentence—even for high treason—to castration. Some claim that this sentence reduction served mainly to increase the number of eunuchs in the palace and the number of educated, influential men amongst the eunuchs; and that the attempt to isolate eunuchs from state affairs only tended to increase their desire for power. Thus, Kuang Wu Ti may have unwittingly sown the seeds which would one day destroy his dynasty, for the history of the Second House of Han is largely a record of the ups and downs of organized eunuch power.

In A.D. 58, after thirty-three years of Kuang Wu Ti's sound and sober policies, his son Ming Ti inherited a revitalized nation. One of Ming Ti's first decrees required all schools to promulgate the state cult of Confucianism. Confucius now officially became Patron Saint of Scholars, with religious rites performed at temples erected in his honor. Many now worshipped the Great Sage as a deity. (Confucius was not the last historical figure to be so deified in China, for down through the centuries many a great hero or illustrious personage was canonized and worshipped by imperial decree.)

Like most Chinese emperors, Ming Ti embarked on an elaborate building program, refurbishing the North Palace in Loyang and adding an audience hall that would accommodate 10,000 persons. This structure sat at the top of a great tier of steps, its stately, curving rooftops visible for some thirteen miles around. Covered passageways linked the North and South palaces to conceal the emperor's movements. Modern-day excavations in Loyang show that the two palaces occupied half the city area, the remainder being taken up by the imperial park, administration buildings, royal storehouse and armory, and residential districts for ranking officials and aristocrats. Commoners lived outside the city gates, around the marketplaces, while the peasantry lived in outlying rural farm villages. Ming Ti is also credited with constructing a dike thirty miles in length to control the disastrously flood-prone Yellow River.

Ming Ti is best known, however, as the emperor who introduced Indian Buddhism into China. Records say that in A.D. 61 a golden statue was revealed to Ming Ti in a dream—an image of the Buddha, one of his clairvoyant ministers assured him, the North Indian prince and sage who had founded the religion around 500 B.C. Fascinated by this revelation, Ming Ti dispatched envoys to India to gather information on the alien faith. They returned some years later, bringing copies of Buddhist scripture and two Indian missionaries. As a place suitable for them to live, teach, and translate their holy books, Ming Ti built the White Pony Temple in Loyang, said to be China's first Buddhist shrine. Foreign merchants, missionaries, and travelers coming along the Silk Roads from Afghanistan and Central Asia—where Indian Buddhism already flourished—were also instrumental in fostering the growth of the new cult in China.

Members of court circles became intrigued with the new exotic religion, which eventually would spread to all classes, and which at times would come to rival native Taoism and even Confucianism. Buddhism is the religion which most palace eunuchs would come to prefer—and often use surreptitiously to further their quest for riches.

Ruler Ming Ti also set out to restore China's lost prestige among the defected vassal states of Turkestan and the nomad tribes of Mongolia. Several nearby Mongolian chieftains were already allied with China against their kinsmen further north. With their assistance, Ming Ti sent expeditions far into Outer Mongolia and pushed the marauding enemy horsemen all the way to the Altai Mountains. By A.D. 88 the nomads were so decisively defeated by Han armies that, for over a century, China's northern frontier was secure from barbarian attack.

In A.D. 78 Ming Ti launched one of the most famous military men in Chinese history on a brilliant career which was to span the next three decades. General Pan Chao was from an illustrious family, his scholarly father having started, before his death, a definitive history of the Han Dynasties. This work was completed by Pan Chao's sister, who is now known as China's first and foremost female scholar—she was also known as the "Mistress of Poetry, Eloquence, and History." She had originally been a lady-in-waiting to the Han empress, and her well-known *Admonitions to Court Ladies* set the Confucian standard for ages to come of decorous, subservient female conduct, wherein a woman was even prohibited from addressing her husband by name. Nonetheless, Pan Chao's sister strongly advocated female education, pointing out that while court ladies were quite knowledgeable in the art of painting their faces, they were deplorably lacking in the means to nourish their intellect.

Ming Ti sent General Pan Chao to recover Chinese prestige in Turkestan and Central Asia. On reaching the nearest vassal state, Pan Chao and his entourage received a warm welcome. Within days, however, he sensed a complete reversal in the local ruler's attitude. Rightly suspecting that a representative of the Mongolian enemy had arrived to undermine his efforts, Pan Chao sought out his rival, chopped off his head, and presented it to his host. From then on Pan Chao was treated with awe and respect throughout the entire area. Within two decades his armies had regained control of China's western outposts and compelled some fifty Turkestani rulers to again send regular tribute to the Han throne. In A.D. 102 Pan Chao returned to Loyang a hero, and died peacefully soon thereafter.

Under favorable policies of Ming Ti and his successor, Chang Ti, the landholdings and influence of the great manored families steadily increased. Archeological research on their tombs confirms that by this time the burial of human sacrifices with deceased notables had been stopped. These intended servants of the deceased in the Afterworld, who used to be buried with them, along with live horses and real carriages, were now represented in graves by small replicas modeled in clay, wood, or sometimes bronze. Also buried with the rich gentry were miniature examples of everything used on their lands—tools, coins, domestic animals, peasant laborers, farm buildings—leaving an amazingly clear record of agricultural practices in these times. One interesting pottery replica—an open-pit latrine in which hogs are rooting—is reminiscent of just such a toilet into which Han Empress Lu threw her rival, some 200 years before.

Wall reliefs and frescoes found in tombs of this era picture the gentry riding in processions of fine horse-drawn carriages and enjoying banquets and entertainments in the great manor houses, while peasants work the land, often carrying weapons as members of their master's private militia. The peasantry also produced all the foods and handmade craft items necessary to make each manor house a self-supporting entity, and labored to cover the elaborate graves of their lords with earthen mounds as high as small mountains.

In A.D. 79 Han ruler Chang Ti ordered an official commission of scholars to compile an edition of all the writings attributed to Confucius and his school of philosophy. This monumental work from then on had canonical authority and firmly established the Confucian intelligentsia and scholar-officials as an organized power group. These intellectuals would eventually be locked in deadly combat with palace eunuchs to control government.

For almost a century under the Second Han Dynasty, China enjoyed increasing prosperity and cultural development, and prestige throughout Asia. Then, after having reached the peak of success (*yang*), affairs began to deteriorate in a slow 100-year decline to ultimate collapse (*yin*). Eunuchs contributed substantially to this decline, as circumstances in the palaces presented them with repeated opportunities to usurp control of state affairs.

Ten-year-old Ho Ti was placed on the Han throne in A.D. 88, the first in a series of child rulers under the regency of dowager empresses whose clans took turns controlling the emperors' private and public affairs. When they came of age, these often weak-willed monarchs repeatedly tried to overthrow the blatant domination of consort-regent families by putting palace eunuchs in positions of power. By Ho Ti's time, the general increase in luxury and size of the imperial court was paralleled by a like increase in the harem. The vast numbers of palace women made necessary a veritable army of eunuchs, most of whom were low-born menials. However, a considerable number in the eunuch corps were former scholar-officials condemned and castrated for offenses. Some of this group served faithfully as mediators between the inner and outer courts. Some also devoted their spare time to Confucian studies, work on various technical advances, or the study of alchemy under renown Taoist practitioners.

One enterprising eunuch, Tsai Lun, who had been in palace service for fifteen years prior to Ho Ti's reign, had an inquisitive mind and used every opportunity to study the treasured treatises in the imperial archives. He was pleased with the recent change in monarchs, for Ho Ti's empress was genuinely interested in scholarship and literature. She befriended and encouraged Tsai Lun, and no doubt was responsible for his promotion to chief of the eunuch staff.

This administrative post made eunuch Tsai Lun aware of the inconvenience of engraving records and literary works on cumbersome wooden or bamboo strips and plaques, and of the expense entailed in the more recent method of writing with ink on scrolls of rolled silk cloth. Largely through a desire to please his benefactress, after countless experiments combining old rags, fish net, tree bark, and hemp, Tsai Lun succeeded in A.D. 105 in producing a usable form of paper. "Tsai Lun's paper" came into universal use in China, and 600 years later the Chinese taught the manufacture of paper to the Arabs. Paper would be unknown in Europe until the twelfth century.

In A.D. 114 eunuch Tsai Lun's patroness, now dowager empress, saw to it that he was titled a marquis, and was later responsible for his appointment as Lord High Chamberlain of the eunuch corps. But at her death, the aging eunuch found himself out of favor with a new empress whose scheming involved him in unsavory palace intrigues. Finally, saddened to see his prestige from a long and successful career undermined, the eunuch who invented paper retired to his home and committed suicide. He took the required bath, combed his long hair into a top-knot, donned his official hat and robes, and drank poison mixed in a little bowl of wine. Tsai Lun's biography represents one of the rare instances in Chinese history where a palace eunuch is praised.

Many eunuchs in Ho Ti's palace had far less integrity than had Tsai Lun. Having become emperor as a child, with his mother, Empress Teng, as regent, Ho Ti came to deeply resent his maternal uncle, the real power behind the throne. On reaching his majority, Ho Ti enlisted the aid of his chief eunuch, Chen Chung, to murder this uncle. After this, for the remainder of his seventeen-year reign, Ho Ti was unable to free himself from the clutches and domination of his wily co-conspirator. It is said that eunuch Chen Chung's easy acquisition of power served to encourage other eunuchs to try to insinuate themselves into positions of influence.

When Ho Ti died in A.D. 105, his 100-day-old son was put on the throne, with Empress Teng again as regent. This infant died in a matter of months, but she continued to act as regent for the next emperor, An Ti, who acceded to the throne at age thirteen. During her entire regency,

Empress Teng—following rules of Confucian decorum for women—held no audience with ministers of state, but suffered her eunuchs to be the sole medium of communication with the ministers, affording them a voice in every national question and an important role in every court intrigue.

When Emperor An Ti died in A.D. 125, a group of powerful eunuchs led by one Sun Chen successfully proclaimed the Han prince Shun Ti emperor, thus foiling a counterplot of the relatives of the new empress, allied with a second group of influential eunuchs. All three eunuch leaders of this second alliance, and all their conspirators were put to death by the party of the victors.

From this time on, eunuch cliques held power by teaming up against the consort family and factions of scholar-officials. The unprecedented political influence of the eunuchs during Shun Ti's reign (A.D. 125-144) was recognized as a dangerous threat to control governmental affairs. Before this, under young or inept rulers, affairs of state had always been administered either by a dowager regent and her male kinfolk or seasoned ministers.

Now, however, the eunuchs squared off against the great authority of the renowned Liang consort-family, which had made one of its daughters Shun Ti's empress. This notorious clan dominated government for twenty years, producing three empresses, seven imperial princes, six imperial concubines, three grand generals of the armies, and fifty-seven ministers of state and governors of provinces. Shun Ti's Empress Liang was one of four concubines regarded by the ruler with equal affection. Unable to decide which should be his legitimate consort, Shun Ti was about to have lots drawn, when wiser heads prevailed upon him to select his consort according to family background, virtue, age, and appearance. The Liang concubine won out in the final interview by coyly suggesting that the emperor would be granted "a large number of descendants and a hundred happinesses" if he chose a wife who was not of a jealous nature. No doubt she was well aware that Chinese males especially feared and detested any jealousy and discord among their wives and mistresses.

Overweening control by the Liang family, however—especially by the empress's brothers, who threatened to seize the throne—greatly hastened the eventual triumph of the palace eunuchs. For, to counteract the encroachments of the Liangs, the emperor now bestowed upon trusted eunuchs high official rank and titles. This aroused fierce resentment among orthodox officials, intellectuals, and even the populace.

In A.D. 135 Shun Ti's eunuchs pressured him into issuing an edict granting them the right to legally adopt uncastrated sons. This unprecedented concession enhanced the eunuchs' already considerable greed for wealth, for now they could leave the fortunes they accumulated to heirs, in the time-honored Chinese tradition. This adoption right for eunuchs was destined to be rescinded and reinstated several times in dynasties to come.

It is reported that during Shun Ti's reign one enterprising palace eunuch alone acquired thirty-one homes and some 1,500 acres of lucrative tilled land. Other eunuchs became masters of even larger agricultural domains and controlled droves of personal slave workers, while many made fortunes in big business ventures. Now palace eunuchs took wives, set up proper households, and established their relatives, retainers, adopted sons, and grandsons in central and provincial offices to carry out their self-seeking policies.

When Shun Ti died, in A.D. 144, Empress Liang and her grand marshal brother still were powerful enough to put on the throne and act as regents for a two-year-old Han prince, who died, however, in less than a year. Then they enthroned another Han child, whom they soon poisoned in the belief that he would oppose Liang family ambitions. Finally, in A.D. 147, Empress Liang's brother made a fifteen-year-old Han prince called Huan Ti emperor, while continuing to lord it over the nation as the most powerful official of state. To fortify his position and that of his clansmen— who by now held most high offices—Grand Marshal Liang married off one of his younger sisters to Emperor Huan Ti.

For the next twelve years Huan Ti chafed as an ineffectual figurehead under the domination of the overbearing grand marshal, but at Empress Dowager Liang's death in, A.D. 159, he saw his chance to plot revenge. Enlisting the aid of a palace eunuch named Chao and four of his eunuch henchmen—all of whom detested the Liangs for undermining the throne, upon which their lives depended—Emperor Huan Ti had them assassinate Grand Marshal Liang in a sudden ambush attack. Almost as suddenly, the entire Liang family was ejected from their posts and executed, their great wealth confiscated, and their landholdings auctioned off to replenish the government treasury. While he was at it, Huan Ti also deposed the childless Empress Liang, thus ending the power of her clan altogether.

On the very day of the surprise coup against the Liangs, Huan Ti ennobled eunuch Chao and his four cohorts, and bestowed upon each of them lands with tax revenues from thousands of households. Then, further dismaying loyal officials, he presented the "Five Eunuch Lords," as they now called themselves, with huge cash awards. Leading eunuch Chao died soon thereafter, but his four accomplices continued to completely dominate the court by acting as a council of state. Huan Ti relied upon them in all matters. The eunuchs convinced him they had saved him from his most formidable enemies—the Liang clan. Before long eunuch power was greater than that of the Liangs had ever been, as was their lust for riches.

Under Huan Ti and his young successor, Ling Ti, the eunuchs took over all key positions, controlling the economy, administration, military, judiciary—even ideology. These posts they filled with their own relatives, fellow eunuchs, and craven officials. Legitimate officials were forced to buy appointments and promotions from palace eunuchs with bribes in gold. Honors, rewards, titles, and influence were now bestowed only upon those whom the eunuchs recommended to the emperor, and only after they had paid the demanded price. Provincial officials, having purchased their posts, could retain them only with continual contributions to the eunuch overlords, an outlay which they recouped by misappropriating tax revenue collections and cruelly exploiting the populace with ever-increasing taxes.

Countless needy or ambitious fathers, seeing that riches were so readily available to palace eunuchs, had themselves or their sons emasculated to enter imperial service. Hordes of eunuchs now organized and consolidated themselves under a "eunuch elite"—the clique especially favored by the emperor.

Despised and resented as they were by upright officials, in the emperor's eyes the eunuchs were his best choice as loyal confidants, since they would protect him from the domination of nobility, the tyranny of consort families, and the moral supervision of pompous Confucian officials, all of whom now saw their influence rapidly waning.

The history of the Second Han Dynasty described court eunuchs at their height of power: "Wearing high official hats and long swords, tying crimson cords around their waists and carrying gold ornaments on their person, the eunuchs were posted throughout the palace. A score of them bestowed titles of nobility upon themselves, and now as grandees owning fiefdoms, they feel entitled to receive their retainers facing south [as does only the emperor when meeting his courtiers]. Their palatial mansions stretch in rows from the capital to the suburbs. Their adopted nephews and other junior family members take up more than half the government payroll. Gold and treasures from the South, bolts of pure white silk and misty-colored gauze [both mediums of exchange], fill their private storehouses to overflowing. Ladies of the bedchamber and waiting women, singing boys and dancing girls, staff the eunuchs' homes. Their fine dogs and horses are richly caparisoned. Interior walls and pillars of their mansions are covered with hangings of embroidered yellow and red silk. The wherewithal for these luxuries is ultimately fleeced from the masses in taxes. Vying with each other in their extravagances and covetousness, the eunuchs scheme to bring honest and virtuous officials into trouble, and to foster factionalism at court."[1]

Eunuchs acquired such wealth that even kinsmen of Han empresses allied with them in lucrative business dealings, as did big merchants and industrialists who profited greatly by supplying the "purchasing eunuchs" with overpriced goods to satisfy palace extravagance, which the eunuchs encouraged.

Yet the eunuch take-over by no means went unopposed. Certain outraged brave officials who attempted to save the nation from sinking under a morass of eunuch corruption and graft issued a veritable stream of remonstrances, memorials, and petitions to the throne. They succeeded in having only a few of the most conspicuously corrupt discredited.

Army generals' loyalty to the throne cooled as they watched their officers being degraded for inability or unwillingness to pay stiff bribes to the eunuchs. Unfortunately, a combined effort between the military and officialdom to purge the eunuchs from court never came about due to lack of cooperation, for intellectuals had always looked on army officials with a jaundiced and perhaps fearful eye.

At last, thousands of indignant scholars from the imperial academy rallied with like-minded officials in government to form an association ostensibly devoted to the spread of Confucian doctrine, but actually used as a forum to express bitter opposition to eunuch control. The scholars' league also had strong public backing, for the populace suffered as much from eunuch exactions as did the bureaucrats.

The first disastrous collision occurred in A.D. 166 when eunuch leaders accused the scholars' league of scheming to discredit the emperor's rule. Convinced of this by his eunuchs, Huan Ti issued an edict for the arrest of several hundred members of the league on grounds that they had "conspired to organize illegally to criticize government policies and to abuse good customs and traditions." Interestingly, it was the empress's father, a man of considerable authority, who finally intervened and saw that most of the accused were freed from jail. Even so, hundreds of scholars were sent back to their native states and prohibited from holding public office for life. These moves drew angry opposition from the public, who rose up to champion the accused scholars as martyrs, who were glorified as "The Pure Critics," while palace eunuchs were scorned as the "muddy faction."

The whole structure of government began to crumble. The inquisition against the league of scholars and officials by Emperor Huan Ti and his eunuchs was soon to be followed by another, more serious one. Palace officials, who considered the administration their rightful domain, had long stood as a power bloc opposed to consort-regent clans who so often dominated the emperor and government. Now, for the first time, the reigning Dowager Empress Tou and an influential brother enlisted the aid of officials and the association of scholars to help purge eunuch supremacy once and for all from court.

Rallying this time around the dowager empress's brother, who was considered a match for the powerful eunuch leaders, thousands of scholars staged a clamorous demonstration against eunuch abuses. Especially they decried blatant excesses, such as those of eunuch Hou Lan, who had confiscated so many houses and landholdings that he was able to build himself ten fine mansions and a pretentious mausoleum for his own future burial.

Predictably, the consortium of eunuchs who controlled the young emperor were not long in wreaking a fearful vengeance against their detractors. Using the murder of a palace eunuch as a pretext to commence an imperial investigation, eunuch leaders soon accused the dowager empress's brother and over 100 intellectuals of sedition. All were executed or imprisoned, while their relations "to the fifth degree" were exiled and barred from ever again holding office. Dowager Empress Tou was banished and imprisoned in a deserted palace, and nearly a thousand more scholars were thrown into jail, tortured, or killed. For good measure, the eunuchs coerced the impressionable young Emperor Ling Ti into signing an edict proscribing the scholars' league altogether, and removing from office all officials thought to be associated with it.

For the rest of his short life, Ling Ti acquiesced completely to the will of the eunuchs. He addressed favorites among them in familiar terms of endearment and respect such as "Mother" or "Father," and was even enticed to share in their profits from the sale of official positions. Cloistered within the palace by his eunuchs, the emperor never realized they were ruining the nation, nor that out in the countryside the exploited, overtaxed peasantry were preparing for the first stage of one of the most devastating rebellions China was ever to see.

For some decades, Taoist occultists, alchemists, and mystagogues had been attracting disgruntled peasant followers by attempting to heal the sick with magic talismans and secret potions, and promising longevity and a better life for those who pledged loyalty and paid cult dues. Around A.D. 175, one such charismatic medicine man, a wonder-worker named Chang, along with his two brothers, founded a new, more formidable secret society cult. In emotion-charged ceremonies lasting several days, Chang succored crowds of the poor and "miraculously" cured victims of a then-raging pestilence with magic amulets and potions, faith healing, ecstatic trances, confessions of sin, and orgies in which male and female devotees scandalously "mingled their breath" as taught in Taoist sex manuals.

Chang organized his vast following into a structured church hierarchy, trained them in Taoist military arts, appointing himself as "Heavenly General," and sent a stream of missionaries out across east and central China. With remarkable rapidity, Chang brought the peasantry of eight provinces completely under his spell.

When the central government finally became alarmed enough to plan action against Chang's sect, Chang himself—warned in advance and bedazzled by the power he now held—made the first move. Issuing an alarm to his huge flock, and avowing that, according to the stars, the year A.D. 184 was the beginning of a new millennium, he raised a cry for an all-out revolution. With fanatical zeal, some 360,000 devotees donned yellow headdresses as their badge of loyalty. At Chang's signal, the so-called "Yellow Turban Rebellion" exploded across the face of a nation already debilitated by gross mismanagement by eunuchs at the capital.

Unwary provincial authorities were everywhere overwhelmed and slaughtered. In a plan to capture the emperor, Chang even sent cult members to cultivate the cooperation of eunuchs controlling the Loyang palace, but word of this plot leaked out and his agents were put to death. In a matter of months, the mushrooming number of peasant hordes pillaging and killing throughout the provinces reached alarming magnitude, leaving devastation and untold thousands dead. The imperial court depleted the national treasury to muster large armies, and though in one year alone the armies slaughtered half a million Yellow Turbans, they were unable to completely eradicate them. Their failure was in large part due to the interference of court eunuchs in military plans and operations. Some eunuchs were even taking bribes from the rebels.

During the chaos, large segments of the population migrated in all directions, swept along before the carnage. Contemporary writers tell of piles of whitened human bones strewn over the plains, of starving women forced to abandon their children in the fields where they hid, and of northern Mongolian tribes taking advantage of China's turmoil to resume their raids, decapitating every male in some Chinese border villages and carrying off their womenfolk in oxcarts.

Only after two years of wholesale massacre did imperial armies finally flush out and kill two of Chang's brothers. Rebel leader Chang died soon thereafter. But by this time the Yellow Turban Rebellion had reduced the central government to complete impotence. Military generals, whose soldiers now looked to them as the only real authority, vied with one another over territories and power as virtual warlords, continuing to pursue remnants of the Yellow Turbans for the next twenty years. Through it all, they seethed with anger, remembering their discomfitures due to court eunuch perfidy at the height of the rebellion.

At Emperor Ling Ti's death in A.D 189, a consortium of ten powerful eunuchs conspired to put the younger of two Han princes on the throne, contending that the eldest and rightful heir was too weak and sickly to rule. The mother of the princes, regent Empress Ho, with strong backing from her brother and chief advisor, Ho Chin, held out against the eunuchs in favor of the legitimate heir. She and her family even tried to gain eunuch favor—and thus a solid foothold at court—by marrying her youngest sister to a chief eunuch's adopted son.

Ho Chin, who was a military commander and a competent one, was soon convinced by intellectuals and his generals that if eunuch control was to be overcome, the military would have to step in. Empress Ho was afraid to agree to so drastic a plan against the powerful eunuch corps. Accordingly, Ho Chin ordered a large army into the capital, hoping that only a display of might would convince court eunuchs to capitulate. However, ostensibly to discuss their differences, the eunuchs enticed Ho Chin into the palace alone and unarmed. Ho Chin had planned to remonstrate with the eunuchs and convince them to avoid bloodshed by retiring peaceably into private life, but he was cut down in the great audience hall by eunuch assassins.

Meanwhile, Ho Chin had stationed 500 of his troops outside the palace walls to await the outcome of the talks. At length, angered by the delay, the troops raised a great clamor for Ho Chin's appearance. In answer, the eunuchs threw his severed head over the palace wall into their midst. Enraged, the soldiers burst through the imperial gates, surged through the palace, and massacred every eunuch they could find. Over 2,000 eunuchs perished, along with many non-eunuchs who, because they were beardless, were mistaken for eunuchs.

At the height of the slaughter, a handful of eunuchs hurriedly dragged Empress Ho and her two princely sons through a rear palace gate and fled with them into hiding. Next day, they were discovered by the soldiers of a brutal, ambitious general, Tung Cho, who had answered Ho Chin's summons to the capital, but had conveniently brought up his army only after a semblance of order was restored. Tung Cho, who had borne a long-standing grudge against the empress, imprisoned and finally killed her. Then he did away with the older prince and put the younger prince, whom the eunuchs had backed, on the throne as his puppet. Emperor Hsien Ti, the last emperor of the Second Han Dynasty, was to sit on the throne in name only for the next thirty years, harassed and captured in turn by one warlord after another, as they fought each other for control of the empire.

The coarse, obese General Tung Cho made himself master of the Lo-yang capital. But within a year, threats from other, freebooting generals forced him to retreat west to Chang An with the captive Han emperor in tow. Before abandoning Loyang, he instructed his troops to burn and pillage the entire city. The imperial palace, royal tombs and monuments, libraries with precious works of art and literature carefully collected by four centuries of Han rulers, all were lost in fires that blazed for weeks.

Along the route to Chang An, Tung Cho managed to withstand attacks from rivals and roving bandits. For two years, he held sway over a puppet court in Chang An, crushing all opposition in the name of the helpless emperor, whom he treated with scant respect. He even arrogated to himself the right to approach the Imperial Presence at a normal pace, fully booted and carrying his sword, rather than unarmed, shoeless, and at the swift, scurrying gait demanded by court etiquette.

Finally in A.D. 192, disaffection erupted among Tung Cho's military men, incensed over his mindless cruelties and bloodthirsty fits of temper. Conspiring together, they had one of their lieutenants—actually Tung Cho's own adopted son—murder him. Then they threw his naked corpse to the populace, who subjected it to unspeakable indignities. They placed a lamp-wick in the dead tyrant's navel, lighted it, and watched it burn on body fat for days.

Meanwhile the provinces were being decimated by hostilities among rival warlords, who carved out private domains and thumbed their noses at the ineffectual court at the center. At last, in A.D. 196, the famous strongman and commander, Tsao Tsao, descended upon Loyang at the head of a formidable army. This man had been called up by the throne to put down the Yellow Turbans. At that time, he gathered a force of a million men and in one year alone captured or killed 300,000 peasant rebels. Now in Loyang, Tsao Tsao—using fair means and foul—overcame all rival contenders and set himself up as protector of the Han throne. This controversial, totally unscrupulous leader, whose father was a palace eunuch's adopted son, was nonetheless a talented scholar, an adroit politician, and an excellent leader of men. Though Tsao Tsao failed in an eight-year campaign to unite the entire nation, he brought under firm control all the northern provinces, the most populous and prosperous part of China at the time.

Tsao Tsao relocated the nominal Han Emperor Hsien Ti back to Loyang and set himself up as dictator over the imperial court and government. In A.D. 208, he made himself minister of state, and married his daughter to the puppet monarch, who was allowed to retain the throne only so long as it suited Tsao Tsao's purposes. When high officials accused Tsao

Tsao of plans to make himself emperor, he flatly denied the allegation in an eloquent treatise wherein he highly praised his own victories and accomplishments for the House of Han, pointedly reminding his accusers that his long-standing dedication to the elimination of eunuch corruption and intrigue had earned him the enmity of the entire eunuch corps.

Even so, when Tsao Tsao died, in A.D. 220, his son, Tsao Pei—following his father's wishes—became minister of state and immediately set into motion the abdication of the last Han emperor. Under Tsao Pei's direction, Emperor Hsien Ti issued an edict declaring his own unworthiness and praising the great virtues of the Tsao family, who now had been mandated by Heaven to found a new dynasty. As etiquette demanded, Tsao Pei repeatedly declined the honor, but after false modesty had run its course, he accepted.

To establish the legitimacy of his take-over, Tsao Pei ascended the huge stage he had built outside the palace, and in sight of the assembled court, received the seal of empire from the "retired" Han ruler, and then mounted the imperial throne. Emperor Tsao Pei's first act was to make ostentatious official sacrifices to Heaven to receive divine approval. Then he took two of Hsien Ti's princess daughters into his harem and became the founder of the new Wei Dynasty. At least he spared the Han emperor complete humiliation by granting him a token title of nobility and allowing him to live on in anonymity for another fourteen years before he died a natural death.

Thus ended four centuries of Han Dynasty rule, the first—but by no means the last—of China's great imperial houses to be fatally undermined by organized eunuch power.

Note

1. From "Biography of the Eunuchs," in *Basic Annals of the Later Han Dynasty*.

8

Eunuch Influence Wanes Under Barbarian Rule

THREE KINGDOMS AND TARTAR INVASIONS
(A.D. 220-581)

No sooner had Tsao Pei set up the new Wei Dynasty to rule North China than two rival Chinese leaders did the same in the south. A distant relative of the Han family became sovereign in the Szechuan region, while a powerful army commander established himself at Nanking as master of the coastal areas below the Yangtze River. Thus commenced the celebrated "Three Kingdoms" era, sixty years of treachery and bloodshed during which the three contending states tore at each others' throats for supremacy. This era is glorified in romantic Chinese literature as a time of heroics and high adventure. Each ruler maintained a huge army, a retinue of officials, and a palace teeming with consorts, courtiers, eunuchs, concubines, and hangers-on. Their military generals connived and schemed to outwit one another as much as they did battle. Peasants fought their wars and tilled the soil to feed the great armies and populous courts, and life within the three royal palaces followed familiar court patterns.

In the north, ruler Tsao Pei's family was beset from the start with female intrigue. Lady Chen, a ranking concubine and mother of the heir apparent, was the object of the empress's bitter jealousy. The empress finally succeeded in convincing Tsao Pei to have her killed. Immediately after issuing the order for Lady Chen's death, Tsao Pei had a court diviner interpret a frightening dream wherein he had seen a vaporous green cloud issue from the earth and attach itself to the heavens. Warned that the dream meant a palace lady of noble birth would die unjustly, Tsao Pei hurriedly dispatched a eunuch to rescind his order, but he was too late. Lady Chen had already been put to death, probably by eunuchs, who traditionally inflicted punishments meted out to harem women. Despite this story, later historians suspected that Tsao Pei deliberately had Lady Chen murdered as a precaution to prevent her male relatives or her personal palace eunuchs from taking control should she become regent for her son.

Though Tsao Pei regularly consulted his court diviners and fortune tellers, he often belittled their superstitious prognostications. He banned the practice of burial in jade-piece shrouds, saying it was "vulgar and stupid." Rich nobility were buried in such shrouds, which were thought to preserve the corpse forever. One prominent court seer foretold that Tsao Pei would live to be eighty. But when he lay dying of illness at age forty, after only six years on the throne, he weakly remarked that the diviner must have calculated his eighty-year life span "half in days and half in nights."

Tsao Pei's court was dominated by the great gentry families that had brought him to power. A powerful army general of these, the land-rich Ssu-ma clan, succeeded in overcoming and annexing the rival Szechuan kingdom in A.D. 263, but by this time the Szechuan ruling house was racked by inner dissensions that included a series of assassinations. Later, General Ssu-ma staged a formal abdication ceremony to force out the last of Tsao Pei's descendants, and made himself emperor of the new Chin Dynasty. By A.D. 280 he had conquered the last of the "Three Kingdoms" in Nanking and united the whole empire once more. But no Chinese dynasty deteriorated more rapidly than the Chin.

The Chin court at Loyang became a veritable vipers' nest of plots and intrigues. One empress had the entire family of a Chin dowager empress assassinated to place her own clan in power. In another instance, one of the twenty-five Chin princes governing outlying feudal states murdered an empress, made himself emperor, and opened the way for rival princes to butcher each other and take over the imperial throne in a rapid succession of palace coups. Throughout this period of upheaval, the bureaucracy somehow carried on.

Eunuchs in Chin Dynasty courts seemed to exercise little influence over government, but they were heavily involved in palace conspiracies. Around A.D. 310, Emperor Huai Ti's concubine, the daughter of a chief minister, plotted with her father and ranking eunuch Chia-Yu to have the emperor murdered and replaced by her son. Accordingly, eunuch Chia-

Yu secreted an assassin into the palace, but in the abortive attempt on the Chin ruler's life, the assassin was seized by palace guards and thrown into prison. To prevent the jailed assassin from revealing the identity of his conspirators, eunuch Chia-Yu soon had him fatally poisoned. Though prison officials and many others knew or suspected that Chia-Yu had arranged the plot to murder the emperor, none dared accuse such a powerful eunuch.

In an attempt to control the squabbling Chin princes and restore peace in the provinces, the emperor declared nationwide disarmament, but many peasant soldiers, instead of turning in their weapons, emigrated from their war-torn areas to join barbarian nomadic chieftains north of the Great Wall. At least these Mongolian tribal leaders maintained strict order in their domains, all the while hungrily watching China dissolve in civil wars and anarchy.

Eventually, wave after wave of fierce Turko-Mongolian hordes, known to history as Huns or Tartars, swept down to invade North China, plundering and killing as they came. Some of these chieftains had already been employed by Chin Dynasty princes to help fight their family feuds, and thus were fully familiar with Chinese ways and weaknesses, as well as the lay of the land.

One Hun chieftain, in payment for his former assistance, had even been allowed to establish his encampment and tribes in the heart of Shansi province. He declared that he was distantly related to the old Han Dynasty family, having descended from a long-ago Han Dynasty princess who had been sent as a hostage-bride to his ancestor, a great Mongolian khan. In A.D. 308 this chieftain solemnly made himself head of his own dynasty in Shansi and set up a magnificent Chinese-style court. His son and successor, having grown up in the court at Loyang, and having been taught Chinese scholarship and warfare, in A.D. 311 launched his cavalry against the Chin Dynasty capital and met with only weak resistance. His Hun horsemen, whose most usual employment was looting for treasure, savagely slaughtered 30,000 inhabitants of Loyang, burst into the palace, killed the crown prince and his brothers, and took the emperor captive. Then they set fire to the palace, plundered the imperial tombs, and hauled their royal Chin prisoner north to their ruler in Shansi. The captive Chin emperor was forced to act as a servant to the Tartar khan, who soon had him killed in a fit of cruelty.

Meanwhile, some of the Chin family had escaped the Tartar hordes and fled westward to set up court at Chang An, proclaiming one of their princes the new Chin emperor. But in A.D. 316 mounted horsemen of the Shansi Tartar returned *en masse* in a surprise attack, circling the city's great walls and cutting off all food supplies.

After half the inhabitants had died of starvation or resorted to cannibalism—and even the palace food stores were gone—the Chin emperor prepared for surrender. With his body bared and a piece of imperial jade in his mouth, he rode out through the palace gates in a simple sheep-drawn cart, followed by a wagon bearing an empty coffin, conforming to well-known rituals of total submission. The barbarian victors accepted the jade, burned the coffin, and once again carried a captive Chin emperor off to their chieftain. There, though he was given a concubine and the title "Duke of Ease and Comfort," the fallen Chinese emperor was forced to guard the khan's royal carriage during his great hunts, and act as wine-bearer at his banquets. After one of the Chinese prisoners wept to see his emperor so humiliated, the disgusted Tartar khan had the Chin ruler put to death.

With the fall of the two Chin capitals, northern Chinese gentry and scholar-officials fled south in great number, seeking safety in Nanking, where another Chin prince had established a regime. He was to rule in comparative peace, the beginning of a 200-year era called the "Division of North and South." Most northern Chinese, however, had to remain in the north and accept the rule of alien barbarians.

For three terrible decades the khan fought off other rival Mongolian invading hordes from further north, as fleeing Chinese peasants abandoned their fields, which would become so desolate and overgrown that remaining families had to beseech their barbarian ruler for protection from wolves and jackals.

In time, a descendant of the khan was overthrown by his own lieutenant, Shih Lo, a crude Mongolian savage of lowly birth who despised the Chinese and ransacked the country anew. He was bested in savagery, however, by his debauched nephew and successor, Shih Hu, in whom native barbarism was combined with vices he had learned from a decadent Chinese civilization. Shih Hu, whose name meant Tiger, was a man of violent contradictions, for cruel as he was, he made a learned Buddhist his chief advisor, and saw that the gentle faith of Buddhism flourished under his patronage. Yet he was capable of the most diabolical atrocities. He killed his grown son who appeared overly anxious to inherit the throne. If Chinese sources are to be believed, he took special pleasure in sumptuous palace banquets at which he would decapitate several concubines, serve their roasted bodies to guests, and pass the uncooked heads around on a platter to prove he had sacrificed the most beautiful.

Chinese peasants, especially, suffered from Shin Hu's mindless excesses, some 280,000 of them being conscripted to construct his splendid imperial palace. A lavish summer pavilion was air-conditioned by ventilating shafts connected to underground pits where ice was stored. In the palace's great ornate bathhouse, water spewed from the mouths of nine stone dragons into a great jade pool, and drained through the mouth of a tremendous bronze tortoise.

Ruler Shih Hu had a passion for ingenious mechanical contrivances. He had a cart constructed in which a standing human figurine turned automatically to constantly point southward, the direction sacred to emperors. Another mechanized platform displayed a life-size image of Buddha being constantly laved with water that spurted from the mouths of carved dragons, and scrubbed down by a group of mobile wooden figurines of monks.

In his later years, when Shih Hu became so grossly obese that he could not mount a horse to attend his beloved hunts, he was borne forth by twenty men on a litter which contained a revolving couch, allowing him to shoot in any direction. All his huge game chariots were topped with seventeen-foot lookout towers, and forty two-story slaughterhouses mounted on wheels were used to process the kill.

Long in advance of each royal hunt, Shih Hu ordered his censors across several provinces to prohibit the taking of game by Chinese subjects. This practice led to wholesale abuses. Under false accusations by imperial game wardens of poaching, terrorized peasants were forced to hand over a daughter, a horse, or an ox, or face death.

It is written that when Shih Hu sent recruiters throughout his seventy feudal states to collect some 30,000 female candidates for his harem, as many as 3,000 young Chinese women hanged themselves rather than submit to the barbarian. When Shih Hu came forth to view the thousands of females nonetheless brought into the capital, he was so pleased that he bestowed a royal title on each recruiter. A ranking palace matriarch minutely examined the most perfect and beautiful girls for the harem. According to the records, Shih Hu also maintained all-girl orchestras, and battalions of female soldiers clad in sable and gold ornaments, with bows and arrows painted imperial yellow.

Of all Shin Hu's cruelties, perhaps the most monstrous was the manner in which he executed his young brother who was found guilty of killing a favored cavalry general. Maddened with grief and rage, Shih Hu ordered his brother bound in tight chains and thrown into a dungeon, where he was forced to lap up his food from a wooden trough like a farm animal. Day and night his screams could be heard throughout the palace grounds, as jailors sliced his skin with swords enough to draw blood but without killing him. For the prisoner's execution, Shih Hu had built a tall pyre-scaffold topped with a ladder and high pole to which pulleys were attached.

Two men—the murdered general's best friends—pulled the condemned man up the ladder by his tongue and hair, affixed a chain from the pulleys to his chin, and as he was slowly raised up the pole by this mechanism, hacked off his limbs and repeatedly stabbed his body and eyes.

Having viewed the scene from a special central platform and with his ranking concubine at his side, Shih Hu ordered the pyre ignited and saw his brother burned to ashes. Next he had all the victim's wives and children killed, except one favorite five-year-old boy who now lay terrified in Shih Hu's arms. Though the boy's cries caused even the attending eunuchs and retainers to weep, court ministers determined that the child must not remain alive, lest one day he challenge the throne. In the end, Shih Hu released himself from the clutches of his child nephew and watched him be led away to his death.

Shih Hu was more or less typical of the several Mongolian chieftains who fought and ruled over parts of North China for the next two centuries. Though countless scholars, peasants, and landless gentry periodically fled to Chinese realms in the south, millions remained in the north to serve the alien rulers as administrative officials, concubines, palace eunuchs, peasants, farmers, serfs, and slaves. It was an era of which the Chinese have not been proud.

Strangely enough, it was during this violent epoch when the gentle religion of Indian Buddhism took permanent hold and proliferated on Chinese soil, first among the rulers and educated elite, then spreading to the populace. As the faith had slowly advanced toward China through Afghanistan and Turkestan, carried by merchants and monks, it had absorbed the shamanistic and magical practices that especially appealed to Mongolians and to many Chinese.

Perhaps in these troubled times Chinese subjects needed the solace of the promise of redemption of the faithful in a beautiful, multi-colored paradise. But above all, Buddhism was tolerant, welcoming converts from all classes—men, women, and eunuchs alike—allowing them to live by their old Confucian codes, make offerings to their ancient gods of the soil, and employ Taoist mediums to speak with ancestral spirits and drive out evil spirits. (The Buddhist heaven was also open to those rich enough to generously endow the monasteries, pagodas, and lovely cliff-temple grottoes now springing up in North China.)

To combat Buddhism, Taoists were now openly copying their rivals, setting up a huge hierarchy of Taoist deities, and great cloisters and temples financed by rulers and wealthy patrons. Thus, popular Taoism thrived and endured side by side with the proliferating Buddhism; both faiths were destined to become absorbed as an intregal part of Chinese culture. Of course there were die-hard Taoists and Confucianists who bitterly opposed the alien religion, claiming that Buddhism was "unfilial," encouraging the faithful to become monks and nuns who practiced celibacy, "an abomination against the state and the ancestors." Condemned also was the Buddhist practice of "eating impurities," such as in the Indian remedy of taking cow's urine—or one's own—as medicine. Opponents of Buddhism also feared that the monks' ancient practice of collecting alms in begging bowls would encourage the naturally industrious Chinese masses to resort to begging. Despite periodic persecution of the "alien religion," by the end of the fourth century, Chinese chronicles assert that nine out of ten families in North China had embraced Buddhism.

Of all the Tartar rulers of North China who sponsored Buddhism during this period, the most ardent were those of the important and long-lasting Toba-Wei Dynasty. At the beginning of the great Hun invasions, a Toba chieftain and his Mongolian horsemen tribes had settled on Chinese soil, in Shansi again, just below the border. By A.D. 409 they had conquered the entire fertile plain of east China and were wisely employing Chinese officials to administer the conquered area. Though a Taoist himself, the Toba-Wei founder issued the following decree: "During the long time of its existence, Buddhism has brought benefit to the dead as well as the living. The Buddhists' claim to knowledge of the supernatural is un-questionably valid, since the monks have proved it by irrefutable evidence. Officials are hereby authorized to build new Buddhist pagodas and monas-teries in my capital so that the monastics will have a proper place to live."[1]

The Toba-Wei Dynasty founder (and some of his successors) aped the occasional practice of Chinese emperors of having a consort put to death as soon as her son was proclaimed heir. This proved disastrous in one case, when the absence of a dowager empress opened the way for the new emperor's childhood wet nurse to try to fill the vacuum. (Chinese upper classes traditionally were very solicitous of their babyhood wet nurses, providing them an important lifetime place in their homes or palaces.) The unscrupulous wet nurse of the Toba-Wei emperor who ruled from A.D. 424 to 451 coerced him into bestowing upon her an imperial title equal in rank to that of a dowager empress, and to ennoble all her family. She even teamed up with palace eunuchs and forced the heir apparent's mother to commit suicide, lest she eventually outrank the wet nurse. This was not the last time an imperial wet nurse would raise havoc with a dynasty.

During this same reign, a renowned and respected Taoist alchemist, having studied magic as a recluse in a mountain sanctuary, claimed that the ancient Father of Taoism, Lao Tze, had descended to him in person to ordain him as head of Taoists on earth, presenting him with a complete set of the Taoist holy books. He also maintained that a direct descendant of Lao Tze had appeared to him and ordered that he take the sacred Taoist title of "Master of Heaven." Convinced of the validity of these miracles, the Toba-Wei emperor built a temple in the capital for this charismatic sorcerer and his disciples, and in person visited the shrine, where, in A.D. 442, he was ceremoniously presented with a supposedly Heaven-sent book of Taoist charms. So overawed was the ruler by this charismatic that he made his title of Master of Heaven official. When the Taoist alchemist died, in A.D. 448, his disciples swore that his corpse, when encoffined, had shrunk to a mere six inches in length—proof that he had disappeared to enjoy life forever among the Immortals.

Most of this emperor's lifetime was devoted to driving rival Gobi Desert tribes far westward into the mountains around Lake Baikal. Though he also won many battles against southern Chinese kingdoms, no Toba-Wei emperor ever succeeded in conquering the south of China, where Chinese culture was being carefully preserved.

During one of his campaigns in Chang An to suppress a rebellion, when the Toba-Wei ruler stopped over at a large Buddhist monastery, he was greatly agitated to learn that the monks therein were storing up military weapons, evidently to assist the rebels, and furthermore were distilling large quantities of strong liquor, keeping valuables for rich devotees, and secretly carrying on illicit affairs in their monastic cubicles with wealthy matrons of Chang An. Then and there, the emperor decreed, "Buddhist monastics advocating absurdities from foreign lands and speaking falsely of supernatural appearances cannot be relied upon to bring good customs."[2] He ordered that noblemen who patronized the monks should turn them over to the authorities by a certain date or face death along with their families and the monks involved.

In a stronger edict, in A.D. 446, he decreed that the long-ago Han Dynasty ruler who claimed to have seen the Buddha in a dream and then brought the religion to China had "served the evil spirits of an alien land [i.e., India] and violated the eternal Chinese law of Heaven and Earth, a great tragedy. Having received from Heaven the mandate to rule," he continued "I strive to eliminate falsehood and reestablish truthfulness, so peace and prosperity of ancient times will return. Therefore, all who worship Buddhist deities or have their idols and statues made, will be executed. All Buddhist images and books shall be burned, while monastics, regardless of age, shall be put to death."[3] The Toba-Wei crown prince, an ardent Buddhist, saw that most of the monks escaped into hiding with their precious scriptures and idols of silver and gold. The prince could not, however, prevent the destruction of many beautiful Buddhist temples, pagodas, and precious libraries in the capital.

Despite these brief periods of persecution, Buddhism persisted and steadily increased in popularity. From now on, however, most Toba-Wei emperors restricted the numbers allowed to become monks and nuns, in an attempt to weed out those whose sole aim was to avoid legal prosecution, taxes, military service, or corvee labor for the government.

The next Toba-Wei ruler, whose reign commenced in A.D. 466, openly declared himself a Buddhist and within six years abdicated in favor of his five-year-old son, Emperor Hsiao Wen Ti, to retire to a cloister in the imperial park. There he took vows as a contemplative monk, forgoing all interest in state affairs.

Hsiao Wen Ti, whose rule ended in A.D. 499, is cited as a paragon of virtue and tolerance who, despite his Tartar blood, was everything that Confucian scholars admired in a monarch. It is written that as a small child Hsiao Wen Ti's filial piety was so sincere that he volunteered to suck the pus from his father's (the emperor's) boil. At an early age, this prince ceased to participate in imperial hunts, adhering to Buddhist doctrine against the taking of life. When he became emperor, Hsiao Wen Ti humanized harsh punishments by reducing sentences of bodily mutilation to imprisonment, so that for a time at least the eunuch corps was composed of only those who had voluntarily been castrated.

Hsiao Wen Ti also greatly reduced the number of animals sacrificed in official state religious rites and for the worship of imperial ancestors, and condoned only those taboos and prayers clearly authorized in the ancient Confucian classics. He loved to discuss the philosophy of Taoism with the learned, and believed in the ancient Confucian doctrine that if a ruler were truly good and virtuous, his example alone would convert even savages into civilized subjects. Thus, it is claimed, when a vindictive eunuch reported to the dowager empress that Hsiao Wen Ti himself had committed some trumped-up offense, and she ordered that her son be punished by flogging, the emperor calmly underwent the whipping with no attempt at vengeance on the eunuch for his false charges, "even after the dowager's death."

By these times the Toba-Wei people, from emperor to tribal herdsmen, had all but forgotten their barbarian ancestry and considered themselves Chinese. Northern Chinese accepted the Toba conquerors, worked for them, civilized them, and intermarried with them in great numbers. There is no doubt that the injection of Tartar blood reinvigorated a Chinese civilization which was already old.

In A.D. 493 Chinese officials and the gentry convinced Hsiao Wen Ti to move the court south to Loyang because of the expense and difficulty of transporting sufficient food supplies to his court in Shansi. By now, the entire civil administration was run by Chinese Han officials. A year later, Hsiao Wen Ti issued an amazing decree, prohibiting the use of any language, dress, or custom other than Chinese—an attempt to eradicate the last vestiges of Tartar and other alien influence throughout his North China domain.

Not all Toba-Wei monarchs were as saintly as Hsiao Wen Ti, however. From A.D. 515 to 528 the dynasty was ruled by Dowager Empress Hu, the last strong sovereign of the dynasty. This unscrupulous, strong-willed woman, though a dedicated Buddhist, rid herself of a female rival by forcing her to enter a Buddhist convent, and there had her put to death. She ruthlessly executed her lovers when she tired of them, and poisoned her own son when he objected to taking orders from her many paramours. This last crime, however, was her undoing, for it caused her officials to plot a coup. Before they could do her in, she hastily shaved off her hair and took vows in a Buddhist nunnery, but the insurgents found her there and took her life by hurling her into the river.

In spite of her amoral conduct, Dowager Empress Hu is known for her generous endowments toward building the beautiful Buddhist Lungmen cave-grotto temples near Loyang. There she commissioned craftsmen to sculpt amazing bigger-than-life figures of Buddhist deities into the cliff's rock face, considerably enhancing the reputation of the Toba-Wei era as a period of truly great religious art, much of which is still intact today.

After the time of Dowager Empress Hu, the thoroughly sinicized Toba-Wei regime became as corrupt as any native Chinese dynasty had ever been. In addition to the splendor and utter wastefulness of the imperial court, extravagances of Toba-Wei princes further drained the economy. To show off his wealth and "generosity," one prince acquired 300 talented concubines for his harem, together with innumerable eunuch chamberlains. He was greatly piqued to find himself outdone by his prime minister cousin, who took into his harem some 500 courtesans, each of "heavenly beauty and nationwide fame."

From A.D. 530 onward, popular uprisings against misrule by the failing Toba-Wei government became formidable. The few remaining Toba pastoral tribes, having become more and more impoverished in agrarian China, also revolted and overran Shansi province and Loyang, massacring great numbers of Chinese and their own pro-Chinese Toba kinsmen. In A.D. 534 the rebels were thwarted by a Chinese general who, with the help of the gentry, moved the impotent Toba-Wei emperor far to the east, where he reigned for only sixteen years before being deposed by the same general, who then formed his own short-lived dynasty.

In A.D. 555 this new ruler, impatient with the rivalry between Buddhist and Taoist leaders, commanded the sects to hold a joint symposium to debate the worth of their respective religions. When the Buddhists easily bested the Taoists, he ordered all Taoist priests to become Buddhist monks or face execution. After four brave Taoists gave up their lives, the rest promptly shaved their heads and took their vows in Buddhist monasteries. From then on, there were no Taoists whatever in this petty northern domain.

At the same time, remnants of the former Toba imperial family established one of their members as ruler of a kingdom to the northwest. In A.D. 547 the founder of this brief regime emphatically abolished castration as a punishment throughout his entire state, decreeing that henceforth all liable to punishment by castration should not be castrated, but should merely pass into control of the state as slaves. This regime, too, was soon overthrown by a man of the Chinese gentry who founded yet another minor dynasty. One of its over-proud rulers, in A.D. 578, named his favorite concubine "Great Empress," and retitled himself "First Heavenly Emperor." Pleased with himself, he soon took on three more legal consorts, titling them "First Heavenly Empress," "Heavenly Empress of the Right," and "Heavenly Empress of the Left."

One of the most important results of this long era of Tartar rule and the Division of North and South was the great migrations of cultured northerners to the southern kingdoms. Prior to this time, South China had been sparsely settled almost entirely by non-Chinese aborigines, few of whom had been touched by "superior Chinese culture."

Back in A.D. 317, when North China was first overrun by Tartar hordes, the Chin Dynasty, together with fleeing northern gentry, had set up court in Nanking below the Yangtze River. Within a century the Chin Dynasty had overcome the Szechuan area also, and successfully repulsed all attacks from barbarians from North China. Despite their ability to hold this large southern realm, all was not well within the Chin courts. The dynasty was distracted and enfeebled by continuing factional intrigues, intra-family usurpations, and finally a series of weak, juvenile, or debauched monarchs.

One remarkable character to emerge during the early days of the Chin realm in Nanking was a famous Taoist alchemist and prolific writer, Ko Hung, who placed great emphasis on the magical practices now rapidly transforming Taoism into a religion of the common people. His works and teachings promulgated Taoist doctrine and methods with regard to the casting of spells, the use of magic charms, the cult of immortality, and alchemical processes to transmute cinnabar, mercury, or other common substances into gold. His concoctions for rejuvenation guaranteed that "white hair will once more become black, lost teeth will grow in again, and physical vigor will return." Ko Hung wrote of one of his recipes: "He who takes this elixir will not grow old but will return to youth and never die."[4]

Ko Hung also codified a Taoist merit system: "He whose actions are evil and unjust will be punished with a foreshortened life span; he who does 1,300 virtuous deeds will become a celestial immortal; and he who performs 300 good deeds will become an ordinary earthly immortal." His "internal elixir" theory for long life prescribed the preservation of "the three precious things of the male body: the breath to be inhaled more than exhaled, the saliva to be swallowed, and the sexual fluid to be drawn inward and upward."[5] When Ko Hung was eighty-one, a friend whom he had invited to his mountain hermitage arrived to find nothing but the alchemist's empty clothing. Ko Hung's adherents ever after avowed that he had taken one of his own drugs for eternal life and ascended on high as an Immortal.

In A.D. 365, a Chin ruler called Ai Ti died at age twenty-four from imbibing a Taoist elixir which evidently contained more poison than magic. Another southern monarch, seldom sober and noted for his all-night orgies, was smothered to death with his bed covers by maidservants under orders from a ranking thirty-year-old concubine whom he had repeatedly teased with drunken threats to replace her with a younger woman.

The southern Chin Dynasty at Nanking fell in A.D. 419, to be followed by a dreary succession of ever shorter and weaker regimes, each considering itself champions of "true Han Chinese civilization."

Buddhism gradually became the predominant religious and intellectual force of the South as well as of the North. Old feudal patterns of great manor houses became established as the lifestyle of the landed gentry gradually became more luxurious and elegant, and the gentry themselves became effete. Historians claim that at this time South China was the most refined civilization in the Far East. Emperors, nobles, and the idle rich wiled away their days composing poetry and other literary works, while Taoist philosophers and dropouts retreated to mountain lairs to dream, drink, compose poetry, and brazenly flout all the proprieties of an overly refined society.

These brief southern dynasties were plagued with continual regicides, murders of whole royal families, bloody usurpations, and hopelessly debauched rulers. In A.D. 473, when a monarch's princess sister peevishly complained about the unfairness of his having 3,000 concubines from which to choose, he presented her with thirty male lovers. In A.D. 498 another ruler rounded up thirty virile men for his widowed mother's use, and for himself took in twenty young street toughs to share his bed, his table, and his wife.

Evidently the only southern sovereign of any consequence whatever during the Division of North and South was Liang Wu Ti, who ruled in Nanking from A.D. 502 to 549. He was the second longest-lived emperor in imperial Chinese history. He credited his longevity to the fact that "I have abstained from sex for the past thirty years."[6] For a long time, Liang Wu Ti was a monarch of greatness, combining the virtues of a first-class military general with an avid interest in promoting learning, culture, and especially, Confucian literature. Strongly disapproving the abominations committed by previous southern rulers, most of his early edicts were aimed at reinstilling in the state and the Chinese family traditional Chinese moral values.

Whether Liang Wu Ti grew discouraged with this unrewarding crusade, or whether charismatic Buddhist clergymen won him over, is not clear. At any rate, in his old age he lost interest in statesmanship, turning all his attention to Buddhism. Following Buddhist tenets, he ate only one meal a day of strictly vegetarian foods, forbade the immolation of animals even for official sacrifices, and could no longer bring himself to order capital punishment. The last two measures caused him to lose favor with many of his Confucian officials.

Liang Wu Ti loved to be called "Bodhisatva," after the most popular of Buddhist deities. By A.D. 517 he had ordered the destruction of all Taoist temples in his domain. Ten years later he renounced the world, entered a Buddhist cloister as a monk, and allowed himself to be ransomed back to the throne only after his monastery received a huge donation from government treasuries. His several repetitions of this pattern greatly increased the wealth of the Buddhist "church."

During Liang Wu Ti's reign, the number of Nanking city pagodas and monasteries increased to 700. Elite society considered it fashionable to attend Buddhist lectures, elaborate religious ceremonies, and festivals, which Liang Wu Ti sponsored and which sometimes drew crowds of 50,000. Eventually, he commanded all his court officials to adopt Buddhism and to denounce Taoism as false doctrine.

Liang Wu Ti died at the venerable age of eighty-six. In A.D. 557 his last ruling descendant, having surrounded himself with an immense and tremendously valuable collection of Chinese literary works, the envy of southern intellectuals, was burned alive when his palace was razed, along with his library. The loss was forever mourned by Chinese literati. The victor in this take-over, one of Liang Wu Ti's generals, did not long sit on the throne.

Soon thereafter, both the northern barbarian Tartar regimes and the southern Chinese dynasties were overcome by the founder of the Chinese Sui Dynasty, who once again united the entire empire and paved the way for China to reach the apex of her civilization.

Notes

1. J. Li Dun, *The Civilization of China.*
2. Ibid.
3. Ibid.
4. C. P. Fitzgerald, *China: A Short Cultural History.*
5. J. R. Ware, *Alchemy, Medicine and Religion in China of* A.D. *320.*
6. Wang, Chia-yu, *Lives and Loves of the Chinese Emperors.*

9

Eunuchs in a Palace of Debauchery
SUI DYNASTY (A.D. 581-618)

For bringing to an end almost three centuries of war and division, and the humiliation of barbarian Tartar rule, Emperor Yang Chien, founder of the Sui Dynasty, has always been revered as a great unifier. He arose as an official and military general in the court of the Tartar regime in North China. Yang Chien was Chinese, though he inherited some Tartar blood through his mother's relationship to the ruling family. In A.D. 581 he ousted his seven-year-old monarch (who died four months later under suspicious circumstances) and founded the new Sui Dynasty. He set up his court in Chang An, the traditional western capital.

Within a few years, Yang Chien and his armies had overtaken the whole of the North and were rapidly pushing down towards Nanking. There, in A.D. 589, he forced the last southern ruler into an inglorious surrender, making himself master of all China.

Practical-minded and extremely frugal, Emperor Yang Chien resolutely set about bringing strict order to society, and to restoring peace and prosperity to the nation. Not a highly educated man himself, he brooked no nonsense from intellectuals. He was wary of using scholarly Confucianists in government posts, dealt ruthlessly with corrupt officials, and excluded the landed gentry from politics altogether. In accord with his attitude of distrust of others, the hard-working emperor personally attended to even the least important of government affairs.

To revive the shattered economy, Yang Chien set an example by living simply—almost as a miser. When he compelled the rich gentry to curtail their extravagant lifestyles, that influential element turned against him.

Early after his accession to the throne, Yang Chien's edict—for the first time in Chinese history—abolished castration as a form of official punishment throughout all China. This decree by no means put an end to the employment of palace eunuchs, however. On the contrary, in the court of Yang Chien's successor, which greatly surpassed that of Yang Chien in size and luxury, the demand for eunuchs became greater than ever. But since castration by this time was considered an indignity to which no upper-class Chinese male would voluntarily submit, raiding expeditions were organized to capture young boys of aborigine tribes, especially those of the southern coastal areas, to be made into eunuchs. Starting in A.D. 602, Yang Chien's fourth son on several occasions captured aborigine youths and sent them as eunuchs to the imperial palace in Loyang. (Under the next dynasty, such raids would be continued, and the practice of castrating Chinese criminals would be revived.)

Within a short time, Yang Chien's successful military campaigns had brought such prestige abroad that China was again receiving homage and tribute from Central Asian states. Though he won battles against the marauding Turkomans from the north, who by this time had overrun all Mongolia, he gained more than he won in the battles by the shrewd Chinese strategy of setting the Tartar tribes to fighting each other. His luck ran out, however, when it came to the Koreans, who balked at the idea of again becoming vassals of China and were attempting to team up with the Mongolians.

The following excerpts from a letter written by the Sui Dynasty founder to the ruler of Korea in A.D. 597 indicates the frustrations that kingdom was causing him, and also illustrates how profoundly emperors of China believed in their own omnipotence.

"Having received the Mandate of Heaven to love and cherish all peoples of the empire, I entrusted you with responsibility of governing that corner of the earth by the sea, hoping you would continue to promote the great civilization of China so all people in your kingdom would live a peaceful and enjoyable life. As my vassal, each year you have sent tribute bearers to China and pledged your fealty to myself, the sovereign of all men. However, doubt still exists about your sincerity, since you, as my vassal, have not followed policies parallel to my own.

"First, since you well know some of the northeastern barbarian Tartars have become our tribute states, why do you use force to chase them from their homes or forbid them to move about? How can you be so brutal and merciless after they, like other peoples who know where righteousness lies, have sworn their loyalty to me? Second, why do you bribe and seduce bowmakers from China to ship weapons to Korea, when they would be yours just for the asking? Why use illicit smuggling unless you are preparing for war against China? Third, why have you repeatedly subjected my envoys and inspectors to house arrest and prevented them from seeing or hearing anything, when I wish them to learn conditions in your country so I may be able to provide you with necessary instructions to govern successfully—unless you have evil designs? Fourth, why have you sent cavalrymen across our border to kill and injure Chinese, engaging in false propaganda and conspiratorial activities? Why, when I have granted you territories and royal titles—as is known to all peoples of the world—have you sent spies into China to seek information, if you really mean to remain a loyal subject of mine?

"Perhaps all your misdeeds may be my own fault in that I may not have taught you as well as I should have. If this is true, you shall have my forgiveness, providing you correct all your mistakes and carefully observe the duties required of a vassal and abide by the law of my Celestial Empire. Were I not an extremely patient and tolerant ruler, I could easily have sent just one general to punish you and the matter would long have been settled, but I have not given up hope that you can be reformed."[1]

Despite his pretence of omnipotence, Emperor Yang Chien's great military forces were disastrously repulsed by Korea the following year.

In A.D. 604, when Yang Chien, at the age of sixty-four, was confined to his apartments due to recurring illnesses, his son, the heir apparent, trying to conceal his eagerness for the throne, wrote a confidential letter to his father's close aide inquiring after the emperor's health. By accident the letter fell into the hands of the ailing ruler, arousing his anger and distrust of his son. The deciding blow came when an imperial concubine complained that the heir apparent had tried to force his attentions upon her. In a rage, Emperor Yang Chien vowed to depose his son as crown prince, but encouraged by members of the disgruntled gentry, his son seized the initiative and had the emperor poisoned. Then the son took the throne as the next Sui monarch, Emperor Yang Ti.

Yang Ti had neither the frugality nor wisdom of his father, but for all his faults and vices, he was fully aware of the renewed greatness of a unified China and of her destiny as the dominant power in Asia. A man of vacillating moods, he alternated between times of feverish activity in colossal public works projects and military campaigns, and periods of inertia and utter depravity. He was a dedicated patron of advanced learning, and instituted the highest literary degree: doctor of Confucian studies.

It appears, however, that one of his primary objectives was to live a life of incredible ostentation and eroticism, possibly to enhance the imperial image, though his excesses shocked upright officials to the core.

One of Yang Ti's first acts was to move the capital east to Loyang and set up a court that was the most magnificent, bizarre, and licentious in the Far East. Besides a ranking empress, he had two deputy empresses, six royal consorts, seventy-two ladies of lesser titles, and 3,000 concubines conscripted from throughout the country. For good measure, he forced two of his dead father's courtesans to enter his harem, an act which Confucian purists looked upon as incest.

Yang Ti's notorious "Palace for Displaying Benevolence" was actually an entire park some seventy-five miles in circumference, walled, and heavily landscaped with gardens and forests of flowering trees. Within the park he had had excavated a five-mile-long lake, out of which rose three man-made "Isles of the Immortals," on which were constructed magnificent Taoist shrines. The lake was fed by the elaborate zig-zagging "Dragon-scale Waterway," its banks studded with exquisite pleasure pavilions accessible only by boat and furnished with talented young damsels awaiting the imperial favor. In autumn, when the leaves fell, trees and shrubs in the gardens were decorated with hand-made fabric flowers and greenery, while artificial lotus blossoms were used to replace the natural blooms on the lake.

Completion of the main palace, designed by Yang Ti's leading architect, required eighteen months of labor by 50,000 artisans and workmen. Its tiered golden roofs towered over the treetops, and each of its three stories was encircled by ornate verandas from which harem girls entertained the ruler with song and instrumental music, as breezes played with their diaphanous gowns. Yang Ti named the sprawling main edifice the "Labyrinth Palace." He delighted in its countless, ingeniously deceptive arches and doorways, from which a maze of intricate passageways led to lavish apartments housing "several thousand lovely harem girls."

Disapproving Confucian historians recorded that the great Main Hall of the palace was walled in mirrored bronze punctured with concealed openings which emitted fragrances of perfumed incense. From the ceiling hung silken lanterns painted with nude female figures which appeared to undulate as candlelight flickered within them. This huge chamber accommodated 100 dining tables and four enormous silk tents where bevies of maidens amused themselves and languished on fur-covered couches. On the Son of Heaven's frequent visits, eunuchs knelt down to kowtow, remove his robes of state, and drape his torso with a leopard skin. Thus clad, Yang Ti sauntered among singing, flirting concubines, drinking wine from golden goblets. Then he would enter the tents to indulge in a favorite drunken sport where, with closed eyes, he seized any girl within reach and copulated with her, before chasing after another.

Yang Ti, like some of the barbarian rulers before him, was fascinated with complicated mechanical contraptions, which were designed by a junior official to enhance imperial pleasures. His "Virgin Wheelchair" was used in deflowering young maidens, while his "As-You-Wish Chariot"—rigged with movable pulleys—made love-making resemble riding in a boat at sea, Yang Ti claimed.

He seemed to be addicted to long, luxurious journeys around the empire—"inspection tours," which were little more than extravagant pleasure jaunts. For cross-country travel, his huge entourage was accompanied by a fleet of "Seven Precious Chariots," each curtained with seven layers of strings of costly gems, behind which an ever-ready imperial concubine lounged on silken cushions.

Along the route from his capital to the scenic southern pleasure city of Yangchow, Yang Ti had forty spacious lodges constructed for his stopovers, and when he tired of these he ordered others built towards the north, through Shansi. His incessant caravan trips, which necessitated an immense court following, were a crushing burden to the populace along the routes, whose unpaid duty it was to provide food and supplies for the entire entourage.

His several thousand harem concubines were under the jurisdiction of an avaricious chief eunuch named Hsu-yuan, who enriched himself by collecting bribe money and costly gifts from ladies he promoted to the emperor for favor. Concubines paid dearly in the hope of bearing an imperial son, which would put them in line for higher rank, possibly even the position of empress.

A story has it that one young concubine languished for years without ever laying eyes on her master, for she had no money to bribe eunuch Hsu-yuan. Rather than face more years of such a melancholy existence, she committed suicide by hanging herself. When eunuch Hsu-yuan reported her death, Emperor Yang Ti asked to view the corpse and was astounded to see that she was an outstanding beauty. Angrily he reproached the eunuch for failing to present her to his bed. It is related that Yang Ti wept and embraced the lovely dead concubine until, exhausted with grief, he fell asleep with her corpse in his arms. Yang Ti's displeasure with the chief eunuch emboldened other concubines to reveal the eunuch's long-standing malpractices, and he was promptly sentenced to decapitation.

Early in his reign, while holding audience to receive tribute from a southern aborigine tribe, Emperor Yang Ti became intrigued with one of the tribute-bearers—an eighteen-year-old dwarf named Wang-I. Pleased with the lad's appearance, conduct, and intelligence, Yang Ti took him into his service as a personal attendant and companion. Emperor and dwarf became so inseparable that when Wang-I learned that he could not accompany his master into the harem, he had himself castrated by an older eunuch after being heavily sedated with liquor. When Emperor Yang Ti heard that his favorite had sacrificed his manhood to better serve him as a eunuch, his partiality toward the dwarf increased. It is said, however, that Wang-I never took any personal advantage of his favored position, but always did his best to direct his master away from excesses and towards virtuous rule.

Later, during a rebellion, the dwarf eunuch dared memorialize the throne, pointing out that the uprisings were caused by Yang Ti's lack of concern for his subjects' welfare. At this affront, the emperor ordered Wang-I brought before his presence. Wang-I failed to appear, however. Believing he had rightly performed his duty, only now to find himself about to be sentenced to death, the dwarf had cut his own throat. He died hoping his suicide might convince the monarch to abandon his extravagant depravities. Though Emperor Yang Ti deeply mourned the loss of his little eunuch, he did not curtail court luxuries and the resulting oppression of his subjects.

One of the most crushing drains on the nation's finances and conscripted peasant labor force was Yang Ti's tremendous public works projects, especially his great waterway systems. His Grand Canal made possible the convenient transport of rice and goods from the Yangtze region to Loyang and points northward almost to present-day Peking. Especially benefited by this project were the northern landed gentry, who could now more profitably ship their grain into the palace, where thousands had to be fed or paid in grain.

For Yang Ti's maiden voyage on the new canal, several hundred singing girls stationed on each bank held ropes and pulled the luxurious imperial Dragon Barge upstream. Their multicolored gowns "reflected from the water like rainbows," as the emperor pursued amorous activities on board to the accompaniment of the palace orchestra.

Between A.D. 611 and 613 Yang Ti, still seething from China's loss of face when his father was defeated by Korea, personally led two great expeditions against that kingdom to avenge the national honor. He was repulsed so soundly in both campaigns that "bringing the Koreans to their senses" became his overriding obsession. When he launched a third attack, a sea battle, he was disastrously defeated. The retreat of his forces resulted in such terrible losses that even the gentry turned against the emperor, while the overtaxed populace began angry uprisings.

Continuing his father's policy of stirring up discord between two rival
Turkish chieftains ruling Mongolia, Yang Ti found himself paying exorbitant
bribes to each. In A.D. 615, while on a tour along the Great Wall, he
and his imperial entourage encamped at a frontier military post on the
edge of the Gobi Desert. Without warning, a renegade Mongolian leader
and his horsemen appeared and completely encircled the imperial encampment. For a solid month, the emperor of China was immobilized by a
siege, completely at the mercy of the Turkish horsemen. He only escaped
with his life because of the ingenuity of a youthful Chinese commander,
Li Shih-min, who duped the enemy by leaking the falsehood that large
Chinese reinforcements were on the way. The barbarian chieftain's wife,
a Chinese "hostage princess," assisted her native countrymen by convincing
her Turkish master of a second fabrication—that another Mongolian tribe
was descending to attack him from the north. Though he had the upper
hand, the Turkish chieftain raised his siege and departed, allowing Yang
Ti and his party to beat an ignoble retreat back to Loyang.

After this embarrassing and costly escapade, revolts against Yang Ti
and his misrule broke out everywhere. The severity of the revolts forced
him to flee for safety to the southern city of Yangchow, together with
his court, an elite corps of personal guardsmen, and much of the army.
There he settled in to abandon himself once more to debauchery while
the nation's recently reestablished unity dissolved in anarchy. Against better
advice, Yang Ti had new palaces built so that, if rebels took the north,
he could found a new capital in the south. When imperial finances ran
short and food supplies from the region became exhausted, his homesick
soldiers deserted in great numbers, while his disheartened generals and high
officials, in league with Wei Shih, chief of the eunuch contingent, planned
a coup.

One court lady, on learning of the plot, reported it to the empress,
who gave her permission to inform Emperor Yang Ti. This unwelcome
news so upset him that he had the informer put to death for "exceeding
her authority." As other palace women continued to relate rumors of a
coming coup, the empress told them: "The empire has so deteriorated that
nothing we can do will make a difference. Telling the emperor the truth
only worries him more and gains nothing."[2]

On the appointed day for the coup, eunuch Wei Shih forged a decree
in Yang Ti's name ordering all the imperial palace guardsmen to take a
holiday. As they happily absented themselves, the conspirators gathered
their troops and followers outside the palace, while conspiring attendants
assured Yang Ti there was nothing to fear. When the emperor realized
the palace was being stormed, he hurriedly changed his imperial robes for

less ostentatious attire and fled to the nearby palace of the crown prince. Eunuch Wei Shih opened the palace gates to his co-conspirators and their troops, who were informed by a concubine of the emperor's whereabouts. They found him peeping from behind a window curtain, deeply shaken to see among the rebels several trusted lieutenants who had served him since boyhood.

The usurpers forced Yang Ti to mount a horse and be led back to the main palace between rows of whooping soldiers. There he was seated in a chair, remonstrating and pleading with his captors, while his eleven-year-old favorite son leaned against him wailing in terror. Suddenly, an exasperated conspirator beheaded the boy with one blow of his sword, spewing his blood over the emperor's cloak. Yang Ti recovered himself enough to say: "A Son of Heaven must die with dignity. I would prefer a cup of poisoned wine." When this was not brought forth, the emperor undid his silk sash and handed it to his tormentors. Roughly, they bound his neck to the chairback and watched him strangle to death.

Thus, the national unity forged by Yang Ti's father came to an abrupt end, but it was not forgotten. Thinking Chinese had learned that national consolidation was China's only hope for salvation. For the next few years, warlords fought each other for supremacy, until there arose a soldier of genius to reunite the empire. This was Li Shih-min, the young commander who had saved Emperor Yang Ti from annihilation three years earlier when his camp was surrounded by northern horsemen.

Note

1. J. Li Dun, *The Civilization of China.*
2. Ibid.

10

Eunuch Power Waxes Anew
EARLY TANG DYNASTY (A.D. 618-713)

Though Li Yuan, a respected military governor under the Sui regime, became first ruler of the great Tang Dynasty, it was his second son, Li Shih-min, who is heralded as the real founder.

Li Yuan remained staunchly loyal to the failing Sui Dynasty, while his son Li Shih-min proved himself a leader of men by first overawing and then forging alliances with aggressive Tartar chieftains beyond the Great Wall. Unlike his careful, righteous father, the ambitious Li Shih-min early foresaw that the Sui Dynasty was doomed. When self-seeking regional commanders conquered Loyang and forced the Sui court to flee south, Li Yuan took over military command, vowing to avenge the honor of the Sui Dynasty. Ostensibly toward this same goal, the young Li Shih-min gathered an immense army of devoted men, aided by his horseback-riding sister, who sold her jewels to hire thousands of mercenaries.

By A.D. 617, Li Shih-min's forces had retaken Chang An, the secondary Sui capital, where he installed on the throne a grandson of the assassinated Sui monarch. Within a year, with the ultimate object of forming a new dynasty, Li Shih-Min, using typical Chinese strategy, tricked his father into deposing the infant Sui emperor. He bribed a Sui palace eunuch to present his father with a lovely concubine from the Sui harem. The father, unaware of the girl's origin and that he would be committing a most heinous crime against the Sui throne, accepted the gift. Only when it was too late did

Li Shih-min have his horrified father informed of her origin. Thereafter, Li had no trouble convincing his father that he could escape execution only by overthrowing the Sui Dynasty. All went according to Li Shih-min's plan: His father took the palace by storm in A.D. 618 to become Emperor Kao Tsu, "founder" of the new Tang Dynasty, with the capital in Chang An.

With his father securely installed on the throne, over the next several years Li Shih-min brilliantly led his troops and his Mongolian allies in the grueling task of destroying regional warlords, overcoming marauding barbarians, and reuniting the nation. When at last in A.D. 621 he took the main Sui capital at Loyang, the vast Labyrinth Palace—a symbol of Sui corruption—was razed to the ground in an inferno that blazed for months.

Like a man of destiny, Li Shih-min returned to Chang An riding slowly through the streets on his richly caparisoned war horse, resplendent in coat of arms, helmet, and golden breastplate, with a great bow and quiver across his shoulder and sword in hand. Crowds of officials, gentry, and common folk gathered to hail the young hero of the House of Tang. His popularity and immense self-assurance must have given even his father pause. He certainly would have aroused resentment in his eldest brother who bore the title Crown Prince.

Li Shih-min's father proved himself a capable, energetic ruler, dedicated to staffing a huge Tang bureaucracy with qualified men and restoring the agrarian economy. He encouraged learning and promoted Confucian ideals. However, the continuing proliferation of the "foreign" Buddhist religion worried him, especially after an upright official memorialized the throne, complaining: "Chinese converts to Buddhism confess their sins, give large sums to the poor, and feed the begging monks, hoping to earn extravagant rewards in this life and the hereafter. They are duped into believing that Lord Buddha can grant longevity, happiness, riches—even freedom from punishment for crime. Thus, our people are being corrupted, using the religion merely to satisfy selfish aims."[1] Emperor Kao Tsu decreed the suppression of monasteries, defrocking of priests, and destruction of Buddhist temples. His officials, however, were loath to fully implement so harsh an edict, which, within three years, had to be rescinded. Though again much damage had been done to Buddhist shrines, libraries, idols, and artifacts, the religion not only survived, but flourished anew after the temporary set-back.

The first Tang emperor imposed severe restrictions on his eunuchs, keeping them to menial palace duties and strictly forbidding them any part in state affairs. He denied them positions above the fourth rank, and restricted the number of fourth-rank posts to less than a hundred. Following his lead, succeeding rulers during the first half of the Tang Dynasty kept the threat of eunuch power at a minimum, though eunuch numbers and influence steadily rose.

Meanwhile, Li Shih-min increasingly asserted his authority as protector of the Tang Empire, arousing distrust in his father and extreme jealousy in his two brothers, who soon were engaged in plots against him. They held a banquet in Li Shih-min's honor, had his wine poisoned, and were galled to see him survive. Assassins hired by the brothers to kill him met with failure when Li was forewarned. At last, Li Shih-min boldly set out for the palace in full military regalia to face a volley of arrows from his brothers. Unscathed himself, Li shot down one brother, while his lieutenant killed the other. Standing over their bloody corpses, Li removed his helmet and said to the onlooking crowd: "My children, have no fear for my safety. Those who wish to assassinate me are dead."[2] Then his faithful aide cut off the heads of the slain princes and held them up for all to see.

On learning of the matter, Emperor Kao Tsu, distraught with grief and anger, ordered a rigorous inquiry. Courtiers who secretly backed Li Shih-min presented a list of heinous crimes purportedly committed by the dead brothers, including the capital offense of debauching the monarch's wives. When Li Shih-min appeared before his father to beg forgiveness, pleading that he had acted only in self-defense, the weary emperor declared his abdication in favor of his indefatigably ambitious son. Li Shih-min, complying with proper filial etiquette, wept and repeatedly threw himself at his father's feet, begging him to keep the throne, but the old man was adamant. As a dutiful son, Li was "forced" to accept the throne. He acceded in A.D. 626, to be known as Emperor Tai Tsung. His first act was to have his dead brothers' womenfolk and sons put to death—all except two of their wives, whom he kept for himself. The old emperor retired complacently to one of the outer palaces and lived on to enjoy honors and tranquility.

Emperor Tai Tsung is touted by most historians as the outstanding monarch of the imperial era, unsurpassed as a general, administrator, and scholar. He ushered in the Great Age of China, which perhaps owed its advent not only to his genius and vigorous leadership, but also to the civilizing stimulation of Buddhism, as well as the infusion of fresh blood from Tartar allies.

Having spent years of his boyhood at the corrupt Sui Dynasty court—as was the custom for noblemen's sons—Tai Tsung benefited from having observed at first hand the folly of the exercies of power without restraint, of neglecting the popular welfare, and of an arrogance among officials that caused them to disguise the true state of the nation. Tai Tsung inspired his ministers and generals to dedicated, loyal service, and the unified nation prospered as never before. His conquests and strong administration secured a long internal peace and fostered a highly sophisticated culture.

In A.D. 627 Tai Tsung's armies drove the enemy Tartar hordes who menaced northern provinces into Outer Mongolia. Peace was concluded on a bridge near the Chinese capital, following the traditional blood-sacrifice of a white horse. A few years later, when he had brought Inner Mongolia into the Tang Empire, Tai Tsung held a great audience of all the barbarian chieftains, who prostrated themselves and knocked their heads on the ground nine times in subservience to the powerful Chinese emperor.

After all Turkestan was forced back under Chinese dominance, Uighur tribes from grasslands beyond the Gobi Desert came with tribute of their finest, most spirited horses, in which Tai Tsung, an expert horseman, took the greatest delight. Tai Tsung was a generous victor, allowing Turkish allies to settle within China's northern border, often granting titles of nobility to defeated alien princes and accepting their sons into his imperial university— showing such generosity even to Koreans, whose country he never completely subjugated.

During the Tang era, travelers, merchants, and missionaries flocked to the magnificent Chang An capital from as far away as Europe. Never before had China been so open to foreigners. When a Nestorian Christian missionary from the Middle East arrived in A.D. 635, Tai Tsung heard his teachings with interest and issued the following decree: "The Way has more than one name; there is more than one Sage. Religious doctrines vary in different lands, but their benefits reach all mankind. This man of great virtue has brought scriptures and images from afar to present in our capital. After examining his doctrines, I find them profound and pacific. Let this faith be preached freely in the Empire."[3] Muslims from Arabian states, Zoroastrians from Persia, Manichaeans from Central Asia, all were tolerantly received.

Tai Tsung patronized Buddhism, possibly because he was beholden to the "fighting monks"—the inventors of the famous lethal kung-fu martial arts of self-defense—for their assistance at the time of his early conquests. Thirteen Shaolin monk-soldiers with their "fists of steel" had once saved his life on the battlefield. As a reward, he gave their order an immense tract of land and the right to consume the meat and wine forbidden to other monks, rights they retain to this day. During the Tang era, some 2,500 kung-fu monks dwelt under the palatial roofs of the immense Shaolin monastery not far from Loyang. The awesome Shaolin "Pagoda Forest" nearby, where some 250 tall, ornate stone obelisks still stand above the graves of the martial monks, was started during this period.

By A.D. 640 the Tibetans in their high plateaus and Himalayan fastness below China's southwest border had become strong enough to harass the great "South Route" so important to Chinese trade with the West. The fierce, near-savage Tibetan king sent an embassy with tribute to Tai Tsung and boldly demanded a Chinese princess to wed. When he was refused, he invaded China's frontier. Chinese armies drove him back, but he was mollified only after Tai Tsung sent him the lovely bride Wen Chen, who was a princess of the royal family and a devout Buddhist.

The hardships of her caravan journey across treacherous passes, where baggage horses slipped from high narrow ledges cut into steep rock cliffs, are still narrated in Chinese legends. Princess Wen Chen arrived at the bleak stone palace of Tibet to find another royal princess, this one from Nepal, just south of the Himalayas, ensconced as a queen. Since this Nepalese woman, too, was an ardent Buddhist, the two young queens soon became fast friends and allies. Both were horrified at the bloody animal sacrifices and wild demon dances performed as religious rites by animistic shamans at the Tibetan court. In time, the two brides persuaded their temperamental master to allow Buddhism to be introduced into Tibet. From this beginning, all Tibetans would be eventually converted to Lamaism—their own peculiar brand of Indian Buddhism. Both queens died young, and both were deified as Buddhist goddesses, Green Tara and White Tara, emanations of the revered Chinese Goddess of Mercy. In Tibet and Nepal today, their idols sit at the feet of the Buddhist God of Mercy, of whom each Tibetan Dalai Lama is believed to be an incarnation. In the remote hills of Nepal, the writer has seen the story of these two beautiful Buddhist queens of Tibet enacted during village religious festivals.

Despite his tolerance of all religions, Tai Tsung himself was basically a simple Confucian. In his older years he gave himself over to a life of peace and scholarship, studying the works of the Great Sage. "By using a brass mirror you may see to adjust your cap," he said, "but by using antiquity as a mirror one may learn to foresee the rise and fall of empires."[4] In A.D. 630 he decreed that temples to Confucius be erected in all districts. There his officials twice each year had to perform religious rites by sprinkling the blood of sacrificed cattle over the altars. Local dignitaries participated in these ceremonies "with reverential attitude," chanting somber, antique music and performing ancient, stylized Confucian court dances.

When his ministers recommended harsh punishments for criminals, Tai Tsung told them: "Were I to diminish expenditures, lighten the tax burden, and employ only honest, caring officials so that people have food and clothing enough, this would do more to abolish theft than the employment of severe laws."⁵ He further decreed that no Tang emperor should ever ratify a death sentence until he had fasted and meditated on the case for three days.

The strong bond of confidence between Tai Tsung and his ministers was a stumbling block to ambitious eunuchs who traditionally rose to power on palace intrigue and outer court dissension. He denied imperial titles to his eunuchs, clothed them in simple yellow robes of the lowest ranks, and allowed them to act as messengers only within the capital. In A.D. 632, his empress sent one of her eunuchs with a present of silk and money to a minister for a job well done, and the emperor frequently had his eunuchs bear medicines and wishes for a speedy recovery to high officials suffering illness.

While a few eunuchs at this time may have been alien prisoners of war, by far the most were children of poor Chinese or southern coast aborigines. The recruitment of eunuchs from aborigines was started during the Sui Dynasty. It is recorded, however, that Tai Tsung had one alien northern tribesman who was a professional musician castrated so he could instruct the ladies of the harem in playing musical instruments.

Later in his reign, Tai Tsung reversed his policy and began sending eunuchs as messengers and envoys into the provinces and sometimes even beyond China's borders, a practice which brought the eunuchs into prolonged conflict with Tang officials. In A.D. 640 Tai Tsung ordered a eunuch envoy to a neighboring state, but when the eunuch applied at the office of border surveillance for a pass, the Chinese official indignantly refused the request. The eunuch reported this slight back to the emperor, who angrily ordered the official dismissed. At this point, a respected elder statesman intervened to advise that "It has always been impossible to treat eunuchs on intimate terms. They tell untruths on the slightest provocation, and are always ready to provoke trouble. To employ them on missions to distant lands is highly unwise, a practice which should be curtailed. The whole matter requires careful consideration."⁶ Tai Tsung accepted the warning (to the great admiration of Confucian officials), and withdrew his dismissal of the passport officer.

About this same time, Tai Tsung's best-loved son and heir was causing him great sorrow with scandalously profligate behavior. The prince's degrading and intimate relations with the eunuchs of his own household staff, and the extravagant favors he granted them, brought vigorous official protests from all sides. Even the eunuch superintendent of the prince's own palace, Yu Chin-ning, reported his excesses to the throne, and was rewarded with an unsuccessful attempt on his life by the prince's henchmen. Soon the heir apparent, who enjoyed unlimited grants from the treasury by order of his indulgent father, abandoned any pretext of filial virtue. Now he made no attempt to hide his vicious inclinations. A report of his sexual intimacy with a singing boy caused the distraught emperor to have the boy executed. The heir's resentment toward his father for this action, as well as his jealousy of a younger brother, goaded him into an unsuccessful attempt to overthrow the throne and assassinate the brother. Among those implicated was the prince's principal supporter, who saved his own head by revealing the entire conspiracy.

Heartsick, Emperor Tai Tsung deposed the crown prince and executed or banished all his accomplices and household eunuchs. Only head eunuch Yu Chih-ning was spared, because of his early revelations of the heir's shocking conduct.

Six years later, the imperial succession devolved upon a weak and ultimately incapable younger son who would be known as Emperor Kao Tsung. Tai Tsung designated the same eunuch Yu Chih-ning as one of the loyal, capable men who should guide the inexperienced prince when he became emperor.

When Tai Tsung was fifty-three, after one of the most successful reigns in Chinese history, he died at the Chang An palace—some say from taking so-called drugs of immortality. He was entombed in the imperial cemetery, having already had carved around his mausoleum statues of chieftains and kings he had conquered, as well as replicas of his beloved war horses. So loyal were his military officers that one veteran Tartar captain had to be restrained from killing himself so he could keep eternal vigil over the great man in the next world.

One historian wrote: "When Tai Tsung died, the grief of the people knew no bounds. Even foreign envoys cut themselves with knives and lances to sprinkle their blood over his grave."[7] In compliance with Tai Tsung's death decree, centuries-old scrolls of beautiful, rare calligraphy and other priceless antique works of art from his vast collection were interred beneath his coffin to pleasure him in the hereafter.

His son Kao Tsung ascended the Tang throne in A.D. 650, a well-meaning twenty-two-year-old prince, but fortunate indeed that his father had left him an administration so strong that the empire continued to prosper and expand despite his weakness of character. Fortunately also—for the nation at least—Kao Tsung early acquired as his consort the notorious Empress Wu, who was infinitely more shrewd and assertive than he was in the management of state affairs.

Almost from the beginning, Kao Tsung's reign was plagued with palace scandals. His sister, a princess of loose morals, married to the son of a chief minister, plotted to gain control of her husband's family inheritance as well as Kao Tsung's throne. She enlisted Taoist and Buddhist soothsayers to make dire prophesies against the emperor, while a ranking eunuch, Chen Hsuan-Yun, acted as her collaborator within the palace. In the end her entire plot came to light, with the result that the princess, the eunuch, and all her fellow conspirators were executed.

Next, Kao Tsung's Empress Wang, fearing his preference for a more attractive harem rival, conspired to divert his attention by promoting a concubine of her choice. She remembered a certain concubine Wu who had entered the former emperor's harem as a thirteen-year-old beauty. While still a young prince, Kao Tsung had coveted her. At his father's death, according to established custom, concubine Wu and other harem ladies had been forced to shave their heads and enter religious cloisters. It is not clear how Empress Wang rescued this ambitious charmer from life as a nun. Some accounts say Emperor Kao Tsung himself asked to have her brought back to the palace, after having once again succumbed to her wiles when he visited her convent during a religious festival.

In no time, concubine Wu was elevated in rank to become Lady Wu, the imperial favorite and dominating influence in the harem, blinding the impressionable emperor with her grace and wit as she ruthlessly schemed her way toward ultimate power. As one discerning contemporary wrote, "Lady Wu, with her lovely eyebrows arched like the antennae of a butterfly, yields to no woman, but coyly hides her face behind her long sleeve and applies herself to slandering others, knowing her vixen charms hold the power to bewitch the emperor."[8]

By A.D. 655 Lady Wu had borne Kao Tsung a girl child, and when the empress called at her apartments with customary congratulations and took the baby in her arms, the new mother showed demure appreciation. But when the empress departed, Lady Wu quickly smothered her own child in its blankets. Within minutes, the emperor arrived to view his new daughter, pleased to find the mother seemingly glowing with pride; but when he drew back the cradle covers, he gasped in horror at the sight of the dead infant. Feigning shock and grief, Lady Wu tearfully accused her nursery attendants, all of whom tremblingly denied guilt by pointing to the empress as the last to have touched the baby. Their testimony, and Lady Wu's concurrence, convinced the emperor. He had his empress deposed, imprisoned in outside apartments, and replaced by the "bereaved" mother, who thus became Empress Wu.

Strong-willed and intelligent though she was, Empress Wu was paranoid over any perceived threat to her ill-gained position. When she heard that Emperor Kao Tsung had visited his former empress in her prison quarters (which also housed a concubine whom Empress Wu hated), she had both women beaten with 100 strokes of the cane, their limbs cut off, and their remains thrown into a wine vat. Soon thereafter, the unhappy emperor's health began to fail.

By the end of a year, Empress Wu and her principal backer, a rapacious chief minister, had assassinated or forced to commit suicide all officials who had opposed her promotion to empress. When this same minister was tried and banished for blatantly selling official positions, the new chief minister attempted to oust Empress Wu. He enlisted a ranking eunuch, Wang Fu-sheng, to convince the emperor that Empress Wu was freely admitting a Taoist priest to the inner palace, where he was performing black magic rites to bring about Kao Tsung's death. The emperor at once called the minister to a secret audience and was strongly advised that Empress Wu must be deposed. To this the emperor finally consented, ordering the minister to draft the necessary edict. Empress Wu, forewarned by her spies, rushed to the emperor and found him perusing the edict, but in the face of her wrath, all his resolution vanished. "This was never my desire," he sighed, "the chief minister advised me to do it."

Empress Wu had the minister and eunuch Wang Fu-sheng beheaded and their accomplices banished, and brought the minister's wives and daughters into the harem as slaves. Never did she forget how close she came to being deposed. From now on she watched powerful ministers with suspicion, and held tight reins on the eunuchs. Taking no further chances, she observed all Kao Tsung's official audiences from behind a screen and saw to it that, without her personal approval, no state action was taken or decision made.

Focusing on such events, Chinese annalists have systematically portrayed Empress Wu as an ogress, for in orthodox Confucian doctrine, a female usurper of ruling power can spell nothing but disaster. However, after A.D. 660, when the emperor's eyesight became impaired, guided by her strong leadership and political acumen, a wise and just administration promoted a series of reforms. Military expenses were reduced, taxes cut, salaries of deserving officials raised, retirees given a viable pension, and vast royal lands near the capital turned over to husbandry.

Under Empress Wu's guidance, Chinese generals helped the Koreans rid themselves of Japan's overlordship to become united under a king who remained loyal to China. Tang armies repulsed northern Tartars who for centuries had "thundered down like predatory wolves to lay waste the lands of Chinese subjects who were timid as sheep."[9] One Mongolian inscription boasts, "In the early years of the Tang Dynasty we had so many victorious expeditions into China that our slaves became slave-owners themselves."[10] By the end of Empress Wu's reign, China had regained her influence in

Central Asia, and the Japanese were so enamored of the glories of Tang China that they were aping everything in Chinese culture—even planning their capital city as a copy of Chang An.

As Kao Tsung became progressively enfeebled, the control of state matters in the hands of Empress Wu, he restlessly drifted from one imperial pleasure palace to another, a mere figurehead of power. Even his eunuchs were slighted with impunity by officials. In A.D. 675 the officer in charge of palace parks found one of the emperor's eunuchs "misconducting himself" among the shrubbery and had him severely beaten. When he addressed a memorial to Kao Tsung to justify his action, he received a personal reply saying that should such an incident recur, the official was at liberty to inflict punishment without approval from the throne. Some years later, the emperor sent a eunuch envoy south to collect a species of exotic bamboo for his beloved palace gardens. On his journey, the eunuch treated local officials with such insolence that a prefect arrested him and wrote the emperor a strong letter deploring both the eunuch's conduct and his trivial mission. Kao Tsung's meek reply, written in his own hand, approved the arrest and asked the prefect to replant the bamboos where they were found.

Historians of this era have recorded their suspicions that Empress Wu had a hand in promoting her husband's poor health and even his death in A.D. 683. Records say that in Kao Tsung's last months "his head swelled up and he became like a blind man."[11] When his physician advised draining the swelling, Empress Wu cried out that to lay hands on the imperial person was a capital offense against the throne. Under the doctor's strong insistence, she finally allowed him to puncture the emperor's bloated head. When his condition markedly improved, she professed great gratitude by personally presenting the surgeon with 100 pieces of silk. A month later, however, the emperor died in the palace "without witnesses," a most unusual occurrence since tradition mandated that the entire imperial family attend a dying emperor to attest to his final words and wishes.

Empress Wu placed her son by the emperor on the throne, the twenty-seven-year-old Chung Tsung, but kept all ruling power to herself. Before the year was out she had deposed and exiled the emperor and his wife to a remote province. There they lived for the next fifteen years closely guarded by a repulsive local prefect whose very approach reduced the former emperor to almost suicidal terror. Meanwhile, Empress Wu installed another son, Jui Tsung, on the throne, but soon threw him out as well.

In A.D. 690 she abandoned all pretense, put an end to Tang Dynasty rule, and founded her own dynasty with herself as "emperor"—the only woman in imperial Chinese history to assume that title. When Tang family members challenged her, she executed or exiled almost all of Kao Tsung's close male relations. After a failed coup led by two Tang princes, she wiped out twelve collateral branches of the imperial Tang clan and had the two princes' severed heads brought before her in the palace.

Most historians agree that during Empress Wu's fifteen years as "emperor" the stage was being set for a disastrous future rise in eunuch influence. By A.D. 693 the outer court had broken down into several factions that were hopelessly divided not by political issues but by petty self-interest and bitter personal animosities. The practical Empress Wu turned for advice and assistance to favorite Buddhist monks, certain eunuchs, and her ruffian secret police, who terrorized all officialdom and even spied on the eunuch corps. In A.D. 693 she had the deputy chief of the eunuch staff, Fan Yu-hsien, indicted for treason and publicly beheaded after he was found paying a private visit to her son Jui Tsung. Such draconian punishments, it is said, caused the eunuchs to band together for mutual protection.

In A.D. 699, when six royal military stables were founded within the palace grounds, Empress Wu gave full responsibility for one of them—the Flying Horse Stable—to a eunuch, along with an impressive official title. This stable evolved into a full-fledged troop of cavalry commanded and evidently staffed by eunuchs. After the orthodox body of censors strongly disagreed with Empress Wu's plan to send these eunuch forces against marauding Tibetans, the empress became disaffected with the censors and henceforth completely ignored their advice and guidance.

Such weakening of the traditional legitimate bureaucratic system would lend a foothold for the eventual reestablishment of eunuch power. Now, also, under Empress Wu's policies, the Buddhist church had become so fabulously powerful and wealthy that even monks expected—and received—a voice in political affairs. The empress herself had endowed influential Buddhist leaders with enormous sums in appreciation for their support when she usurped the throne, and other influential ladies of the palace made generous donations as well. Monasteries grew so wealthy that they acted as banks, backed by huge stores of valuable metals, and with revenues collected from countless shops belonging to the church. So extensive was Buddhist ownership of granaries and mills that the religious hierarchy could control prices of flour and processed rice. Thus, under Empress Wu, a considerable measure of political and economic controls escaped bureaucratic hands.

After she became "Emperor Wu" at age sixty-seven, this remarkable woman took on a series of intimate favorites in a sort of male harem, which shocked all officialdom. It is said that her eunuchs, her overbearing nephew, and an influential female private secretary provided her with a string of virile lovers such as one lusty, big-limbed lout of a peddler, whom she allowed to frequent her private apartments. So thoroughly did she indulge this strapping fellow that he became arrogant, once beating an imperial censor who had confronted him for aggressive behavior almost to death. No amount of official complaints ever convinced Empress Wu to punish the brute.

More notorious still was the Buddhist monk Hsieh Huai-I, who had taken vows of celibacy, it is said, at Empress Wu's instigation so that he could have free entry to her apartments. His legal adoption by the family into which the empress had married her daughter also gave the monk access. Hsieh Huai-I quickly rose to become chief advisor of the empress, abbot of a monastery, a contractor of vast public works, and finally supreme commander of the empire's military forces. He was allowed to be accompanied at all times by his own private eunuch staff. One outraged official proposed that since the monk had all the privileges of a eunuch and spent most of his time in the inner apartments, he had best be castrated to protect the chastity of harem ladies. Empress Wu ignored this proposal, and kept the monk with her for most of her remaining years.

In her seventies, Empress Wu showered special favor on two smooth-cheeked brothers, the Chang brothers, former boy singers, the nature of whose private relationship with their imperial mistress has never been precisely determined. One of the brothers, she declared, had "a face as beautiful as a lotus flower," while it is said she valued the other for his talents in the bed chamber. As her personal companions, she made them members of the Palace Guard, and in A.D. 698 raised one of them to head a newly created directorate. The Chang brothers and their friends became members of her "inner circle" of favorites with privileged access to the inner palace, through whom she now transacted most official business.

For several years orthodox officials made every attempt to remove the Chang brothers from their position of royal favor, submitting accusations against them of bribery, of a form of extortion in which they forced citizens to sell them their lands, and of treason. In A.D. 704 this last charge was definitely proven against one brother, but the empress sent a eunuch with an order for his release from sentence. Within a year, the empress—greatly weakened by infirmity and old age—would allow no one but the Chang brothers at her side.

By then a powerful Tartar chieftain, who had formerly allied himself in loyalty to the Tang Dynasty, had united all his countrymen and threatened Empress Wu with invasion unless she established the rightful Tang ruler on the throne. Before his armies could reach the border, however, she appeased him by bringing her son Chung Tsung back from fifteen years in exile, though she reinstated him only as her crown prince. With the

Mongolians temporarily stalled off, she continued as "emperor," with her Chang brother favorites as principal aides.

By A.D. 705 disgruntled and disgusted officials were conspiring against her. At last, a veteran chief minister and four colleagues took up arms and entered the palace in the dead of night, abetted by a section of the palace guards. They seized her timorous son Chung Tsung, acclaimed him once again Tang emperor, and led him by force to the empress's apartments. She was awakened from sound sleep to find her beloved Chang brothers lying slaughtered at her feet. This indomitable woman regained her composure enough to make a last attempt to shame and intimidate her quaking son, but the assailants held a dagger at her throat and forced her to abdicate. Late that same year, she died in "retirement" at the great age of eighty-two, "after having been in complete authority for more than half a century and done the empire a power of good," as one modern writer puts it.[12]

Ministers who were relieved to be rid of Empress Wu soon had reason to regret the reestablishment on the throne of Emperor Chung Tsung, who possessed none of his mother's strength of character. Even more ineffective than his father, Chung Tsung allowed himself to be completely dominated by females, especially his consort, Empress Wei, who, emulating the dead Empress Wu, immediately set about seizing power. It is said that during his fifteen years in remote banishment, had it not been for his wife's admonitions, Chung Tsung would have committed suicide. In gratitude, he had promised her a free hand should he ever be recalled. Perhaps this accounts for her treacherous intrigues and numerous infidelities that were soon to rock the court.

Empress Wei took as her lover the handsome Wu San-ssu, nephew and high official of the deceased Empress Wu. This scoundrel was also bedding Wan-Erh, private secretary of the old Empress Wu, who had taken her in as a thirteen-year-old slave girl after having executed her father for treason. This talented, intellectual, scheming girl became one of Empress Wu's close confidential advisors, and now Empress Wei kept her on in the same capacity. Among them, this trio gleaned a fortune in payoffs by selling some 2,000 supernumerary official posts. For a price, they also elevated some 1,000 eunuchs to positions above their lawful rank.

Conniving with the Empress Wei, Wu San-ssu married his son to her adored princess daughter by the emperor who had been born on their journey into exile. When Wu San-ssu proposed to officials that his new daughter-in-law become heir apparent to the throne, the court was stupefied. One astute old minister of lowly birth, whom the spoiled princess afterwards referred to as "that pigheaded farmer from Shangtung," was able to block the appointment. This setback did not deter Wu San-ssu, who never gave up his ambitions. Luckily, the legitimate crown prince, son of Chung Tsung by another consort, got wind of the plan, and with an experienced general and 300 palace soldiers, marched on the Wu mansion and killed both Wu San-ssu and his son.

Next this crown prince and his followers stormed the palace, where they found Empress Wei, the now-widowed princess, secretary Wan-Erh, and Emperor Chung Tsung barricaded in the tower of a palace gate-pavilion. From this height, the emperor, in a rare show of courage, made an impassioned, eloquent plea to the armed men, asking for loyalty and mercy, finally convincing them to turn on their leaders. The eunuch, Yang Ssu-hsu, in charge of some of the rebel troops immediately cut down his own general. The crown prince escaped, only to be killed at a later time. For his bravery and loyalty to the throne, eunuch Yang Ssu-hsu received a high honorific title, was promoted to deputy chief of the eunuch corps, and remained on intimate terms with the imperial family.

For the next three years, Empress Wei and the princess enjoyed the spoils of power, the empress with a series of lovers, while the princess and her lady friends brazenly sold official positions and permits for joining monasteries. As one official complained, "There is not enough gold and silver in the imperial treasury to provide seals of office and gifts of silk for all these new appointees."[13]

Meanwhile, Emperor Chung Tsung sat on the Dragon Throne and signed away imperial revenue with abandon. In one year alone he assigned to a few favored individuals land yielding tax revenue from 40,000 households. It is said that by the end of his five-year reign a huge percentage of taxes which normally accrued to the state was going into private hands.

Eunuch numbers increased under Chung Tsung and his dominating womenfolk, as well as the scope of their duties. Eunuchs now were being trained as soldiers for branches of the Imperial Guard, which was under eunuch command. The princess herself granted her favorite eunuch, Hsieh Ssu-chien, the innovative title "Grand General of Surveillance." His duty would be to guard the gates of half the capital city. In A.D. 707 censors charged eunuch Hsieh with abuse of office and demanded his execution. The trial was halted, however, by order of a chief censor who toadied to Empress Wei's family and also stood in awe of the powerful eunuch. In the next reign, this eunuch would attain a position of still greater authority.

This same year, Emperor Chung Tsung sent a number of eunuchs to buy up huge quantities of live fish which riverside peasants had netted or raised in ponds to sell. His object was to set the fish free, thereby gaining religious merit, according to the Buddhist tenet against the taking of life. Though an official protested against such "misplaced charity" and waste of funds, the imperial family's "ransoming" of live creatures continued and became an increasing source of pocket money for the eunuch middlemen in these transactions. These lucrative religious practices encouraged many palace eunuchs to become Buddhists.

Despite wanton extravagance and internal upheavals at court, Chung Tsung's reign did not endure long enough to impair administration of the provinces. They remained tranquil and obedient under officers who had been appointed by the former Empress Wu.

In A.D. 710 warnings came to the emperor that Empress Wei intended to take his life and assume the throne herself. But before he could act to save himself, he died from eating poisoned pastries served by the empress and the princess. Whereupon, the son of former Emperor Jui Tsung enlisted Palace Guard units, seized the palace, killed Empress Wei with a volley of arrows, and impaled her head on a spike and hurled it to the crowd beyond the palace walls. In the subsequent melee, the princess, all her conspirators and relatives, and even the remaining members of former Empress Wu's clan, were massacred.

The victorious prince then reinstated his father as emperor. But within two years, Jui Tsung abdicated in favor of his more capable son, Hsuan Tsung. This alert, energetic, cultivated Tang ruler would oversee forty years of peace, plenty, and an unprecedented flowering of Chinese culture.

Notes

1. T. Mitamura, *Chinese Eunuchs.*
2. R. Grousset, *The Rise and Splendour of the Chinese Empire.*
3. D. Bloodworth, *The Chinese Looking Glass.*
4. Will Durant, *Our Oriental Heritage.*
5. Ibid.
6. J. K. Rideout, "Rise of the Eunuchs During the Tang Dynasty," in *Asia Major,* New Series, Volume I.
7. Will Durant, *Our Oriental Heritage.*
8. R. Grousset, *The Rise and Splendour of the Chinese Empire.*
9. Ibid.
10. Ibid.
11. Ibid.
12. D. Bloodworth, *The Chinese Looking Glass.*
13. Twitchett and Fairbank, *Cambridge History of China.*

II

The "Brilliant Emperor" Enhances Eunuch Status

TANG RULER HSUAN TSUNG'S REIGN (A.D. 712-756)

Emperor Hsuan Tsung ascended the Tang Dynasty throne in A.D. 712 at age twenty-eight. He was destined to be known as the "Brilliant Monarch" or "Shining Monarch," and would preside over China's golden age, when her culture flourished and influence spread as never before or since. Hsuan Tsung is also the emperor who, in his older years, very nearly sacrificed the empire to the smiles of a beautiful woman. It was this ill-fated love affair, rather than his outstanding reign, which has immortalized his name among the Chinese people. Modern historians also point to him as the Tang ruler whose leniency with court eunuchs set in motion the disastrous rise in eunuch influence which would eventually bring down the dynasty.

Hsuan Tsung started out like several great Chinese sovereigns before him, making every effort to curb extravagance, trying to be a virtuous ruler. He closed the imperial silk factories and forbade even palace ladies to wear jewels and embroidered silken gowns. The granting of superfluous titles and appointments, which was rampant in the preceding Tang reign, was outlawed—except for those bestowed on eunuchs. Concern for his subjects prompted him to found in the Chang An capital a hospital for sick and crippled street beggars, and to oppose the death penalty, but with little success. Once, during a severe drought, he stood on a mat for three days exposed to the open sky entreating Heaven to send rain to the land, emulating revered Shang Dynasty kings of 1500 B.C.

Three years after his enthronement, Hsuan Tsung was compelled to do away with his aunt, the Taiping princess, daughter of his deceased grandmother, Empress Wu. The princess had helped him to power for her own ambitious reasons, and now was interfering in political matters and plotting to control the throne. With the backing of his chief eunuch Kao Li-shih and his Korean "slave general," Emperor Hsuan Tsung had all the sons and supporters of the princess slaughtered in one night on the palace grounds. The princess escaped to hide out in a religious cloister, but was soon apprehended and given "imperial permission" to commit suicide at her home.

In payment for helping rid the emperor of his last adversaries among the imperial relatives, eunuch Kao Li-shih would remain a prominent figure in Hsuan Tsung's long reign.

Under Hsuan Tsung's vigorous rule, Tang armies extended Chinese borders almost to their present vast proportions. Riches and tribute flowed in through eastern harbors and along the Silk Roads from Central Asia in such quantity that Chang An became the largest, wealthiest, and most culturally refined city in the world, with nearly two million inhabitants. Never before or since was China so carefree, so open to foreigners, and so fascinated with alien ideas.

Soon forgotten were Hsuan Tsung's early austerities. Preserved today in Buddhist cliff-grottoes at Dunhuang near the west end of the Great Wall are some of the finest extant Tang murals, depicting the polished, sophisticated lifestyles of the upper classes—scenes of gorgeous weddings, costly funerals, lavish festivals and royal hunts, polo matches where aloof lords and elegant ladies ride in regal splendor. Also depicted are great merchant caravans led by big-nosed foreigners from the West, Tibetan kings and alien rulers come to pay obeisance to the Chinese Son of Heaven, surrounded by their eunuchs—and everywhere fine horses for which the Tang is famous.

Never before had China known such refinement of manners, abundant food, and comfortable homes. Now half the people in her flourishing cities routinely dressed in silks and furs. As one court poet wrote: "What hospitality! What squandering of money! Red jade cups and exotic foods on tables inlaid with green gems!"[1] Artists carved exquisite figurines from chunks of raw ruby. The rich were buried on beds of pearl. So peaceful and prosperous were the people, and generous with hospitality, it is said, that one could travel the length and breadth of the empire without having to carry money.

Under the patronage and avid encouragement of Emperor Hsuan Tsung blossomed an epoch of China's greatest poets, a time of outstanding achievement in all the arts. Hsuan Tsung himself was a musician, painter, and poet. His Pear Garden Academy attached to the palace trained musicians and dancers for imperial ceremonials and stage shows, for which he was posthumously canonized as the Patron Saint of Theatrical Performers.

In A.D. 717 Hsuan Tsung endowed a special library in his auxiliary capital at Loyang for the collection and classification of precious ancient manuscripts in danger of extinction. This "Palace Library Where the Sages Assemble" was overseen by a trusted eunuch with the title Imperial Commissioner.

Records of eunuchs prominent during Hsuan Tsung's reign make clear that by this time new sources had been found for palace *castrati.* Continued was the practice of executing Chinese subjects guilty of crimes against the throne, together with all their male relatives above fourteen years of age. However, sons of the condemned below puberty were castrated and trained for the palace, while the daughters and wives became slaves or concubines in the harem.

The preceding Sui Dynasty is credited with starting the practice whereby regional imperial officials castrated boys from backward aborigine peoples, especially in southern coastal regions, for presentation to the throne. Now a lucrative, widespread slave traffic developed, operated by Chinese entrepreneurs who bought up and castrated not only aborigine boys but also sons of Chinese subjects reduced to poverty or slavery. These young victims were forwarded to the imperial palace or sold to wealthy Chinese who kept concubines, eunuchs, and slaves.

During Hsuan Tsung's rule it became established practice that local officials all over the empire furnish a specific quota of emasculated youths as part of their area's annual tribute to the throne. Chinese scholars explain that in the Tang era this practice was not considered inhumane, for anyone, even palace eunuchs, could attain wealth and influence if they met with "good luck"—considered a very important element in Chinese life.

In A.D. 749, for reasons not entirely clear, Hsuan Tsung decreed that all eunuchs in private homes be sent to the household department of the imperial eunuch corps within five days. Perhaps this edict was predicated on poetry of the day that lamented the cruelties undergone by hapless young boys torn from their homes by local officials. This same decree also limited the number of slaves allowed to private individuals according to their rank. These "reforms," however, proved short-lived.

Despite an ancient precedent specifically denying education to palace eunuchs, the lenient Hsuan Tsung allowed a number of low-ranking young eunuchs to be taught by professional scholars. A special department in the palace kept their records and supplied their food. Evidently it was now recognized that castrated males with fairly comprehensive schooling were needed to instruct harem ladies in subjects ranging from Confucian classics to games of draughts. In A.D. 741 the "Palace School of Literary Studies" was enlarged and staffed entirely by eunuch instructors.

Under Hsuan Tsung's relaxed policies many eunuchs became so wealthy that they were able to make huge personal donations to Taoist, and even more so, Buddhist, religious organizations. Two prominent palace eunuchs were given official control over the countless religious institutions and activities in the capital, allowing them to extract lucrative commissions from builders after forcing monasteries and temples to undergo costly repair works. Other palace eunuchs busied themselves rounding up great quantities of live birds, fish, and other wildlife for release by devout Buddhist wealthy imperial relatives.

By far the most prominent eunuch in Tsung's palace was the aforementioned Kao Li-shih, who was born into an aborigine tribe south of Canton. A former Tang official had had him castrated and sent as a chamberlain in the palace of Empress Wu. Eunuch Kao's shrewdness earned him favor until Empress Wu became annoyed over some minor infraction and dismissed him to the palace of her powerful nephew. There he was adopted by an older eunuch—although eunuch adoptions at this time were illegal—and assumed his mentor's surname, Kao.

Eventually, Kao Li-shih was taken into the retinue of a minor Tang prince who recognized his talents and valued him highly as a personal secretary and servitor. When this prince made a bid for the throne, Kao Li-shih figured prominently in exterminating the ruling consort family. And when the prince became Emperor Hsuan Tsung, eunuch Kao was instrumental in doing away with the plotting Taiping princess. For loyalty and support such as this, Emperor Hsuan Tsung made Kao, in turn, chief of his eunuch staff, supervisor of religious affairs in the capital, head of the inner-palace secretariat, and general of the palace armies, and eventually raised him to the third official grade, a rank heretofore expressly prohibited to eunuchs.

Eunuch Kao was on such intimate terms with Emperor Hsuan Tsung's family that he addressed the Son of Heaven familiarly as "Honorable Master," and in turn was called "My Old Servant." To the young heir he was "Elder Brother," while other princes and princesses called him "Venerable Sir"—all phrases of affection and respect widely used for valued servants in ordinary Chinese homes. Without doubt there were countless unrecorded eunuchs through imperial times who were likewise highly regarded.

Emperor Hsuan Tsung allowed wealthy eunuchs to buy mansions and estates, to reside outside the palace, and to take wives and adopt sons. Here we find the distant beginnings of the powerful "eunuch families" who would wreak such havoc under Tang emperors to come. Thus, unknowingly, Hsuan Tsung was setting the stage for the eunuchs eventually to rise once again as a destructive political force. Eunuch Kao Li-shih was the leading actor on that stage, a role that required someone with his exceptional tact, intelligence, and the complete confidence of the Son of Heaven. As chief eunuch, all state business to and from the throne now passed through channels under Kao's personal control. Not even ranking ministers could approach the emperor without eunuch Kao's consent.

High-ranking officials were indignant at eunuch Kao's success in promoting the status of palace eunuchs in general. He saw to it that eunuchs now were inducted into office with the same dignified ceremonies and regalia that had always been the sole prerogative of ministers of government bureaus. Now eunuch envoys ranged at large in the provinces, armed with authority over the highest local and military officials, all of whom knew that their advancement depended upon favorable reports turned in by these detested "eunuch spies." As a result, eunuchs returned from inspection tours with "their pockets bulging with bribe money," which demoralized upright officials.

Kao Li-shih became so wealthy and so influential with the throne that even the highest ministers competed to be in his good graces, many paying dearly for his favor. When, at his own expense, Kao constructed a Buddhist monastery and Taoist temple of unexampled magnificence in the capital, officials looked on with resentment and envy. Upon completion of these projects, Kao invited to the opening ceremonies scores of ranking officials and titled noblemen, who accepted with alacrity. Each guest who rang the temple bells was obliged to present the host Kao with a "donation" of 100,000 coppers—and some dignitaries tolled the bells as many as twenty times.

In subtle ways, eunuch Kao was able to foster the bitter factionalism which had developed in the outer court and was now preventing effective administration. Aware that such dissension could only lead to greater dependency on himself, Kao paid a private visit to one clique leader who had been convicted of taking bribes and of employing sorcerers to cast malignant spells against his opponents, and then carried back to the emperor the pitiable tale of finding the once-respected minister sitting on a common grass mat eating from a crude clay bowl, uncombed and unwashed, half-crazed with worry as he awaited sentence. Seeing Hsuan Tsung wring his hands in compassion, as well as from doubt about the justice of the conviction, Kao pressed his advantage by quietly reminding him of the accused's stellar past service. In the end, the emperor ruled that the minister should retain his office. In this way, eunuch Kao kept the befriended official in a position that would insure continued political infighting.

By A.D. 727, Emperor Hsuan Tsung had become so weary of bureaucratic strife that he dismissed the disputing party leaders and turned to Kao Li-shih and his eunuch cohorts and a few personal courtiers to act as his agents and supporters.

One man in the emperor's confidential retinue filled eunuch Kao with apprehension—General Wang, Kao's only rival as imperial favorite. Wang was of Korean blood, his forebears having been taken slaves in a war to subdue the Korean vassal state. When Hsuan Tsung was still a prince, Wang had been presented to him as a personal slave. Trained as a professional soldier and an expert in breeding spirited war horses, Wang soon became invaluable to his master. When he became emperor, Hsuan Tsung bestowed upon Wang a series of appointments in the palace guards, made him director of imperial stables and pasture lands throughout the realm, and ultimately named him Grand General in the military. Wang's appearance was required daily at the palace, an honor that was greatly envied.

The Korean general had gained ascendancy when, against objections of prominent ministers, Emperor Hsuan Tsung allowed him to marry his daughter to a top commander, putting Wang on intimate terms with prominent military families. Within a year, Wang boldly demanded nothing less than the presidency of the imperial war board. When he was turned down by the secretariat, he did not hesitate to broadcast his anger. Indignant ministers sent secret memorials to the throne, warning that the Korean was using his personal influence with the emperor to allow his military cohorts to indulge in flagrant illegal gain, yet nothing was done about these abuses. Soon, even a eunuch-controlled section of the palace guards was prepared to take orders from Wang, much to the resentment of eunuch Kao who headed up a rival eunuch clique in the palace.

Festering with indignation over General Wang's arrogance and insults, eunuch Kao awaited the opportune moment to take revenge. It came when Emperor Hsuan Tsung sent him to Wang with a congratulatory gift on the birth of a son—an honorary appointment for the infant to an official position. Kao returned to report the ungrateful Korean had demanded to know why his son did not rate yet a higher rank. Seeing the ruler's displeasure, eunuch Kao warned that unless quick measures were taken to "curb these alien slaves" there would be dire troubles for the throne. Hsuan Tsung degraded the Korean general and his close colleagues to minor offices at distant frontier postss, and soon "gave permission" for Wang himself to commit suicide.

After eliminating the disturbances in the military, Hsuan Tsung reportedly avowed, "With Kao Li-shih in control, I can now rest at ease." To keep the eunuch close to him, the emperor had him move from his private mansion into a spacious apartment within the palace.

In his middle years, having brought peace and prosperity to the empire, Hsuan Tsung turned to Taoist philosophy and mysticism—a definite swing away from the Buddhism that had long been in favor at court. A Taoist temple should be built in every large city, the emperor decreed, and all nobility must possess a copy of the Taoist scripture, which now included the emperor's personal commentaries. He established academies for Taoist studies, and added Taoist learning and poetry writing to examination requirements for official positions.

Hsuan Tsung became so involved in Taoist supernaturalism and magic practices that he convinced himself and the entire court that the sixth century B.C. founder of the religion—the deified Lao Tze—had appeared to him in person to reveal the whereabouts of a true likeness of himself. At the insistence of the emperor, sycophantic charlatans duly located an image, replicas of which were soon installed in temples nationwide. Perhaps the emperor was under the influence of Taoist hallucinatory drugs of immortality when he declared that, while burning incense at his private altar, he had actually been wafted up for a sojourn amongst the gods and spirits.

In his early sixties, Hsuan Tsung became morose, having lost all interest in his thousands of powdered and rouged ladies in the palaces of Chang An and Loyang. It was eunuch Kao Li-shih, ever sensitive to his master's needs, who discovered a concubine of great beauty in the harem of the emperor's eighteenth son. This was Yang Kuei Fei, who would become by far the most famous of the "Eight Celebrated Beauties of Old China." In appropriating this concubine for the emperor, eunuch Kao compensated the prince with the gift of another concubine, and for appearances sake had Yang Kuei Fei briefly enter a nunnery.

When eunuch Kao presented Yang Kuei Fei to the emperor, at first sight Hsuan Tsung completely lost his head over this willful, capricious, fun-loving charmer who, now in her late twenties, made him feel young again. "One glance from her is enough to destroy a town, and another glance will destroy a nation,"[2] the emperor said, echoing a Han Dynasty emperor's exclamation recorded a thousand years previously.

From now on, Hsuan Tsung completely neglected the rest of his harem to keep Yang Kuei Fei by his side day and night. Under her influence, he relegated his once-favored empress to an outside palace where she languished in the company of a few eunuch servants. When the emperor sent his eunuch to her bearing a conciliatory gift of pearls, she returned them with her own poetic composition: "Alone in sorrow in the Cold Palace, I am loath any longer even to paint my eyebrows like willow leaves. My scarf is smeared with tears mingled with faded rouge. Since there is no cure for loneliness, of what use is a bushel of pearls?"[3]

To keep his pleasure-seeking new paramour entertained, constant palace theatricals were arranged where hundreds of costumed dancers whirled and twisted "like fairies and butterflies" to music of the royal orchestra. Yet none was so lovely as Yang Kuei Fei when she alone danced with white cockatoos under the willows in the imperial gardens. Court poets won everlasting fame as they competed to sing her praises, rhapsodizing that she was "a Heavenly apparition with the radiance of a full-blown flower upon her face."

Soon Yang Kuei Fei's ruinous extravagances became the talk of Chang An. For her, the emperor built the opulent Palace of Longevity on a man-made lake island at the capital. This pleasure retreat boasted sixteen marble bathing pools, rooms plastered with gold and gems, and furnishings more magnificent than any seen before. When she wanted lichee fruit out of season, Hsuan Tsung sent riders galloping in relays to the far south of China. He bestowed her with jewels appropriate to an empress. Envious court ladies competed to emulate her seductive plumpness, her bejewelled false hair-pieces, and her elegant gowns.

From Yang Kuei Fei the aging emperor learned the art of dissipation. Word leaked from the palace that one of her favorite amusements in the harem was to arrange riotous mock battles where Hsuan Tsung personally commanded an "army" of over a hundred eunuchs. She opposed him, leading the same number of harem girls, who removed their high collars and used them as battle standards. As the two armies clashed in a drunken fray, the first side to admit defeat had to consume great quantities of wine. These scandalous orgies became known far and wide as "the battle-lines of profligacy." Thus in his late years, the general respect previously accorded to Emperor Hsuan Tsung began to wane.

Countless females of Yang Kuei Fei's family clan usurped free run of the palace. Her male relatives by the score appeared at court, eager for a share in imperial power and riches. At Yang Kuei Fei's insistence, Emperor Hsuan Tsung made her brutal, incapable brother his prime minister. He also installed such numbers of her male kinfolk in high positions that soon the Yang family was wealthier and more powerful than nobility. To curry their favor, courtiers showered them with gifts and competed to do their bidding.

"No longer weep at the birth of a girl-child," the people said, "for she could become a royal concubine and bring glory to the entire family, while a son cannot even become a baron."[4]

In his lust for wealth, Yang Kuei Fei's brother, the prime minister, extracted bribe money from mandarins in return for favors, spreading graft and corruption like cancer throughout the government. As faith in Tang rule weakened among upright officials and the populace, dissatisfaction grew among military officers who could not, or would not, pay the Yang family for promotions.

One military man, however, became a favorite playmate of Yang Kuei Fei and the emperor. This was the Turk, An Lu-shan, born in Manchuria to a Tartar mother and a father from Samarkand. An Lu-shan had been captured as a boy and sold as a slave to a Chinese general who recognized his promise and promoted him through the ranks to become an officer in charge of troops. Sources describe An Lu-shan as a grossly obese prodigy of evil, but he also proved himself an astute general, piling up victories over northern barbarians in China's behalf.

A sly, hard-to-manage Mongolian slave boy had come into An Lu-shan's possession. General An wielded his own sword to castrate the lad, who bled so profusely that he lay half dead until the wound was healed with hot ashes. Once subdued as a eunuch, the boy became an inseparable companion of his master. So intimate was their relationship that, as An Lu-shan became increasingly fat and his belly rested on his knees, the little eunuch had to support his enormous paunch with his head so attendants could tie the general's waist sash. This is the eunuch servant who, in the end, would do his master in.

During trips in from the field, An Lu-shan became an habitue of the pleasure-bent palace where court ladies found him fascinating. His ingenious pretense of uncouth barbarism and ignorance of court etiquette, as well as his audacious pranks and crude jokes, soon made him the most popular guest at court—especially with concubine Yang Kuei Fei. She took An Lu-shan under her protection, encouraging him to gain the emperor's favoritism through flattery and bawdy buffoonery.

Tongues wagged when Yang Kuei Fei legally adopted this hulking Turk as her own son, giving him free access to her private apartments. When the emperor was informed the two of them were having an affair, he shrugged off the suggestion as preposterous. Under Yang Kuei Fei's prodding, Hsuan Tsung made An Lu-shan a military governor with the strongest troops in the empire at his command. Yang Kuei Fei's grasping brother was consumed with envy when the emperor elevated his beloved concubine's adopted son to "Prince-Second-Class," a title that by law was reserved for those of royal birth.

By A.D. 761 Tang China's great armies were becoming worn out with conquests of expansion, heavy peasant conscription, and decreasing financial support due to palace extravagance. In this year alone, a Mongol horde defeated General An Lu-shan north of present-day Peking, a southern aborigine kingdom in Yunnan all but wiped out another imperial force, and another suffered disaster at the hands of Arab and Turkish armies in Central Asia.

As one anguished Chinese poet wrote: "Five thousand of our best men in sable and brocade, lost in the Hunnish dust!"[5] Another Tang poet mourned: "Sad, sad, our soldiers leave their native land headed beyond the frontiers where the net of misfortune awaits them. The Sovereign already possesses a vast empire! Why should he wish to extend it further?"[6]

In his determination to bring down An Lu-Shan, Yang Kuei Fei's jealous brother tried to convince the emperor that the general was plotting a revolt against the throne. Hsuan Tsung dismissed all such warnings as nonsense. When even the crown prince insisted the allegation was true, the emperor reluctantly summoned General An back to Chang An where he kowtowed to the emperor and wept, completely convincing the ruler of his loyalty.

When accusations continued, the weary emperor at last dispatched a eunuch inspector to the field. There An Lu-shan paid him a large sum to carry back a convincing report of his innocence. However, when the general learned that his Chang An mansion had been impounded by imperial guards, and that the eunuch inspector had been executed for accepting his bribe money, he refused to leave camp even when summoned by an edict written in the emperor's own hand. Instead, he assembled his 100,000 troops, most of them tough Tartar cavalry, and boldly advanced toward Chang An, easily overcoming Loyang on the way.

News of his approach threw the Chang An court into panic, for all knew that the capital armies—now more ornamental than a potentially effective fighting force—were no match for the Turk's seasoned troops. Hurriedly the emperor was carried off to safety across the southern hills to Szechuan, guarded by a platoon of palace soldiers and accompanied by Yang Kuei Fei, her brother and family members, and a few eunuchs headed by Kao Li-shih.

When the weary entourage reached a hill-station in Shensi, the guardsmen, grumbling with cold and hunger, refused to go further. Some accounts say their resentment mounted against Yang Kuei Fei and exploded into mutiny as they blamed her for the rebellion—for had she not brought General An Lu-shan to power? Others claimed that the soldiers became enraged when they watched her brother consorting with Tibetan officials and mercenaries. Supecting that he was conspiring to betray the empire, they fell upon him and decapitated him.

When Emperor Hsuan Tsung himself tried to reason with the maddened troops, they surrounded him with drawn swords, and, to his horror, demanded the head of concubine Yang Kuei Fei. After long and fruitless pleading for mercy, the ruler was at last convinced by his terrified entourage that nothing would appease the soldiers, and that refusing them would cost his own life. Utterly helpless, the emperor allowed chief eunuch Kao Li-shih to lead his beloved to a nearby pavilion. There, at age thirty-seven, Yang Kuei Fei was strung up on a pear tree with her silken white scarf until she strangled to death. The emperor, a broken man, was carried in the royal sedan chair to Szechuan, soon to abdicate in favor of his eldest son, Su Tsung.

Known as the "everlasting sorrow," the story of Yang Kuei Fei's tragic death would be told and retold down through the centuries in poetry, stage plays, operas, and today even in Chinese films.

Her protege, General An Lu-shan, took the Tang capital with little opposition. He then pitched his armies against forces collected by the new young emperor, launching the most devastating civil war Imperial China had ever undergone. Not until A.D. 757, with the aid of alien horsemen tribes from Mongolia, was the Tang ruler able to defeat An Lu-shan's forces in a great battle outside Chang An.

An Lu-shan himself managed to withdraw to the west where, soon thereafter, his disloyal son bribed the Turk's little Mongolian eunuch into killing his master. General An died of a knife wound in his tremendous belly. One of his officers took over to lead the rebels for several more years in senseless killing, burning, and looting, until the unnecessary war finally wore itself out.

Emperor Su Tsung brought his father back from exile in Szechuan to the war-ruined capital, a quavering, white-haired old man. Now titled "Grand Emperor," Hsuan Tsung retired to an outer palace to nurse his grief for three more years before succumbing to severe depression—or as some claim, to Taoist drugs of immortality. Eunuch Kao Li-shih, his faithful aide for half a century, died shortly thereafter.

Though the Tang Dynasty would rule on for another 150 years, it would not recapture the heights of glory and vigor experienced during Emperor Hsuan Tsung's best years. The undue influence of eunuchs Hsuan Tsung engendered with his lenient policies would grow to such grotesque proportions in the decades to come that it would eventually bring down the House of Tang.

Notes

1. Will Durant, *Our Oriental Heritage.*
2. Elizabeth Ten-Chen Wang, *Ladies of the Tang.*
3. H. T. Lee, *The Story of Chinese Culture.*
4. Ibid.
5. E. H. Schafer, *Ancient China.*
6. R. Grousset, *The Rise and Splendour of the Chinese Empire.*

12

Second Disastrous Upsurge of Eunuch Power

LATE TANG DYNASTY (A.D. 757-907)

Su Tsung was an energetic and well-meaning Tang prince whose six-year reign was marred by the An Lu-shan rebellion which raged across China. Only the South was left unscarred by battle, but the southerners remained so loyal to the dynasty that to this day the Cantonese refer to themselves as the Men of Tang.

When old Emperor Hsuan Tsung fled from insurgents to Szechuan and abdicated, Su Tsung took refuge in Shensi where in A.D. 756 his own troops declared him emperor. He rallied the people to the northwest, held off the rebels, and sought desperately needed aid from China's barbarian neighbors and tribute states. Even in disaster, the prestige of Tang China was sufficient to win support. Various foreign chieftains—even an Arab caliph of Central Asia—sent small contingents, but it was the war-trained Uighur barbarians dispatched by the khan of Outer Mongolia who saved the day. By A.D. 757 Uighur cavalry, together with Chinese loyalist troops, had reclaimed the two capital cities from the rebelling troops and followers of An Lu-shan.

Yet the cost to China for barbarian assistance was very high—as well as deeply humiliating. The Uighur horsemen considered Loyang their special prize and sacked the city thoroughly, burning whatever they could not carry off. They only desisted when the city elders paid them off with 10,000 rolls of choicest silk. Even then, Uighur soldiers continued to roam the countryside for some time, "torturing people and insulting local officials."[1] To a lesser extent, the Uighurs looted in the main imperial city, Chang An, too. It is also recorded that war-weary Chinese imperial troops joined them in the plunder.

Emperor Su Tsung set up court in Chang An, but the revolt was far from suppressed. Rebel troops returned to occupy Loyang again, and it required a force of Uighur cavalry led by the khan himself to recapture it for the Tangs. The city was retaken and the Mongolian khan escorted away the Tang emperor's own princess daughter as his reward. Uighur lieutenants and troops stayed on, selling stolen horses to the government at exorbitant prices and lending money to the people at grueling interest rates. For a time, Tang China was little more than a tribute state to the Mongolian Uighur allies.

At last, the senseless fighting petered out, leaving, in all, some thirty-six million dead. Several rebel leaders surrendered only after being bought off by the imperial government, while others were pacified by permission to remain on as military governors over their captured territories. Though the Chinese throne's overriding authority had been considerably weakened by the rebellion, the nation gradually pulled itself together. The great, lumbering bureaucracy resumed its myriad functions throughout the empire according to timeworn tradition; millions of peasants industriously tilled the soil; and the educated elite pursued their refined pastimes, while the ruinous animosity borne by officialdom toward palace eunuchs steadily mounted.

Throughout Su Tsung's rule the dominating figures at court were two close allies: a keen-witted eunuch named Li Fu-kuo, who had risen to prominence in the preceding reign and had now gained the unbounded confidence of the new emperor, and Empress Chang, an overbearing former concubine risen to exalted position through eunuch Li Fu-kuo's influence over the monarch.

Eunuch Li made a great show of Buddhist piety, eating only vegetarian foods and counting his beads even while conducting official business. This must have impressed Emperor Su Tsung, who was himself so devoted to the religion that he often made his eunuchs and guards dress up as Buddhist deities to take part in religious performances at his private palace chapel.

Though eunuch Li Fu-kuo had learned only the rudiments of writing and figures, Emperor Su Tsung granted him a number of official commissionerships, along with control over all palace administration and considerable say with regard to palace armies. All official memorials and imperial edicts to and from the throne had to pass through this eunuch's huge office staff, and needed his personal approval before promulgation. Thus he was able to insinuate himself into court politics to a far greater degree than previous emperors' eunuchs ever had. Secure of backing from Empress Chang, eunuch Li was able to override courtiers of the highest pedigree, arousing their extreme animosity.

After five years of eunuch Li's dominance, even Empress Chang became disenchanted with him and sought to do him in, but her plan was thwarted by the emperor's untimely death in A.D. 763. Thereafter, she directed her malice toward the legitimate crown prince, plotting to have him killed and replaced by her own son. This conspiracy was foiled by her erstwhile cohort, eunuch Li, who, together with a eunuch subordinate named Chen Taun-chen, led a detachment of palace guards into the empress's apartments and had her brutally murdered.

Thus the rightful heir became the next Tang ruler—Emperor Tai Tsung (not to be confused with the second Tang emperor of the same name). Because of his debt to eunuch Li—whom he thoroughly disliked—the new emperor allowed him to remain a power in the palace. Within a year, however, Tai Tsung had become so fearful of the eunuch's growing encroachment into state affairs that he had him killed by a band of assassins. Eunuch Li's subordinate, eunuch Cheng Tuan-chen, enjoyed special favor with the emperor for only a year before he was banished as a traitor for trying to keep the throne from learning of an imminent attack by marauding Tibetans.

Emperor Tai Tsung granted high honors to another eunuch, Yu Chao-en, whom his father had valued for his service as a leader of the Chinese army that aided Uighur barbarians in recapturing Loyang during the great rebellion. Tai Tsung allowed eunuch Yu to formally adopt an uncastrated professional soldier thirty years before such adoption was decreed legal. Eunuch Yu rancored lofty court officials by boasting of his literary skills, though all knew his staff of scholars wrote his compositions. He flaunted his new-found wealth and power, fearlessly pushing his way into the most sacrosanct areas of government.

At one point the Tibetans seized and occupied Chang An, looting and terrorizing the capital for fifteen days, and the emperor had to flee for safety. Eunuch Yu Chao-en and his reliable troops protected him during this embarrassing episode. Once the Tibetans were driven off and the emperor was able to return to Chang An, he showed his gratitude by incorporating eunuch Yu's army into the palace guards, with Yu as commander. Distasteful as this appointment was to high officials, now for the first time in decades the court could field an armed force completely under imperial control, and was no longer dependent on vacillating provincial military governors to come to its rescue.

Eunuch commander Yu Chao-en, like most eunuchs down through history, was a munificent devotee of Buddhism and successfully encouraged the emperor to follow suit. Tai Tsung built a costly temple dedicated to his deceased mother and paid over a thousand monks and nuns to say masses there every year. His own donations to Buddhism and those of his imperial womenfolk reached astronomical figures.

In A.D. 770 eunuch Yu Chao-en fell from grace, the victim of a convoluted political intrigue from which he failed to extricate himself. He was executed and all his backers killed or dispersed. A bureaucrat replaced him as head of the capital forces, and not until twenty years later—again in wartime—would eunuchs be given top military responsibility.

Emperor Tai Tsung regularly sent palace eunuchs to spy on military governors in the provinces, where some governors, backed by their armies, were asserting their independence from the throne. He also allowed eunuchs control over his personal treasury where large amounts of government revenue had been deposited for safekeeping during the great rebellion. Financial expert officials had no choice but to cooperate with eunuchs in order to conduct monetary business, and all their protests against eunuch interference went unheeded.

From then on the Tang Dynasty would be plagued with a series of short-lived, short-reigning rulers. The next emperor's reign of over twenty years was an exception. Te Tsung ascended the throne in A.D. 779, a ruler intensely concerned with government administration. He aimed at nothing less than restoring the initiative, authority, and power of central rule. Wary of delegating authority, and distrustful of the bureaucracy and military alike, he turned to loyal eunuchs for support in important affairs. The considerable advancement of eunuch influence during his reign laid the foundation for their usurpation of highest authority in decades to come. For this he has been severely, and perhaps unfairly, condemned.

Te Tsung inherited from preceding Tang monarchs the practice of having key eunuchs transmit official information and imperial decisions to and from the throne. However, he allowed his eunuchs much more control of this function and thus more political power. He also inherited the practice of allowing trusted eunuchs to head up parts of the palace guards and capital army units. Te Tsung put these vital branches of the military under command of the two eunuchs who had been the only men to rally to his desperate call when rebellion threatened shortly after his enthronement. He referred to these two eunuchs as his "claws and teeth," and gave them such high-ranking titles that they could repeatedly face down the highest court ministers. Soldiers in these eunuch-commanded troops received legal and financial exemptions on such a generous scale that wealthy subjects paid bribes to the two eunuchs to enroll them or their sons as nominal recruits. As a result, the total muster of forces swelled to tens of thousands, only a fraction of which was legitimate fighting men. Nonetheless, the central core of these armies remained strong and mobile, and control over them was the primary basis of the power Tang Dynasty eunuchs were to exercise for the next 100 years.

A third opportunity for eunuch advancement arose—again based on established practice—when Emperor Te Tsung used them to report on activities at frontier military headquarters and provincial administrations. Border commanders by this time were boldly making their own decisions, while some governors were even failing to remit their territory's tax revenues to the throne. Thus, Te Tsung found it necessary to increase the numbers, responsibilities, and powers of the eunuch reporters, arming them with coveted seals of office and the prestigious official title of "Imperial Army Supervisors."

These eunuch supervisors became the key liaison agents between throne and province in all political, military, and sometimes even administrative matters. This opened the way for all sorts of grave abuses, most significant of which was the eunuchs' malefic role in the selection of regional governors, wherein they used intimidation and bribery to sell their support. Field commanders also had to pay heavy "squeeze money," the common term for extortion, to the "eunuch watchdogs" for turning in favorable reports.

Time and again the throne received bitter complaints of baleful eunuch interference in provincial affairs, but Emperor Te Tsung invariably upheld his eunuch supervisors. In one instance, during a steadily intensifying conflict, both the provincial governor and eunuch supervisor sent messengers in a race for the capital with their version of a bitter dispute over such interference. En route, the eunuch's man was murdered by the envoy of the governor, who then wrote a memorial protesting the eunuch's intrusion into regional affairs, dispatched it on to the throne, and committed suicide. (Such suicides were a form of revenge against a rival, upon whom blame would now fall.) Despite an outcry of court ministers against the eunuch supervisor in this affair, Te Tsung did no more than recall him and give him a comfortable post at court.

Te Tsung's edict of A.D. 791 permitted eunuchs of the fifth grade or above to legally adopt one uncastrated male child under the age of nine. In this way, extended "eunuch families" rose to influence, as the adopted sons were married off and begot other sons. Now eunuch "patriarchs" could bequeath their titles, position, and wealth down through the generations, as did orthodox officials of the great families.

Thus, under Te Tsung, eunuchs were no longer shadows lurking in the background of the imperial palace. Officials throughout the empire were gradually forced to deal with this despised class. Intense hatred for the eunuchs throughout officialdom was transferred to some extent to Emperor Te Tsung himself. He was never forgiven for allowing the eunuchs to usurp duties which had traditionally belonged to Confucian officials.

A series of edicts from the very beginning of Te Tsung's reign attempted to put an end to the traffic in slaves and castrated youths, but so lucrative an enterprise was impossible to contain. Provincial castrated youths, on arrival at the capital, entered the imperial household under the supervision of senior eunuchs, who often formally adopted their young charges, thus binding them in "family loyalty." On emerging from a training period, they became "serving eunuchs," a general designation for all who as yet had no official appointment or grade. They were first assigned to the huge palace household staff or to the same staff of the heir apparent's harem. By this time imperial edicts conferring official appointments on deserving eunuchs were drafted by officials from the grand secretariat and presented in a solemn ceremony, similar to that for the proud official class.

Despite the advancement of eunuch influence during Emperor Te Tsuing's reign, the emperor himself never allowed a eunuch to challenge his supreme will. In his last years, though, he frequently closeted himself in his apartments for long periods, inaccessible to government officials and court politicians, and let his eunuchs assume key roles, increasing their influence in national affairs. His reemployment of eunuchs as custodians of the inner palace treasury did restore them powers he had previously curtailed. Evidently, he did this so finances could be controlled by the throne, rather than by the bureaucracy, in troubled times.

Far from completely abdicating his responsibilities, as his detractors accused, Emperor Te Tsung in A.D. 798 instigated such severe penalties against provinces that refused to submit taxes that one military governor openly revolted. The governor's troops actually occupied the capital and forced the emperor to seek safety in Shensi until order was restored. After this near-fatal setback, Te Tsung increasingly relied on his eunuch supervisors to investigate the loyalty of governors and generals in the territories.

Where Emperor Te Tsung did make a mistake was in maintaining his disabled son as heir. Some time before Te Tsung's death, a small group of concerned officials began gathering in secret with the crown prince and his retinue to fume and criticize defects in current policies. They condemned outrages committed by grasping eunuchs and noted the resulting misery of the people, while laying plans for seizing control from the entrenched eunuchs and corrupt officials once the crown prince was on the throne. Strangely, their clique also included a eunuch, Li Chungyan, a personal aide of the crown prince.

Upon Te Tsung's death, in A.D. 805, and the accession of the crown prince as Emperor Shun Tsung, this cabal set into motion their long-deliberated plan. Shun Tsung was suffering from an illness which severely curtailed his ability to speak or conduct court business. For several months after his enthronement, he isolated himself in his apartments, attended solely by his favorite concubine and eunuch Li Chung-yan, while the cabal set about wresting control of government from the eunuchs. Once in charge, they severely warned the court eunuchs against any further instances of fraud and bribery, and abolished the corrupt office- and influence-peddling system which had so long enriched the eunuchs. They also sent almost a thousand harem ladies and musicians to nunneries or back to their homes, in an effort to reduce the need for excessive eunuchs in the palace.

Within a year, Emperor Shun Tsung's health suddenly worsened, whereupon his personal followers began bickering among themselves and their influence at court rapidly waned. Diehard opponents demanded that Shun Tsung appoint an heir at once, lest another incapacitated ruler come to the throne.

The ultimate blow to Shun Tsung's power group came when one of its leaders attempted to take over command of the metropolitan armies, which required dislodging court eunuchs from their newly won military commands. This attempt failed not only because of eunuch opposition but also because of strong objections from frontier military generals, many of whom owed their jobs to eunuch supervisors.

At last a temporary coalition of most of the eunuchs together with some officials and military governors was able to secure the abdication of the ailing Shun Tsung in favor of Emperor Hsien Tsung. No sooner was this new Tang ruler enthroned than he removed the remnants of the former emperor's clique from their posts. Thus, the power group made no lasting gains, but they are given credit for their daring attempt to curb the steadily increasing power of the eunuchs.

Like most Tang emperors from then on, Hsien Tsung was beholden to the palace eunuch faction that had helped remove the preceding monarch and backed him as next emperor. In A.D. 809 Emperor Hsien Tsung appointed his favorite and most powerful eunuch, Tu-tu Chen-Tsiu, as commander-in-chief to lead a campaign against rebelling subjects in Hopei. This was an unprecedented step that enraged the highest ministers. In reply to their complaints, the emperor boasted that he "could remove eunuch Tu-tu as easily as plucking a hair."[2] After the campaign failed, however, Hsien Tsung heeded the advice of the ministers and did not appoint eunuch commanders for active warfare. (Eunuch Tu-tu remained on as a force in the palace, but when Hsien Tsung died, he was murdered by a group of younger eunuchs who had backed the candidacy of the new emperor.)

In A.D. 810 Emperor Hsien Tsung established a new, highly prestigious position for eunuchs called "Commissioner of Privy Affairs." The commissioner headed up a palace council coordinating all eunuch-operated activities. The position provided an invaluable link between eunuchs in the palace and those commanding metropolitan military forces. Eunuch Liang Shou-chien was the first to fill the position. (At the end of Emperor Hsien Tsung's reign, this eunuch would murder a contending prince to settle the issue of succession.)

In A.D. 819 Emperor Hsien Tsung became greatly excited over news of a sacred Buddhist religious relic enshrined in a monastery temple in Shensi. It was purported to be an actual finger bone of Lord Buddha, capable of working miracles. With great enthusiasm, the emperor made extravagant arrangements for a dignified delegation of monks to proceed to Shensi to escort the marvelous object in solemn, stately procession back to the Chang An palace. There, from a high, especially built ceremonial tower, Emperor Hsien Tung planned to receive the precious relic amid great pomp and lavish donations in celebration of its introduction into the palace.

Horrified Confucian officials sent vigorous protest to the throne, warning in the name of ancient Confucian wisdom against the growing tide of mysticism, magic, and rampant superstition which had infiltrated and enriched the Buddhist church. The most stinging and famous protest came from Han Yu, one of the Tang Dynasty's greatest philosophical essayists, who had now reached the highest ranks of officialdom. His petition to the emperor read in part: "This barbarian called Buddha, who did not even speak our language nor wear civilized clothes, has been dead and decomposed for twelve hundred years. Now a dried and rotted bone, said to be from his finger, is to be admitted to the sacred precincts of the palace, though this disgusting object may well give off evil emanations. Your humble servant asks rather that this relic be burned and cast into the river.

"How could the superior wisdom of Your Majesty stoop to participate in this charade? The people are easily beguiled, and should they behold their emperor worshipping at the feet of a Buddhist idol, they will rush to become monks by scorching holes in their skulls, burning their fingers, ready to cut off an arm or slice off their flesh as an offering. Thus would our sacred Chinese traditions and customs be severely injured, and ourselves become the laughing stock of the world. And should this Buddha really have the power, as claimed, to avenge my derogatory remarks by inflicting some misfortune, then let the vials of his wrath fall upon my head, as I now call upon Heaven to witness that I shall not repent my stance."[3]

Despite all the official condemnation, Emperor Hsien Tsung was not to be deterred from welcoming the sacred "Buddha-bone" into his palace—but no emperor would again risk holding such a Buddhist ritual for another fifty years.

Emperor Hsien Tsung died in A.D. 820. For many centuries afterward it was accepted that he was murdered by palace eunuch Wang Shou-cheng, who had risen to a position of prominence in this and the following reign. Some researchers question this story, however, since the records also indicate that near his death Emperor Hsien Tsung displayed symptoms of mental instability, as did several subsequent Tang rulers who expired from overdoses or the cumulative effects of elixirs and drugs of immortality—a propensity of Tang sovereigns that the eunuchs are said to have encouraged. Whatever the real cause of the emperor's death, it is known that in the factional fights over the issue of succession, one powerful eunuch was murdered, while another killed a contending prince to keep him from the throne.

The new emperor, twenty-four-year-old Mu Tsung, was never accorded that mixture of fear and respect essential to emperors for the proper functioning of the Chinese system. Partly this was due to his libertine lifestyle. He was devoted to vigorous hunts, rough games of polo, lavish banquets, and "indecent" entertainments, and was even inclined toward "sexual excesses"—activities hardly to be condoned by morality-conscious Confucian ministers.

The imperial eunuch staff registry for the year A.D. 820 shows that there were now 4,618 eunuchs in official grades; of these, 1,696 held offices of third rank or higher. Historians say that from this time on, the power of the Tang Dynasty eunuchs exceeded that of the monarchs, and that the eunuchs readily "enthroned emperors, slayed emperors, and deposed emperors."

After only three years on the throne, Mu Tsung fell from his horse playing polo with his eunuchs and was left an invalid, unable to attend to state affairs. Many of his responsibilities were taken over entirely by eunuchs Wang Shou-cheng and Liang Shou-chien, both of whom had helped put him on the throne. Physicians could not cure him and he died the following year. As a result of a hurried decree of investiture arranged by the two powerful eunuchs, his fifteen-year-old son Ching Tsung was put on the throne in A.D. 824.

Emperor Ching Tsung is most noted for catering to the corrupt habits of a large group of young eunuch companions, allowing them extraordinary familiarity and privileges inside and outside the palace. Gangs of undisciplined young eunuchs from the palace were allowed to roam the streets blatantly committing atrocities, intimidating and harassing the populace. In one well-known incident, a high-ranking magistrate was near-fatally beaten by a gang of eunuch thugs when he tried to stop their public brutalities. On his ruffian eunuch friends the young emperor squandered palace treasury funds, and with them indulged in orgies and entertainments that shocked and disgusted the most inured of palace hands.

So lax was palace discipline and security that in the very first year of Ching Tsung's reign 100 armed common laborers, in an uprising led by a canal worker and a fortune teller, forced their way into the palace and the throne room. Ching Tsung barely escaped their clutches before being rescued by eunuch-controlled palace troops. For gross negligence in their security duties, eunuch palace guards were but mildly scolded, while one eunuch army leader was richly rewarded for valor in the affair.

It is unclear what prompted an imperial decree of A.D. 826 that once again forbade court officials and territorial governors from keeping eunuchs for their private use. Perhaps published writings of this era exposed the gross injustices perpetrated in the procurement of eunuchs from the territories. One contemporary poem is a lament for a boy who was torn from his family by a local official who castrated him and forced him to labor as a slave in the official's household, where he suffered the most inhumane treatment.

One night in A.D. 826, Emperor Ching Tsung brought some eunuch friends back to the palace for an evening of entertainment. When Ching Tsung became thoroughly intoxicated, his eunuch friends escorted him into his chamber and murdered him. It is said this act of regicide was actually committed under orders from powerful eunuch Wang Shou-cheng and his colleagues, who deemed it their duty to save the dynasty from the young emperor's utter irresponsibility and uncontrolled excesses.

Immediately, two factions of eunuchs became embroiled in bitter controversy over the choice of succession. The well-entrenched Wang Shou-cheng succeeded in enthroning Wen Tsung, a seventeen-year-old half-brother of the murdered emperor.

Unlike the two preceding rulers, Emperor Wen Tsung was devoted to scholarship and literary pursuits. He began his reign in A.D. 827 by sending many palace women back to their families, abjuring all luxuries, and holding regular audiences with his ministers, sessions that had been sadly neglected of late. Despite his good intentions, Wen Tsung was most influenced by the advisor with whom he last conferred, changing his attitudes toward rival court factions as frequently as he changed ministers.

Wen Tsung was exceedingly frustrated over his inability to control such old palace denizens as eunuch Wang Shou-cheng, who had put him on the throne but had also murdered his uncle. In A.D. 830 the emperor discussed the eunuch problem in private with a trusted scholar-official, after which he made this confidant a chief minister, commissioning him to slowly but systematically proceed to undermine eunuch power. Before the man could begin, eunuch ears caught wind of the plan and the eunuchs struck out against him, claiming to have proof that he was plotting to depose the emperor.

As controversy over this matter mounted, the emperor, isolated from reliable advice and fearing for his own life, vacillated. In the end he gave in to the eunuchs and allowed the minister to be tried, along with many "suspected accomplices" rounded up by the eunuchs. Only with great difficulty did a handful of government officials persuade Wen Tsung to move the investigation out of the inner palace where eunuchs had the upper hand. Though the hapless minister was nevertheless declared guilty, at least he was spared execution. He died a year later in banishment.

Haunted by this failed effort to free the court from the grip of the eunuchs, the young emperor became increasingly frustrated. As his health worsened and he suffered from partial loss of speech, he bemoaned the fact that getting rid of all the outlaw bandits in Hopei would be easier than expunging eunuch and factional leaders from court.

By A.D. 835 Wen Tsung had devised another scheme, this time in collusion with an old hand at court intrigue—a veteran palace physician who now had fallen foul of many eunuchs, but purported to still be a loyal ally of chief eunuch Wang Shou-cheng. The emperor also brought in another collaborator, a respected official. Again, he made both men chief ministers, and the three of them plotted to secretly lure eunuchs away from protection of the eunuch-controlled palace armies and assassinate them.

The minister-official secured assistance from those colleagues allowed to keep their own personal guard detachments, while the doctor quietly assembled another strike force. Together they succeeded in stripping eunuch Wang Shou-cheng of his offices and army command, cast him in prison, and there had him assassinated. This they were able to accomplish only by consorting with a rival eunuch, Chiu Shih-liang, who had recently been made commander of a capital army. This eunuch commander did not realize that the two men planned to take his life also, once he had served his purpose.

In accordance with the plan, one morning at the emperor's regular predawn court audience, a eunuch chamberlain rushed in by prearrangement to report to the emperor that a most auspicious heavenly portent had appeared to bless his reign. During the night, the eunuch announced, "sweet dew" had fallen from Heaven upon a pomegranate tree in the palace courtyard. Emperor Wen Tsung thereupon sent eunuch Chiu Shih-liang out with a contingent of eunuchs to authenticate this marvelous phenomenon. Just as they reached the courtyard, however, wind blew aside the flap of a tent where armed troops were hiding. The sudden clank of their swords alerted the eunuchs, most of whom were able to run back into the safety of the inner palace.

There the eunuchs confined the emperor to the harem while eunuch Chiu Shih-liang summoned his detachment of the dreaded palace army, which massacred every courtier and official in the precincts. More than a thousand were slaughtered, while all their official seals of office, documents, and records were destroyed.

In the following weeks, eunuch-led troops rounded up the main conspirators, together with their underlings and entire families, as well as many other innocents. Confessions of treason were exacted under torture, and three chief ministers with their entire households were publicly beheaded in the western marketplace. Eunuch Chiu and his men allowed the bloodbath to continue for almost two months before a limitation on further prosecution was proclaimed.

The overwhelming eunuch victory completed the demoralization of officials who escaped the massacre. From now on eunuch Chiu and his backers concentrated on preventing further palace coups, increasing palace security, even searching out conspiracies within their own eunuch ranks. Weapons of inner-palace eunuch guards were confiscated, and the distraught emperor was forced to decree that chief ministers must henceforth forego personal bodyguard contingents.

The humiliating failure and fiasco of the "Sweet Dew Plot" seems to have broken Emperor Wen Tsung's spirit. Realizing his inability to shake off the eunuch yoke, he became listless, sullen, altogether bored with court matters, and began drinking heavily. He mourned: "The most inept of our ancient kings were controlled by their feudal lords, while I—far worse—am dominated by eunuchs who should be mere household menials."[4]

When Wen Tsung's old illness struck again in A.D. 839 and his health rapidly declined, the court again became viciously divided in a struggle over the choice of successor. One faction, led by concubine Lady Yang, now a powerful figure among the imperial women, and including all her clansmen, a clique of eunuchs, and a chief minister's party, favored her princely son. Another claimant was backed by the eunuch overseers of the palace armies. This group eventually carried the day. Emperor Wen Tsung, unable to make up his mind anyway, was given no say in the matter. When he died early in A.D. 840, ranking eunuch Chiu Shih-liang and his allies forged a decree on behalf of their candidate, Wu Tsung, and enthroned him as emperor. Then they executed Lady Yang along with the losing princes and their supporting party leaders. Eunuch Chiu wanted to decapitate all remaining members of opposing factions. Only because of the appeal of an imperial relative, Prime Minister Li, did the new emperor spare their lives.

Prime Minister Li and eunuch Chiu Shih-liang became the most outstanding and powerful court figures. Minister Li was a master of tact and diplomacy, especially when it came to maintaining his own supremacy over powerful eunuchs like Chiu Shih-liang. To do this, he was not above placating the eunuch at the risk of irking his official colleagues. He even had a chancellery official demoted for trying to deny eunuch Chiu's swaggering adopted son privileges which were accorded only to highest dignitaries.

Because he was in large part responsible for Emperor Wu Tsung's enthronement, eunuch Chiu had a very real hold over the ruler. As controller of all religious establishments and commander of armies in half the capital, eunuch Chiu had become fantastically wealthy even before Wu Tsung appointed him army inspector-commissioner in charge of all eunuch activities. Incredibly, in A.D. 841 eunuch Chiu was allowed to erect an ornamental monument to his own glory in the grounds of the outer imperial palace which housed his private offices. Its engraved inscription read, "Stele of the glorious record and virtuous administration of Lord Chiu." Emperor Wu Tsung himself graced the elaborate dedication ceremonies.

However, it appears that Emperor Wu Tsung was not completely dominated by his eunuchs. The following year, evidently seeking more support for Wu Tsung's reign, courtiers proposed that the emperor adopt a new reign title, which would occasion an empire-wide celebration and a general act of clemency. Eunuch Chiu and his cohorts demonstrated loudly against the plan, certain that the edict would also allow Prime Minister Li to eliminate many of their privileges and sources of illegitimate income. The eunuchs were temporarily stilled when, in a climactic scene, the volatile emperor thundered that he was master of his own court and sole author of edicts and imperial acts of clemency.

As imperial armies fought to drive off raiding Mongolian hordes and control rebellious military governors, the interference, graft, and abuses of eunuch army supervisors in the campaigns became intolerable. Their hampering of successful military action finally became so flagrant that Prime Minister Li, with his usual persuasive tactfulness, was able to induce two high-ranking eunuchs, both inner-palace council members, to restrict the eunuch supervisors' authority and activities. Even so, in parts of the territories, eunuch supervisors continued to keep huge personal staffs and military escorts sometimes numbering in the thousands.

By this time Emperor Wu Tsung had fallen deeply under the influence of a fanatical Taoist advisor and his sorcerer and alchemist followers who encouraged bias against other religions. The emperor turned first on the Manichaeists. In a decree of A.D. 842, he caused seventy nuns to be put to death in Chang An, their temples pulled down and lands confiscated, and the priests of the religion forced to abandon their robes for typical Chinese dress.

This same edict was meant to include Buddhists as well, but chief eunuch Chiu Shih-liang, a generous patron of Buddhism, was able to forestall the Buddhist persecution, at least until his health began to fail. After repeated petitions to the throne for retirement, the emperor finally accepted eunuch Chiu's resignation (for to have agreed at once would have violated proper Chinese etiquette). In truth, the emperor and Prime Minster Li had greatly desired to be rid of this powerful eunuch. On the day he resigned, they gave all his official positions to his rival, eunuch Yang Chin-I, who had once been an aide to Minister Li. Within a fortnight, eunuch Chiu died of his ailments. His four principal eunuch supporters were immediately executed along with all their adopted family members and slaves.

Before long the emperor and Minister Li struck out at eunuch Chiu's extended family as well, the official excuse being that his adopted son, in a drunken act of bravado, had insulted the Imperial Presence by declaring: "Although the emperor is so revered and noble, it was my father who set him on the throne."[5] Wu Tsung struck the son dead on the spot and decreed that eunuch Chiu's womenfolk and female relations be seized, their heads shaved, and all permanently exiled to guard and maintain the imperial Tang tombs.

When officials were ordered to confiscate eunuch Chiu's vast properties, they found his rooms and storehouses overflowing with incredible wealth— ivory, silk stuffs, gold, silver, and copper coins, and costly antiques and exotic rarities beyond count. Every day for over a month, thirty oxen carts were required to transport this bounty to the palace, the total value of which exceeded the annual budget of the entire empire. When Emperor Wu Tsung came forth to view the treasure, he clapped his hands together in wonderment and cried, "Our imperial storehouses have never before contained such things!"[6]

It is believed that long use of Taoist elixirs caused Emperor Wu Tsung to become increasingly irrational and religiously fanatical. His extensive "Terrace of the Taoist Immortals" had finally been completed—a structure 150 feet high, supporting a seven-sided pavilion, above which rose a five-tiered ornamental tower. Overjoyed with the results, Wu Tsung prepared for the first ceremonial mounting of the edifice by ordering seven Taoist adepts to concoct an elixir of immortality. Among the attending dignitaries were two ranking eunuch commanders who were evidently less credulous than some, for one turned to the great ministers and said: "Today we have come to the Terrace of Taoist Immortals. We wonder if you, my lords, will now take the elixir and seek to become immortals also."[7] The embarrassed ministers only hung their heads in silence.

During the second mounting of the terrace, Emperor Wu Tsung inexplicably turned to one of the ceremonial singers and ordered him to shove eunuch commander Yang Chin-I off the uppermost level. When the terrified singer hesitated and the emperor demanded the reason for his disobedience, he quaked, "The eunuch commander is an important dignitary in the land and I dare not cause his death." For this timidity the emperor laid twenty strokes of the cane across his back. Next he turned upon his Taoist priests and demanded to know why, after two mountings of the terrace to drink the elixir, not one of them had risen up into immortality. The glib priests quickly explained that evil emanations coming from nearby Buddhist temples were blocking their attempts, after which Wu Tsung mumbled that he wanted no Buddhists around whatsoever.

Next Wu Tsung announced to his officials that the nearby open pit from which earth was taken for the tower's construction was causing the people fear and uneasiness, and must be filled in. To do this, he planned that at the next sacrifice to the terrace a feast would be held to which all the Buddhist monks and nuns in the city would be invited. Once assembled, all would be decapitated and their heads used to fill the pit. Wu Tsung was only dissuaded from this insane act by a brave official who pointed out that Buddhist monastics could better benefit the throne if they were simply made to return to lay life to become productive subjects once again.

In this same year, A.D. 845, Emperor Wu Tsung, prodded by Taoist fanatics, would instigate the most strenuous persecution against Buddhism that any religion would ever undergo in China. Why the ministers and officials wholeheartedly encouraged this persecution is not known, for many of them were practicing Buddhists. However, it is known that there was a direct relationship between the harsh anti-Buddhist measures and the determination of the emperor and the court to curb eunuch power. Some historians speculate that the destruction of this extremely popular and wealthy religion was encouraged as a way of striking a blow at the eunuchs, most of whom were Buddhists. Also, powerful eunuchs had been given control over all Buddhist institutions in the city, from which positions they siphoned off considerable wealth for their own pockets.

Wu Tsung's edict declared that Buddhist monks and nuns, "as numerous as blades of grass," were living off the people, their temples eclipsing the imperial palaces in splendor. The census for these years showed over a quarter million monastics, who controlled some 4,600 monasteries, 40,000 pagodas, and untold thousands of temples, including slaves and attendants, much of the nation's best lands, and much wealth, all existing tax-free. The edict, which was fully backed by officialdom, ruthlessly ordered that nearly all Buddhist edifices should be demolished or burned, and all clerics should return to lay life except a very few who would be allowed to maintain and run a temple or two in each large district. The imperial government confiscated Buddhism's great stock of precious metals contained in ceremonial bells, idols, and artifacts. These were melted down to produce coins, which ironically the people then refused to use lest they commit sacrilege against Buddhist deities.

So much wealth ended up in state coffers—which had badly needed replenishing—that some historians conjecture that this had been another reason officials encouraged the great persecution. Never again would the Buddhist hierarchy be strong enough to rival the state in political and economic power. But as a faith, Buddhism would remain an important part of popular culture, and as a philosophy it would leave its humane and gentle imprint on the Chinese soul.

During the persecution of Buddhism, Wu Tsung also struck out at eunuch power, determined to transfer command of metropolitan armies back to the civil bureaucracy. Significantly, Minister Li's old aide, eunuch Yang Chin-I, agreed with the plan, though he himself was commander of half the capital armies. This was not the case with the doughty old commander of the other half, eunuch Yu Hung-chin. When the imperial edict ordered both eunuchs to turn in their official seals of office, eunuch Yang complied at once, but aging eunuch Yu sent a memorial to the throne, declaring that "on the day I was presented the seal of command, I led my troops forth to receive it, and on the day I have to surrender it, I will muster my troops again."[8] Alarmed at this threat, the emperor quickly rescinded his order.

In A.D. 846, when Emperor Wu Tsung, like several of his predecessors, lost his ability to speak and died from elixir drug addiction, his successor,

Emperor Hsiuan Tsung, promptly beheaded the fanatical Taoist advisor who had advocated the eradication of Buddhism, and reinstated the religion to its former status.

As a minor prince, Hsiuan Tsung had been scorned not only by his father as least-favored son, but also by the imperial kinfolk as an illegitimate child. He was forced to be reared among the Sixteen Princely Residences, a compound which housed a great number of minor imperial relatives and princes. Now as emperor, he refused to formally install any of his wives as empress, or to appoint an heir from among his twelve sons, saying that he did not want to be "made idle," i.e., pushed from the throne by overly ambitious consorts or offspring. He even forced his eldest son (who would eventually become the next emperor) to live in the Sixteen Princely Residences as he himself had done.

During these years, so many new eunuch recruits were furnished from the poorer southern coastal areas, that Fukien province became known as "the eunuch nursery." One foreign merchant in China at this time wrote of his surprise to learn that almost all palace eunuchs were of Chinese stock, rather than aliens, as preferred by rulers elsewhere in Asia. Only a few, he noted, were from China's aborigine tribes.

After a dozen years on the throne, Hsiuan Tsung became chronically ill from consumption of elixirs and remained in his apartments, inaccessible to officials, attended solely by eunuchs, herbal physicians, and Taoist adepts, all of whom shared responsibility for his condition. Since he had named no heir, a consortium of three astute eunuchs claimed the emperor had privately communicated to them an order that his third and favorite son should succeed. When the emperor died (the fourth Tang ruler in four decades to succumb to Taoist elixirs of immortality), the eunuch trio concealed the death until they could make arrangements to meet with their greatest rival, eunuch Wang Tsung-shih, outside the palace. He was a prominent and powerful general of palace armies. The three conspirators handed him a forged imperial edict ordering him to assume immediately an important command conveniently located at a great distance from the capital. Eunuch Wang was suspicious of the edict and secretly made his way into the palace where he learned that the emperor had died. Without hesitation, he took control and had the three conspirators executed. Then he had his own faction produce a hurried "last testament," bearing the imperial seal, which summoned the eldest prince from the Sixteen Princely Residences to be enthroned as Emperor I-Tsung. Historians came to disdain this Tang ruler as a mediocrity who devoted his life to sensual pleasures, labeling him "cruel, capricious, unstable, and senselessly extravagant."

During the first year of his reign (A.D. 859) I-Tsung faced extremely stubborn resistance from bureaucrats and most ministers, who suspected the legitimacy of his rule, some claiming that he was not even the dead emperor's son. By this time, palace eunuchs were in charge of all imperial palaces, parks, and estates. They supervised the post-relay services, imperial guest houses, and all religious affairs and establishments in the capital. Eunuchs had acquired a strong voice in government as commissioners of privy affairs in the palace, controllers of the emperor's private treasury, and supervisors over provincial armies and governors, and all communications between them and the emperor. But the most important power of eunuchs was their command of palace armies, including the emperor's personal guard and the main forces at the immediate disposal of the government. With this power they could directly influence or control the imperial successions, and—through rulers beholden to them for having put them on the throne—could easily maintain their power and privileges.

In A.D. 861 Emperor I-Tsung, trying to gain favor with the highest ministers, asked that the officials who had served his father should concoct a bogus, back-dated memorial, stating that he was the legitimate heir. His aim was to show that his succession had official approval of senior ministers, not just of senior eunuchs. The ministers turned him down, but softened their refusal by agreeing that, ideally, ranking imperial eunuch secretaries and the chief ministers should "participate together in the administration of the empire's affairs." The emperor was delighted. He interpreted this as official sanction for continuing to give a conspicuous political role to his eunuchs.

Taking undue advantage of this windfall, top eunuchs raised the hackles of all officialdom by referring to themselves as "policy-making elder statesmen." Two ranking inner-palace eunuch secretaries and two powerful eunuch executives of the palace household staff proclaimed themselves "The Four Ministers," implying equality with the four orthodox chief ministers of the secretariat, exacerbating the hostility of officials toward the eunuchs.

In the last years of I-Tsung's rule, he was opposed by officials and ranking eunuchs alike when he insisted upon putting his obnoxious, inept, and corrupt favorites in highest positions. Official protests only infuriated the emperor, prompting him to allow his favorites to carry out a purge of all who opposed them, banishing some, and driving others to suicide.

Ministers were appalled by I-Tsung's blind extravagances when he fell under sway of Buddhist monks who persuaded him to make incredibly extravagant donations to their religion. In A.D. 871 he held a feast in the palace in which he lavishly dined 10,000 monks. Two years later he decided, against strenuous official objections, to again hold the ceremony venerating the sacred finger bone of Buddha, which had aroused such an official furor fifty years earlier. This time the ceremonies were conducted with far greater cost and imperial pomp, and were marked by the emperor's act of clemency for prisoners throughout the empire. During the rituals, wealthy families vied to impress the emperor with their lavish displays of expensive offerings to the Buddha-bone, while members of the court were compelled to make huge charitable gifts toward the affair.

From I-Tsung's reign on, the nation suffered from a dangerous drain on the treasuries because of continuing and ever-increasing palace extravagance. In addition, already groaning under imperial tax burdens, peasants of the central plains were hit year after year by floods or droughts. To avoid starvation, droves of the poor banded together and turned to banditry. Repeatedly these roving bands overpowered local militia, and imperial troops had to be used to suppress them, further depleting Tang treasuries. Thus began a vicious circle which would plague the Tang Dynasty to its end: increased taxation drove peasants to banditry, requiring expenditures from state treasuries to put them down.

In A.D. 873 another minor, I-Tsung's twelve-year-old son, was put on the throne. At that time, his only interests and knowledge centered on sports and gaming. As Hsi Tsung neared twenty, he attempted to take a firm stand in court affairs, only to earn the reputation of being strong-willed and inclined toward cruel punishments. He is condemned as an ill-prepared, incapable monarch, but in truth he ruled in such difficult times that perhaps it was beyond the ability of any emperor to reverse the Tang Dynasty's slide toward collapse.

Hsi Tsung owed his enthronement to several powerful eunuchs, including the senior general of palace armies, Liu Hang-shen, from a prominent old "eunuch family," several members of which had been highly respected at court. This eunuch helped the new boy-emperor in his attempt to rid the court of his father's worthless and widely detested favorites.

Another prominent eunuch inherited from past reigns was Yang Fu-kung, whose "eunuch family" was among the most powerful, its members having served as senior generals in palace armies for almost a century. Eunuch Yang's long career was quite similar to that of regular court officials, especially after his adoption by an eminent inner-palace secretary, who sent him to a series of regional posts as imperial army inspector. Eunuch Yang had played a significant part in suppressing rebellions under the previous emperor, after which he was brought to the capital and elevated as chief eunuch of the imperial household, soon to succeed to his foster father's secretarial post in the emperor's privy council.

Eunuch Yang Fu-kung represents a segment of the eunuch institution that had now become an established part of Tang Dynasty administration, loyal to the dynasty rather than to a particular emperor. Ten of Yang Fu-kung's adopted sons held positions in the territories, ranging from prefect to military governor.

By far the most powerful of Emperor Hsi Tsung's eunuchs, however, was the notorious Tien Ling-tze, who had no eunuch-family background, and had held but a minor post in the preceding reign. Tien Ling-tze was well educated. More importantly, he was a highly skilled manipulator of other people. The key to his vast authority lay in the extremely close personal relationship he had been carefully cultivating with the new boy-emperor, who now looked upon him as a foster father. Eunuch Tien encouraged Hsi Tsung's boyish pastimes, while he himself systematically set about usurping control, quickly becoming by far the most dominant figure at court. By A.D. 875, besides managing all imperial appointments, he had been made head of a palace army, and at court handed out official posts and rewards without need to consult higher authority. Usurping the right to participate in government planning, he grandly proposed that money be raised for the dwindling Tang treasury by confiscating the wealth of rich merchants. Since all who protested his various schemes faced execution, even the highest ministers were afraid to oppose him. His utter ruthlessness politically, in conjunction with his firm control over the emperor, made him profoundly feared and resented throughout officialdom.

Eunuch Tien Ling-tze's dominating presence helped destroy any sense of common purpose among legitimate officials, and dashed any hopes for recovery of Tang imperial authority. As a result, eunuch power and influence increased to intolerable limits in Hsi Tsung's reign. Number one eunuch Tien Ling-tze made his insensitive elder brother (who had been a common peddler) military governor of Szechuan, a most unfortunate choice that was to cause severe unrest in that province.

Although similar appointments were being meted out by ordinary, i.e., non-eunuch, court ministers to their relatives, the regional bonds and alliances forged by the palace eunuchs led to more flagrant abuses in this regard, for their adopted sons were beholden for their appointments solely to their foster fathers rather than ordinary government channels.

When Emperor Hsi Tsung commenced his reign, another popular rebellion was broiling in the east, where drought and severe famine, coupled with requirements of prolonged military duty and heavy taxation, had reduced the peasantry to starvation. The insurrection was at first led by a peasant who soon commanded an outlaw force of several tens of thousands. In time, the rebels overran fifteen prefectures. Government troops sent against them were ineffectual, for they were mostly peasants themselves, who more often than not deserted to join the rebels in looting and plundering the wealthy.

In A.D. 875 this frightening horde of plundering malcontents was joined by a charismatic intellectual, Huang Chao, whose family had made a fortune in the salt industry. Huang Chao was embittered by repeated failure to gain public office after taking the civil service examinations. He felt himself a victim of gross injustice directed against the merchant class, and perhaps rightly so. This eloquent man, by befriending swarms of the destitute, easily gathered an immense peasant following, and within a few months had united all the rebel hordes, with himself as supreme commander. He titled himself the "General Who Mounts to the Heavens," and led his forces forth to pillage fortified towns and overrun government and military districts at will.

By A.D. 879 rebel leader Huang Chao had his rabble hordes so well organized militarily that they were able to capture the great southern city of Canton. There they killed most of the inhabitants, including thousands of foreign merchants, simply because they were rich. Huang Chao distributed all plunder fairly amongst his men, and issued a telling public proclamation condemning sleazy imperial administration, unchecked eunuch control of the central court, and the disintegration of public morality.

Huang Chao next moved his vast armies northward, appointing his own governors in captured regions, with dire warnings to each against accumulating wealth. He threatened to wipe out the entire families of any district magistrate caught accepting bribes. By the following year, his rebel armies controlled the whole of eastern China and were advancing toward the Tang capital.

When news of Huang Chao's approach reached court, Emperor Hsi Tsung ordered his "Divinely Planned Armies" to block the rebel advance— a futile decree, since his eunuch-controlled troops were swollen with Chang An's wealthy who drew army pay but had never seen military service. Sons wept with their fathers when they were called up, while most hired the equally untrained poor to fight in their stead. Panic-stricken officials fled the capital in every direction as Chang An's defenses collapsed after the imperial army commander, eunuch Tien Ling-tze, and his troops had hurriedly carried off the emperor to seek safety in Szechuan. The great Tang imperial city fell to the insurgents with hardly a fight.

Rebel commander Huang Chao entered Chang An in grand style, having been met outside the city walls by a delegation of groveling Tang dignitaries who hoped to save their necks by joining up with the victor. Huang Chao was carried through the city gates in a royal gold-colored sedan chair. When he ascended the supreme imperial hall, several thousand palace maidens hailed him as "King Huang." Members of the royal family were killed outright along with captured officials who refused to capitulate, while Huang Chao's lieutenants raced to occupy choice city mansions and fought over the women occupants. Huang Chao declared himself the new emperor and his wife the empress, dismissing all remaining Tang officials above the third rank and replacing them with lower-grade bureaucrats whom he could control.

It has always been considered a disgrace for a Chinese monarch to be forced to flee his capital, but the circumstances of Emperor Hsi Tsung's flight from Chang An were particularly humiliating, pointing up his utter subjugation to the will of eunuch Tien Ling-tze. On learning of the rebel armies' approach to the capital, eunuch Tien, unbeknownst to any government official, in the dead of night called up 500 of his troops and fled west, with Emperor Hsi Tsung, four imperial princes, several royal consorts, ladies-in-waiting, and palace eunuchs in tow. The primary concern of this eunuch was to secure his own paramount position by keeping the Tang emperor and inner court safe and under his thumb, for this was his power base.

The court-in-exile arrived in Szechuan to find that area in the grip of local disorders caused by the corruption and brutalities of Tien's brother, whom the eunuch had made governor. Unrest soon developed into military insurrection, due in part to eunuch Tien's preferential treatment of his own troops over local forces, which previously had ranked among the most loyal to the throne. One disgusted Szechuan general defected and led his troops into banditry. After numerous solemn promises guaranteeing him immunity from punishment if he would cease this renegade activity, he brought his men back to the faithless governor, who immediately had him cruelly tortured and killed.

Throughout Emperor Hsi Tsung's four-year exile in Szechuan, a steady stream of fleeing Chang An officials arrived to rejoin the court. Some owed their positions to bribes and alliances with eunuch Tien and his subordinates. Others, like the strong chief minister and his faction, hated Tien and did everything in their power to oppose him, a situation which rendered the makeshift government all but impotent. The emperor, far from being in charge, was virtually a prisoner of eunuch Tien.

Back in the capital, chaos reigned. In A.D. 881 troops loyal to the throne, allied with barbarian Tartar chieftains, succeeded in wresting the capital from Huang Chao, only to embark on their own round of ransacking the city. Huang Chao and his armies soon managed to retake Chang An and this time, angered that the populace had welcomed imperial troops, ordered a bloodbath wherein 80,000 citizens were slaughtered. Shredded remnants of the Tang court again sought help from the northern Tartar leader, Li Ko-yung, who in A.D. 883 descended on Chang An with his well-trained Mongolian horsemen, famed as "the crows of Li Ko-yung" in reference to their black military garb. In the face of crack Tartar cavalry, the rebel hordes melted away, while Huang Chao—the usurper who had terrorized half the empire for three years and driven the Tang court into exile—was chased into Shantung where he saved face by committing suicide.

Historians rate Huang Chao's rebellion far more devastating to the Tang nation than the previous An Lu-shan civil war. This second insurgency marked the beginning of the end of the House of Tang, for never again would the dynasty regain its former strength.

The savior of Chang An, Tartar chieftain Li Ko-yung, brought Tang Emperor Hsi Tsung back from exile in A.D. 885, and was himself rewarded with military governorship of a northern Chinese state. The emperor returned accompanied by eunuch Tien and his full-scale army recruited in Szechuan—fifty-four regiments, each of a thousand men. They found the abandoned city "overgrown with weeds and bushes, the home of hares and foxes."[9]

From now on, North China disintegrated into a kaleidoscope of constantly changing alliances, hostilities, loyalties, and mutual treacheries involving eunuch Tien's imperial troops, forces of Chinese military governors, many of whom had been appointed by court eunuchs, and armies of Tartar military governors who had earned their territories by assisting or rescuing the Tang throne.

One Chinese strongman, Chu Wen, whose defection from rebel general Huang Chao had earned him a provincial governorship of his own, was now rapidly becoming paramount military leader in the north. His failed attempt to massacre the Tartar Li Ko-yung and his bodyguards resulted in a desperate ongoing feud between the two that was to last for forty years through two generations.

By this time the ineffectual Tang court had lost all control of the provinces, too weak even to enforce recommendations from its eunuch army supervisors out in the states. The governors, by bribing the eunuchs, were able to influence or take sides in intrigues and struggles at the palace, and also openly interfered in court decisions using military pressure.

To pay and feed his huge capital army, eunuch Tien put pressure on governors of nearby areas, and soon found himself at war with a temporary alliance of mutual arch-enemies, Li Ko-yung and Chu Wen. The eunuch's forces were so ignominiously defeated that he fled west, taking the emperor with him again. Time and again, different alliances sent word beseeching the emperor to execute eunuch Tien and return to the capital, but when Emperor Hsi Tsung attempted to reinstate Tien's old eunuch rival, Yang

Fu-kung, as imperial secretary, eunuch Tien and his army simply moved a makeshift court further west, pursued and harassed by contending forces.

At last, chief bureaucrats in Chang An agreed with military governors that Emperor Hsi Tsung must be deposed. When the attempt to do so failed and almost half the conspiring officials had been executed, a compromise was reached with eunuch Tien's refugee court, and Tien agreed to forsake his command. At long last, Tien fled to Szechuan and set himself up as army supervisor under his corrupt brother who was still governor there.

Eunuch Yang Fu-kung immediately took over all eunuch Tien's offices and banished all Tien's supporters. Yang Fu-kung's adopted son and two other governors made possible Emperor Hsi Tsung's return once again to the partially restored capital in A.D. 888, but by this time the tormented emperor had fallen so gravely ill that within two months he died, at only twenty-seven years of age. Eunuch Yang, with his extensive court experience and influence, succeeded in putting the dead ruler's twenty-one-year-old brother Chao Tsung on the throne.

Though Emperor Chao Tsung was an able young man, fully aware of the reasons Tang rule was failing, he was powerless to reassert authority over the territories or even to control events at court. Early on, however, he made it clear that his chief ministers should control court affairs—eunuch control would no longer be tolerated. He was especially resolved to be rid of eunuch Yang Fu-kung, who had put him on the throne, for this eunuch had driven his uncle into exile and had him murdered.

Emperor Chao Tsung was able to accomplish this resolve only by resorting to subterfuge: He bestowed his own imperial family surname, as well as high office and authority, upon eunuch Yang's adopted son, making him commander of the most important imperial armies in the capital. In this way, eunuch Yang's son, now a "loyal adopted member of the royal family," was transformed overnight from Yang's principal supporter into his strongest rival. Eunuch Yang managed to escape from the capital and rally military support from several other of his adopted sons, whom he had made regional governors, but his combined forces were so severely beaten by Tang armies that in A.D. 892 he fled for safety to his private estate in Shansi. He was soon captured and brought back to Chang An to be executed. This was the most serious setback the eunuch establishment had suffered in many decades. As for eunuch Yang's adopted son-turned-nobility, he was soon assassinated by top eunuch generals who claimed he was planning to take control of palace armies and possibly the government.

Respect for the Tang Dynasty rapidly deteriorated. In A.D. 893 one

Tartar governor dared send a letter to Emperor Chao Tsung openly sneering at his failed military ventures and his inability to control his top-ranking palace eunuchs. The letter also taunted the emperor over his vulnerability to a take-over, asking contemptuously where the court would flee next time. Burning with anger, Chao Tsung ordered recruitment of several thousand raw urban youths to fill out the depleted crown regiments and sent them against the Tartar—a hopeless endeavor. The battle-hardened Turk easily routed the imperial troops and, to complete the court's humiliation, demanded the immediate execution of the emperor's most trusted minister and four prominent eunuchs. Chao Tsung had no recourse but to comply.

In A.D. 897, when the capital again fell under attack, Emperor Chao Tsung, while attempting to flee to the Tartar general Li Ko-yung for protection, was intercepted en route by a wealthy Chinese district prefect named Han Chien. For unknown reasons, Han Chien, using thinly veiled threats, forced the emperor to remain with him, forbidding him all outside contacts "lest he become confused." Soon, claiming the imperial princely sons were plotting to assassinate him and abduct the emperor, Han Chien forced eleven Tang princes into Chang An and took their troops under his command. Then his men surrounded the imperial compound, causing some terrified princes therein to shave their heads, hoping to pass as monks, while others made desperate attempts to escape. Abetted by an imperial eunuch, Prefect Han Chien finally captured and killed all eleven Tang princes.

Soon Han Chien, faced with the threat of being overwhelmed by Chu Wen, who obviously had designs on the throne, was forced to ally himself with the two foremost Tartar governors to restore the Chang An palaces and move the Tang emperor back to the capital. From his stronghold in Loyang, Chu Wen now issued an invitation to Emperor Chao Tsung to come under his "protection." Though he could have easily taken the palace by force, Chu Wen seemed to prefer to bide his time and control the throne by placing 10,000 of his troops in Chang An as palace guardsmen. By A.D. 900 he had allied himself closely with the emperor's chief minister, who abhorred the eunuchs and needed Chu's authority to bring about the execution of the two principal eunuch commanders.

These two executions made the eunuchs realize their dangerous position so long as the dreaded chief minister and Chu Wen were able to exploit the monarch's resentment of eunuch control. Therefore, the eunuchs, long accustomed to control succession to the throne, conspired and deposed Emperor Chao Tsung, confining him to inner-palace apartments. In his stead, they installed the heir apparent, and carried out savage reprisals against real or suspected adversaries. Within two months, however, when the powerful Chu Wen and his armies were preparing to intervene, the frightened eunuch consortium hastily returned control of the court to the chief minister and restored Emperor Chao Tsung to the throne. All the eunuchs involved in the coup were executed. In celebration, Emperor Chao Tsung decreed a major act of clemency in an edict which—curiously—included a posthumous pardon for the officials condemned and killed by eunuchs fifty years before in the ill-fated "Sweet Dew Plot."

From this time on, hatred and intrigues between ministers and eunuchs grew to grotesque proportions. Governor Chu Wen, who for all intents and purposes controlled the palace, heeding the urgent advice of the still-powerful chief minister, had his soldiers herd several hundred ranking eunuchs into their household section of the palace and brutally massacre them. Next, Chu Wen had the helpless emperor decree that military governors everywhere should execute all eunuch army supervisors in the field. (Though Chu Wen was later to become emperor of his own dynasty and rule over most of North China, his extermination of eunuch power is heralded as the most important act of his career, for it ended more than a century of eunuch domination of the Tang court.)

Within the year, facing constant hostilities from rival governors and deeply resenting that his old enemy, Li Ko-yung, had captured one of his prefectures, Chu Wen had two of his marshals murder Emperor Chao Tsung. To avoid any consequent political embarrassment, he had both marshals executed. He then put on the throne the dead ruler's ninth son, the twelve-year-old emperor Ai Ti. Before long, he invited Ai Ti's princely brothers to a palace banquet, at the end of which he had all eight of them strangled. Thus he removed all possible threat from the rest of the Tang imperial family.

Chu Wen also ruthlessly executed all old Tang ministers who had opposed him, and had thirty other bureaucrats killed and their corpses thrown into the Yellow River in a special defilement for their non-cooperation.

Young Emperor Ai Ti sat uneasily on the throne as a puppet for three years before Chu Wen, now suffering from recurring illness and paranoid over threats from enemy governors, forced the boy to issue a decree of abdication in his, Chu Wen's, favor, making it clear to one and all that the Tang Dynasty had at long last forfeited the Mandate of Heaven. In A.D. 907 Chu Wen founded the new Liang Dynasty with himself as first emperor, and nine months later had the last Tang emperor put to death.

Though the Chinese have glorified the Tang era, the historians also repeatedly and pointedly reminded all future emperors of the sordid take-over of court eunuchs that brought about the ruination of the once-great dynasty.

Yet, in time, the eunuchs would rise again.

Notes

1. J. Li Dun, *The Agless Chinese.*
2. Twitchett and Fairbank, *Cambridge History of China.*
3. Excerpted from H. T. Lee's *The Story of Chinese Culture.*
4. Twitchett and Fairbank, *Cambridge History of China.*
5. E. O. Reischauer, *Ennin's Travels in Tang China.*
6. Ibid.
7. Ibid.
8. Ibid.
9. R. Grousset, *The Rise and Splendour of the Chinese Empire.*

13

Eunuchs' Brief Return to Power

FIVE DYNASTIES ERA (A.D. 907-960)

Predictably, Chu Wen's claim to sovereignty as founder of the new Liang Dynasty ruling North China was repudiated everywhere by contending military governors. The whole of the South broke away into numerous independent kingdoms that managed to coexist in comparative peace and quiet. In the war-torn North, in just fifty years five different dynasties overthrew each other in rapid succession to rule over all or parts of North China. Historians consider these decades some of the darkest in Chinese history.

With Chang An in ruins and Loyang all but depopulated, ruler Chu Wen made his capital the strategic city of Kaifeng in Honan, some thirty miles below the Yellow River. The hundreds of Tang Dynasty eunuchs and many Tang officials he massacred he replaced with his personal military men and old provincial retainers, most of whom were of lowly origins. When they proved incapable of running the bureaucracy, he finally recalled former Tang officials, though they were understandably most wary of undertaking a dominant role in a regime so strongly at odds with their own gentry class.

Emperor Chu Wen succeeded in gaining the cooperation of some military governors, but never was able to overcome his long-time, hated rival, the Turk Li Ko-yung, whom the Tang had made military governor of

Shansi, where his strong cavalry armies still remained firmly entrenched. When Li died in A.D. 908, his capable son took over to carry on the feud with Emperor Chu Wen, and to rally the people under the slogan, "Restoration of the Tang!"

Thus, Chu Wen's brief dynasty was never to rule in peace. Incessant battles with the Turkish regime and strong Chinese governors lay waste the land, devastated the countryside, and further impoverished the people. Anarchy spread as hungry peasants joined brigand hordes to roam North China, pillaging and killing. After a few years of this anarchy, the area became so depleted of soldiers that Chu Wen had to conscript all able-bodied men—even the aged. As emperor, Chu Wen ceased his former practice of branding soldiers' faces so that deserters could easily be found. The punishment for desertion was decapitation.

In A.D. 911, despite advancing age and bouts of illness, Chu Wen, in desperation, personally led his forces against a coalition of belligerent provincial governors, only to suffer a humiliating defeat and worsened health. He retreated back to Kaifeng to face a palace coup led by his own illegitimate son whom he had made commander of his personal bodyguard. This son was supported by a marshal who as a retainer of Chu Wen had replaced the last Tang chief eunuch as senior inner-palace attendant. In the coup, Chu Wen was killed and the faithless son set himself up as emperor. Within eight months he too was assassinated by supporters of the legitimate heir. This third and last Liang Dynasty prince ruled North China only for ten years before the son of Turk Li Ko-yung overthrew him in A.D. 923 and founded an equally brief dynasty known as the Later Tang.

By this time three generations of the Turkish Li family had held sway in Shansi and were almost completely sinicized. Having long since been awarded the imperial Tang surname of Li in compensation for repeatedly rescuing that failing dynasty, they were looked up to as Chinese aristocracy. Many Chinese scholar-officials from both the old Tang and Chu Wen's courts did not hesitate to seek positions at the Li court, which was established in Loyang. As emperor, the new Li ruler was completely enamored of palace entertainments. From among the many actors, musicians, and entertainers who frequented his palace, enjoying great favoritism and familiarity, Li chose several to become high officials or commanders.

He is most remembered, however, for bringing eunuchs back into positions of power after their twenty years in oblivion under Chu Wen and his successors. This was an attempt to restore all the traditions of the former Tang Dynasty. Some Tang eunuchs who escaped Chu Wen's massacre had fled to their home provinces as heads of newly rich adopted families, while others had remained unemployed in the capital city. Now back in their traditional roles, the eunuchs became so overconfident that their aggressive and arrogant behavior soon provoked the hatred of officials, governors, and commanders alike. Yet there were many in high positions who were entirely willing to promote themselves and their desired ends by blatantly bribing ranking eunuchs as well as the theater-loving emperor's favored actor friends.

During this dynasty, the failure of the eunuchs to completely recapture their former all-pervading power was ultimately due to their inability to regain sole control of the palace armies. This command the leading eunuch had to share with the emperor's most trusted old retainer, Kuo Chung-tao, who had become prime minister and predominant figure at court. Early on, minister Kuo tried to placate the arrogant, newly hired eunuchs by creating for them a special "Commission of Internal Affairs." Eunuchs appointed to positions as commissioners had no duties other than to "check imperial cash, grain, and registers," functions already being performed by regular officials. The appointment of the eunuch commissioners was likened to the "hiring of nine shepherds to tend ten sheep."[1]

Turkish Emperor Li's intensive and aggressive measures to regain control over outlying territories aroused resentment from governors who still held significant military power. One of the measures was to reintroduce the intimidating eunuch field supervisors, backing each eunuch with an imperial army contingent. In the palace, the eunuchs worked doggedly to regain their former prominence, and openly challenged the highly capable chief minister Kuo and his colleagues in all their honest endeavors. Under the eunuchs' goading, Minister Kuo himself finally led imperial forces in a failed campaign to put down a mutiny instigated by the Szechuan governor. While retreating home from this disaster, a large section of his troops rebelled. For this fiasco, Kuo was soon executed, along with several colleagues, which led to turmoil that was aggravated and encouraged by eunuch cupidity and intrigues. Hatred for the eunuchs led to further mutinies by outlying governors.

As insurrection spread everywhere, four governors murdered all the imperial eunuch supervisors in their areas. One of the emperor's provincial ex-retainers (so greatly favored for once having saved his master's life that he was rewarded with a favorite court concubine) was now made an expeditionary commander, but failed to defeat the mutineers.

Another retainer, the emperor's domestic servant since their boyhood, was given complete command of capital troops, only to turn traitor, refusing help when the emperor's own bodyguards mutinied. Both these men had originally gained influence by developing close relationships with the emperor's well-placed eunuchs and actor favorites.

When an adopted member of the emperor's family, Li Ssu-yuan—now a governor as well as army chief commander—objected to the appointment of the ruler's old, unqualified ex-retainer as commander of capital troops, he survived accusations of disloyalty solely because of the friendship he had developed with the chief eunuch. In the end, the emperor entrusted the capital troops to the leadership of Li Ssu-yuan.

Historians have never been able to agree on the strange part Li Ssu-yuan played during the mutinies and a coup against the emperor. For some unknown reason, he was "overcome" by his own men in the imperial armies and was finally handed over to the mutineers. Soon afterwards, when they released him, he captured several thousand horses from the imperial grazing grounds, as well as an imperial boatload of priceless silk—a medium of exchange—on the Yellow River. He then marched toward the capital "to explain his actions" to the ruler. There, another disloyal relative of the emperor, now an executive officer, turned half the imperial armies over to Li Ssu-yuan. Even the governor of the Kaifeng area gave the city's resources to Li. By A.D. 926 a senior palace official—an adopted son of a wet nurse in former ruler Chu Wen's family—had opened the gates of the capital to Li and his forces.

An actor favorite commanding capital troops led the palace mutiny and allowed the emperor to be killed by his own bodyguards. In this way, Li Ssu-yuan became the next ruler of North China. He claimed that victory came to him as a "complete surprise," yet there is every indication that he himself was far from innocent in this usurpation. Six days after becoming emperor, to mollify the provincial governors, he decreed that all remaining eunuch supervisors in the territories be executed and replaced by his own men.

It has been maintained that the insurgencies and the coup against Emperor Li Ko-yung were largely provoked by his long and staunch support of his eunuchs. With his death, the two-and-a-half years of borrowed time enjoyed by palace eunuchs came to an end.

In the early years after the beginning of Li Ssu-yuan's reign, the only remaining palace eunuch of any influence at all was Meng Han-chiung, whom Li had brought in with him from his provincial palace. In A.D. 931 eunuch Meng and two other ex-retainers were able to accomplish the execution of a powerful palace commissioner who had dominated the court for five years. Two years later, eunuch Meng and one of these same retainers ruthlessly crushed a coup instigated by yet another Li family prince. When ruler Li Ssu-yuan died soon thereafter, eunuch Meng and his collaborator became the most powerful figures at the court of Li's son and successor. For a time, this new monarch was completely dominated by eunuch Meng and palace commissioners.

In A.D. 934, when one governing prince refused to be transferred and led a revolt, several commanders of the imperial armies joined his cause. Within twelve days they had placed the rebelling prince on the throne as emperor. This ruler did away with the position of palace commissioner altogether, which ended the career of eunuch Meng. All eunuchs throughout the palace were ousted and replaced by relatives of provincial governors and senior army officers.

Meanwhile, beyond China's northeastern frontier, a Tartar horde known as the Khitans had for decades been steadily consolidating a great federation of nomad tribes. By this time, the khan of the Khitans had transformed his old tribal league into a strong military organization with a central command. His capital was in Manchuria. In A.D. 937 a North China military general—also of Turkish descent—successfully bribed the Khitan khan and his 50,000 crack cavalry troops into helping him overthrow the ruler of North China and set up another new dynasty. The cost of the khan's assistance was dear: The new North China ruler had to cede sixteen northern districts, including the modern Peking area, and also pay him a large yearly tribute. He even tried to cement good will by adopting the barbarian khan as his "father."

The painful consequences of the new North China ruler's "treasonable acts" were soon felt. His son and successor, resenting the alien khan's intrusion in Chinese affairs, refused to pay the onerous tribute, thus provoking the Khitans to war. Early in A.D. 947 they swooped down *en masse* to conquer Kaifeng, the North China capital. The khan thoroughly sacked the city for five straight months, disarmed North Chinese armies, and confiscated thousands of horses. During this Tartar invasion, some Chinese governors were killed, another preferred suicide, four were taken to Manchuria as Khitan captives, while twelve others collaborated with the conqueror.

The barbarian Khitans withdrew only after their great khan died and his succession had to be decided in Manchuria at a great gathering of all the chieftains. Besides, they despised North China's burning hot summers. With their departure, another Chinese commander of Tartar blood immediately moved in to fill the vacuum and set up his own petty dynasty. Yet he was never able to wrest the sixteen lost Chinese districts from the Khitans, a corridor which would open the way for more Tartar invasions. Though his dynasty lasted only three years, this Chinese ruler, with his strong armies, brought all the northern provinces—except for the sixteen districts—under control. But China had not heard the last of the barbarian Khitans.

In A.D. 950 another Chinese general took over the throne by force to found the last of the petty Five Dynasties. He ruled for only ten years. In A.D. 960 he was overcome by his own commander-in-chief, the greatly revered founder of the renowned long-term Sung Dynasty that was soon to reunite all China in Chinese hands.

Amazingly, during this inglorious Five Dynasties era of incessant coups and convulsion in the North, intellectual pursuits thrived, leaving a legacy of one invention that was soon to herald a new way of life for China: printing from engraved wooden blocks. Though he may not have been the actual inventor, a Chinese politician and sometime prime minister named Feng Tao is credited with introducing and popularizing block printing in courts of the North. Feng Tao had served seven ruling families, whether Chinese or alien, in rapid succession, by adroitly steering clear of trouble in one take-over after another. He even composed a poem praising himself as the "Ever-Gay Old-timer," enumerating with obvious relish the various honors and dignities he had acquired in the course of his lively career. Due to his influence, the Five-Dynasties rulers avidly patronized the printing of books, which would soon bring a great diffusion of knowledge throughout the nation—"the second flowering of Chinese culture."

Another institution credited to the Five Dynasties era is the binding of women's feet. Though nobody knows exactly when this crippling fashion originated, according to one strong tradition, it was first introduced in the court of the sensual poet-ruler of a petty Chinese regime at Nanking. A story has it that as this libertine watched his most beloved concubine dance atop a six-foot, lotus-carved golden pedestal, he became entranced by fleeting glimpses of her unusually tiny, beribboned feet. "With every step a lotus grows," he sighed.[2] From then on he saw that gold-leaf blossoms were strewn in the streets as she rode by in a sedan chair. Soon all the envious ladies of the harem were binding up their feet to make them appear smaller, poetically calling them "golden lotuses."

Mothers started tightly wrapping small daughters' feet to stop their growth, gradually bending the toes completely under, to meet the heel, which painfully forced the arch to grow "high and round like a crescent moon." The yards of tight white bindings used to wrap the feet cut circulation. When putrification set in, the odor was suppressed by soaking the feet in herbal medicines. The ideal was for girls to reach marriageable age with three-inch-long, useless feet, which produced a hobbling gait, causing the hips to undulate enticingly. Even a glimpse of these stump-like appendages encased in beautifully embroidered, minuscule slippers sexually excited Chinese males. In time, no man of culture would consider marrying a girl with normal feet, as "golden lotuses" became a symbol of feminine chastity, docility, and gentility. Foot-binding eventually spread to all classes, rich and poor, except for women of non-Han Chinese blood and female laborers. So deeply was foot-binding imbedded in Chinese mores for the next centuries that it was only eradicated with great difficulty in the 1900s. As late as 1974, the writer met white-haired Chinese grandmothers in Taiwan villages hobbling about on stub feet, their high, deformed arches protruding above tiny soft black slippers.

Another legacy of these times was ending open participation of eunuchs in affairs of state for the next several centuries. A famous essay found in the history of the Five Dynasties, written by one of the following dynasty's most respected statesmen and man of letters, says: "Eunuchs come about because of a monarch's love of sexual indulgence [necessitating a huge harem and attendant eunuch corps]. Yet the harm eunuchs cause the nation is much more serious than excessive sexual indulgence. This has been true throughout history. There are numerous ways eunuchs can bring harm to the nation. Since they are closest to, and on most familiar terms with, the monarch, they have an advantage which none others possess. Eunuchs are even allowed to be harsh and dictatorial. They constantly do small favors to please the ruler, and keep their promises in unimportant matters so as to win his complete trust. Once a monarch trusts eunuchs and takes them into his confidence, they manipulate or sometimes control him through a simple device: they terrify him with tales of evil consequences that might ensue if he does not take their advice and counsel.

"Even though the ruler has loyal scholar-ministers in court, he will not trust them, for in his judgment, they are too remote and unfamiliar, and thus not so reliable as the eunuchs who surround him every day from morning to night, groveling to please his every whim. As he draws closer and closer to the eunuchs, his alienation from orthodox ministers becomes greater and greater. Meanwhile, the eunuchs keep him increasingly isolated from his officials. The more isolated he becomes, the more fearful. The more fearful he becomes, the more he is subject to eunuch control. Eventually, he realizes that even his own life is at the mercy of the eunuchs, who decide whether he should live or die in accordance with their ambitions. Danger thus lurks behind every door or curtain in his palace in the form of eunuchs he thought he could trust.

"Once the danger becomes obvious, often the monarch will try to make an alliance with his alienated ministers for the purpose of eliminating the eunuchs. If for some reason the ruler and his ministers decide to wait for a propitious moment to take such a drastic step, the danger to his life will continue to deepen. If, on the other hand, the monarch and his ministers decide to take immediate action, eunuchs whose listening ears are everywhere can hold the monarch hostage. In this situation it is extremely difficult for the ministers to initiate an alliance with the monarch, however capable they might be. Even if such an alliance is formed, it is unlikely that concrete action will follow. Even if action is taken, it is doubtful that the purpose can be achieved, for in the end it will bring about damage and defeat to the allies as well as the eunuchs, and may even cause the ruler to lose his kingdom. Even if the dynasty does manage to survive, the monarch himself may be killed. This in turn will give some strong, unprincipled man the needed excuse to slaughter all the eunuchs so as to allay the anger of the populace. Instances of this type appear time and again in our histories: the eunuch curse is not confined to a particular generation or period.

"No sovereign wishes to cultivate danger for himself or to deliberately alienate his loyal officials. Nevertheless, the danger comes about because the situation described above slowly but inevitably feeds upon itself until it becomes a reality.

"Regarding overindulgence in sex, a monarch will, of course, suffer evil consequences if he ignores this fault. However, once he acknowledges his problem, he can easily eliminate the danger by dismissing excessive harem woman. The eunuch threat, however, cannot be easily eliminated, even after the danger they cause has been recognized. This is what I mean when I say that the harms caused by eunuchs are much more serious than those resulting from a monarch's overindulgence in sex! How can future monarchs afford not to be alert to the danger of eunuch power?"[3]

Interestingly, even this greatly respected author-statesman does not advocate complete abolishment of the court eunuch system. The next dynasty—the long-reigning Sung—well aware of past history, was almost entirely free of eunuch interference in government.

Notes

1. Wang Gung-wu, *Structure of Power in North China During the Five Dynasties.*

2. Wang Chia-yu, *Lives and Loves of Chinese Emperors.*

3. Excerpted from J. Li Dun, *Essence of Chinese Civilization.*

14

Powerful Ministers
Dominate Eunuch Corps
TWO SUNG DYNASTIES AND
BARBARIAN CONQUERORS (A.D. 960-1279)

Emperor Tai Tsu, founder of the Sung Dynasty, was the last in a succession of North China army commanders who overthrew their petty state
rulers during the chaotic Five Dynasties era. Despite this somewhat unorthodox beginning, his House of Sung would hold sway for the next
300 years and prove to be one of the most revered of Chinese dynasties.
For the Sung accorded more closely than any of the other dynasties to
the Confucian ideal: Scholarly ministers firmly guided the emperors and
held a tight rein on court eunuchs, consort families, and even the military—though not always to China's advantage.

Official historians have tried to absolve Emperor Tai Tsu of guilt in
seizing his ruler's throne, emphasizing that he had led many successful
campaigns for his monarch against encroaching barbarians. The take-over
was not Tai Tsu's doing, they say, but his army tent was surrounded at
dawn one morning by his own officers, wielding drawn swords, who "forced"
Tai Tsu, barely awake, to don a yellow imperial robe and hear his men
proclaim him emperor. Though he pretended to be loyal to the little boy
monarch in Kaifeng, Tai Tsu allowed himself to be mounted on his horse
and led out towards the capital, surrounded by his cheering troops. En

route, he did at least halt the cavalcade to demand pledges from all, promising that in the take-over, neither the child ruler, regent mother, minister colleagues, nor the populace should be harmed, nor should the Kaifeng treasury or arsenals be pillaged. Only when all his men swore to obedience did Tai Tsu continue. When his forces surrounded the Kaifeng palace, the reigning queen-regent bowed peaceably to the inevitable, and with little more ado, the Sung Dynasty was founded.

Wisely realizing that military men who would "mutiny" once to put him in power could mutiny again, Emperor Tai Tsu soon afterwards invited to a palace banquet all senior officers who had backed him. "Happiness," he told them, "is to have enough wealth to enjoy life and leave to one's descendants. If you, my men, will forego your commands and retire to the provinces, you may have your choice of best lands and finest mansions. There you may ally your offspring in marriages with my imperial family, thus negating any suspicion between us, and so spend the rest of your lives in peace and tranquility."[1] Next day they all resigned, saving face by professing poor health. All were given honorific titles and richly endowed for life—an arrangement unheard of in all past imperial history.

By buying off his top generals to safeguard his regime, Tai Tsu seriously reduced the strength of his armies. His policy of subjugating military authority to that of powerful court ministers would be continued under most of his successors to such an exaggerated degree that Sung China was to suffer one humiliation after another at the hands of invading barbarians. Even so, the Chinese elite—having never considered military prowess on a par with cultural achievement—glorified the Sung Dynasty for its pursuit of classical culture, erudite literature, archeology, and art. The Sung was an age when learning flourished, the recent invention of block printing disseminating throughout the empire the so-called Neo-Confucianism, which incorporated a more rational, perhaps more moralistic philosophy, than the previous state doctrine.

Tai Tsu is especially revered for bringing all China once again under Chinese leadership. To do this, he invited rulers of the long-independent petty kingdoms of South China to surrender in return for immunity and generous remuneration. Most submitted willingly, but the poet-king at Nanking held off, asking instead to retain his throne and be allowed to pay tribute as a vassal state. To this Tai Tsu replied: "And what crimes have your subjects committed that they should be kept in exile from the Empire?"[2] In A.D. 975 he took the Nanking regime by force, brought the ruler as a captive to Kaifeng, and made him a permanent "guest" in the Sung palace.

"Alas," wrote the fallen poet-king, "when I took leave of my ancestral temple in Nanking, our royal band played such a mournful tune that my tears drenched the sleeves of my beloved."[3] This was his new queen, with whom he had been openly dallying long before the death of her sister, the legitimate consort. Of their notorious romantic trysts he had written, "In the Painted Hall of Paradise Palace, a heavenly beauty is taking a nap. No one speaks. She moves on her pillow. Black shines her hair like a blackbird's feathers. From her flowered robe one senses strange perfumes. When I tiptoe up, her jewelled pearl moves and she awakes from a dream. On her serious face a small smile gathers as we gaze at each other in endless love."[4] The "Unwilling Duke," as Sung Emperor Tai Tsu titled his prisoner, was to spend the rest of his life in the North Palace, "his face daily bathed in tears."

The Sung founder is greatly admired for his attempts to bring a more benevolent government to his subjects. His edict of A.D. 970 held that a responsible local official should investigate the cause of death for all deceased slaves. Thereby he strove to eliminate the practice where owners reprimanded errant slaves by beating them to death with rods bristling with metal blades. Now all such offenders would be severely punished. He further forbade the buying up of Chinese boys and girls to be hired out as slave labor. All violators of this edict were to be flogged and exiled to distant frontiers.

To avoid repetition of the former Tang Dynasty's collapse at the hands of a multitude of eunuchs, Tai Tsu banned the lucrative trade in forcibly castrated boys, and—it is claimed—reduced the number of palace eunuchs to fifty. His immediate successors would more or less follow this precedent. The result was that eunuch political influence was minimal all during the Sung.

At the same time, however, Tai Tsu officially recognized the right of individual subjects to choose voluntary emasculation. Thus, while cultured men attained high position through official literary exams, those lacking the means for education could choose castration as a road to wealth. Applicants had first to present themselves to military authorities, who recorded the date set for their castration. If and when they were appointed to eunuch rank in the palaces, the day of their emasculation was marked as their "birthday"—the beginning of their "second life."

Tai Tsu's highly respected empress mother insisted that he bequeath the throne to his brother rather than to his young son, reminding him that he himself became emperor by easily overthrowing a child ruler. Nonetheless, there has always remained a strong suspicion of foul play at the time of the succession. Sung annals say that when ailing Emperor Tai Tsu summoned his brother to hear his deathbed instructions, eunuchs and attendants outside the chamber affirmed they saw the brother's candle-lit shadow dart across the room, and heard the sound of a hatchet crashing into the floor, just before Tai Tsu expired. What actually happened has never been authenticated, but it is pointed out that when the brother became the second Sung emperor, the three men who could have contended with him for the throne all died soon thereafter. (Even as late as the 1700s, Chinese emperors pondered this frightening deathbed story as they agonized over their own choice of heir.) Some modern historians note that the Sung founder's failing health and death could have been due to his heavy drinking.

Unlike the founder of the Sung Dynasty, the new emperor, Tai Tsung, was not averse to warfare. Rankled that the barbarian Khitans still occupied China's northern border area, which had been ceded to them by a feckless Five Dynasties ruler, Tai Tsung made two long and costly attempts to recover these lands. In the first, he was forced into an ignoble retreat; in the second, in A.D. 986, he barely escaped with his life when his forces were not even able to reach the present-day Peking area before being disastrously routed by Khitan armies.

Tai Tsung also tried to recapture lands in China's northwest from the Tangut people. These territories had been granted them long ago by the Tang Dynasty for assistance in curbing rebellions. Here again, Sung armies met with abysmal failure, leaving the monarch no choice but to tolerate the aliens who were firmly entrenched on Chinese soil.

Both the Khitans and Tanguts founded their own dynasties after the Chinese example, and both would absorb many Chinese subjects and customs. (In 1982 a tomb from this era was unearthed in Inner Mongolia containing the corpse of a Khitan princess wrapped in a shroud of copper wire mesh, following old Chinese custom.) The Khitans extended their empire and influence so widely westward across Asia that even a far-away Arabian ruler asked for the hand of one of their princesses. The Khitan realm was known in eastern Europe as "Kitai," that is, "Cathay," the name of China to Westerners.

Unsuccessful in battle, Sung China concentrated on peaceful commercial enterprises as well as intellectual pursuits and development in humanitarian directions. Slavery was so widespread by A.D. 991 that Tai Tsung decreed that Chinese children sold as slaves to northern barbarians should be purchased back by Sung frontier officials with funds from the imperial treasury. He also ruled that southern coastal children sold into slavery by indebted parents to pay off moneylenders should all be freed and returned to their homes.

The third Sung emperor, Chen Tsung, grandson of the founder, received poor press from historians. When his Taoist adepts provided Heaven-sent messengers and letters fallen from above which purportedly sanctified his divine right to rule, ranking ministers were not convinced. Nor did they approve his early decree attempting to make the supreme deity of Taoism equal in rank to the Confucian Heaven.

During this unfortunate Sung emperor's reign, wars against the northern Khitans dragged on with but few Chinese victories, until suddenly the barbarians pushed down to the Yellow River, just opposite the capital, Kaifeng. Panic-stricken palace courtiers urged Chen Tsung to flee to safety, but he refused. Instead, in the year 1004 he sued for peace, surrendering all claim to Chinese districts held by the Khitans. In addition, he agreed to pay the Khitans a heavy yearly indemnity: 100,000 ounces of silver and 200,000 bales of finest silk. This tribute was soon to be doubled after the Khitans helped Sung armies in another failed attempt to drive out the Tanguts ensconced in present-day Kansu. As a result, the Tanguts, too, now demanded yearly Chinese tribute of even more silver and silk than was being sent to the Khitans, in addition to 30,000 pounds of tea.

Thus, Emperor Chen Tsung is accused of selling out to both northern enemies and weakening the Sung nation by ceding away Chinese lands and paying outrageous tribute. However, by agreeing to these humiliating terms, China's northern frontier was secured for the next 100 years, leaving her free to prosper and indulge in literary pursuits by some of Imperial China's greatest minds.

Attempting to carry on his predecessor's much-admired policies, Chen Tsung also ruled against the heavy traffic in Chinese slaves, decreeing that subjects indebted to the government would no longer be forced to make payment by deeding their male and female slaves to the state. He further decreed that both ringleaders and accomplices proven to be dealing in slavery would be executed, while those of proven intent to do so, but who had not as yet succeeded, would be flogged, branded, and banished to the hinterlands.

One of the few stories of treachery among Sung palace inmates verifies that eunuchs were still used to mete out inner-palace punishments. Emperor Chen Tsung's chief eunuch, Chen-lin, by chance intercepted a harem slave girl leaving the palace gate carrying a mysterious box. It proved to contain a live male infant just born to a favored imperial concubine. The terrified slave explained that her mistress—yet another concubine— was so jealous of her rival's new son that she had secretly abducted him and ordered the slave to throw the boy into the river. Shocked, eunuch Chen-lin hurriedly carried the baby to the emperor's uncle, who agreed to secretly rear it as his own. The slave girl returned to her mistress in the harem and claimed that she had drowned the boy as instructed.

Before long, however, the treacherous concubine, alarmed by rumors that the baby still lived, ordered eunuch Chen-lin to flog the slave until she confessed the truth. To conceal his own role in the affair, the eunuch was forced to comply, while the slave, not daring to confess her disobedience, died in silence under the prolonged beating.

When Sung China's prosperity began to erode late in the eleventh century, emperors began entrusting highest office to some of China's most celebrated men of letters, thus beginning a long era when mandarin officials held more complete control of government than in any other period of Chinese history. The most innovative prime minister was Wang An-Shih, a cantankerous, unwashed, brilliant scholar-statesman whose astute ideas proved to be too liberal for his day. It is recorded that this eccentric, dedicated administrator once became so unbearably dirty and odorous that two colleagues had to force him to bathe.

However, Wang An-Shih's sweeping reforms brought great improvements, improving governmental administration, fiscal stability, military preparedness, and, with agricultural incentives, the welfare of the peasantry. Yet within twenty years all his innovations were thrown out, as staid, conservative ministers came back into power. These were men from the well-to-do classes most hurt by Wang's reforms. They bitterly denounced his measures as blasphemous in that they were unsanctified by any precedent from the revered past. Their maddening complacency in objecting to any change fostered a stagnation and defeatist attitude for which Sung China would soon pay dearly.

These same conservative Confucian erudites are also blamed for encouraging the unrelenting puritanical double standard long ascribed to by Chinese males. They insisted that Confucius himself had taught that females should bow unquestioningly to the will of father, husband, and sons, all of whom were to be treated like gods. Female chastity became an obsession among Chinese males, who nonetheless deemed it their unquestionable right to keep multiple wives and concubines, and to openly patronize the many luxurious public brothels. "It is a trifling matter to die of starvation, but a grave one to lose one's chastity," said an accepted Sung moral dictum applying to women only. One scholar wrote that by Sung times the binding of women's feet was quite common, for this crippling fashion kept wives, concubines, and daughters confined to the home, and so "less apt to succumb to outside sexual escapades." Even the Sung's most respected historian-statesman contended that women should read only the "proper" Confucian classics, and be denied access to "sensual arts" such as poetry and music.

The most notorious Sung Emperor, Hui Tsung, occupied the Kaifeng throne from 1100 to 1125. Though he was an inept ruler, this talented voluptuary painted exquisite scrolls of birds and flowers, while personally presiding over his famous artistic academy and his invaluable collection of bronzes, paintings, jades, and manuscripts, antique and recent. Palace eunuchs arranged his celebrated "secret" visits to elegant prostitutes of nationwide fame. The beauty and accomplishments of one of these led contemporaries to write that she was "delicate as an orchid, graceful as a peony."

In time, Emperor Hui Tsung also became so deeply enamored of occult Taoism that he squandered ruinous amounts on favorite Taoist practitioners, elaborate costly religious ceremonies, and elegant temples and monasteries. In the year 1113, his wildest dreams were answered when there miraculously appeared before him in the distant heavens a glorious, shining palace—home of the divine Immortals. This beatific vision goaded him to waste years trying—quite unsuccessfully—to force an amalgamation of Taoism, Buddhism, and Confucianism into one official religion.

In the following year, because imperial male progeny were not abundantly forthcoming, Emperor Hui Tsung's Taoist officials convinced him that if a high earth-and-stone hill were constructed in the northwest corner of Kaifeng, it would produce certain wavelengths that would increase the number of imperial princes. Once this elaborate project was completed and apparently was successful—palace women did indeed begin bearing sons—the delighted emperor built around "Longevity Hill" one of the most magnificent and costly garden parks ever constructed in Imperial China. During the several years of its construction, palace agents traversed the land collecting unusually shaped rocks, and rare trees and plants, all of which cost so much in money and the labor of the populace that many households went bankrupt because of the project. This and like palace extravagances—to say nothing of the ongoing tribute payments to the Khitans and Tanguts—severely drained Sung treasuries of resources sorely needed to refurbish neglected armies.

While Hui Tsung wiled away his time in sensual pleasures, he left government in the hands of his favorite ministers, who seemed oblivious to the danger of attack from yet another barbarian enemy gathering strength to the north of the now-sinicized Khitan realm. These were the Jurchen tribes, fierce horse-breeders and hunters who had now firmly consolidated their peoples in the Manchurian hills and forests and had already raided the Khitans on several occasions. By this time, the Khitans had made Peking their southernmost capital. No longer uneducated nomads, they had entirely assimilated Chinese culture and institutions. Much of their old fighting spirit was lost as they grew soft seeking wealth and gracious Chinese-style living. Indeed there was little to distinguish them from the Chinese. A disastrous series of droughts, floods, and inner-palace conspiracies had further weakened Khitan rule.

The hardy Jurchen horsemen had successfully combined considerable knowledge of the art of war, gleaned from Korean, Khitan, and Chinese contacts, with a driving, feral energy that their more civilized neighbors had lost. In his ringing oration declaring vengeance against the Khitans for harboring a Jurchen traitor, the Jurchen chieftain slashed his forehead to let blood run down through his tears in a shamanistic tribal ritual that goaded his warriors to fight with demonic strength and endurance. Though the Khitans valiantly held off the Jurchen predators for many years, in the end, against such dedicated ferocity, they were doomed. Already in 1115, a mere 10,000 Jurchen horsemen had destroyed an army of 700,000 personally led by the Khitan ruler.

It was at this juncture that Sung Emperor Hui Tsung foolishly let craven court eunuchs and advisers convince him to ally his forces with the Jurchen predators, in the hope of reclaiming China's lost territories from the Khitans. Contrary to the prohibition that had been in effect many years now, Hui Tsung entrusted army command to a favorite palace eunuch. In the ensuing battles, Jurchen forces drove out the Khitan ruling family, while their eunuch-led Chinese "allies" were not even able to protect their own subjects near the Chinese-Khitan border.

With the fall of the Khitan-controlled Peking area to the Jurchen in 1125, Sung China suddenly found herself with no buffer state between herself and her new barbarian "allies." Just as suddenly, Sung Emperor Hui Tsung abdicated to his son Chin Tsung, hied himself off to safety in a monastery in south China, and assumed a Taoist religious title. By this time the Jurchens knew that Sung rule had become incompetent, corrupted by the baleful influence of palace eunuchs and backward-looking ministers. They also learned that their fickle Chinese allies at the court in Kaifeng were secretly fomenting a revolt against them, while at the same time demanding territorial concessions from them. Infuriated, the Jurchen chieftain sent two great armies to descend on Kaifeng. When the besieged emperor of China sued for peace by agreeing to cede more garrison posts and pay a tremendous annual tribute, the Jurchen victors accepted the offer and warily withdrew towards the north.

As soon as the enemy had turned their backs, two Sung court eunuchs, Liang Shih-cheng and Tang Kuang, persuaded the Chinese ruler to attack the withdrawing barbarians, prompting the maddened Jurchens to return in full force. For one terrible month they besieged the Kaifeng capital, again forcing the Chinese into an ignominious capitulation. In his 1126 communication of surrender, Emperor Ching Tsung addressed the Jurchen ruler as "Uncle," meekly acknowledging himself as an inferior "Nephew." Unimpressed, the Jurchens issued an ultimatum exacting reparations which pauperized Kaifeng overnight—10,000 horses and all weaponry in the city, plus millions in gold, silver, silk, gems, and artistic treasures. Soon afterward they also demanded Sung China's imperial libraries, official records, printing plates, medicines, astrological and mechanical apparatus—all the accoutrements of the older, more advanced civilization.

When next the Jurchen conquerors demanded that both the acting and "retired" Sung rulers proceed to Manchuria as prisoners, the old emperor, now back in Kaifeng, tried to take poison. A Sung official wrenched the potion from him and forced both him and the emperor to leave for the Jurchen territory in a clumsy calf-drawn cart. Next, the Jurchens rounded up most of the Sung imperial family, nobles, officials, courtiers, even palace eunuchs, concubines, and artisans—3,000 persons in all—and herded them off to the northern wilds.

One loyal Chinese scholar who accompanied Emperor Chin Tsung to Manchuria volunteered to return to the defunct Sung court to raise money to ransom the monarch out of captivity. After a frantic collection, Kaifeng officials produced an enormous outlay of gold and silver, which the Jurchen victors scornfully rejected as insufficient. To the further humiliation of Sung China, the Jurchens brutally decapitated the Chinese go-between in this negotiation and mounted his head on a pole.

Neither of the captive emperors would ever again see his native land. One of the few reports on them simply said that two years after their arrival in Manchuria, both were allowed to visit the Jurchen ruler's elaborate, Chinese-style imperial tombs. Ex-Emperor Hui Tsung died in the cold north nine years later, and his disgraced son lived on for a few more decades.

The Jurchens controlled their vast conquests by stationing military contingents throughout North China, and used willing Chinese and Khitan collaborators by the thousands to run their administration. It is estimated that 100,000 North China families—including high officials and scholars— willingly emigrated or were moved to Jurchen Manchuria, while entire villages of Jurchen barbarians were transplanted to occupy North China.

An early Jurchen edict prescribed: "Now that all peoples have submitted to our dynasty, it behooves us to have unified customs. We expect all subjects to shave their heads and wear the short Jurchen tunic with lapel opening to the left. Those who dare disobey will be considered loyalists to the Sung and severely punished."[5] For violating this edict, a few brave Chinese were executed, but the edict failed to make Jurchen customs supreme—nor could the Jurchen prohibition of marriage between conquered and conquerors ever be enforced.

Though the Jurchen occupation of North China lasted for over 100 years, the Chinese have always claimed ultimate victory: In the end the Jurchen "became Chinese," captivated by the more civilized Confucian culture.

At the fall of North China to the Jurchens, an escaping remnant of the House of Sung established a court in the South. They made their capital the splendid rich city of Hangchow in a coastal bay below the Yangtze, setting up young Kao Tsung, ninth son of the captured ex-Emperor Hui Tsung, as first emperor of the new Southern Sung dynasty.

Most historians are convinced that in the early years of the Southern Sung regime, the Sungs could have recovered North China had not the pacifist Confucian ministers controlling the new emperor ruthlessly stifled brave Sung generals. On the other hand, numerous forays against the Sung by the Jurchens—who were unaccustomed to the steaming, low-lying expanses of rice paddies and great rivers of the South—met with failure. Eventually, however, the weak and indolent Sung ruler capitulated. In an uneasy peace pact of 1141, Sung Emperor Kao Tsung formally gave up all claim to North China and promised to pay the Jurchens yearly tribute as a subjugated state. Appeals of outraged Chinese patriots to abrogate this mortifying treaty were considered offenses against the Southern Sung emperor's authority, and the protestors were put to death.

Despite this "armistice," as late as 1161 a Jurchen ruler was personally leading his forces south in yet another attempt to cross the Yangtze. Though his dramatic appeal to his armies—delivered with tears and blood streaming down his face from a self-inflicted wound—fired his men to a ferocious fighting pitch, his efforts failed. The Sung navy made the difference. When the Southern Sung's last drive north against the Jurchen also failed abysmally, the Chinese minister who initiated the campaign was put to death and his head was sealed in a box and delivered as an appeasement to the Jurchen enemy court—a spectacular and craven departure from proud Sung tradition against putting high officials to death.

A stalemate was ultimately reached, which at least left the Southern Sung realm free to flourish in comparative security for another century. As the rich South became richer, its sophisticated, refined lifestyle surpassed even that of the former Sung in Kaifeng. Sumptuous palaces and mansions, and elegant pavilions proliferated on the shores of Hangchow's river and beautiful West Lake, affording splendid views of pagoda-studded, wooded islands and hazy distant peaks. Colorful pleasure boats plied the city's Venice-like canals, which were everywhere spanned by lacy stone bridges. In such a setting, artists produced the famous Southern Sung scroll paintings of unsurpassed perfection, ingeniously combining sky, water, space, and pine-covered mountains in the classic Chinese tradition.

In the South's burgeoning economy, Sung palace inmates and residents of Hangchow competed in a veritable frenzy of accumulating and displaying wealth and luxuries. One prince gave a banquet in the emperor's honor where 180 exotic courses were served. Well-to-do imperial ladies and palace eunuchs further enriched themselves by letting out their considerable properties as warehouses and pawn shops at exorbitant rents. Desire for wealth among contesting factions of Sung officials led to nepotism, patronage, and corruption on a grand scale. Yet at the same time, Sung philosophers brought Neo-Confucianism into full flower, to remain the leading school of Confucian thought throughout the remainder of imperial times.

So rapidly did the Jurchens ruling North China become sinicized that by 1141 the monarch in person was offering official sacrifices at his own Confucian temples. By 1153 the Jurchens even abandoned their Manchurian palace and moved their capital to Peking, which they transformed into a city more beautiful than Kaifeng. Decrees of various Jurchen rulers to force their countrymen to retain their native language and customs met with failure, vastly outnumbered as they were by the Chinese and sinicized Khitan subjects who filled most government posts.

Records show that 170 families of the Jurchen imperial clan and top military echelons—982 persons in all—came to own almost 28,000 non-Jurchen slaves, all captured or surrendered in battle. In time, many of the once-hardy Jurchen aristocracy, now spoiled by easy living, were reduced to abject laziness, alcoholism, and habitual gambling, becoming paupered parasites on the hardworking, tax-paying North China populace. Neglected even were the great mounted hunts which had once kept Jurchen cavalry at the peak of military fitness.

At the Jurchen court in Peking, eunuchs of the powerful, Chinese-style Bureau of Palace Attendants served as "ears and eyes" for the ruler. High-ranking officials turned in by spying eunuchs and censors for offenses against the throne were flogged on bare back and buttocks in full view of the entire court. One Jurchen ruler watched with relish as fifty accused persons—including prime ministers, top officials, generals, monks, a cook, and a princess—were mercilessly beaten with whips and rods. These often-fatal floggings became a fixed Jurchen institution, and contributed to growing disaffection of the Chinese with Jurchen rule. (Yet this form of punishment would persist in Chinese dynasties to come.)

By the early 1200s, while the Southern Sung basked in its refined cultural and intellectual heritage, the Jurchens themselves were being harassed by a terrifying new enemy who had forged a federation of nomadic horsemen tribes from across Mongolia and Siberia. These were the Mongol hordes, the most savage, pitiless race known to history. Jenghis Khan had just become the Mongol's undisputed chieftain, a conqueror so utterly ruthless that he reportedly was born with a clot of blood clenched in his fist. "Man's highest joy is conquest," he once declared. "Defeat your enemies, pursue them, seize their possessions, ride their horses, and rape their wives and daughters."[6] He fixed his great headquarters encampment at Karakorum in Upper Mongolia, over a thousand miles northwest of Peking, and now was looking southward for new lands to pillage for booty.

When Jenghis' intentions became apparent, the Sung ruler in South China sent a foolhardy message demanding his submission. The tough Mongol khan spat in the direction of the Chinese Dragon Throne and at once began his march south across the Gobi Desert. First he had to subdue the Tanguts in Northwest China and the Jurchens in North China. So sinicized by this time were the Tanguts and the Jurchens that Jenghis Khan lumped them together with the northern Chinese and considered them all one race: the Chinese enemy.

For five solid years Jenghis Khan laid waste to North China, so completely flattening ninety Jurchen-ruled cities that "horsemen could ride over vast devastated areas in the dark without stumbling."[7] It was the worst destruction and wholesale slaughter that China had ever seen. The Jurchen defenders held out so heroically in a losing cause that even the ruthless Mongols admired them as brave adversaries. Jenghis took the Jurchen capital at Peking in 1215, burned the city to the ground, and massacred the inhabitants. The Jurchen ruler managed to flee across the Yellow River to set up court in the old Sung capital of Kaifeng. During the carnage, droves of northern Chinese defected to join up with the Mongols, while others fled south to their brethren under Sung rule.

Jenghis would have slaughtered the Tangut population and turned their vast cultivated land into grazing grounds for his horses, camels, and herd animals, had it not been for a sinicized Khitan nobleman whom he had taken captive and made his administrative advisor. This highly cultured Confucian convinced the khan that "although one can conquer by horseback, one cannot rule from horseback," and that the people and their fields must be spared to sustain and enrich the Mongols. The Chinese still consider this Khitan gentleman a Confucian hero. As a result of his intercession, most lands were left to the plow, and most of the people were taxed instead of butchered.

Jenghis left the task of subduing North China to his able cavalry generals, while he pushed on far westward to wreak vengeance on Central Asian states whose rulers had dared kill a few of his envoys and tradesmen. There his superbly disciplined, fearless, hard-riding warriors put to the sword entire city populations if they dared lift a hand in self defense. Women and children were carried off as slaves. Male prisoners were nailed to wooden donkeys, chopped to pieces, flayed alive, or boiled in cauldrons, as Persian historians have recounted in blood-curdling detail. Jenghis became master of the "hinge of the world"—Tashkent, Bokhara, Samarkand—while his generals and sons went on conquering and plundering into Persia, Poland, Hungary, and Russia. He is known as "the Scourge of Asia" and much of Europe.

All considered, Jenghis ruled the largely Muslim peoples of Central Asia with tolerance, except for his strong objection to their traditional Islamic ritual of butchering animals by slitting their throats and letting them bleed to death. "When an animal is to be eaten," Jenghis decreed, "it must be slaughtered according to the Mongol code: its feet must be tied, its belly ripped open, and its heart squeezed by hand until it dies. If anyone slaughters an animal after the Mohammedan fashion, he himself is to be slaughtered."[8] Yet Jenghis systematically spared the lives of builders, artisans, merchants, and financial adepts for employment in his newly subjugated lands, distributing some 30,000 Islamic craftsmen amongst his relatives, generals, and nobles.

In 1227 Jenghis returned triumphant to North China to punish the Tangut people in Kansu for refusing to furnish men for his troops. In the ensuing battle, a fall from his horse left him with a badly wounded knee. Shortly thereafter, to escape the heat as well as a dangerous omen foreseen in an unfavorable conjunction of the planets, and instructing his officers to remain and subdue the area, Jenghis and his entourage headed north toward his homeland. En route he became fatally ill from the wound and died in the mountains of Kansu. His corpse was carried on to Mongolia for burial outside Karakorum where, it is written, forty beautiful women of Mongol nobility, together with his favorite steed and forty war horses, were sacrificed at his tomb.

Today the government of China is rehabilitating Jenghis Khan's reputation from that of a bloodthirsty monster to a folk hero, a brilliant conqueror who commenced the reunification of China. This is being done to placate China's thousands of Mongol subjects, especially those near Inner Mongolia's strategic borders, where they are now being trained in Chinese-style cadre organization.

Jenghis' son Ogotai, the next Great Khan of the Mongols, using conquered Central Asian and Chinese artisans, built a splendid capital city at Karakorum and carried on his father's conquest with added ferocity. In 1230, one of Ogotai's generals, a brilliant tactician fresh from conquests in Persia and Europe, began the siege of Kaifeng, where the Jurchen ruler still held out. Urgently the Jurchen ruler beseeched the Southern Sung Chinese for help, his famous message warning, "We are to you as lips to the teeth; when the lips are gone, the teeth will have to face the cold unprotected."[9] This prophetic appeal was ignored, and the Southern Sung, in their utter folly, chose to join up with the Mongols. After a long siege, the Mongol khan took Kaifeng in 1233, forcing the Jurchen ruler to flee to a neighboring fortress to make a final stand. At this juncture, the Sung Chinese army tardily appeared to assist their Mongol "allies." When the besieged Jurchen ruler saw Mongol soldiers mounting the fortress ramparts, he committed suicide, while his brave generals, rather than surrender, chose to have their legs severed by the Mongol conquerors.

When the Mongol khan prepared to completely raze Kaifeng, the Khitan minister who had previously interceded with Jenghis Khan to spare the Tangut people and lands attempted to do so once more. Impatiently Ogotai demanded, "Are you going to weep for the people again?" The intrepid Khitan persevered and convinced his master to spare the city and its people. Within a year, the remainder of North China had fallen to the Mongols, and the court of Southern Sung China finally realized that now it was "exposed to the cold": the Mongols were overlooking their border just above the Yangtze.

This might have ended Mongol conquest in China, had not the fickle Southern Sung court, in a repetition of history, belatedly opted to turn against their Mongol allies in a hopeless attempt to reclaim the North. The Mongols readily took up the challenge and started an invasion of South China in 1236. Within a few years, however, they temporarily quit China for conquests in Western Europe, as well as to participate in a great gathering of all the tribes at Karakorum to settle the matter of succession following the death of the Great Khan.

The deceased khan's avaricious wife in Karakorum ruled as regent over the Mongol empire for four years after his death. Resenting the Khitan minister's policies to protect conquered peoples from overtaxation, she replaced him with a Muslim merchant from Central Asia. She also took as her most intimate and influential confidante a conquered Muslim slave girl named Fatima. Soon this scheming trio had rid the court of all their opponents and were cruelly overtaxing subjects, to the delight of the greedy empress regent and the deep resentment of many Mongol noblemen.

In 1246, when Ogotai's son assumed the Mongol throne, the detested

Muslim merchant was promptly executed for diverting state revenue to his own pocket, and Fatima was accused of using sorcery to bring about the death of an imperial Mongol cousin. Fatima was tortured until she confessed, after which "her upper and lower orifices were sewn up, she was rolled in a felt sheet, and thrown into the river to drown."[10] The new khan threw out all Muslim advisors in the government and replaced them with Nestorian Christians from the Middle East. This khan died two years later, en route to do battle against ambitious relatives who held sway in southern Russia.

The next Mongol khan, Mangu Khan, grandson of Jenghis, dispatched his ferocious armies to put an end to the Sung Dynasty holding out in South China. He put his younger and better known brother, Kublai Khan, in charge of the armies and much of North China. Kublai proved to be a wise administrator and an astute military leader. In 1253 Kublai finally established for the Mongols a stronghold in South China by sending his armies 3,000 miles down the far western marches of Tibetan lands to conquer the independent-minded Chinese state of Yunnan, just above Burma. (Over 700 years later, in 1983, some 1,400 subjects of this province petitioned the government of China to officially recognize them as a separate ethnic minority—the proud descendants of Kublai Khan's armies.)

In late 1259, while the forty-three-year-old Kublai was besieging Southern Sung cities on the Yangtze, he received word that his brother, the Great Khan, had died. Kublai returned to his capital just above the Great Wall, where, in 1260, relatives proclaimed him the next khan of the Mongols. Three times he ritually refused the honor before finally accepting. Kublai's enthronement prompted a four-year war with another and younger brother who challenged Kublai's succession. Kublai Khan marched on Karakorum, destroyed the city, and killed his brother by encasing him between two heavy carpets which were violently shaken until the victim ceased breathing, thus observing the Mongol belief that Sun and Heaven should not witness the shedding of imperial Mongol blood. Other sources say the brother surrendered to Kublai and died of an unknown ailment a few years later. Centuries later, travelers through Mongolia reported that all that was left to mark the site of old Karakorum was a huge, stone sculpted turtle on a plain west of Ulan Bator.

It took Kublai almost twenty more years to end all resistance from the Southern Sung, one of whose generals had courageously held a walled town through five years of continual siege. Sung China may have held out much longer but for a worthless minister who controlled the emperor and whose direction of him nullified all efforts of Sung army generals. This obstinate Confucian chancellor ultimately led a contingent against the

Mongols and was so thoroughly routed that he was forced to retreat after heavy casualties and desertions of his troops. Finally, the Sung court stripped him of his rank and banished him to Fukien, but he was killed en route. After this fiasco, the Hangchow court was left in a state of utter confusion and chaos.

When the Sung emperor suddenly died in 1274, his four-year-old son was enthroned, the aging dowager empress acting as regent. By this time, defections of court officials to Kublai Khan's northern regime had left her with few reliable advisors. Sung defenses slowly crumbled against relentless battering by Mongol forces.

By 1275 Kublai's famous General Bayan was advancing on the Sung capital in Hangchow. When advised to flee to safety with the child emperor, the dowager empress refused to abandon the Sung capital, but did agree to send the emperor's two young brothers south to safety. Then she dispatched an envoy to General Bayan offering to surrender and pay regular tribute of 250 taels of silver and 250,000 bolts of silk to the Mongols. General Bayan refused the offer until the Chinese child emperor offered himself up as a subject of Kublai Khan, and the dowager submitted the Sung Dynasty's imperial seal to the victor. The Mongol then generously accepted the surrender, ordered that the Sung family be respectfully treated, prohibited his men from plundering the imperial tombs, and ordered them to take the Sung emperor, the empress dowager, and the empress mother to Kublai at his summer palace beyond the Great Wall. Kublai and his wife treated them kindly, though he could not resist confiscating some imperial Sung treasures: royal robes of state, jade tablets of authority, and exquisite jewelry. He granted the deposed empero the title of duke, and years later exiled him to Tibet, where he became a Buddhist lama. The empress dowager lived comfortably on in Peking until her death, while the empress mother joined a Buddhist nunnery and died there many years later.

When South China fell to Kublai's armies in 1276, a group of Sung loyalists and naval commanders escaped from Hangchow to join up with the last pretender to the Sung throne, a five-year-old princely brother of the fallen emperor. Though by this time all was obviously lost to the Mongols, for the next three years this naval contingent avoided Mongol ships by hiding out in harbors and islands along the South China coast. Finally, in the spring of 1279, the royal Sung flotilla was surrounded by superior Mongol vessels in a secluded coastal bay. Seeing the end of all hope, a devoted courtier on the Sung imperial vessel approached the now eight-year-old boy "emperor" to explain, "Your brother basely surrendered the Southern Sung nation to the Mongol enemy, and that disgrace must be redressed,"[11] and mounting the child on his back, he jumped into the waves in an "honorable" double suicide. The 300-year-old House of Sung perished with the child, leaving the Mongol Kublai Khan to rule the whole of China—the first alien emperor to do so.

Notes

1. C. P. Fitzgerald, *China: A Short Cultural History.*
2. Ibid.
3. H. T. Lee, *The Story of Chinese Culture.*
4. C. Birch and Donald Keene, *Anthology of Chinese Literature.*
5. Jing-shen Tao, *The Jurchen in Twelfth Century China.*
6. R. Grousset, *The Rise and Splendour of the Chinese Empire.*
7. Will Durant, *Our Oriental Heritage.*
8. J. D. Langlois, Jr., *China Under Mongol Rule.*
9. Jing-shen Tao, *The Jurchen in Twelfth Century China.*
10. J. D. Langlois, Jr., *China Under Mongol Rule.*
11. H. W. Rathbun, *Echoes of Chinese History.*

15

Eunuchs Subdued Under Mongol Emperors
KUBLAI KHAN'S YUAN DYNASTY (A.D. 1260-1368)

In 1260, when Kublai Khan's followers elected him Khan of Khans over the great Mongol Empire, his domain stretched a staggering 10,000 miles from Peking across Asia into Persia and Russia. Yet, from this vast area, Kublai chose North China—where he had governed under his brother's rule—as his seat of power and personal domain. Even before his armies overcame South China in 1276, Kublai had taken concrete steps to convince the Chinese people that he was indeed "Ruler of All Under Heaven," a universal sovereign and legitimate Son of Heaven. He did so, it is claimed, under the advice of the few Chinese scholars he had taken into his court early on.

Though he retained Shangtu, in Mongolia, just above the Great Wall, as his summer capital, beside the ruins of Peking he entirely rebuilt his splendid "Great Capital," carefully designed after a capital city outlined in the ancient Confucian classics. More importantly, Kublai titled his new ruling House the "Yuan" Dynasty, an esoteric, highly symbolic term, meaning "the origin," taken directly from China's age-old Book of Changes. He also constructed an impressive Chinese-style dynastic temple to worship his imperial Mongol ancestors, and another shrine to pay homage to Confucius—though Kublai himself proved but little inclined to personally participate in Confucian rites and rituals.

In the first decades of his reign—as his kinsmen and generals increasingly asserted themselves as independent rulers over Mongol-conquered lands toward Europe—his primary concern became the return of prosperity to a reunited China. No Chinese Son of Heaven ever took his duties more seriously or performed them more successfully. This alien Mongol was a civilized ruler—a far cry from his grandfather, the plunder-bent Jenghis Khan.

Kublai may have erred, however, when he ranked, by official decree, the one million Mongol countrymen who followed him to China—heads of government agencies and military units—as non-laboring, untaxed elite, above and apart from the indigenous Chinese, even forbidden to intimacy with Chinese. This decree was humiliating to the Chinese, and since his successors throughout the entire Yuan era would continue this policy, the Mongols were never to become an integral part of Chinese society, as had former barbarians.

To the further humiliation of the Chinese, Kublai ranked just below the Mongol conquerors—also granting them special tax exemptions and privileges—yet another million foreigners who functioned as Kublai's agents entrusted with the administration of China's finances and rapidly expanding foreign trade, as well as the collection of taxes from the Chinese populace. Evidently, Kublai was unwilling to place these vital functions in the hands of conquered Chinese. Most of this second privileged category were Muslims from conquered Central Asian lands. The Venetian adventurer Marco Polo, a Roman Catholic, fell in this category of alien agents. He was favored at Kublai's court for seventeen years before returning to Italy with unbelieved, but generally accurate, tales of China's stupendous wealth and advanced civilization.

"Native" inhabitants of North China—Chinese, Jurchens, Khitans, Tanguts, and Koreans—some ten million hard-working, taxpaying subjects in all, composed a third and lower class. Thousands of Chinese of this rank who could read and write but had not graduated as classical Confucian scholars became government clerks who essentially ran Kublai's Chinese-style bureaucracy. For few of the nomadic conquerors were literate—Kublai himself was illiterate—and few had a taste for mundane administrative detail. Multitudes of Northern Chinese—either out of admiration for their conquerors or a desire to ingratiate themselves—readily adopted Mongol custom and dress, learned the Mongol language, and even assumed Mongol names.

Lowest in rank and least favored of all were some sixty million Southern Chinese, though they contributed eighty percent of Yuan China's taxes.

Since Southerners had so long remained loyal to the Chinese Sung Dynasty, they were never entirely trusted by the Mongols. Rarely were the proud Confucian scholars who congregated in the South allowed posts of rank in the Peking bureaucracy. Most of these unemployed erudites instead gave themselves over to literary pursuits, teaching in newly founded academies dedicated to upholding Chinese tradition, as they gradually learned to live with and accept "barbarian" rule. These southern Confucianists are credited with the preservation of Chinese culture—almost unchanged—through some eighty years of Mongol occupation.

Kublai made every effort to preserve Mongol customs and ceremonies among his Mongol compatriots. Before leaving Peking each summer for his northern capital, he performed a ritual to secure another year of good fortune. In the ritual, four shamans sacrificed a horse and some sheep, while Kublai bowed to Heaven, honoring his ancestral spirits by calling out Jenghis Khan's name and scattering mare's milk from a special breed of horses. In a ritual at the end of the year—aimed to forestall bad luck—participants shot arrows at grass and straw figures representing the Mongol's enemies, or at a dog, the Mongol's symbol of good luck, after which shamans performed rites and muttered prayers for prosperity and the prevention of pestilence and afflictions. Members of the Mongol imperial family who were stricken with illness were placed in a round "yurt" tent, before which two sheep were sacrificed daily until the patient recovered. Before going into battle, Kublai always poured out a libation of fermented mare's milk and invoked heavenly assistance against the enemy. At the New Year, and again on his birthday, elaborate and costly feasts were held, where thousands of Mongol guests gorged themselves with food and indulged in excessively heavy drinking, for which the Mongols were noted.

We know from records of foreign travelers to Yuan China that thousands of eunuchs served in Kublai Khan's palaces. One good indication that they seldom had a role in state affairs is that the histories seldom mention them. Kublai and his ruling descendants seemed to prefer their own countrymen, their related noblemen, or imported aliens such as the Muslims as their agents and personal confidants.

Bodily mutilation as punishment for crime was rarely resorted to during Mongol rule in China. Castration as a penalty for an offense was strictly prohibited, though beheadings were common, as were floggings before the court.

Most Yuan palace eunuchs were volunteers from North China; many from Fukien province were from certain impoverished families that for generations had contributed castrated sons to Peking. Mongol emperors also requisitioned eunuchs as tribute from vassal states like Korea and

Northern Vietnam.

Besides their harem and household duties, palace eunuchs, with their high falsetto voices, were widely used as female impersonators in Chinese dramas and stage shows, which the Mongol court especially favored. So popular were theatricals written in the vernacular during Mongol rule that even unemployed Confucian scholars "lowered themselves" to write scripts for this type of entertainment. Several of today's best-loved Chinese "operas" date back to Yuan times, and many still employ male actors in female roles.

There was one Chinese eunuch—a model of decorum—whom Kublai completely trusted as a man of character and ability. Li Pang-ning had been a minor eunuch in the last Sung court. When the Sung were overcome, eunuch Li stayed on under Kublai, who soon noticed his alertness, vigilance, and exemplary behavior. Ordered to learn Mongolian and other alien languages, eunuch Li quickly mastered them and was soon serving the Great Khan in his personal retinue. He was first attached to the Treasury of Imperial Vestments, but was soon promoted to several higher administrative posts. Under Kublai's successor, this valued eunuch received still higher appointments. It is said that during Kublai's ten-month-long illness, eunuch Li Pang-ning never left his side day or night.

In 1300 the next Yuan emperor wanted to appoint eunuch Li Pang-ning manager of affairs over three provinces, but the eunuch declined, saying: "I was a humble eunuch of the Sung, but Kublai Khan gave me special dispensation to serve at court with high rank and liberal rewards, an honor more than I deserved. Now, how dare I accept this even higher position? Only high ministers assist the emperor in governing the empire! I, a lowly eunuch, should not put the position to shame. What would the people and later generations think? I dare not accept this appointment."[1] For such dedicated subservience, the ruler ordered one of his ministers to immediately advise the empress dowager and crown prince of eunuch Li Pang-ning's exceptional virtue, and heaped high honors upon him.

When the new Yuan emperor planned to follow precedent and send officials in his stead to conduct sacrifices at the imperial ancestral temple, it was eunuch Li who explained that it was the past ruler's poor health which prevented him from personally conducting these all-important rituals—"But you, Your Majesty, have just ascended the throne and should officiate to show your filial piety as an example to All Under Heaven."[2] Without a word, the emperor entered the Palace of Abstinence to commence the required fasting and cleansing period in preparation for the sacrifices, appointing eunuch Li as commissioner in charge of ceremonies. Thereafter, the emperor bestowed upon eunuch Li his greatest recognition in granting posthumous titles and imperial rank upon the eunuch's deceased father, grandfather, and great-grandfather.

When the Yuan emperor who ruled from 1312 to 1321 was still a crown prince, the Mongol grand counselor and associates held governing power, which they feared they would lose to this capable prince if he became emperor. Therefore, the grand counselor suggested to the present emperor that he pass the throne on to his brother instead of his son. Aware of the fears of the grand counselor, eunuch Li warned the emperor not to contradict ancient doctrine by doing as the counselor suggested. When the ruler answered, "I have made my decision," the eunuch withdrew in silent humility. Old advisors suggested that eunuch Li should be executed for interference, but the ruler told them, "Imperial succession is decided by Heaven's Mandate. How can a mere eunuch's words or opinion bring harm?"[3] All the while, the emperor intended to follow the eunuch's advice. When the crown prince became emperor, he piled further honors on eunuch Li and rewarded him with 1,000 pieces of silver—which Li piously refused—for his long service. This is one eunuch who died a natural death after an exemplary career.

A book of fanciful essays written during the Yuan era points up the era's curiosity and theories regarding the results of castration. The Chinese author has the mythical "Yellow Emperor" demanding to know why normal men were able to grow beards after puberty, while eunuchs whose genitalia are amputated in boyhood never develop facial hair. In reply, the legendary "Inventor of Healing" informs his questioner that surgical castration leaves the seminal ducts sealed, prohibiting the sexual fluid from being ejected. Instead, he said, the semen spreads out near the surface of the eunuch's body, causing the skin to become "arid" or infertile, unable to nourish the growth of a beard. This ingenious explanation evidently satisfied readers of the day. The same essayist informs us that in these times sterile married men, incapable of producing offspring, were referred to as "natural eunuchs," while castrati were simply called "imperial palace" after the place of their employment.

Marco Polo describes how each of Kublai Khan's four legitimate empresses, all of Mongol descent, maintained her own sumptuous establishment within the palace grounds, each presiding over hundreds of youthful castrated pages training under the countless older, experienced eunuchs who ran her household. Each empress also retained some 300 young female attendants, as well as numerous ladies of the bedchamber, a personal court totaling several thousand. By these four top-ranking empresses, Kublai sired twenty-two princely sons who were destined to become overlords of outlying regions, while his twenty-five lesser-rank sons, born to harem concubines, were sent out as leaders of Mongol armies.

Kublai's vast harem required constant replenishment, even though hundreds of concubines languished magnificently dressed and heavily perfumed in the richly appointed ladies' apartments. Kublai especially preferred virgin girls from a tribe of Tartars in far western Mongolia, noted for beauty, fairness of skin, and exemplary deportment. Every year or so he dispatched agents armed with specific written instructions regarding required qualifications for new recruits to the harem.

As multitudes of these beauties were brought to the Peking palace, a set of eunuch inspectors selected out thirty or forty of the most qualified for Kublai's personal favor. Next, elderly palace ladies observed the chosen girls throughout the night, and lay with them to detect any unnoticed imperfections such as uncleanliness, snoring, disturbed sleep, bad breath, or unpleasant odor from any part of the body—and to ascertain that each retained her virginity. Finalists who passed this rigorous scrutiny were divided into groups of five who took turns of three days and three nights in Kublai's private apartments "where they performed each service required of them, and he did with them as he liked."[4] After the third night, they were replaced by another team of five, until all the new concubines had served the imperial pleasure.

Female recruits who failed to pass final muster were assigned to various sections of the imperial household to be instructed in mundane tasks such as cookery and sewing. Kublai also generously gifted these less successful virgins as concubines to deserving Mongol nobles and lords. Marco Polo maintains that Chinese parents of daughters forcibly taken from their homes were not aggrieved; rather, they considered the girls especially honored.

Marco Polo decried the general inferior position of females throughout Chinese society, pointing to the widespread practice of infanticide—the poor often drowned unwanted girl babies or left them exposed to the elements to starve to death. Daughters were a serious burden who must be married off with unaffordable dowries. The birth of a son, however, was greeted with joy, for he would add to family income, support aging parents, and perform the essential ancestor-worship rites for deceased parents. Today's government of China is still trying to eradicate the age-old practice of female infanticide and the dowry system.

At its height among the Chinese during the Mongol era was the practice of *suttee*, in which a widowed woman committed suicide, usually by burning alive on her deceased husband's funeral pyre, to accompany him to the Afterworld and thus uphold his honor. Chinese doctrine at this time held that a widow's remarriage brought everlasting disgrace to the deceased husband and entire extended family. Thus, wealthy families often had ornate honorary monuments erected in remembrance of the righteous daughter-in-law who had voluntarily committed *suttee*.

Opulent and omnipotent as Kublai Khan's China appeared to foreign envoys, merchants, and missionaries who streamed into his palace from as far away as Europe, the nation was not without internal problems. Deeply resented by the Chinese people were the leniencies and special privileges which Kublai granted to Buddhist lamas from Tibet who had convinced him to make their religion the official faith of the imperial family. Tibetan Lamaism—a Tantric, magic-ridden, miracle-working version of Indian Buddhism—appealed to the Mongols, whereas Chinese Buddhism, with its intellectual and aesthetic tendencies did not. Tibetan lamas increased their inordinate hold over the Mongol court by officially proclaiming that both Kublai and the deceased Jenghis Khan were divine reincarnations of ancient Buddhas listed in their mythological scripture. The visiting Grand Lama was honored during imperial conferences with a special seat beside the throne, while highest ranking officials remained standing on either side of the audience hall.

It was not the Tibetan religion itself which offended the Chinese. It was the lamas' arrogance and other offenses against the people which evoked bitter resentment. Marco Polo had nothing but contempt for the Tibetan "idolaters," declaring that they were completely wicked, "the greatest thieves and criminals on earth." Under patronage from the throne, lamas poured into China, often in groups of a hundred or more, demanding the same treatment they received in Tibet, where they completely dominated all levels of society. Demanding free transportation for themselves and their saleable goods aboard Kublai's extensive horse-relay transport system, they overran government lodges meant only for traveling dignitaries. The lamas also appropriated private homes, exacting free lodging, food, and, it is said, a free hand with the womenfolk.

Chinese officials were compelled to greet the detested arriving lamas at the outskirts of Peking with deep kowtows and the drinking of toasts, rites normally accorded to important envoys. People were especially aroused when the Tibetan clerics demanded and obtained freedom from Chinese prisons for numerous and often dangerous criminals, citing as their motive Buddhism's doctrine awarding religious merit to those who released captive creatures. The Chinese knew that many a freed murderer had paid the lamas to secure his liberty. In general, corrupt practices and even murders committed by the lamas went unpunished. Yet if a Chinese subject dared raise a voice or a retaliating hand against an offending lama, he was in danger of having his tongue or arm severed in punishment.

Tibetan lamas would remain the most venerated figures at court throughout the entire Mongol reign. It is well known that one of the causes of the ultimate fall of the dynasty was the palace's endless, costly religious rituals and excessive monetary donations. One emperor paid a fortune to have the lamas copy their holy books for him in gold. Lamas enticed Mongol rulers to build magnificent Tibetan-style temples, altars, and monasteries, inflicting a drain on the treasuries that would slowly impoverish the nation. Toward the end of the dynasty, two-thirds of the empire's budget was being spent on the lamas.

Another source of Chinese discontent was the proliferation of alien Muslims from subjugated Islamic lands brought in by Kublai and his successors to manage government finances. Especially clever as tax collectors, money lenders, and merchants, the Muslims were despised as avaricious, aggressive, miserly competitors. Marco Polo was convinced that the reason many Chinese deeply resented their Mongol masters was that they allowed their Saracen agents to lord it over the people and "treat them like slaves."

The most villainous of all Kublai's Muslim administrators was the notorious Achmad, who was from a town near Tashkent in Central Asia. For twenty long years Kublai granted him such unlimited control over most phases of government that many Chinese were convinced that he used sorcery to cast magic spells over the emperor. Achmad ruthlessly overburdened the people with inordinate tax increases to meet the Mongol court's insatiable need for funds. For himself, Achmad demanded heavy money bribes or the gift of a comely virgin daughter from those seeking office or favors. Records state that he boldly ravished other men's wives to indulge his "disgusting" sexual appetites. He put most of his twenty-five equally corrupt sons in office to help him amass a stupendous fortune, drove his opponents out of office, and resorted to unlawful means to expand his authority and wealth. Even many of the Mongols feared to oppose Achmad and his great power.

Finally, in 1282, when Kublai was away at his summer capital above the Great Wall, Chinese army officers (one of whom bore a special grudge in that his mother, wife, and daughter had all been "dishonored" by Achmad) assassinated the hated Muslim. When this shocking news reached Kublai, he returned to Peking in a rage and executed every man thought to be involved in the murder. Soon afterward, however, on learning of the gross iniquities and crimes perpetrated by Achmad, Kublai had his body exhumed and strung up on a pole in the bazaar. Finally, the corpse was thrown into the street, where horse-drawn carts were driven over it and the remains left for dogs to eat. Kublai next had Achmad's enormous accumulation of treasure and valuables confiscated and transferred to the imperial coffers. Later, he had all Achmad's sons who had participated in his exploitations flogged to death.

For a number of years thereafter, hoping to cut his Muslim agents down to size, Kublai enforced the death penalty for circumcision or the slaughtering of animals in the Islamic fashion.

By 1287, however, a Muslim named Sanga, who replaced Achmad as chief administrator, had convinced Kublai to revoke all his anti-Muslim measures so that merchant caravans from the Islamic world would again be willing to bring their lucrative trade to China. Court officials hated Sanga because of the inordinate power he wielded in several bureaus, including the Office of Buddhist and Tibetan Affairs. He was the most dominant figure in government. Sanga's repeated atrocities to satisfy his "disgusting carnal appetite" horrified officialdom, especially when he demanded slave girls and concubines from Korea—only the emperor did this—for his own household.

It was Sanga, together with his alien protege, a notorious Buddhist lama named Yang, whose insulting treatment of the southern Chinese aroused them to such a resurgence of Sung-loyalist feeling that the newly united nation was threatened with rebellion. Immediately after the fall of South China, these two miscreants transported the Sung empress, together with several members of her family, north to Peking to serve as hostages in the Mongol palace. Next, Sanga saw to it that lama Yang was given unlimited control over all Buddhist affairs in the South. With a vengeance, lama Yang set out to recover all buildings and lands that had once belonged to the Chinese Buddhist church but had long since been converted into imperial Sung palaces, mausoleums, and shrines. Ruthlessly, Yang demolished six royal palaces and over 100 elegant Sung tombs, altars, temples, and even the shrines where the great imperial sacrifices had been held. Yang's most serious transgression was his defilement of the Sung royal corpses. It is said that he hung the body of one of the last emperors on a tree for three days, later decapitating and burning it, and reburying the bones amidst skeletons of horses and cows. In the most brutal fashion he ransacked the corpses and Sung burial vaults for valuables, confiscating great quantities of priceless funerary relics. His take included quantities of paper money, a fortune in gold and silver, jade belts, imperial ceremonial vessels, precious shells, and fifty ounces of oversized pearls.

When Yang started construction of new Buddhist temples on the old palace grounds, his intent was to use as a cornerstone a revered stele inscribed with the Confucian classics in the Southern Sung founder's personal calligraphy. He was only prevented from this desecration by the intervention of an indignant ranking official who would not tolerate such misuse of a venerated cultural relic. The lama further oppressed and exploited the southern Chinese by forcing them to provide beautiful young women in payment for favors and services. Even Mongol officials condemned Yang's transgressions. One southern Chinese Buddhist monk publicly insulted lama Yang by loudly refusing an invitation to his home and denouncing him to his face as a grave robber.

The year 1291 brought disgrace not only to the Muslim Sanga but also to his henchman Yang. Sanga was arrested, convicted of corruption and extortion, and executed, while Yang was found guilty of unauthorized appropriation of private lands, money, and valuables for his personal use. Lama Yang was one of the few Lamaist clerics ever indicted and convicted of a crime in Yuan China.

All Yang's booty went to the national treasury, while his bevy of "wives" taken as bribe payments was transported to Peking for the Mongol harem. For years to come, the government was plagued with the tangled matter of placating some 23,000 southern peasant households whom lama Yang had listed as tax-free temple tenants, but who had actually been tilling some 3,000 acres for Yang's personal profit.

During the 1280s and 1290s, the aging Kublai Khan suffered disastrous defeats in renewed military expeditions against Japan, after that nation beheaded Mongol court envoys who had come demanding submission. When his expedition of 140,000 Chinese and 25,000 Korean troops approached Japan, a typhoon struck, dashing all Mongol hope for victory. Some 63,000 men were drowned or slaughtered on shore by the Japanese. Small wonder the Japanese called the saving storm a "Divine Wind" (kamikaze) sent by the gods. Infuriated with this devastating humiliation, Kublai was only stopped by overwhelming opposition of advisors from launching another attack, which would have brought China to financial ruin.

Meanwhile Kublai's close relative ruling in Manchuria, Nayan, a Nestorian Christian, had turned traitor and teamed up with Kublai's nephew ruling in Turkestan, Kaidu, a long-time bitter enemy. In 1287, after court diviners had prophesied victory, Kublai, at age seventy-two, carried on a palanquin mounted on the backs of four caparisoned elephants, led Mongol troops into battle. True to the predictions, he captured Nayan and had him executed according to Mongol tradition, which dictated that no imperial Mongol blood should fall on the ground for Sun and Heaven to witness. Nayan was completely wrapped and tightly bound in a carpet to be dragged about and tossed into the air until he died. As for the archenemy nephew Kaidu, he would continue to attack China's borders for seven years after Kublai Khan's death.

In 1294 Kublai died, alcoholic, obese, gouty, and despondent over the deaths of both his favorite wife and favorite son and chosen heir. He had reigned thirty-four years. A solemn caravan wound its way north to the Kentei Mountains for the burial. The precise site was never recorded and is still undiscovered. No grandiose tomb remains for one of the greatest figures in history. His grandson who succeeded him ordered officials to build a temple altar a few miles from Peking honoring Kublai Khan, and also dignified his memory with the posthumous title of Founder of the Yuan Dynasty.

None of Kublai's seven descendants who took the throne ever measured up to him in stature or ability. Most of them were too young, short-lived, incompetent, or depraved to be effective leaders. Within thirty years after Kublai's death, his great Yuan empire was falling into serious decline, as factions of the imperial family and powerful Mongol grandees battled each other for the throne in a series of bloody coups, regicides, and assassinations. Six Mongol heirs took the throne in quick succession, only to meet violent deaths after reigns of just a few years. General respect for the throne, which had been carefully nurtured by Kublai, gradually waned, as officials high and low were emboldened to indulge in rampant graft and corruption. The greed of officials exhausted the poor, causing them to rise up in revolts. Rich landlords conspired with corrupt officials to evade taxation, leaving an increased burden on destitute farmers.

The Mongol grip on the populace was further weakened as poverty increased due to a series of floods, landslides, droughts, and severe food shortages. When dikes along the Yellow River burst, inundating vast areas, the government impressed 170,000 peasants to forego the tasks of their meager livelihood to repair the extensive damage. By 1319, over seven million people were starving.

The last Mongol emperor was put on the throne at age thirteen in the year 1333, just as popular revolts were beginning throughout the East and South. Unfortunately, this ruler was a blatant voluptuary who took pleasure in the company of catamites and fell deeply under the sway of avaricious Tibetan lamas, who completely dominated his palace. In the name of religion, the lamas encouraged shocking, erotic religious dramas at court and gory sacrifices of animals and humans whose hearts and livers were offered up to appease Lamaism's all-powerful, bloodthirsty goddess Mahakali. Orgiastic rites overseen by the lamas called for sexual intercourse between devotees and consecrated temple girls—rites not unusual in Tantric temples of India and Tibet, but horrifying to the Chinese.

This emperor's repeated missions sent to Korea in search of Korean concubines finally caused such turmoil in that country that the Mongol throne was forced to grant a Korean petition seeking an end to such raids. One Korean concubine was so highly favored that the last Mongol emperor raised her to rank of empress. It so happened that she was from the same village as a Korean eunuch named P'u Pu-hua who was then in Mongol palace service, and he became her favorite eunuch. When the Korean empress's son became crown prince in 1355, she saw to it that eunuch P'u was appointed to a high official position.

By 1358 rebel fighting had so ravaged large areas of North China that refugees by the thousands flocked into Peking, where they lived under such deplorable conditions that they were dying like flies. This tragic situation gave eunuch P'u an opportunity to make a name for himself. He convinced the emperor, the crown prince, and the Korean empress, along with members of court and officials, to contribute vast amounts in the starving refugees' behalf. Eunuch P'u personally donated jade and gold belts, bars of silver, thirty-six bushels of rice and wheat, and two valuable fur coats. Now people willing to carry corpses to an excavated burial site could be paid. By 1360, 200,000 refugees had been buried, while the sick were given medicines, and their dead relatives were provided with coffins.

By this time the Mongol emperor had ruled nearly thirty years, and was allowing the crown prince to act as his personal aide and principal administrator. The Korean empress sent eunuch P'u to convince a Mongol counselor of the wisdom of having the emperor abdicate in favor of the crown prince. When the counselor refused to cooperate, she had him expelled. Eunuch P'u quickly allied himself with the counselor's replacement, and soon the two were intercepting civil and military reports which warned the throne of impending danger in the provinces. The Commissioner of Buddhist and Tibetan Affairs joined them in their evil activities. Finally, in 1363, a group of powerful censors condemned the trio in a memorial to the throne accusing them of treachery, and requesting their dismissal. The crown prince, acting for the emperor, hesitated—for the empress had wholeheartedly defended the accused—and finally had the censors demoted.

Angry memorials continued to be issued, as a number of ministers resigned, protesting the power of the eunuch and his associates. Finally, the crown prince was compelled to report the matter to the aging emperor, who had eunuch P'u and the Commissioner of Buddhist and Tibetan Affairs stripped of all rank. Not satisfied with this, a censor memorialized the throne: "These two men are the source of disaster, and must be cut down and uprooted. Their corruption, like decay of a great tree, comes from within. Under a nominal dismissal such as this, they will only continue their evil plans. If Your Majesty is weak and indecisive, their power will only grow until it is too great to be curbed. I prefer starving at home to serving with such men in court."[5]

Another censor, an uncle of the emperor, advised the crown prince:

"Eunuch P'u Pu-hua is arrogant, does not respect his superiors, and is seeking power, receiving bribes, and allowing his followers to become officials through underhanded means. P'u's behavior is the same as that of notorious eunuchs who brought past dynasties to ruin. I hope Your Highness will report this matter to the emperor and expel these criminals from government so their wrongs can be righted."[6] These accusations greatly angered the emperor, for the Korean empress had denounced all the censor's allegations. Nothing was done about the allegations, except that the censor uncle was ordered back to his fiefdom.

Soon the empress had the emperor reappoint eunuch P'u to high position, where he at once accused the censor uncle of conspiring with the throne's strongest army commander. When ordered into exile, the doughty commander refused to obey, knowing it was eunuch P'u who had instigated the order. Now, fearing the strength of the commander's forces, the emperor issued an edict which impeached eunuch P'u and his cohort, the Mongol counselor, for covering up each other's corruption and for keeping vital information from the throne. Both were "exiled," though neither left the capital. Before long, the angry commander marched his forces on Peking and refused to withdraw until eunuch P'u and his cohort were apprehended. Helpless, the emperor handed the culprits over. The commander himself beheaded the Korean eunuch P'u, and the cohort was also duly executed.

Around 1350, after monks of the Chinese Buddhist secret society called the White Lotus had been driven underground by the Mongols, this sect began promising divine aid to the exploited poor and training them for battle. The White Lotus contingent soon joined up with other rebelling peasant groups to raid and kill the rich and powerful. By this time the ineffectual Mongol government was riddled with internal strife, while the long-idle imperial armies had lost the militancy and horsemanship of their Mongol ancestors. They were powerless against small roving bandit groups.

In a feeble attempt to assert control over the agitated populace, the Mongols made the mistake of reinstating vexatious petty laws that prohibited the Chinese from wearing certain colors and from using their ever-popular written characters denoting "long life" and "happiness." Soon the Mongols were stationing spies in every district to watch movements of Chinese householders, and threatening to exterminate millions who bore certain Chinese family names. These acts infuriated the rebellious masses, who now turned their vengeance against the government as well as the wealthy.

By the early 1350s, all eastern China was in open revolt. Several insurgent leaders set up petty kingdoms of their own, and rival rebel leaders and their hordes began fighting each other over territories lost or gained.

Meanwhile, one farsighted leader, a former peasant named Chu Yuan-chang, was quietly and methodically gaining the upper hand. He was the only rebel leader who, from the start, was wise enough to envision conquest of the whole empire. Powerful landowning gentry families that at first had gathered armies to fight off attacking rebels eventually realized that Mongol rule had disintegrated and joined the insurgents. With their backing, rebel Chu came to control all South China. Nanking became his headquarters and capital city.

For twelve more years, Chu fought on to consolidate his holdings, as the Mongol court continued to expend its energies in bloody family feuds and assassinations. When, in 1368, Chu's armies finally marched on Peking, the feckless last Mongol emperor and his entourage had already abandoned the city and fled north toward Mongolia, leaving their capital to fall with hardly a struggle.

The victorious peasant leader, Chu Yuan-chang, was declared emperor and founder of the Ming Dynasty which would reign for the next 300 years. In the end, the Ming would fall to the most infamous group of eunuchs in all Chinese history, and later to another barbarian conqueror from above the Great Wall.

Notes

1. *Yuan-shih* (*History of Yuan Dynasty*), translated for the author by Li Jing, History Department, Rice University.

2. Ibid.

3. Ibid.

4. M. Komroff, *The Travels of Marco Polo.*

5. *Yuan-shih (History of Yuan Dynasty).*

6. Ibid.

16

Setting the Stage
for Another Eunuch Take-over
EARLY MING DYNASTY (A.D. 1368–1522)

The destitute peasant rebel, Chu Yuan-chang, who fought his way up to found the Ming Dynasty, is best known as Emperor Hung-wu, the title of his outstandingly successful thirty-year reign. He fixed his capital at Nanking in the South, firmly united a nation devastated by decades of bloody revolts, and proved to be the kind of ruler fourteenth-century China needed: tough-minded, fearless, and down to earth. These qualities and his abiding knowledge of the Chinese people stemmed no doubt from his hard-working peasant upbringing, together with the loss during youth of his parents and brothers to plague, a tragedy that forced him to enroll in a monastery for a time as a mendicant Buddhist monk. When insurrections broke out everywhere against the Mongol regime, Chu did not hesitate to shed monastic garb to lead his countrymen with the cry: "Throw out the Mongol barbarians and return China to Chinese rule!"

Having risen rapidly in revolutionary ranks and earned the hand of the strongest rebel leader's daughter in marriage, in some dozen years, through adroit maneuvering, Chu became the most powerful leader of all the insurgents. He was especially noted for demanding uncompromising rigid discipline in his huge, tightly organized army. Now that he was emperor, he never deviated from his conviction that China must be ruled with an iron hand. If today his policies seem unduly harsh, it must be acknowledged that he succeeded in setting up a government on such solid foundations that his House of Ming would reign for the next 300 years, despite the dire weakness of some of his successors.

To maintain Ming military preparedness and utmost respect for command, Emperor Hung-wu was pitiless in his punishment of errant army officers, whose positions were inherited by their sons. His edict of 1389 decreed that any officer who taught his sons to sing songs rather than training them in horsemanship and using the bow was to have his tongue cut out. One officer lost his upper lip and most of his nose when his son was found playing the flute and singing. Punishment for an officer who wasted his own time at chess or football was the amputation of arms and feet. An officer caught paying kickball with one of the guards lost a leg in penalty.

To prohibit military generals from accumulating power, Hung-wu ruled that no longer would they command their own "personal" forces: instead they would be rotated from army to army at the discretion of a central War Board. He was especially proud of his establishment of army camps wherein, he declared, "I keep a million soldiers without causing my subjects to contribute one grain of rice!"[1] Imperial troops worked the camp farmlands to support themselves, eliminating the age-old practice of having Chinese armies feed themselves and their horses by raiding peasant homes and crops.

When his generals and ministers became too influential for comfort, or appeared to be guilty of coveting the throne, Emperor Hung-wu had them mercilessly executed by the hundreds. In 1380, concluding that the position of prime minister was far too powerful, he abolished this vital post. "In the future," he proclaimed, "anyone who dares suggest the restoration of this position will be punished and cut into pieces and his whole family put to death."[2] This policy, which made the emperor a feared, absolute dictator, worked well only so long as the reins of government were held by someone of Hung-wu's ability and drive.

Self-conscious about his peasant background and lack of formal education, the Ming founder kept scholar-officials subdued to his will by continuing the humiliating punishment of court flogging at the least suspicion of disrespect. A palace eunuch supervised the adminstering of this dreaded punishment, and all court officials in their red robes of state were required to line up and observe. On the left stood thirty eunuchs; on the right the emperor's bodyguard of thirty men; while in the center waited 100 muscular soldiers holding bamboo whips or rods. After the decree of the monarch had been read out specifying the number of blows due the offender, a hempen sack was tied over the victim's shoulders to prevent any movement and his feet were fastened apart, leaving the buttocks bare to receive the beating. During the flogging, the culprit's head lay on the ground, where his face and mouth became clogged with dirt. A majority of the flogging victims died as a result. Those who survived had to have great amounts of dead flesh removed during a recuperation that took several months. This type of punishment was commonly administered throughout Ming Dynasty rule.

A keen student of China's long and rebellious history, Hung-wu forged his nation into shape by providing farmlands and generous tax incentives to the war-weary peasantry upon whose labors national prosperity had ever depended. At the same time, he saw to it that the landowning gentry could no longer connive with provincial sub-officials to evade land taxes. Nonetheless, Hung-wu stressed to the masses that their mandated duty was to serve and honor their superiors—the intelligentsia, gentry, imperial officials—all of whom, unlike the peasants, were exempt from forced labor on government projects.

The institution of human slavery was rampant all through the Ming era. The state itself was the greatest slave owner. Though Hung-wu condoned slavery, he ordered the freeing of innocent Chinese youths who had been sold by their parents to avoid starvation during the recent rebellions. Also, later, he had his officials buy back children sold during a terrible famine. In order that his Mongol subjects might be more rapidly sinicized, as a means to assure their loyalty, on penalty of enslavement to the government, in 1372 Hung-wu strictly forbade Mongols from marrying among their own countrymen.

It is claimed that the chief source of slaves was from captured alien prisoners of war. Some were taken into Ming armies, while most were awarded by the ruler to deserving officials as their private property. Noblemen, royalty, officials, the gentry—all had the privilege of buying and selling slaves, which many possessed in great number. One of Hung-wu's chief complaints against a condemned army general was that he had personally accumulated several hundred slaves.

One contemporary writer tells how the gentry, sparing no effort to make their own lives comfortable, allowed their slave-workers so little food and clothing that they rarely had a full meal or protection from bitter cold winter winds, adding that the gentry ordered their slaves about in the most inhuman manner, beating them mercilessly if they happen to displease. Commoners were prohibited from owning slaves, but evaded the law by listing homeless or destitute persons who came into their possession as adopted family members, and used them as farm or household slaves.

Hung-wu was especially hostile to the merchant class, despising and fearing their ability to "accumulate wealth without labor," and to monopolize the markets. If someone from the family of a simple farmer entered a trade, the entire family was denied the right to wear silk, as were all merchants. This age-old disdain of merchants is interesting, considering that Chinese tradesmen would in time be known to Europeans as "the Jews of the Orient"—astute, clever money-makers.

Acutely conscious of the disruptions caused by imperial consorts and their families in past dynasties, Hung-wu enforced severe rules of conduct to control his multitudinous court ladies. His aim was to keep them from extravagance by keeping them removed from all outside contacts, including their own family members. When court ladies requested replenishment of clothing, cosmetics, supplies of any kind, a palace administrator specially charged with overseeing needs of the harem first had to obtain the emperor's personal approval. Next, a court eunuch had to compile a report on the matter. Only then might the provisions be obtained from the official in charge of palace supplies.

Wives of ranking ministers were strictly barred from the palace except for twice-monthly ceremonial visits to pay homage to Hung-wu's reigning empress. This was his long-time wife, who proved so virtuous, the histories claim, that she declined his offer to grant high rank to her male relatives.

One of the Ming founder's cardinal principles was that both empresses and concubines be chosen from among the common people, never from noble families. Though kinsmen of the consorts were granted honors and riches, they were forbidden any say whatever in government. Lest any palace lady be tempted to flout his authority, Hung-wu had a red plaque prominently displayed in the palace, proclaiming: "Any female who dares send messages of any kind outside the palace without the ruler's express permission shall be put to death." That Hung-wu's strict controls over palace women were in general adhered to throughout the Ming era is seen in the almost complete absence of harem intrigue and consort family interference in state affairs.

Aware that court eunuchs had brought on the ruin of the former Han and Tang dynasties which he so greatly admired, Hung-wu issued the following proclamation to the Civil Office in 1369: "In ancient Chou Dynasty times the courts employed less than 100 eunuchs. Thereafter in succeeding dynasties eunuch numbers steadily increased to several thousand, resulting in dire upheavals. Since it is no longer possible to return to ancient custom, we must now take precautions to prevent recurrence of past abuses.

From now on, eunuchs shall be employed solely to perform menial household tasks. If we look for men of integrity among them, we will scarcely find one or two in a hundred; if we try to use them to gather information, they will blind us to the facts; if we give them responsible duties, they will invariably cause serious damage. It is best to make eunuchs fear the law! Never allow them to be educated or to excel in anything, lest they grow proud and uncontrollable. If eunuchs are kept in fear of the law, they will conduct themselves discreetly, and remain subdued."[3]

In 1377 a eunuch who had long served in the inner court once stepped out of line and commented on a government matter. Hung-wu dismissed him on the spot, proclaiming to a gathering of ministers that although it was said that the fall of the Han and Tang dynasties were crimes of the eunuchs, it was the rulers who actually brought on their own downfall by wrongly giving undue trust and affection to certain eunuchs. He insisted that, even though eunuchs may have wished to cause trouble, if they were denied a role in both the administration and military command, they could do no harm. "Now," he said, "although this eunuch has for a long time served me, I cannot be indulgent with him. He absolutely must go as a warning to other eunuchs."

In 1384 the monarch had a famous inscription engraved on an iron tablet and installed in front of the Nanking palace that warned: "Eunuchs are forbidden to interfere in government affairs. Those who attempt to do so will be punished by death."[4] He fixed eunuch salaries at one-tenth of a bushel of rice each month; decreed that their rank should never exceed the grade of fourth class; forbade them to wear the uniform of orthodox officials; and forbade officials of all departments to communicate with palace eunuchs by written document.

It is known that in Hung-wu's time palace eunuchs were still taken from subdued tribal or aborigine peoples, as well as from impoverished Chinese families. Many of his eunuchs, however, were aliens. In 1384 the vassal king of Northern Vietnam presented thirty of his castrated subjects to the emperor of China as tribute. Seven years later, Emperor Hung-wu himself demanded 200 eunuchs in tribute from Korea. Seemingly in violation of his own decree, Hung-wu once sent two of his Mongol eunuchs to the northern border to barter with alien tribes for army horses—possibly because none of his legitimate envoys knew the barbarian's language.

If the Ming founder's edicts controlling the use of palace eunuchs had been adhered to by his successors his dynasty may have played a much different—and, possibly, longer—role in history. Later in the dynasty, Ming eunuchs would come to surpass in infamy and power the eunuchs of all other dynasties. This deplorable state of affairs was in large part due to the complete reversal of Hung-wu's eunuch policy soon after his death.

Six years before the end of his reign, Hung-wu suffered a tragic loss: His son and heir apparent died—a gentle, pleasant man in whom the aging monarch had placed great hope. The deceased prince's child, still a mere boy, was then named heir, but the possibility of a subsequent coup against an underage ruler so worried Hung-wu that he commenced another purge against ministers and generals whose loyalty he suspected. These men, along with thousands of their associates, were put on trial and systematically executed.

When Emperor Hung-wu died within a few years, a group of loyal ministers—fearing that his sons might challenge the authority of the newly enthroned boy-emperor—proposed that all Ming princes in the provinces be stripped of their armies. This provoked a revolt led by Yung-lo, the Prince of Yen, the most powerful of the Ming founder's sons, who ruled the Peking area. He marched his armies south in great force to meet with fierce resistance, but he captured the Nanking capital in 1402 and declared himself emperor. During the take-over, the young emperor mysteriously disappeared, presumably burned to ashes in the razing of the Nanking palace. Since this supposition could never be verified, for some time the usurping conqueror lived with the nagging worry that his nephew might have fled unharmed and could one day return to challenge him for the throne.

Fortunately for Ming China, the victorious Prince of Yen inherited his father's vitality, forceful character, and leadership ability. Yung-lo's rule followed the founder's sound, if ruthless, principles, which tended to strengthen the foundations of the dynasty and restore China's prosperity and her recognition throughout Asia as a great power.

Historians agree, however, that Yung-lo made a grave mistake when he completely rejected his father's policy of curtailing duties of palace eunuchs. His drastic reversal of this policy came about when Yung-lo was besieging the Nanking palace. He met with strong opposition from the Nanking court ministers, who considered his attempted take-over contrary to the Mandate of Heaven. However, the Nanking court eunuchs came to Yung-lo's aid. They readily deserted their young emperor to act as informers, providing Yung-lo with invaluable military and palace intelligence. Once securely ensconced on the Nanking throne, Yung-lo, unable to trust ministers and officials who resented him, lavishly rewarded the eunuch turncoats with important official posts, high rank, special privileges, and even military commands.

Hence, though Yung-lo himself kept the eunuchs under rigid control, the positions he awarded them gave them the opportunity to start consolidating such power that under weaker Ming emperors to come they would all but rule China.

In his frantic determination to eliminate all enemies, Yung-lo promptly had all ministers who opposed his usurpation slaughtered or made slaves to the state, at the same time inflicting cruel tortures on all their family members, relatives, friends, and backers. Thousands perished in Yung-lo's tyrannical purge. Taught by the relative ease with which he himself had been able to take over the throne, he further protected his position by depriving his princely brothers of their armies, forbidding them to leave their territories to visit each other or the ancestral Ming family tombs, or even come to the rescue of the ruler himself unless he expressly so ordered.

Eunuchs sent by Yung-lo into the provinces to open up and supervise gold and silver mines were so inexperienced that the attempt failed miserably at great expense to the government. One mine under eunuch supervision barely produced eight ounces of gold for the imperial treasury, in return for the labor of 6,000 miners under deplorable conditions for months. And beyond doubt, eunuchs whom Yung-lo placed in army commands, untrained as they were in military affairs, were responsible for a decided decline in military discipline and preparedness. As early as 1419, Yung-lo found it necessary to threaten orthodox army generals and War Board members with capital punishment unless improvements in the armies were quickly forthcoming.

Yung-lo tried to enforce his father's policy of putting to death Chinese subjects who had themselves or their sons castrated for palace service. Even persons who failed to report such cases were liable to execution. Yet, given the incessant palace demands for ever more eunuchs, this practice was never stamped out, especially in famine-struck areas, where the poor, rather than submit to starvation or slavery, looked upon castration as their only means of staying alive.

During the early years of his reign in Nanking, the ever-suspicious Yung-lo used the palace guards as spies throughout the city, to listen and watch for the slightest signs of disloyalty. After moving the Ming capital north to his old headquarters at Peking in 1421, Yung-lo established a permanent secret police corps totally under the charge of his eunuchs— the first of its kind in China. He allowed his eunuch police to operate their own prisons, which came to be feared as places of horror where countless loyal ministers or anyone considered in opposition to the eunuchs lost their lives in tortures using unspeakable devices. The eunuch-controlled police organization was to remain a fixed institution all down through Ming rule, doing untold damage to officials and the entire nation.

Once when Emperor Yung-lo went on a hunting expedition, he left his favorite general in charge of the palace, an important trust, for which the general felt deeply honored. Foreseeing the very real danger that some envious official might seek to do him injury by falsely accusing him of misconduct with the palace ladies, the loyal general had himself castrated. Just as he anticipated, when the emperor returned, an enemy minister falsely reported that the general had had intercourse with several imperial women. In reply to this accusation, the general related how he had made himself a eunuch and showed Yung-lo his emasculation. Struck by such personal loyalty, Yung-lo made the general chief of the eunuch staff. When this eunuch died, the emperor deified him by official decree and had his images placed inside altars in a temple dedicated to the god of war. Ever afterwards, eunuchs considered the general their patron saint and worshipped at his shrine. At the same time as he canonized the eunuch general, Yung-lo bestowed a large piece of land some four miles from Peking for use as a cemetery for palace eunuchs.

Yung-lo did not hesitate to use his eunuchs as important diplomats and envoys throughout the empire and even to alien countries. By far his most celebrated ambassador was eunuch Cheng-ho, whom he dispatched abroad as commander over seven different naval expeditions between 1405 and 1422. Each voyage required some fifty enormous, specially built sailing vessels carrying 27,000 men, many of whom were eunuchs. In behalf of the emperor of China, eunuch Cheng-ho called on and intimidated rulers of states throughout the South Seas and visited Ceylon, India, Persia, Arabia, and even the African coast, where he obtained a live giraffe for the Son of Heaven's exotic menagerie.

Nobody knows Emperor Yung-lo's purpose in sending out these mighty sailing flotillas, especially in the face of strong disapproval from top ministers, who apparently resented the inordinate power given commander Cheng-ho, who was not only a eunuch but a Muslim from Yunnan as well. Other, isolationist officials abhorred the tremendous expenditures for contacting barbarians in faraway lands who should be of no interest whatever to the Chinese empire. It is possible that, being a usurper, Yung-lo sought to bolster his reputation and power at home and abroad with this magnificent display of naval force, inducing Asian rulers to pay him homage as well as tribute in curious and rare items from their distant lands. Indeed, as a result of eunuch Cheng-ho's missions, sixteen Southeast Asian countries for a time sent spectacular embassies, consisting of as many as 200 men, bearing exotic and valuable gifts in tribute to the Chinese Son of Heaven. Of these magnificent state visits, one contemporary minister exclaimed, "Since olden times, no one has ever seen such splendor as in our day!"[5]

It was also speculated that Emperor Yung-lo originally sent Cheng-ho in a vain search for the young nephew he had ousted from the Nanking throne. Cheng-ho's expeditions opened up and gave impetus to great waves of Chinese migration to Malaysia, Indonesia, and the Philippines, exposing vast Asian regions to the influence of Chinese civilization.

Though Ming histories give him short shrift, eunuch Cheng-ho must have been a most impressive, colorful, and skillful navigator, commander, and diplomat. This writer has observed on the island of Taiwan that Chinese from the mainland consider Cheng-ho a semi-divine hero, honoring his memory on the first of July with special rites and offerings.

Yung-lo also sent a eunuch named Chen Cheng on three diplomatic missions to Central Asia. On one occasion he traveled as far as Transoxiania, the empire of Tamerlane. Another palace eunuch, Hou Hsien, was dispatched as an envoy to Tibet and Nepal, and Bengal, India.

Thus, under Emperor Yung-lo, Ming China prospered, and gained great prestige in foreign places.

Yung-lo completely rebuilt Peking, replenishing his new capital with splendid palaces and shrines exemplified in the still extant Forbidden City, and the incredibly beautiful white marble Temple of Heaven where he and all future emperors of China conducted the great imperial sacrifices. It is said that the silver, gold, gems, and precious treasures sent from the four corners of the empire and alien states overflowed the ten caves used by the imperial treasury for storage.

After personally leading several successful military expeditions to put down incursions of the northern Mongol enemy, Yung-lo died in 1424, while returning from a victory. Some sources intimate that his death resulted from an elixir of immortality he had taken from the hands of Taoist priests in his entourage.

Unfortunately for the Ming Dynasty and for China, none of Yung-lo's successors would ever compare with him or his father for strong, decisive leadership. The most that historians say is that the next few Ming rulers carried out their duties as conscientiously and wisely as their limited abilities allowed. Thereafter, Ming rulers, almost without exception, were so negligent, weak, or self-indulgent that they let decisions fall to eunuch intimates, who maintained incredible power to the end of the dynasty.

Within ten years of Yung-lo's death, the northern Mongols had regained sufficient strength to resume forays into China, while the power Yung-lo had given palace eunuchs was already being felt. By 1428 Ming ruler Hsuan-te had put down a rebellion of one of the Ming princes. During the rebellion, court ministers had seemed to support the rebel. As a result, this monarch, like his predecessor, turned to eunuchs as the only agents he felt he could trust.

Now eunuch commanders and generals became familiar figures in the provinces. They were also frequently used in special assignments to requisition government supplies and supervise state projects. In 1425 Hsuan-te was advised by a censor in Chekiang province that eunuchs he had sent out to requisition court commodities had bilked the people, amassed far more goods than required, and seriously disrupted local trading. "How could we have foreseen that eunuchs would make trouble like this!"[6] exclaimed Hsuan-te, and put an immediate stop to the eunuchs' illegal activities. In 1427 he put eunuch Chang Shan to death for corruption and abuses while on commission out in the countryside; and four years later, when it was discovered that eunuch Yuan Chi had organized a large-scale network of graft, Hsuan-te had him executed by slow torture and ten of his eunuch associates beheaded. Thus, eunuch influence at this time seems to have been a potential threat to government stability, but not actually disruptive.

In 1432 Hsuan-te, apparently alarmed at corruption among the Buddhist priesthood, announced, "The Buddha originally transformed men so they became good, but now Buddhists rarely observe the warnings and laws, and rarely devote themselves to ancestral ways."[7] He complained that Buddhists everywhere were collecting contributions from the people to be wasted on ornate monasteries and shrines, and expensive idols, and ordered the chief censor to promulgate clarifications of regulations governing such matters, with warnings against all violations.

In the following year, annoyed that many of his palace eunuchs were being converted to Buddhism—some even deserting their posts to become monks—he assembled all senior eunuchs and lectured them: "There is an ever-constant way by which a man may establish his character. As a subject, he must be loyal, as a son he must be filial. A loyal and filial man will inevitably enjoy good fortune. Is it necessary to be a vegetarian and recite Buddhist sutras to have good fortune? The Buddha only taught that men should set their minds on goodness. The heavenly palaces and subterranean Hells he spoke of, after all, exist only in the mind. If the mind is fixed on good thoughts, that alone is Heaven; if the mind evokes evil thoughts, that is Hell. This is why the sutras say that Buddhahood exists in the mind. Hereafter, take warning: set your minds on goodness—that is true reverence. Any of you who dare desert and become monks will be put to death, with no hope of pardon."[8] He then ordered the chief censor to warn all local civil and military authorities to keep watch for eunuchs who shaved their heads to become monks, threatening the death penalty for anyone who gave them protection.

Emperor Hsuan-te once again opened a classroom in the palace and appointed four imperial academy scholars to educate almost 300 castrated boys of around ten years of age. Some of these educated eunuchs would become imperial "secretaries" to later Ming emperors, inner-court agents frequently used to communicate—and interfere with—outer-court affairs. Historians point to Hsuan-te's education of eunuchs as a seed from which eunuch dictatorship would grow.

Ming armies and military settlements steadily deteriorated under eunuch supervision. Troops were misused in nonmilitary labors such as transporting the great quantities of food needed to support the growing Peking capital. They were also used as labor in the building of scores of grandiose imperial edifices. Soldiers were soon deserting in such numbers that after a fierce Mongol invasion in 1434 the government was forced to hire mercenaries, a great drain on the treasuries.

Yet the throne continued its flagrant show of munificence and splendor, heaping donations and elaborate gifts upon visiting alien envoys, deserving court ministers, and the ever-increasing numbers of imperial family members. Frequent donations of grain ordered by the throne for areas struck by natural disasters were also taking a toll. The imperial largess was considered vital in these cases, though it was questionable how much of the relief, which had to pass through the hands of dishonest eunuch overseers and sub-officials, actually reached the starving people.

The next Ming emperor, Ying Tsung, ruled from 1438 to 1449 and again from 1457 to 1464. He was brought up in the palace according to protocols of elaborate etiquette, isolated from ordinary human contacts. He soon fell under the influence of his only intimate companions and servants, the eunuchs. During his first reign, a widely despised eunuch who had been educated in the palace school managed to gain inordinate control over the throne. Eunuch Wang Chen had the complete confidence of the emperor and became so powerful that he denied ministers imperial audiences to discuss state business unless the matter suited his own aims. So great was his influence that officials feared to report illegal excesses of the eunuchs for fear of provoking Wang Chen's wrath and retaliation.

By this time the number of arrests and executions by the eunuch secret police force, claiming they were carrying out the emperor's orders, had reached alarming proportions. Judges from the Board of Punishments were rendered impotent, daring not to protest lest they themselves be accused and sent to the eunuch's political prison.

Eunuch Wang Chen encouraged Emperor Ying Tsung to contribute heavily to religious sects, setting an example by lavishing a great part of his own ill-gained wealth on the construction of Buddhist monasteries and shrines. On Wang Chen's urging, the ruler spent several hundred thousand silver tael and the labor of 10,000 workers on the grandest temple ever constructed in Peking. During Ying Tsung's reign, over 200 religious shrines were built in the capital, resulting in an astonishing increase in the number of Buddhist and Taoist monks in Peking. Each abbot and even common monks kept a retinue of sometimes a dozen retainers, who went about the city demanding alms from the gullible and the poor.

By 1449 eunuch Wang Chen had usurped such awesome influence over the throne that he was able to persuade the inexperienced twenty-one-year-old Emperor Ying Tsung to lead a capital army of some one million men into battle against the Mongols threatening at the northern border. Eunuch Wang Chen's underlying reason for the campaign was to honor his own family and display his power in his native area by entertaining the emperor in his home when the great Ming armies passed through Huai Lai city, some fifty miles northwest of Peking. Not far from Peking, they were temporarily halted by violent rainstorms, causing official advisors to plead with the emperor to turn back his ill-prepared armies. Their intervention so angered eunuch Wang Chen, who had made himself commander-in-chief, that he intimidated and humiliated other objecting high ministers now arriving from Peking, forcing them to kneel on the ground for hours to await an audience with the ruler, and to crawl on their knees when entering the ruler's tent.

Despite the opposition, the eunuch and his Ming monarch led the great armies forth to face the Mongol enemy, only to be surrounded at Huai Lai by hordes of swift barbarian cavalrymen and all but annihilated. The main Chinese imperial forces perished; less than 10,000 Chinese soldiers survived. The Chinese Son of Heaven was captured and carried away a prisoner of the Mongols in total disgrace. The commander-in-chief, eunuch Wang Chen, was slain in battle.

When the remnants of the exhausted Ming army retreated back to Peking, the people were panic-stricken. No one at court knew what to do. An emergency government was set up to defend the capital, with a brother of the captured Ming ruler on the throne. After years of fruitless negotiations for a ransom, the Mongols lost interest in it and allowed Emperor Ying Tsung to be brought home alive.

On regaining the throne in 1457, Ying Tsung promptly changed the title of his reign, hoping to reverse the calamitous humiliation to China caused by eunuch Wang Chen. After the Huai Lai disaster, never again would Ming armies recover their former strength.

No sooner was he back on the throne than Ying Tsung found himself faced with an attempted revolt of another powerful eunuch, Tsao Chi-hsiang. This once-favored eunuch had been awarded hundreds of acres of land by the throne, to which he had been adding great tracts by appropriating fields of helpless farmers. After his unmasking and ultimate downfall in 1461, eunuch Tsao's entire landholdings were confiscated by the House of Ming.

Palace extravagances during the second reign of Ying Tsung began to exhaust Ming treasuries. When Ming armies were putting down revolting Miao tribals in South China, 1,565 aborigine boys were captured, castrated, and sent to Peking to enlarge the mushrooming eunuch corps. In 1460 Ying Tsung issued an edict demanding 7,000 additional bolts of silk from provincial factories—above and beyond the huge quota regularly allotted him—to be distributed mostly as imperial largess. Everywhere the common people were becoming bankrupt under the burdens of ever-increasing taxation and governmental corruption at all levels. Certain districts became centers for rebels, vagrants, bandits, and discontents, who terrorized and robbed the local people as well as central government representatives. Their numbers increased as the poor became poorer and joined their ranks, preferring to be killed as rebels than die from hunger under growing injustices of a corrupt throne.

From this time on, Ming China was to pay great sums for mercenary armies not only to protect the border from northern enemies, but also to protect her people in the provinces from their own countrymen who had turned to banditry. The government, suffering from perpetual financial shortages, had to resort to selling offices and titles of honor, which brought inexperienced men whose only interest was self-enrichment into government.

When Emperor Cheng-hua took the Ming throne in 1465, an outspoken court minister advised him that it had now become almost routine for officials to seek promotions through bribes demanded by powerful palace eunuchs. They then had to rely on and continue to pay the eunuchs for protection and favors. "The eunuchs are selling official rank like merchandise," he admonished.[9] However, this monarch was even more susceptible to eunuch domination than his predecessor. Cheng-hua stuttered so badly that he avoided audiences and contact with officials whenever possible, which allowed more power to a eunuch faction headed by arrogant chief eunuch Wang Chih. Before long, ranking court ministers were so afraid of this power-hungry eunuch that they groveled before him with gifts and flattering attention as if he were a prime minister.

One top-ranking censor regularly honored eunuch Wang Chih with innumerable visits. Other high ministers who also wished to ingratiate themselves, begged the censor to arrange an audience with the great eunuch. When the censor had done this, they then asked him if it was necessary to kneel before eunuch Wang Chih on entering his presence. Indignant, the censor declared, "It is unheard of for highest ministers to bend their knee before any official!"[10] However, on the day of the audience, when the censor had entered the eunuch's quarters to announce his colleagues waiting outside, they managed to peek in and observe him on his knees, kowtowing before Wang Chih. Thus, on being admitted, the ministers, too, prostrated themselves before the eunuch. Afterwards, the censor derided his colleagues for their "undignified behavior," until one minister silenced him by saying, "We saw someone just ahead of us kowtow, and were only following his example."[11]

By this time poor parents of large families in certain districts were castrating two-month-old infant sons for palace servitude. Many of these died under the crude home surgery. Of the ones who survived, however, many found such favor with the emperor that they were able to obtain official rank for themselves and all their male family members. Often the wealth accumulated by these eunuchs rivaled that of high officials. Thus, the practice of home castration of male infants increased, especially since it was known that every year the Board of Ceremonies was ordered to admit several thousand new eunuchs to the palace. Eventually, the numbers of eunuchs presenting themselves became so great that thousands were being rejected, though this did nothing to stem the home castrations. Finally in 1492 an order was issued reinforcing earlier Ming edicts: Both those who had their sons castrated and those who performed the operation were to be executed, and anyone failing to report instances of home castration would be exiled to distant borders.

By 1466 living conditions were so bad in certain areas that the destitute were selling great numbers of their children into slavery for a pittance, even to foreign Buddhist monks and visiting merchants. On hearing this, Emperor Cheng-hua decreed that such youngsters should be repurchased at state expense, and that border officials should prohibit aliens from leaving the country with Chinese children in their possession.

Emperor Cheng-hua was a devout Buddhist, but occasionally favored Taoism as well. He donated so much towards building religious shrines in Peking, that soon a long uninterrupted chain of temple rooftops could be seen from as far away as the Western Hills outside the capital. In the twelfth year of his reign, 100,000 monks were ordained; ten years later another 200,000 were ordained. One official calculated that the amount of rice needed to feed the more than 500,000 monks in all the monasteries could easily supply the entire capital population for over a year.

At the urging of his eunuchs, Emperor Cheng-hua ordered the opening of twenty-one new gold mines. Over half a million miners were employed, but at the end of a year, the eunuch supervisors—after lining their own pockets—could present only fifty-three ounces of gold to the throne.

This emperor reorganized and enlarged the palace guards and eunuch police force to spy and punish bribe-taking by officials. This practice of spying had now gotten completely out of control, yet the eunuchs charged with this duty accepted more bribes than the officials they were spying on ever had.

Since the very beginning of the Ming era, Tibetan and Mongolian Buddhist lamas had been visiting Peking as tribute embassies bearing gifts and receiving lavish amounts of largess in return. For the Ming throne could never allow itself to be outdone in a show of generosity. Though the Court of Entertainment supplied the visiting monks with all their daily needs, the lamas unashamedly—and successfully—demanded more. The lamas were welcomed with great enthusiasm and favor by Emperor Cheng-hua, fascinated as he was with their claims of being able to work magic and cast secret spells. He honored them with lavish entertainments, banquets, and gifts, and saw to it that they lived in Peking like princes, carried about in sedan chairs, and accompanied by imperial Chinese bodyguards. Even government officials and nobles had to give way to the lamas in the streets. In this way, much government resources were expended on religion, instead of the needs of the populace.

The Chinese had long feared that punishing criminals had a mysterious influence on nature and the elements. Even the Ming founder had ruled that executions should be carried out only after autumn, when the cosmic forces were in balance, lest an execution should upset the natural order of the universe. When the new Emperor Hung-Chih took the throne in 1488, upset by his predecessor's practice of allowing palace eunuchs to imprison and execute all who opposed them, he meekly cautioned: "If sentences are just, the people will willingly submit; even Nature is in accord with such punishments. But if the innocent are sentenced wrongly, Heaven may punish us by sending natural disasters. Of late the capital has suffered excessive rain and floods, while in Nanking there have been strange phenomena and violent thunderstorms, giving us great anxiety. We are asking ourselves whether they be the result of wrongful sentences [by the eunuchs]."[12]

This Ming ruler, who became known for his efforts to implement reforms, led a frugal, virtuous life, and conscientiously tried to rid government of the universal corruption that was debilitating the entire nation. One of his first moves was to correct the evil effects of palace spending on Buddhism. However, by this time it was impossible to control powerful eunuchs who continued to appropriate treasury funds, or even use their own, to construct religious edifices—a practice which made them appear as grandees.

One official listed the reasons why the land now under cultivation had shrunk to half that at the beginning of the Ming Dynasty: the throne's continuing donations of land to the ever-increasing numbers of Ming princes; the devastation of roving bandits; errors, neglect, and manipulation of official land records; falsified tax returns by dishonest landlords; and extravagant donations of acreages by the throne to favored officials, eunuchs, and religious institutions. Yet covetous nobles, ministers, and influential eunuchs continued to petition the throne for more lands, and often as not received them. Other greedy notables appropriated to themselves both government and private farm lands, covering their crimes by falsely reporting that the ousted farmers had been occupying the land illegally.

Emperor Hung-chih made every attempt to halt all these abuses and to find workable remedies for them. At least he saw to it that lands which had been confiscated by now-deceased eunuchs were returned to the people, along with some government lands which military officers and influential dignitaries had misappropriated from the military settlements. However, the abuses had gotten so far out of control that they were never to be stemmed, even though Ming law threatened offenders with exile for life.

During this reign it was found that widespread desertions by soldiers were due in large part to the corruption of field officers who were pocketing the pay of the troops. By the end of the reign, the once-powerful capital military forces had lost their vitality and were no longer fit for battle. Even the common people saw imperial troops as lax, arrogant, and unreliable. It was said that "as soon as they are brought face to face with the northern Mongols, they at once turn and take flight; hence they are mocked by the enemy, and even cause our local border militia to lose spirit."[13]

Historians found precious little good to say about the next Ming ruler, the fifteen-year-old Cheng-te, who came to the throne in 1506. He became one of the most extravagant, uncaring, and pleasure-bent of all late Ming rulers. He was entirely controlled by the eunuchs who had raised him. A frustrated adventurer, Emperor Cheng-te loved sports and gaming, often roaming the capital in disguise, seeking thrills in the company of eunuchs and sycophantic courtiers.

Early in his reign, a court minister memorialized the throne with a warning against Cheng-te's demands for more eunuchs: "There are already tens of thousands of eunuchs in the imperial complex, yet Your Majesty has now ordered the Board of Ceremonies to present another 500 castrated boys under the age of fifteen. In what service will Your Majesty employ them? It is only human nature for peasants to desire honors and riches. If they are encouraged to castrate their sons in the hope of palace employment, how much more often will they do so when they hear of new edicts demanding ever more eunuchs? I am afraid the damage to the nation will be irreparable."[14] Such warnings received little attention from the Ming throne.

During Cheng-te's reign, when his Palace of Cloudless Heaven celebrated the annual Festival of Lanterns at the end of the New Year holidays, thousands of gorgeous varicolored paper lanterns hung glowing from all the connecting verandas and pavilions. A sudden gust of wind caused one lantern to burst into flames, which ignited the surrounding area in minutes. Emperor, guests, and palace ladies scattered, screaming in terror. Dozens of eunuch workers, unencumbered by the long, embroidered gowns of the celebrities, rushed to man the hand pumps, but by this time even the lanterns decorating the water works were afire. Other eunuchs, aware that the palace was doomed, frantically attempted to salvage imperial treasures, appropriating most of them for themselves. But in accord with the eunuch code, it is claimed, so that all would have an equal chance to grab prize items, the eunuchs took turns at the futile job of pumping water. Even the guards deserted their fire-fighting posts to pillage the buildings for artifacts. As the charred remnants of the palace later cooled in the night air, the chief eunuch reported the total loss to the emperor, who blithely ordered that the palace at once be rebuilt "more beautiful than before, filled with treasures more valuable and magnificent than those which have been lost in the fire."

Completely neglecting imperial duties, Emperor Cheng-te allowed governmental authority to fall into the hands of a notorious chief eunuch named Liu-chin, who soon usurped all but complete control. This eunuch had made himself a great favorite with the empress dowager, who saw that he was raised to a rank just below the emperor. His greatest recommendation for her favor seemed to be his ability to write equally well with either hand. He succeeded in his first year of getting rid of all court eunuchs who were not of his faction.

Eunuch Liu-chin was so rapacious that he stopped at nothing, even the possible ruin of his country, to fill his own coffers. He once had a spring on Ten-Prospect Hill west of Peking enlarged at great expense and labor, hoping that an increased flow of water from the spring would flood the entire area around the capital, thus necessitating the expenditure of enormous government funds to repair the damage, which would be very profitable to him, since he would oversee the spending. After squandering immense sums—including much of his own money—on the project, he was compelled to give the whole thing up as a failure.

This eunuch secured, in entirely official form, the emperor's permission to issue all commands himself. He meted out terrible punishments for officials who stood in his way. On one occasion when he suspected that ministers had denounced him in an anonymous letter, he forced 300 of these top-ranking gentlemen to kneel for half a day in front of the palace before ordering them off to the dreaded eunuch-run prison to be murdered.

Like other Ming eunuchs before him, Liu-chin succeeded in distracting the emperor from his duties, encouraging him to become so preoccupied with licentious pleasures, hobbies, and frivolous interests, that the eunuch was left a free hand in state affairs. He deliberately delayed taking important matters to the ruler until the ruler was absorbed in one of his pastimes, for interruptions so annoyed the Son of Heaven that Liu-chin would be impatiently dismissed with orders to handle the matter himself. Before long Liu-chin was making all imperial decisions, often without the monarch even being aware of them.

Eunuch Liu-chin became an expert in stealing from the palace treasury, and personally collected large amounts of money from the provinces by levying a special tax for his own benefit. He confiscated so many acres from the people and turned them into estates for himself or the throne, that half the land around Peking became imperial property, leaving so little for peasant farmers that they were unable to pay taxes.

When a palace eunuch by chance discovered that chief eunuch Liu-chin planned to use his tremendous, misbegotten wealth to stage a revolt, the eunuch informed powerful officials, who then had the informer appointed as army commander. The eunuch commander and his forces attacked Liu-chin's mansion as he slept, arresting him and all his supporters. A search of his mansion revealed several hundred thousand gold and silver bars and coins, two gold suits of armor, 3,000 gold rings and broaches, and 4,062 belts studded with precious gems. The total value exceeded the annual budget of the empire. All was seized and confiscated for the state treasury.

Meanwhile, spendthrift Emperor Cheng-te squandered government funds on his pleasures, once ordering factories to contribute to the throne some 17,000 bolts of silk and over 300,000 pieces of exquisite porcelain, most of which would be doled out in gifts. Frequently this emperor sent official missions to the southern coast to buy up pearls—on one occasion demanding 800,000 of these gems from the warm southern seas.

In the end, his "Eight Eunuch Tigers," as his chief eunuch attendants were known, had so encouraged his participation in vicious orgies in the exotic palace "Leopard Rooms," that he died a horrible death—the nature of which was never revealed—indulging himself in this cruelly entertaining setting.

About this time, a learned eunuch, Liu Jo Yu, left a detailed account of the functions performed in twenty-four official agencies of the Ming eunuch corps. One department had charge of construction and engineering projects throughout the nation, including supervising repairs of the princely mansions and the tombs of the emperors. A eunuch from Vietnam was the genius who constructed all the ponds, castle gate tower, and palaces in Peking. These building projects proved to be extremely lucrative for the eunuchs, providing ample room for graft. In the first year of the Tien-chi reign, 30,000 of the gold taels granted by the emperor to build an imperial mausoleum were pocketed by the eunuchs. Rumor had it that, in eunuch hands, buildings and fixtures for the imperial court cost several hundred times more than they should have. Another source of graft for eunuchs was in the procurement of elaborate furniture and game boards made from mother-of-pearl, ivory, rosette, and sandalwood for the palace.

Eunuchs also looked after the emperor's horses and elephants, saw to the cleaning up and lighting of incense and altar candles for the emperor to worship his ancestors at the Ming cemeteries, and prepared meals three times a day, to be sacrificed for the imperial ancestors and to be consumed at the court and royal banquets. The ruler's meals were prepared by one of the chief eunuchs. Eunuchs also oversaw the making of imperial seals; the manufacture of the emperor's wardrobe, headgear, and footwear; and the sweeping of roads before the ruler as he journeyed forth in his palanquin. They were in charge of firewood and charcoal for the palace, and kept the ditches dredged and water tanks at the palace for fire-fighting full of water. Other eunuchs, clad in brilliant garments, were employed to play various instruments as they led imperial processions, beat drums for the great yearly Dragon Boat Festival, and stage theatricals, which sometimes used as many as 200 eunuch actors. Others produced toilet paper for the eunuch corps and operated the eunuchs' bathhouse, and only eunuchs were trusted to produce and handle imperial firearms in times of war. Eunuchs looked after the outside "Cold Palace," in which unwanted or accused court ladies were kept in confinement, and oversaw the making of eunuchs' headgear and seasonal garments. They served in the innumerable palace warehouses, acted as timekeepers, and even looked after the palace cats. Twelve grand eunuchs acted as chiefs over the twelve eunuch bureaus and often became exceedingly wealthy doing so, as did many in menial jobs. One scholar was amazed to learn that a fine Peking mansion with magnificent flower gardens where many sweepers worked was the villa of a eunuch whose sole function was to supervise the cart drivers.

One eunuch, titled Chief of the Imperial Bedchamber, dealt exclusively with the nighttime relations between the monarch and his consort and concubines. When the ruler had sex with any of his women, the date was duly recorded by bedchamber eunuchs to serve as proof, in case of conception. As for his favorite concubines, green nameplates of each, called "jade tablets," were prepared and dished up on a silver tray after the emperor was served his evening meal. The eunuch would kneel before him holding the tray high above his head and the emperor made his selection by turning a nameplate face down. The chief eunuch of the bedchamber would then strip the chosen concubine, wrap her in a feather quilt, and carry her on his back to the emperor's bed. He then waited outside the room a given length of time, after which he would shout, "Time is up!" Some say this timing of the ruler's nocturnal pleasures originated as a means to keep emperors from indulging excessively in sex, which, it was thought, might ruin his health.

Thus, by this time, eunuchs had made themselves indispensable in every aspect of palace life and in the running of the Ming government.

Emperor Cheng-te, too, was infatuated with the Buddhist lamas from Tibet who streamed into Peking. He once spent a veritable fortune to bring to Peking a grand lama worshipped in his homeland as the "Living Buddha." This man traveled through China in grand style, and when he arrived in the capital, he and his entire company were honored with costly gifts. Again, when the Board of Ceremonies refused a donation to a visiting lama to bury his superior, the emperor overruled the decision and granted him 2,000 silver taels. Not infrequently, Emperor Cheng-te dressed himself up in lama robes and performed extravagant religious ceremonies in the palace shrine. He was even known to bestow upon Tibetan abbots the high honorary Chinese title of Imperial Teacher.

On top of all the young emperor's extravagances, he indulged his pleasure with extensive, costly army games, constantly assuming new military titles of honor as if he had actually been to war.

Thus, in 1521, when Emperor Cheng-te died—which may be considered the mid-point of Ming rule—the once-great Ming empire was starting to sink into financial ruin and decay.

Notes

1. Albert Chan, *Glory and Fall of the Ming Dynasty.*
2. Ibid.
3. Ibid.
4. Ibid.
5. Ibid.
6. Charles O. Hucker, *The Censorial System of Ming China.*
7. Ibid.
8. Ibid.
9. Albert Chan, *Glory and Fall of the Ming Dynasty.*
10. Ibid.
11. Ibid.
12. Ibid.
13. Ibid.
14. Ibid.

17

Eunuch Infamy and Power
Reach Highest Peak

LATE MING DYNASTY (AD. 1522-1644)

During the next 100 years, the former glory and strength of the once great Ming Empire slowly eroded away as palace eunuchs increasingly usurped control.

Ming Emperor Chia-ching, who ruled from 1522 to 1566, at first showed great promise. As a youth, he dealt severely with his eunuchs and kept them under control. He once had two eunuchs of the secret police executed for atrocities committed in their political prison. Unfortunately though, in the last half of his reign Chia-ching became so addicted to Taoism that the quest for immortality became the ruling passion of his life. As early as mid-reign he tried to abdicate in favor of his son, that he might devote full time to becoming a divine immortal. Dissuaded from resigning, he began sending agents to the four corners of the empire in search of the magic elixir of longevity. He held palace religious ceremonies that lasted day and night for months, and allowed his Taoist priests to severely defame the tenets of Buddhism far and wide.

Such was this ruler's Taoist zeal that scholar-officials who claimed to know the secrets of longevity, or who composed Taoist essays and poems praising the immortals, won rapid promotion. The writings of a shrewd, unscrupulous, power-hungry official named Yen Sung so pleased the emperor that he promoted him to grand secretary, an office this scoundrel held for twenty years, very nearly wrecking the empire during that tenure. Another official, who presented the monarch with a new immortality drug, was at once made president of the Board of Ceremonies, a position the emperor later granted to a Taoist priest, together with a collection of ranks and honors such as no minister had ever received since the dynasty's beginning.

Rumors of auspicious Taoist omens were freely invented to please the infatuated ruler. Every day sycophantic officials brought in good tidings and symbolic curiosities which filled the Son of Heaven with gladness: odd wheat plants having multiple stems; an unusual turtle of five colors; reports of white cranes (a symbol of longevity) seen overhead at the time of imperial sacrifices. All bearers of such tidings received high praise and substantial rewards from the throne.

Other officials and courtiers, seeking imperial favor, went to great lengths to encourage Chia-ching in his belief in Taoist magic. As he relaxed one evening in a palace courtyard, he suddenly spied behind an awning a peach (an ancient emblem of immortality). Attending courtiers promptly declared it had fallen as a good-luck omen directly from Heaven. Overjoyed, the emperor decreed that an extravagant sacrifice of thanksgiving should be held. The next day the excited monarch discovered yet another peach, and received notice of other favorable oddities: a white rabbit had given birth to twins, as had an aging deer in the palace zoo. When all the court officials sent the delighted Chia-ching messages on his miraculous good fortunes, he solemnly honored each one with a thank-you letter written in his own hand.

Ministers who took their duties seriously, aggrieved by the emperor's gullibility and outlandish behavior, tried to remind him of his neglected sacred duties. Doing their best to disabuse him of belief in supernatural and fantastic events, they blamed his eunuchs for encouraging such absurdities, and asked that they be punished. These suggestions only enraged Chia-ching, and he condemned one minister to court flogging and five years in prison, and another to be executed. Furthermore, he kept one imperial prince in confinement for eighteen years for opposing the performance of Taoist rites in the palace, and degraded his own son-in-law to the rank of a commoner when he expressed disbelief in Taoist magic.

For twenty years, Chia-ching withdrew almost entirely from government affairs, leaving all decisions to the highly unpopular Yen Sung. Though not a eunuch, this infamous official evoked bitter public condemnation from honest officials for his blatant misappropriation of state funds. Yen Sung put his equally clever and corrupt son into office to share in accumulating riches and power, until he, too, became so hated that he was derisively called the "little prime minister." When a group of ministers joined ranks against Yen Sung, they faced a difficult task, for he enjoyed the full confidence of the throne. Finally, after twenty years of Yen Sung's gross mismanagement, the coterie of ministers gained the ear of the emperor and convinced him to dismiss the miscreant. Afterwards, factions arose backing various candidates for the position of grand secretary. The consequent bitter bickering put an end to effective government and overjoyed the eunuchs, who saw it as a means to promote their own influence.

As the moral fiber of the nation weakened, lawlessness among the rebellious poor and corruption among upper classes reached incredible proportions. At the same time, Mongols invaded from the north and Japanese pirates sacked coastal cities and carried off hostages for ransom. Concerning the way the Chinese people dealt with these calamities, one scholar wrote: "The poor and rebellious are joining Japanese pirates to make a living, while even the rich have secret dealings with the alien marauders. In the north the poor are taking advantage of repeated Mongol incursions to join them in looting the countryside, causing great harm to our villages. Rich landowners are even more to be dreaded, for they are enriching themselves further by supplying the Mongol enemy with provisions and military secrets."[1]

Another contemporary wrote, "Nowadays, with our great population, one finds many who do no work at all. In the capital alone are countless unproductive eunuchs, court ladies, and prostitutes, while tax-free Buddhist and Taoist priests amount in all to more than 100,000. Imperial relatives out in the provinces tax the people to provide for the upkeep of great numbers of monks and their followers. Even the male and female servants of noble families live like royalty. Cities everywhere harbor untold numbers of prostitutes. Rich wastrels and thieving bandits are more numerous now than ordinary decent citizens whose taxes support them."[2]

Neither Japanese pirates nor popular rebellions in the western provinces proved sufficiently fearsome to cause the Ming throne to curtail its extravagance and munificence. In 1546 Emperor Chia-ching ordered imperial factories to send priceless porcelain pieces in the amount of 300 fish bowls, 1,000 covered jars, 22,000 bowls, 31,000 round dishes, and 18,400 cups. Much of this pottery was to be presented as gifts to officials, courtiers, visiting envoys, and favorite temples.

When one eunuch in the household of Chia-ching's princess daughter, out of sheer spitefulness and revenge, falsely notified the emperor that the husband of the princess was fomenting a rebellion, the husband—knowing that the accused were seldom exonerated—committed suicide. On learning of the eunuch's perfidy, the emperor was so enraged that he ordered he be rolled up in oil-saturated cotton cloth, suspended from an overhead beam by the heels, and then set afire at his feet, so that the flames slowly burned down until death put an end to his torture. This punishment was known as "lighting the human lamp."

By the end of Chia-ching's reign, palace eunuchs were again lording it over officials, daring to commit the most shocking atrocities against them. In 1568 a noted censor found it necessary to decree punishment of a eunuch for extorting money from the people. Infuriated by this humiliation to one of their kind, over a hundred eunuchs gathered at the palace gate where the censor would pass, and when he appeared, rushed out and beat him mercilessly. Other ministers, though horrified by this act of barbarism, were afraid to seek justice against the eunuchs for fear of like reprisals.

Chia-ching's ten-year-old grandson was put on the throne in 1573 as Emperor Wan-li. Fortunately, a strong and capable grand secretary was in control at this time. Under his stern and vigilant guidance, a degree of exemplary government and a measure of prosperity were restored. Upon this man's death, however, Wan-li took the rule into his own hands, and thereafter rapidly degenerated into the most self-indulgent, irresponsible of despots. In reaction to a decade of the grand secretary's strict discipline, officialdom also rapidly degenerated into squabbling factions trying to prevent the emergence of another such strong secretary while seeking to promote their own candidates to that position.

As a child Wan-Li had been under the strictest domination of his mother, the empress dowager, who kept him in her care until he was married at age fifteen. Aware of his domination by the dowager, palace eunuchs took advantage of the child emperor. The eunuch who gave him most trouble was Feng Pao, who was in charge of palace ritual and the privy seal, and was also the dowager's close informer. Feng Pao would report the monarch's transgressions and the dowager would mete out punishments of prolonged kneelings. This continued even after the emperor reached the age of seventeen. But when he became eighteen and was considered an adult, and so no longer under the thumb of the dowager, Wan-li took swift revenge. In 1582 he ordered Feng Pao's arrest, confiscated his property, and banished him to Nanking.

Throughout the last twenty-five years of his reign, Wan-li closeted himself in the palace, lost all patience with the warring factions, ignored the bureaucracy as much as possible, and relied on his eunuchs to perform essential business. So remote and unknown was the emperor to his officials, that one grand secretary, never having laid eyes on the Son of Heaven after years in office, became so flustered when he finally met him that he emptied his bladder on the palace floor and fell into a coma that lasted several days.

Close association with grasping eunuchs from early boyhood had instilled in Wan-li an avaricious desire for wealth, a love for extravagant spending, and a seeming obliviousness to the sufferings of the people and the state of the nation. He encouraged the tax-collector throngs of eunuchs across the nation in their inventions of ever new, even violent and criminal means to bring added revenue to the throne and their own pockets. Desperate warnings and petitions to the throne from deeply concerned officials either never reached the emperor because eunuch intermediaries neglected to deliver them, or they were ignored. Wan-li's utter lack of interest in national welfare encouraged many a disillusioned official to indulge in bribery, corruption, and abuses of every kind. "Heaven is high and the emperor is far away," they said, and proceeded to take advantage of his neglect by every means possible.

Such was the power wielded by eunuch supervisors in the provinces—with the willing consent of Emperor Wan-li—that when their countless gold and silver mining ventures failed utterly, the eunuchs forced rich landowners to pay the wages of the mine workers and guards. The poor, forced to labor as miners while their fields went untilled, had to pay land taxes just the same. Working conditions in the mines were so deplorable that laborers died like flies from accidents and malnutrition. Those who survived often received no pay at all, which provoked continual brawls and lawlessness among thousands of angry forced-labor workers. Unable to produce gold and silver in any quantity, eunuch overseers resorted to the ploy of accusing well-to-do farmers of having stolen the mine's precious ore, and proceeded to seize their properties in the name of the throne. Other landowners were subject to bare-faced extortion of their monies. If they refused to cooperate, the eunuchs had their lands dug up and mansions destroyed, claiming to look for ore beneath the soil. Even graveyards were excavated, tombs opened up, and the bones of the dead scattered about, a heinous crime in the eyes of the Chinese people.

Everywhere Wan-li's eunuch supervisors and tax collectors and their hired ruffians usurped local civil authority, arresting innocents and imposing severe fines upon them. When the eunuchs insulted and violated womenfolk and local authorities tried to stop them, the authorities were silenced by accusations of interfering with imperial orders. Clever eunuchs set up fictitious customs stations on land and water routes, and demanded such high tolls that such commerce practically came to a standstill. They and their paid henchmen even confiscated goods of traveling merchants, and increased the take from farmers by levying extra taxes on such necessities as rice, salt, even their few pigs and chickens. A eunuch tax commissioner for Yunnan province by the name of Yuan Jung was so ferocious that the people burned down the tax headquarters with Yuan Jung in it and killed 200 of his henchmen.

If word of eunuch atrocities reached the throne, Wan-li invariably defended his eunuchs, for he himself shared the booty they brought in. He was especially pleased with the furs and horses they collected, highly praising the eunuchs' special talents for acquiring such "gifts." In 1600 the eunuchs remitted to the imperial treasury tax revenues amounting to nearly a million silver taels, together with an incalculable amount in jewels. Yet it is claimed that the imperial treasury received less than went into the eunuchs' pockets.

Historians agree that the seeds of the eventual fall of the Ming Dynasty were planted by eunuchs during Wan-li's reign. The eunuchs' eagerness for riches and their ruler's insatiable craving for wealth reduced the people and the nation to such dire poverty that there were angry uprisings everywhere against mindless oppression. Concerned officials beseeched the throne to recall all eunuchs and confine them to the capital. Others mourned that the ambition and greed of the eunuchs was increasing every day as they and their hired underlings found new means to exploit the populace.

In 1602 Wan-li suddenly became ill. Fearing his end was near and that he might be punished in the Afterworld—or in Ming histories—he ordered the grand secretary to see to it that all mining and extraordinary taxation perpetrated by his eunuchs was immediately discontinued. The very next day he completely recovered and at once revoked the order, unable to control his rapacity for more riches.

In 1589 an influential judge of the Grand Court submitted a daring memorial to the throne criticizing Wan-li's disreputable private life, incidentally complaining that he had three times presented himself for an imperial audience but was told the ruler was in poor health. He further scolded the emperor for not bothering to accept and read memorials, and for deputizing others to represent him even at state sacrifices and ancestral temple offerings. "I believe I know the cause of Your Majesty's poor health: alcoholic beverages rot one's bowels, lechery undermines one's health, covetousness for wealth makes one lose his ideals, and fondness for Taoist breathing exercises shortens one's life. For the emperor to daily dine on delicacies and dainty dishes and indulge in drinking and feasting in all-day-and-night carousals reflects over-fondness for drink. For Your Majesty to delight in the company of handsome attendants opens the door to their mischief-making; and to listen to every word of advice from the favorite concubine demonstrates that one is besotted by lasciviousness. For Your Majesty to extort money to swell the palace treasury, exact cash and silks from the people, even flog your eunuch agents when their monetary and material offerings fail to satisfy, indicates greed for worldly goods. To fatally beat the palace maidens one day and cane to death the eunuchs the next on unspecified charges, reflects the royal fits of temper.

"Your Majesty, living deep within the recesses of the palace, may imagine that others cannot learn what is going on, but in truth, even when a bell strikes in the palace, its sound is heard beyond its confines and all fingers point to, and eyes focus on, Your Majesty's secluded abode. Officials, wishing to save their skins and keep their jobs, dread the imperial rage; but those who cherish loyalty and justice fear neither punishments of the cauldron for boiling people alive nor the saw for severing people in two. I dare to submit these four admonitions. If my advice could but be accepted, I stand ready for execution for being so bold."[3] The angry Wan-li wanted to deal out supreme punishment for the judge, but was finally persuaded only to discharge him from his post and degrade him to the status of a common citizen.

As early as 1594, when famine, overtaxation, and natural disasters had reduced people in certain districts to eating tree bark and grass seeds, some of the starving tried to stay alive by eating excrement of wild geese flocks, a sample of which one daring censor sent to the emperor in a completely unsuccessful attempt to arouse his pity. That same year one minister warned: "Your Majesty, living in seclusion in the palace, believes the empire is peaceful as before. But, alas, times have changed. General morale is very low. I beg to warn Your Majesty to be on the alert, and implore you to recognize these changes and start reforms. If Your Majesty were to but institute inquiries, you would see the true condition of the empire. Your presence at official audiences would give great hope to the people and help avert the threat of coming disaster."[4]

Instead, Wan-li continued to gratify his obsession for constructing ornate buildings, palaces, and temples, as well as granting petitions from his spoiled and avaricious children seeking ever more land and riches. One prince who owned farmlands in four provinces totaling thousands of acres was using intimidation to extort still more acreage from the people. When he met with fierce resistance from landholders, he had his eunuchs slaughter them. At least in this case, when officials warned Wan-li of a threatening rebellion, he reluctantly agreed to cut the prince's swollen landholdings in half.

According to records, in the year 1598 alone the court took in 4,500 new eunuchs. One writer of the times claimed that now so many people around Peking were castrating their young sons that most eunuchs were rejected by the palace, to grow up as beggars and robbers. He wrote that many of these wretched, unemployed eunuchs hid under ruined city walls. As travelers and merchants passed by, the weaker and younger eunuchs came out to beg, while the stronger demanded money with threats, or used violence to rob them. Authorities were well aware of the forays of these eunuch renegades, but were helpless to stop them.

One censor was brave enough to solemnly tell the emperor that the people looked for the image of the Son of Heaven in their government officials, but when they beheld the face of a eunuch official, they saw the terrifying image of the Buddhist God of Hell. He went on to compare eunuchs to wild beasts that sharpen their teeth looking for the best prey to devour.

In 1614 the same censor reported that a notorious imperial eunuch, Kao Tsai, stationed on the coast, had built two large boats with the intention of cooperating with Japanese pirates who were viciously marauding Chinese cities and villages. The eunuch, he said, was also attempting to arrange business with the "red-haired Dutch devils" who, acting like pirates, had seized islands off the China coast. Though the Ming government strictly forbade trading with foreigners, when the Dutch sent eunuch Kao Tsai a bribe of 30,000 silver taels asking for his influence in arranging mutual business deals in Fukien, the greedy eunuch accepted the money and did all he could to accommodate them. In this instance, however, the Dutch were out of luck: Kao Tsai was unable to bribe the honest Fukien authorities. Nonetheless, reports of eunuchs making secret business deals with foreign invaders continued. The Portuguese—who by this time had settled in Macao and were professing their independence from Chinese authority—were doing illegal business with coastal Chinese by bribing local eunuch supervisors to obtain their assistance, guidance, and protection.

One scholar reported that stealing was by far the chief accomplishment of the eunuchs. More than once, he pointed out, after they had filched from the palace treasury storehouse to the point that it was obvious that items were missing, they would burn the entire storehouse to the ground, pretending the fire was accidental. When a storehouse was gutted by fire in 1566, the eunuch in charge reported that over 188,000 catties of expensive incense had gone up in flames. Not long afterwards, his enemies in the eunuch corps accused him of having stolen the incense and setting the fire himself. When the emperor reluctantly ordered an investigation and the eunuch in charge was proven guilty, helpless officials acknowledged that, had it not been for a quarrel among the eunuchs, the theft would have gone unpunished.

By this time palace household eunuchs were fleecing Peking merchants who sold food to the extravagant imperial kitchen to such a degree that many sellers had fled the capital to try to make a living elsewhere. Those who remained often received no payment at all for the products they delivered, but were so intimidated, they accepted this without complaint, knowing that the money had gone into the eunuchs' pockets. One contemporary scholar wrote that Wan-li's palace banquets were the most sumptuous ever given by any Ming emperor, adding that now influential eunuchs had become so wealthy they were competing with each other in providing lavish entertainments for the Son of Heaven at their own expense. Records show that when Wan-li married, the elaborate ceremonies cost the state some 90,000 taels. Investiture ceremonies for his many princely sons amounted to over 12 million taels, and the marriages of imperial princesses another 120,000 taels. The constant tax increases to cover these extravagances disastrously impoverished the populace.

Some ministers did their utmost to control palace waste. When in 1596 two of Wan-li's palaces were destroyed by fire, a talented official in just two years had them rebuilt at far less expense than was anticipated. He was able to do so only by waging a constant war against eunuch interference in the handling of the treasury monies involved.

Like his predecessors, Wan-li had a passion for pearls, and he commissioned eunuchs almost exclusively to oversee pearl diving at the southern coast. Under the eunuchs' direction, many divers lost their lives in this perilous task. The pearl-gatherers' work song tells something about the current economic situation: "O water, why dost thou produce pearls so I must labor like this? Yet I should not grudge the sacrifice of my life for pearls. I am better off than my neighbor who had to sell all his children to pay his taxes."[5]

In 1598 Wan-li sent a ranking eunuch to the coast at Canton to secure a large quantity of pearls. In seven years, the eunuch completely impoverished the provincial treasury by forcing local authorities to build him a fine mansion and furnish all daily needs and expenses for himself and the several hundred servants and hangers-on in his retinue. When the eunuch finally returned to Peking, leaving hundreds of pearl divers unemployed, to avoid starvation they joined Japanese pirates in raiding coastal towns.

During Wan-li's reign, palace eunuchs became so emboldened that they began to consider themselves above all authority. In 1602, when a scholarly vice-president of the Board of Rites was being carried in his sedan chair near a palace gate, three eunuchs on horseback suddenly galloped forth, and their horses balked and reared at the fluttering of the honorary flags on the official's chair. Infuriated, the eunuchs tore the flags to pieces and began beating the official's bearers and attendants. When the official him-self sought refuge near the gate, the eunuchs drove him out and brutally assaulted him. When palace guards arrived to restore order, they were viciously attacked as well.

Five years later a provincial district magistrate, having finished his busi-ness in the palace, was about to leave the city when several palace eunuchs came galloping after him demanding a donation of "squeeze money." When the magistrate indignantly refused them, the eunuchs beat him so brutally that he died of his injuries while he was being carried by passersby into a nearby house.

During Wan-li's reign the throne also lavished untold sums on religion. Wan-li was as enthusiastic over Buddhism as his grandfather had been over Taoism, even though one minister had warned him, "In and outside the capital are countless magnificently decorated monasteries built with the imperial funds. Would it not be wiser to spare the people from heavy taxes than to finance frequent religious ceremonies and donate large sums to monasteries, the end benefits of which are quite uncertain?"[6] Christian-ity was also condoned at the palace, where the famed European Father Ricci gained entrance under the auspices of eunuch Ma Tang and con-verted many eunuchs and officials to Catholicism. It was Father Ricci who wrote of the Taoist "pope": "The Taoist Master of Heaven spends most of his time in Peking. A recognized favorite of the emperor, he is even admitted into the most sacred chambers of the palace for ceremonies to exorcise evil spirits and catastrophe-causing demons. He is carried through the streets in an open palanquin, wears the paraphernalia of highest magistrates, and receives a fat annual stipend from the crown."[7]

Beginning in 1592, three years of costly wars with Japan were fought in Korea by 200,000 Chinese soldiers to save that tribute state from Japa-nese invaders. These wars further sapped the nation's financial strength, forc-ing Wan-li to demand the minting of copper coins in such numbers that counterfeit coins soon flooded the market, ruining the whole monetary sys-tem. The war with Japan went badly for China, and many Ming troops perished on the battlefield. Chinese armies managed to escape complete annihilation only because the Japanese suddenly withdrew on learning of the death of their emperor. Nonetheless, this war exhausted China and left her an easy prey to rebels as well as enemies beyond the Great Wall.

To make matters worse, by 1619 Manchu tribes of Manchuria had begun invading China's northeastern frontier in earnest. The Manchu people had long been peaceful settlers of Chinese lands in Manchuria, paying reg-ular tribute to China. By 1616, however, because of excesses of Chinese officials, their khan united his tribes and set up his own dynasty, independent of and hostile to China. Leaders of the hardy Manchus were vigorous, imaginative generals and expert organizers. Their Chinese-style government was so honest and effective that northern Chinese had been readily defecting to the Manchus to escape the corrupt, weak rule of Ming eunuchs and officials. Though Ming armies won a few victories over the Manchus, by 1621 the Manchus controlled vast Chinese areas to the extreme northeast, a most humiliating situation for the Ming Dynasty. The Manchus also succeeded in capturing over 300 Chinese generals and officers who then joined the Manchus to fight their former countrymen. From this time on, Ming China would remain constantly on the defensive against the powerful Manchus.

By this time the heinous practice of presenting enemy heads to collect government bounties had become almost universal in Ming armies. Decades previously it had been discovered that corrupt Ming officers had been sending in greatly exaggerated reports of the number of peasant rebels killed in order to claim victories and enhance their reputations. This prompted the War Board to insist on seeing the severed heads of the rebels killed. High government rank was awarded for heads of rebel leaders, and a generous sum for the heads of rebel followers. When the rebels learned of this practice, they started driving members of the local populace before them in the front line of battle. Ming soldiers, eager to collect bounties as easily as possible, slaughtered these helpless noncombatants and turned in their heads, not bothering further with the rebels.

Even as recently as the Chia-ching reign, a scholar had pointed out the evils of the practice of paying bounties for severed heads: "The farmers labor to feed and support imperial soldiers who, instead of fighting the rebels, cut off the farmers' heads to claim a bounty. Then their officers, to cover up their own many defeats, cut off the heads of their own soldiers killed by the rebels to make false claims of victory. Thus, local Chinese farmers nourish bitter resentment toward the imperial armies, as do the soldiers toward their leaders."[8]

This practice spread under Emperor Wan-li, however. In 1583 an official of the War Board severely criticized the corruption of border troops who were gathering heads of civilian Chinese who had died in a famine and turning them in as enemy Manchus. Some troops were even enticing members of the local populace into remote areas and butchering them to collect bounties. In 1618, after the Manchus had killed several hundred neighboring tribesmen in a war that had nothing to do with China, a Ming army commander in an area just below the border, on hearing the news, immediately stole into the war area, cut off the heads of 165 corpses, and presented them to the Ming government, claiming a victory over the

Manchus. In order to earn first class merit, officers were required to submit a total of 165 heads. The government later reduced this number to 120 when it was learned that one commander killed off thirty-five civilians to make up the quota.

When Emperor Wan-li died, in 1620, and the crown prince acceded to the throne, within a week the new young ruler fell ill under mysterious circumstances. It seems a concubine of Wan-li who had wanted her own son on the throne had sent the new ruler—already known as a lecher—eight beautiful girls as a congratulatory gift, and he soon collapsed of physical exhaustion. Then the concubine hovered constantly over his sickbed, conniving with his favorite consort, Madam Li, to prevent high ministers from access to him. Soon the two women had a eunuch physician, Tsui Wen-sheng, give the patient a laxative, which caused his condition to seriously worsen. Angry officials demanded that the older concubine remove herself from the palace, and that the eunuch doctor be punished for prescribing the wrong medicine. A delegation of officials forced their way into the sickroom, but they could do nothing for the monarch, whose condition fluctuated for another two weeks. Finally, just one month after his enthronement, at his own insistence, the patient was given some red pills concocted and highly touted by a minor official. Early next morning the emperor was found dead. For years to come there would be the most ferocious factional disputes over responsibility for the emperor's death, known as the "Red Pill Case." The next emperor, Tien-chi, who greatly favored his eunuchs, had a censor who recommended punishment for the eunuch doctor, who was beaten at court and dismissed.

By this time the sale of government offices by eunuchs and the throne had resulted in officials being appointed who were entirely ignorant of their appointed function, court etiquette, and traditional Ming procedures. It is recorded that on the day of Emperor Tien-chi's accession to the throne in 1621, installation ceremonies were so disgracefully botched by an inexperienced master of ceremonies that the entire court cringed in embarrassment.

The deplorable state of the Ming Empire would have taxed the abilities of the most excellent of rulers: Certainly little could be expected of Emperor Tien-chi, an immature, inexperienced youth with no interest whatever in politics or government. Under long-time encouragement of his eunuchs, he had become completely addicted to his hobby of woodworking and carpentry. Whereupon, power-seeking eunuch go-betweens, aping their predecessors in reigns past, presented important documents just when the emperor was most absorbed in his workshop, knowing he would impatiently wave them away with orders to handle the matter themselves.

When, in his very first year, Tien-chi issued an order for the recruitment of 3,000 new eunuchs, over 20,000 castrated candidates clamored around the Ministry of Rites seeking palace employment. The supervising secretary finally had to demand that they be forcibly dispersed to avoid serious rioting. He further urged that earlier prohibitions against private castrations be enforced more rigorously. In the end, however, the secretary sympathized with the remaining unemployed eunuchs and suggested that they be assigned to service in the many princely establishments throughout the realm. Two years later, when officials complained about the tremendous numbers of eunuchs in service, they were aghast to learn that a palace order had again gone out for 2,500 more eunuch recruits.

One official wrote in consternation: "In recent years ancient tradition has been ignored and the most harmful innovations introduced. Now all imperial authority comes through the hands of the eunuchs. For internal government they are trusted as if they were prime ministers. For external affairs they are employed as army generals, while frontier provinces have to accept eunuchs as their governors. Actors and artisans in the capital look to palace eunuchs for advice on constantly producing fanciful entertainments for the throne. Abbots and monks rely on eunuchs to grant them frequent admission to the palace. Under eunuch protection, certain temples dare to give dire offense to the public with their indecent rituals. And there are grave misgivings everywhere—beyond all imagination—over what palace eunuchs may be doing in secret."[9]

By this time even low-ranking eunuchs had no fear of committing the grossest of affronts against high officials. One duty of the president of the Board of Works was to dole out warm winter clothing for the tens of thousands of palace eunuchs every two years at the onset of cold weather. In 1623, when it was still hot summertime, 1,000 eunuchs accosted the president demanding their supply of winter clothes. On being refused, they rushed to his office and demolished his official chair—a mark of deep disrespect—before overwhelming him with shouted obscenities and degrading insults.

The following year a minister of the same board criticized to the throne the nefarious activities of chief eunuch Wei Chung-hsien, prompting the incensed eunuch to issue an order in the emperor's name that the minister be flogged. Under this chief eunuch's instructions, a group of eunuchs went to the minister's residence, beat him savagely, and carried him away half dead. At a meeting concerning this shocking affair called by the grand secretary, several hundred eunuchs appeared and began "shaking their fists, pulling up their trousers to their thighs, and shouting denunciations at the whole gathering."[10] So overcome was the grand secretary, that his face went red and he was unable to utter a word above the uproar. Suddenly one minister exploded, "This office is a solemn place where even the chief eunuch is denied entrance without order of the emperor! How dare you eunuchs intrude! You are a disgrace to His Majesty and all the imperial ancestors."[11] Startled by this unaccustomed outburst, the eunuchs finally dispersed, leaving the ministers shaken to the core.

Wei Chung-hsien was the most reviled and dangerous eunuch in all Chinese history. He even dared plot to usurp the throne itself. As a young man he was known as an irresponsible, shiftless ne'er-do-well. As an adult, pressed by gamblers for payment after heavy losses, Wei castrated himself, thereby hoping to pay his debts after attaining palace service. He was taken into old Emperor Wan-li's palace as a minor eunuch in the household staff. Quickly he proceeded to ingratiate himself with those who could do him most good, proving himself an adept tactician in palace politics, winning favor and patronage from a succession of powerful chief eunuchs. An excellent cook (a forte of many eunuchs), Wei won special favor with the mother of the crown prince who would soon beome Emperor Tien-chi.

Wasting no time, eunuch Wei managed to become the lover of Tien-chi's comely wet nurse, Mistress Ko. Together they got rid of her former eunuch lover by having him killed. This unorthodox, outlandish romantic alliance between a eunuch and an imperial wet nurse was to form the basis for Wei Chung-hsien's emergence into unprecedented power. It is unknown just what sort of sexual antics this unlikely couple indulged in. It was rumored that Wei's severed parts had at least partially redeveloped. There was also an ugly story that, on the advice of a medicine man, Wei had seven convicts murdered and consumed their brains in an effort to regain his sex drive.

In 1620, within a month after becoming emperor, Tien-chi heaped titles of nobility upon his former wet nurse. After she and Wei had accomplished the murder of the chief eunuch, a man who had earlier befriended Wei, Mistress Ko coerced the emperor into appointing Wei as grand eunuch, from which he would further rise to become the throne's most trusted advisor. At the same time, Tien-chi appointed Wei to several other high posts, including administrator of rites, a position normally occupied only by men of great learning. Tien-chi seemed willing to go to any extreme to please his wet nurse, awarding noble titles and lucrative positions to relatives of both Mistress Ko and her lover. Worried censors, aware that the wet nurse was the key that could unlock the door to a eunuch take-over, admonished the emperor that, since he was soon to be married, he should release Mistress Ko from the palace and send her back to her residence. In reply, the indignant teenage monarch informed them that he could no more dispense with his wet nurse than he could his own mother; and that he would be eternally grateful for the nourishment, love, and protection she had provided him in childhood.

One official reminded Tien-chi that he should demonstrate his filial affection at the tomb of his parents rather than toward Mistress Ko, "so as to dissipate the outer court's suspicions and destroy the threat of interference from intimates."[12] Another worried official advised obscurely: "If one wishes to scour away the Manchu threat, one must first get rid of the female threat. The Middle Kingdom and the scholar-officials represent the male force, *yang;* thus the nation's success derives from employment of the literati. The Manchu barbarians and the inner-palace eunuchs represent the dark, female *yin* force; thus barbarian incursions derive from the employment of eunuchs. But then arose the matter of disposing of Mistress Ko. She spreads rumors to confuse Your Majesty's ear. Thus she corrupts and disorganizes the palace women's apartments and interferes with court administration, fostering the villainous and the depraved, while subverting the good and respectable. The female *yin* force overturns destiny and deceptively causes Your Majesty to worry about the Manchus in the northeast, and to disregard the female threat before your eyes. This is what is called not being able to see your own eyelashes."[13]

Several such protestors were demoted three degrees in rank and transferred to provincial posts. Yet another official dared remonstrate against accepting impeachments of officials by eunuchs: "There already are orthodox officials whose function is to submit impeachments. For eunuchs to do so is unheard of. I am afraid that, whereas today the eunuchs take advantage of imperial favor to enhance their prestige, in the future they might arrogate imperial power unto themselves, so as to the turn the sword of authority against Your Majesty, the giver of such authority."[14]

Wei began his career by murdering every eunuch who did not belong to his clique. Methodically, he threw out of office any and all who opposed him and his ambitions. He did away with the partisans of the Tung-lin faction that had recently rid the government of many crooked officials but left the faction with many enemies. Sensing that Wei was to be the new power base, opponents of the Tung-lin group congregated around the grand eunuch. Wei saw to it that all who rallied behind him received appointments and promotions. The top echelon of Wei's political machine in the palace came to be known as the "Five Tigers," while those in his military contingent were called the "Five Cougars." His power was so pervasive that few cabinet ministers, governors general, or ranking officials could continue to hold office unless they became staunch backers of Wei.

In 1622 Wei talked the ruler into allowing him to recruit and train an all-eunuch army, with himself as chief of the secret service corps. Thus, he was able to collaborate with the imperial bodyguard. In this way, he was able to initiate a veritable reign of terror.

Meanwhile, upright officials did not like what they heard of scandalous goings-on in the palace. Wei and Nurse Ko kept the young Tien-chi occupied in constant pleasures and dissipations: gambling, music, hunting, and long hours at his beloved carpentry, where he resented any interruption. After they introduced him to unknown sexual aberrations and excesses, the ruler's life became one of unrelieved debauchery.

Some claim that Grand Eunuch Wei's rise to power was possible because of the way this emperor had been brought up. Because he had quite unexpectedly been put on the throne, Tien-chi had never been exposed to distinguished Confucian teachers who normally tutored and trained heirs apparent. His upbringing had been entirely in the hands of such palace denizens as the eunuchs and nursemaid Ko. Since earliest youth he had been under eunuch Wei's influence. Evidently Tien-chi had been instilled with no sense of responsibility whatever.

Eventually eunuch Wei, to impress others and for his own safety, was able to increase his personal retainers to 10,000 men. It is said he was always escorted by armed guards, inside and outside the palace. Accompanied by retainers, guards, grooms, cooks, and entertainers, the grand eunuch and his lieutenants often went to the countryside for amusement. He loved to ride his carriage at breakneck speed and bypass—without even acknowledging their presence—all the officials and squires who had come long distances to line up on the road to pay their respects. As he flew past, they all shouted, "Long live the Nine-thousand-years!"—an expression that placed him just one rank below emperors, who were always known as "Ten-thousand-years."

In 1623 a censor addressed the throne, saying: "As for eunuch Wei Chung-hsien's dangerous perversities. . . I happened to pass the Azure Cloud Monastery in the western hills and saw the burial place he is making for himself. Not only does it rival the imperial tombs in grandeur of its design and excellence of materials used, it perhaps surpasses them in size. In front of the tomb are lions and elephants carved of beautiful stone lined up in rows and ranks, no different from those at imperial tombs. Moreover, there are two stone figures standing in attendance on either side of the tomb: one, a civil official in court audience hat and gown, and the other a military official garbed in armor. Now Wei is just a eunuch. It might be possible to countenance his having military personnel in attendance after he is buried, but how could he dare have civil ministers in official attire, as do our emperors? I cannot imagine what position he hopes some day to occupy! To exhibit such extravagance violates all propriety and discipline. I can only deduce that all rumors I hear about his dangerous ambitions are true."[15]

Grand Eunuch Wei built a temple for himself some thirty-five miles west of Peking. It was constructed much like a fortress. Its lofty surrounding stone wall was so broad that a carriage could be driven along the top of it. Within, there were numerous buildings and a high central tower, or keep, with seventy-two circular openings. There was only one entrance gateway to the complex, under which was a deep well covered by a revolving trap. The trap could be sprung on anyone entering, to deposit the intruder below. Additionally, armed guards were stationed on either side of the gate. It is believed Wei intended the temple to be a refuge, in case of danger. A British writer saw this temple still standing in the late 1800s, though with a different use and name.

The crisis for eunuch Wei came in 1624 when a ranking censor, a leader of the good Tung-lin faction, made himself famous by submitting a memorial listing the "Twenty-four Great Crimes of Eunuch Wei Chung-hsien." In the introduction, he wrote in part, "I petition concerning this treacherous eunuch's taking advantage of his position to wield imperial authority; his take-over of power and disruption of administration; his deceiving the emperor and scorning the law; his interference with ancestral institutions. I earnestly beg for a resolute imperial decision to undertake an investigation so as to rescue the throne before it is too late. Who would imagine anyone could be so outrageous and reckless as to disrupt the court's orderliness; deny the ruler's authority, and give rein to selfish interest so as to subvert the good and the honest; to spoil the emperor's reputation; and to brew inexhaustible disasters for the throne. The whole court is intimidated. No one dares to denounce him by name. I, myself, am actually sick at the prospect."

Yet he bravely went on to expose Wei's crimes, as follows:

"Inciting the supervising secretary to denounce the Grand Secretary and Minister of Personnel and bring about their dismissal. Usurping from the Grand Secretariat its privilege of preparing condensations of memorials for imperial consideration, and reporting imperial decisions orally so that their validity is in question. Being hostile to loyal and righteous ministers and bringing about their removal while attaching himself to, and protecting, the unprincipled sycophants. Murdering a favorite, though lowly, imperial concubine while the emperor was visiting outside the palace, and convincing the emperor she had died of a sudden illness. Forging an imperial order that caused high-ranking Madam Chang to commit suicide after she became pregnant by the emperor. Bringing about the death in infancy of the ruler's first-born son, and thus depriving him of an heir to the throne. Murdering untold numbers of eunuchs who had given long and faithful palace service. Punishing and terrorizing imperial in-laws.

Usurping authority over the promotion of officials. Removing a warden from his post in the imperial bodyguard's prison because he would not be a murderer and a toady, clearly demonstrating that the Great Ming laws need not be observed, while the laws of eunuch Wei dare not be disregarded. Making the emperor look ridiculous by countermanding his edicts. Utilizing his control over the palace bodyguard to institute a reign of terror; arresting officials without authorization from the Grand Secretariat. On his jaunts outside the palace, affecting all the regalia of the imperial entourage, he acts as though he has already mounted the imperial carriage. Arrogantly defying imperial authority, as when he made no apology and obviously feared no punishment for staying mounted on his horse in the Imperial Presence, a violation of all propriety."

The brave censor continued his accusations with forceful warnings that Wei had designs on the throne: "Fearful lest the inner court disclose his villainy, he kills some officials and replaces the rest, and intimate attendants are so awed they dare not speak. Fearful lest the outer court disclose his villainy, he expels or imprisons those who cross him, and the members likewise look on and dare not speak. There are some officials of an ignorant and spineless sort who are so intent on gaining wealth and honors that they cling to the eunuch like twigs and leaves, hanging about his gates hoping to be recognized, even pledging themselves to be his patrons and proteges. They advocate whatever pleases eunuch Wei, and attack anything he dislikes—there is nothing they will not do."

The censor ended his missive saying, "If by chance Wei's inner-court villainies are betrayed, there is always Mistress Ko to make amends and gloss over his depraved offenses. Throughout the palace and the capital, all know there is the powerful Grand Eunuch, but forget there is an emperor. Whether in the palace or in the government, whether in great or small matters, there is nothing that is not decided solely by eunuch Wei. Even in the processing of documents it would appear that the emperor is only a name, whereas the eunuch is much a reality." He then suggested that a recent rash of strange natural phenomena—earthquakes in both Peking and Nanking—must be clear warnings of Heaven's disapproval, and further noted that the emperor, instead of punishing Wei, only heaped more favors upon him. As for Mistress Ko, he declared, "She should be ordered to take up residence outside the palace so to preserve the favor in which she is now held by the emperor, but no longer spread her poison in the palace."[16]

In the face of this grievous indictment, Grand Eunuch Wei for the first time was genuinely frightened. He defended himself tearfully before the emperor, even declaring willingness to give up supervision of the powerful eunuch police force. In the end—thanks to strong intervention by nursemaid Ko and his own many henchmen—Wei was not only forgiven, but his accuser was reprimanded for having made false charges against the ruler's most loyal "minister." Immediately after the emperor's decision became known, over seventy ministers jointly petitioned him to retire Grand Eunuch Wei to his private residence and thus stop, once and for all, the scandals in the palace. This petition Tien-chi firmly rejected, which emboldened Wei to purge or execute all his opponents. He then intensified the evil activities of the eunuch police, cruelly punishing anyone suspected of being disloyal to himself, or even having disloyal thoughts. Word seeped out from the eunuch-run prison concerning offenders that they had been subject to a daily series of blows that sliced the buttocks like a knife, 100 excruciating squeezings with the finger-press apparatus, nails driven into their ears, or fifty "body-jerks" in which strong men held the victim's arms and legs and suddenly pulled violently in opposite directions.

Grand Eunuch Wei had the censor who had presented his "Twenty-four Great Crimes" thrown into the prison, where he finally died while undergoing unspeakable torture. Colleagues who attempted to defend the condemned censor were placed on Wei's hit list. One of these died four days after being flogged before the court as a warning to others who might try to speak out.

From now on, the conflict between Wei and his opponents became an open battle, and with Emperor Tien-chi on the throne, a hopelessly one-sided one. In the aftermath of the eunuch's great purge of his opponents, many officials departed in disgrace or fear. Dishonest men whom the Tung-lin faction had previously suppressed or removed were promptly promoted or recalled. They became Wei's henchmen, and presented 700 names of persons who were then blacklisted. Wei's most powerful and most feared outer-court agent was a former high official who had been condemned for dishonesty, but who had rushed to grovel before Wei and pledge himself as the eunuch's adopted son.

It is impossible to estimate the number of officials who fell prey to Wei's reign of terror. One source says he had 365 men in the civil service alone either murdered, unjustly beheaded, beaten to death, forced to commit suicide, or banished to guard the frontiers. Ming histories can only say, "Those who were cruelly murdered are beyond calculation. On the streets men used their eyes only [that is, they dared not speak]."[17]

Thus, within two years, not only most officials in the imperial government, but those at the provincial level, saw the advantage of gaining the grand eunuch's favor and went to preposterous lengths to sing his praises. In 1626 one governor petitioned for permission to erect a "shrine for the living" in honor of eunuch Wei, impelling others, who were eager to show themselves no less loyal, to do the same. Before long, "living shrines" dedicated to Wei—which by tradition were erected only for national heroes—had mushroomed throughout the empire. A flood of written eulogies were soon pouring in, as writers competed to extol Wei's virtues. Even ordinary citizens commenced building temples where Wei would be honored with prayers for his longevity; in some cases the land and materials were acquired by forcibly confiscating farms, lumber forests, and houses of the people. Not a soul dared complain. In this feverish atmosphere of universal adulation, one scholar even petitioned the government to have Wei worshipped side by side with Confucius. Another scholar, who refused to compose an eulogy for the opening of a shrine dedicated to Wei, was sentenced to death, as was another who declined to prostate himself after entering such a temple. Splendid memorial archways honoring eunuch Wei also sprouted up everywhere.

Near the end of Tien-chi's reign, after all dissent had been suppressed, all memorials to the throne necessarily included adulatory phrases and specious praise for Grand Eunuch Wei. By this time, Wei had titled himself supreme duke, putting himself on a par with top-ranking imperial princes. Almost without exception, all imperial digests of memorials, even those drafted by the grand secretaries, now began: "The Emperor and the palace minister [Wei Chung-hsien] hereby decree. . . ." In the most flagrant possible insult to and disrespect for the throne, a mere nephew of the eunuch was allowed to fill in for the emperor in performing the imperial sacrifices.

Everywhere, thinking Chinese trembled in fear, wondering who really was their ruler.

One sycophant even gave Grand Eunuch Wei full credit for a short-lived successful defense against the Manchus, saying, "Wei's virtue blankets the four corners of the universe, and his patriotism surpasses any for a hundred generations!" Another echoed, "Wei cherishes the state as if it were his own family and protects it everywhere, not only against the Manchus!"[18]

Now with eunuch Wei in full power, memorials from censors revealed a significant lack of concern by the throne for disaster-struck areas, but a great deal of concern for ways to increase tax revenues in order to pay for Wei's great construction protects—his special interest. Officials soon saw that eager support for these projects was the quickest means to gain Wei's favor. Beginning in 1625, officials were avidly competing to devise means to save government funds so that they could be diverted to Wei's great projects, some even making contributions from their own resources. By 1627 official concern for the welfare of the people seemed to have vanished completely.

Four years previously, the throne had ignored a memorial from one secretary in which he had warned: "Since the recent troubles with the invading Manchus, military needs have swelled to the point of exhausting the imperial resources, necessitating a phenomenal increase in taxes. The masses of people are cracking their bones, scraping their marrow, and selling their children and wives to make their payments, and this is repeated year after year. . . . Don't wait for rebellion before commencing to restore deficiencies in the treasuries—we must find a way to both strengthen state finances and at the same time relieve the people from dire oppression."[19]

By Tien-chi's time the Ming court was paying heavy bribe payments to the Mongols for remaining neutral in China's wars against the Manchus. One censor warned that the Mongols could not be trusted any more than renegade Manchus enlisted in the imperial Chinese armies, but he conceded that the Mongols might render useful help if they were offered a bounty of fifty taels for each Manchu head they produced.

In 1626 when eunuch supervisors were assigned to each of the northern defense commands, officials who protested were dismissed from civil service. During the same year, when troops under command of eunuch Tsao Hua-chun were battling the Manchus at the border, he issued an order promising that any soldier who brought him an enemy head would be awarded a 50-tael silver ingot as a bounty. Since Manchu facial features were generally similar to those of northern Chinese, Ming soldiers took to killing and decapitating the local populace and presented their heads to eunuch Tsao as those of the enemy. In instances where the facial features were obviously Chinese, the soldiers would beat the severed heads with a wet sandal and steam them slightly until they appeared more like Manchus. When, by mere chance, a number of Manchus were actually captured, the officers carefully kept them safely alive and imprisoned, so that when they lost their next battle to the usually superior Manchu forces, they could kill the captives and present their severed heads as proof of victory.

The military disasters at the hands of the Manchus were accompanied by natural disasters, which were all the more demoralizing to the Chinese because they looked upon them as warnings of Heaven's displeasure with misrule on earth. A series of earthquakes occurred in both capitals; numerous fires destroyed several great palaces, pavilions, and halls; and recurrent floods, droughts, hailstorms, and locust infestations throughout the empire caused the starving people to rise up in violent protest.

In 1627, when Emperor Tien-chi suddenly died, all his power had already been eclipsed by Grand Eunuch Wei. What kept the eunuch from seizing the throne at this juncture—saving China from an ultimate humiliation—nobody knows. Emperor Tien-chi's seventeen-year-old brother was put on the throne, as Emperor Chung-chen. He would be the last Ming ruler.

One can but pity Chung-chen. He took the throne as a well-meaning prince determined to save a sadly deteriorated empire from total collapse. So formidable were the problems he faced—imperial treasuries depleted, imperial armies appallingly undermined by rampant graft of officers and soldier defections, poverty-stricken masses everywhere fomenting revolt and banditry, and the growing menace of the powerful northern Manchu enemy—that he was destined to merely preside for seventeen years over the nation's disintegration. No one can deny he did his best against hopeless odds. Small wonder that he became a disillusioned, frustrated, unbending, ineffectual dictator in his last years.

Having detested eunuch Wei Chung-hsien even as a prince, Emperor Chung-chen's first act was to suppress the eunuch's power. But in his youthfulness, he seemed too insecure to take immediate punitive action against him. Officials held their breath in apprehension; former supporters of Wei now warily submitted criticism of the deposed grand eunuch, trying to feel out the new ruler's inclinations. Only after several months did Chung-chen summon Wei before him to hear yet another indictment listing his unforgivable crimes. The former grand eunuch wept profusely, but nonetheless promptly delivered large bribes to the ruler's personal eunuch and confidant, who had once been Wei's gambling partner, seeking his influence with the new monarch. On hearing of this, the emperor severely reprimanded his eunuch for accepting the bribes, and had eunuch Wei exiled to Anhwei province in total disgrace. Not one official protested. Everywhere those who had previously glorified Wei now rushed to join in his denunciation, hoping to exonerate themselves.

As he journeyed into exile, news reached Wei that the emperor had sent a special prosecutor out to question him and possibly arrest him. Promptly he took his own life by hanging himself. The emperor later had his head severed and exhibited in Wei's native city and his corpse dismembered in posthumous punishment. Wei's paramour and early palace ally, wet nurse Ko, was flogged to death and decapitated. All members of both the Wei and Ko families, regardless of age, were decapitated. Henchmen of eunuch Wei and wet nurse Ko were severely punished, their followers were dismissed, and officials whom Wei had blacklisted or imprisoned—if they had survived their ordeal—were exonerated and recalled to duty.

Thereafter, government was completely disrupted by fierce, continual bickering among officials over the guilt or innocence of officeholders in eunuch Wei's regime. Emperor Chung-chen at last became so disgusted with the bitter infighting among the various factions that he came to find the Tung-lin every bit as distasteful as eunuch Wei's faction had been. This debilitating partisan factionalism continued to the end of the dynasty, causing stagnation in all aspects of government. Under these conditions, Emperor Chung-chen single-handedly tried to establish effective rule, a lonely and probably impossible task.

From the beginning to the end of his reign, Chung-chen harbored an abiding conviction that top ministers and officials were to blame for the nation's woes, and trusted none of them. During his seventeen-year reign he appointed and dismissed fifty grand secretaries. He once announced that the Boards of War and Civil Office were guilty of accepting bribes from every man they appointed to office, forcing new appointees to seek loans that they later repaid with money exacted from the populace. His edict of 1633 clearly pointed out that the appalling number of the destitute who had turned to banditry and rebellion was due to the rapacity, corruption, and cruelty of provincial officials. Everywhere sub-officials were known as "tigers and wolves" because they terrorized and bled the people.

Perhaps in his indictment of official behavior the emperor also meant to include a number of Peking eunuchs who possessed great tracts of farmland near the northern border. This area, which was already suffering from repeated Manchu incursions, was also so harassed by eunuch landlords with trumped-up threats of lawsuits that the inhabitants of whole regions trurned en masse to banditry.

However, when one eunuch reported the corruption of a governor, the emperor appointed eunuch supervisors over provincial officials to watch for and report their misdeeds. For by this time the last Ming emperor, like his predecessors, had turned to his eunuchs as his principal agents, and revived the practice of using eunuch palace guards as his spies. Eunuchs sent out to supervise military districts ruinously interfered with campaign plans and terrorized the local people. The emperor loyally backed his eunuchs in all complaints against them until in 1640 he finally recalled a number of them. But then a month before the end of his reign he again sent out eunuchs to oversee all military districts. When the War Board vigorously protested the lack of central authority and the greed of eunuch supervisors, the distracted ruler refused to listen or retract his order.

Eunuch secret police and palace guards were allowed to accumulate such power that if an official offended a eunuch even unintentionally, he was subjected to exaggerated accusations and thrown into the eunuch-run prisons. By 1641 some 140 top-ranking officials were in jail. The traditional Board of Punishments was incapable of stepping in and enforcing justice, for the eunuchs were allowed to accuse, cruelly torture, and execute anyone who got in their way.

According to old Confucian principles, popular rebellion was a recognized means for the oppressed to rise up against blatant misrule. Indeed, in the Middle Kingdom, rebellion was seen as a warning from Heaven against misgovernment. Now, thousands of poor peasants, forced to rent land from city-dwelling landowners in return for half the harvest—and to be mercilessly exploited by the landlord's retainers and slaves—had become hopelessly indebted to landowners for loans at exorbitant interest rates. Peasants were forced to sell all their belongings and even their children into slavery to meet rapacious landlords' demands. As a result, the masses everywhere were turning to banditry and rebellion.

From 1630 onward, the number of rebels increased with astonishing speed. By 1635 it is estimated that half a million peasants were in open rebellion. They were also joined by great numbers of deserting soldiers, some of whom had not been paid in four years. The leaven of soldiers facilitated the organization of the rebel hordes into well-armed battalions that were able to move swiftly in and out of their strongholds in the mountains and marshes, where the imperial armies could have but little impact on them. Aware of the impatient emperor's incessant demands to put down the rebels at once, provincial officials saw the wisdom of not reporting disorders within their areas, lest they be held responsible and punished, or forced to attack the rebels against impossible odds.

Stagnation and malaise in government had caused flood control measures, dike repairs, and irrigation systems to be neglected, resulting in devastating floods or droughts to great areas already ravaged by bands of rebels and robbers. By now the problem of beggars and vagrants had reached serious proportions. In 1635 an official warned the throne that unless something was done to relieve the sufferings of the populace, all civilians might join the rebels. Already the rebels were being enthusiastically welcomed wherever their mobs passed. Villagers revealed military secrets to rebel leaders, gave them lists of the local rich, and told them they could suffer no more the cruelties of government eunuchs, officials, and local landlords.

During recurring famines, cannibalism became common among the starving. In a battle in Shantung in 1640, when 5,000 Chinese rebels were killed, after the Ming soldiers cut off their heads for bounties, the starving populace rushed forth to cut up the corpses for food. In Shansi, markets sold human flesh. Starving parents killed and ate their daughters, and people were known to kill and roast their parents. One eyewitness wrote of the destitution and cannibalism in the southern city of Su-chou: "The streets are filled with countless beggars, worn and emaciated. Extreme cold has persisted since the New Year, and now it has rained continuously for ten days. People are dying in great number for lack of food. Corpses of the starved are being eaten. Countless others are being buried daily. It is only natural that after a period of prosperity (*yang*), a period of depression (*yin*) should follow, but I never dreamed I would see such utter destitution in my own time."[20] An official report of 1641 stated that in large areas of the north thirty percent of the inhabitants had starved to death, thirty percent had succumbed to plague, and the remainder had become bandits.

The starving people had no resistance to pestilence and plagues, the most violent of which struck Peking in 1641 and 1643. Ten thousand victims died a day. The terrified populace beat metal pans day and night, believing the din would scare away the catastrophe-causing demons. Government relief centers doled out *congee,* a watery rice gruel, to several hundred thousand hungry, but this relief effort fed only a fraction of those in need.

In 1641 the emperor sent his chief eunuch south to personally escort the head of the Taoist church to Peking to pray for winter snow to save the crops. When no snow fell, the Taoist dignitary was dismissed and left the capital, but soon after was summoned back again. Mistaking the second call for his services as an unprecedented honor, the Taoist churchman journeyed forth with a huge entourage and a great display of grandeur, spending six months in an ostentatious progression through the provinces. On his arrival at the capital, he was impeached by the Board of Ceremonies for having failed to produce snow, for having lied about claims of producing rain, for unbecoming worldly interest in luxuries, and for having squandered government treasury monies in a useless, costly procession through the country.

By this time government treasuries had been all but emptied—not only from the stupendous amounts required to maintain the armies and to bring relief to calamity-stricken areas. According to most sources, the throne had in its employ some 100,000 eunuchs nationwide, including the 70,000 in both capitals. The annual cost of cosmetics alone for the 9,000 court women was budgeted at 400,000 taels a year. To celebrate Emperor Chung-chen's accession to the throne, according to Ming custom, two-and-a-half million taels had been spent on banquets and gifts for army soldiers. In 1635 the Board of Revenue reported that government expenditures exceeded tax revenues by a million taels, for constant rebel raids made it impossible to collect taxes from the poor, who more and more frequently were going over to the insurgents anyway. When in the same year rebel hordes destroyed the imperial tombs, the treasuries were so bare that all court officials had to personally contribute towards their replacement.

Mushrooming numbers of imperial princes and relatives throughout the empire, forbidden by Ming code to work for a living, were greatly irked to find their government-provided allowances dwindling, and used every means to exact tribute from the local people. Royal Ming clansmen imperiously demanded their full due and more from provincial treasuries, and if no funds were available, they attacked local officials with abusive language and even assaulted them bodily. In 1638, when complaints reached the emperor that imperial family members were impoverishing the people with exorbitant interest loans, seizing lands of those unable to pay their debts, even kidnapping and enslaving children of the destitute, his edict warned them that the anger of Heaven against such abuses could spell their end. However, when the ruler's fifth son fell seriously ill, it was rumored that the ailing prince had had a vision wherein a goddess had reproached the Son of Heaven for "mistreating" relatives of the empress. The goddess had further warned that, as a result, the ruler might be punished when all of the princes died young. This rumor terrified the emperor, and he at once pardoned the empress's dishonest brother whom he had just degraded and whose treasures he had confiscated. Histories say the story about the dream was concocted by palace eunuchs loyal to the empress.

In the latter half of his reign, Emperor Chung-chen lacked sufficient funds to support his armies. It was a court eunuch who finally proposed that every minister make a personal donation to the war fund. Though early in his reign the ruler had haughtily rejected just such a suggestion made by ministers—telling them that instead they should put a halt to the graft and abuses that had so drained the nation—now he was forced to approve the idea. Indeed, so impoverished had the Ming Empire become that it was soon necessary to solicit funds from ministers, imperial relatives, and even court eunuchs. In truth, though, it was too late for donations to the nation's cause, just as it was too late for reform.

By the 1630s the collecting of bounties by the imperial armies for Chinese rebel and Manchu enemy heads had spawned monstrous abuses. Once when rebels were devastating an area in Shensi, local inhabitants had to goad the Ming general to make an attack. When he did so, and returned with fifty severed heads to claim a victory, the heads were recognized by the people as those of local Chinese women. Again, when a Ming commanding officer tried to coerce a local governor to falsely report victory over rebel forces, and the governor refused to do so without first seeing rebel heads as proof, the commander went off and returned with hundreds of heads, at least eighty of which were identified as those of Chinese students from nearby districts. Conscienceless Ming soldiers turned in their compatriots' heads to deceive their officers; likewise the officers deceived the eunuch supervisors; and the supervisors deceived the court—as the distraught emperor agonized over reliable reports that the number of rebels was constantly increasing.

By this time, Jesuit missionaries from Europe had gained acceptance at the Peking palace and had taught some fifty eunuchs how to produce cannons for imperial armies. The method of production soon leaked out to rebel leaders, as well as to the Manchu enemy, who had already conquered vast Chinese territories in Manchuria. As early as 1633, an army supervisor, eunuch Kao Chi-lien, reported in a memorial to the throne that government troops dared not attack, for the rebels now possessed firearms of better quality than those of Ming armies, and that they were working day and night in their encampments to produce more cannons.

By this time two cunning rebel leaders had emerged to positions of predominance. Each had had military experience in Ming armies, and consolidated and trained such huge battalions of loyal followers that government attempts to overcome them were futile. One leader was the ferocious and diabolically cruel Chang Hsien-chung, the feared "Yellow Tiger." After fighting his way across China, Chang eventually conquered the southwestern province of Szechuan, massacring whole city populations if they offered resistance. When he met with persistent failure in taking the city of Chungking, high above the Yangtze River canyon, he ordered that 10,000 local men have their ears, noses, and right arms cut off, and then be paraded through the streets for all to see. Many historians think Chang was insane. His battle cry was "Kill! Kill! Kill!" Small wonder that many Szechuan towns surrendered without a struggle. Many of the inhabitants of this populous province died during Chang's reign of terror as a self-made "king." In 1647 Chang would be betrayed to the conquering Manchus by one of his own officials and put to death.

The other, more successful rebel leader was Li Tzu-cheng, who at first used the same harsh tactics as the Yellow Tiger, but then, under the advice of Chinese scholars who had succumbed to his influence, soon mended his ways. "One-eyed Li" he was called, in reference to an old injury which, besides costing him an eye, had puckered one cheek and left a scar running down the other. Early on, rebel leader Li began sending his emissaries in advance to areas he was planning to take over, to promise the populace not only exemption from taxes, but equal distribution of farm lands as well. Wherever he went, Li took pains in his public pronouncements to condemn the corruption of the Ming government and of Emperor Chung-chen, "a despot who employs eunuchs to rob the people and to falsely accuse decent officials of corruption." He further assured the people, "Unable to suffer the abuses of such a regime, I have marched my army of justice forth to save my people from their sufferings. Any soldier of mine who unjustly kills a man will be punished as a murderer of my own father, and if he insults a woman, he will suffer as if he had ravaged my mother."[21]

After capturing Honan province in 1640, Li's great rebel hordes moved quickly. When imperial armies were sent to Loyang to put down the rebels, Ming soldiers deeply resented that the Ming prince who ruled that area— one of the richest men in China—refused to give them financial support even to protect his own domain. Already a famine in his area had become so grave that several instances of cannibalism had been reported. But the reports had been blithely ignored by this avaricious prince. When at last he contributed barely enough for a feast to appease the disgruntled soldiers, a brigade general pocketed the entire amount, and the enraged soldiers defected to join rebel Li. With these reinforcements, Li took Loyang after a one-night siege. The Ming prince at first escaped by lowering himself down the city wall with a rope and hiding out in a Buddhist monastery, but he was soon discovered and killed. His palace burned for three days, and with it all his hoarded treasures.

Early in 1641, when Li was attacking the old capital city of Kaifeng, brave local residents determinedly defended themselves during a nine-month siege. Kaifeng did not fall until rebel Li broke the dikes in the Yellow River to inundate the entire city. By the following year, One-eyed Li had won many victories in which his use of cannon was the decisive factor. His armies moved swiftly on good horses he acquired by rewarding men whose first duty was to seize the best horses and mules in each newly conquered area. He was joined by many other rebel leaders and their followers, as well as a considerable number of Ming officials and scholars, for it was known that Li had a genuine respect for learning.

When news arrived that Li's armies were heading for the capital, the emperor put eunuch Tsao Hua-shun in charge of the city's defenses, despite the fact that he had been closely associated with the deposed eunuch strongman Wei Chung-hsien. As One-eyed Li advanced from Sian, he issued a manifesto summoning the populace to war: "The dukes and marquises eat meat and wear silken breeches, and the emperor employs them as his eyes and ears. Their jails are filled with innocent prisoners who could not pay the eunuchs' endless demands for more and more taxes."[22]

Hurriedly, Emperor Chung-chen convened an audience of grand secretaries for advice on raising funds for the deteriorated Ming armies. They reported that all treasuries were empty, and that tax revenue from the beleaguered provinces had ceased to come in. As a last resort, they suggested that funds for the army be taken from the palace treasury. For some moments, the emperor remained silent and tears ran down his face, until finally he was able to speak and confess that the royal coffers, too, were exhausted. The shaken ministers could only weakly suggest that he recall to duty the many military leaders whom he had dismissed when they met failure in battle.

When in April 1644 rebel leader Li arrived to establish his armies outside the gates of Peking, he attempted to negotiate a settlement with the Ming court by sending in eunuch Tu Hsun who had once been one of emperor Chung-chen's closest confidants, though he had long since defected to the rebels. The eunuch frankly advised his former imperial master that the rebels were invincible, and that he had best accept their terms of surrender. When the emperor turned to his grand secretary for his opinion, the man refused to utter a word. The monarch dismissed the eunuch and then flew into such a rage that he overturned the throne, bitterly rebuking the grand secretary for failure to produce any plan at all to save the dynasty.

The next day—the last day of the Ming Empire—was a tragic one for the emperor. He called a final court audience wherein nothing was accomplished and little was heard except the sobbing of the ruler and his officials. The despairing emperor returned to his palace, drank several cups of wine, and ordered that his young princely sons be sent to relatives for safety. Then, turning to his empress, he said, "Alas, our reign has come to an end." Both wept broken-heartedly. As court ladies burst into tears, the emperor waved them away, advising them to look to their own safety. The empress returned to her chambers in silence and hanged herself. Chung-chen summoned his fifteen-year-old princess daughter to gaze upon her and sigh, "How unfortunate and unhappy you are to be born into our family." With this, he drew his sword to decapitate her, but his hand faltered and he all but cut off her arm. He was too unnerved to attempt a second blow. He then wrote out his last imperial missive, begging rebel leader Li to spare his people, and left the palace accompanied by his most loyal personal eunuch, Wang Chen-en. Together they climbed the steps to a lovely open pavilion atop a hill in the Forbidden City, and there, after the emperor had hanged himself, his faithful old eunuch took his own life the same way.

Next day, the faithless eunuch Tsao Hua-shun, who had been placed in charge of city defenses, opened the city gates to the rebels. Li's forces overran Peking with no serious opposition. Though eunuchs had surrendered the city to him, and although he had eunuchs in his employ, rebel leader Li immediately drove thousands of eunuchs from the palace, leaving them to fend for themselves. At the Forbidden City, rebels set many buildings afire. Against a backdrop of flames, smoke, and falling timbers could be heard human screams of pain and the agonized trumpeting of imperial elephants trapped in the burning stables. The president of the board of censors and six ministers committed ritual suicide, while some 200 court ladies followed the example of one imperial concubine and drowned themselves in the royal canal.

The victorious rebel Li declared himself emperor of a new dynasty. But he proved totally incapable of keeping the glowing promises he had made to the people. Nor could he any longer control his own men. Most of the rebel soldiers wanted nothing more than to ravage the conquered capital and return, enriched, to their homes.

Many believe that the self-made rebel "emperor" might have successfully founded a Chinese dynasty had he sought the cooperation of Ming officials and the landed gentry, who—corrupt as they were—still retained much of their old influence and power. Instead, Li utterly humiliated the officials and the gentry, torturing top-ranking officials and putting others to death. Many Ming dignitaries committed suicide, totally unable to meet the rampant demands of Li's lieutenants for money and women. Rebel platoon leaders seized palaces of nobles and enjoyed a life of luxury. In the palace, every day at lavish banquets Li feasted his officers and the Ming officials who joined his regime. One official described the scene as follows: "The rebel leaders push and shove each other in taking their seats, fill their own wine cups to overflowing, and eat with their fingers. They curse, joke, shove and kick each other, and when they walk, they hold each others' hands."[23] Thousands of rebel peasant soldiers roamed the streets robbing homes and raping women. For them the rebellion was over; they no longer felt it necessary to adhere to leader Li's strict military discipline.

Li Tzu-cheng was not able to remain on the throne of China for long. His chances to do so were seriously hindered by the threat of powerful Manchu forces patiently watching for a chance to invade. A second threat was a huge Chinese army under command of Wu San-kuei firmly entrenched in the area where the Great Wall reaches the sea. This was the only strong Ming force still in existence. Commander Wu's forces had successfully acted as a deterrent against recent Manchu advances, but now, on hearing of the fall of Peking, he swore to avenge the suicide of his emperor and destroy rebel leader Li, who had killed commander Wu's father and was now in possession of the commander's beautiful Peking concubine.

Toward these ends, and looking to his own future, Commander Wu now sought assistance from the Manchu enemy in retaking Peking, a proposition they accepted with alacrity. Their combined forces easily entered the capital on June sixth. The conquering Manchus settled in as new rulers at Peking, proclaiming their own child-prince the emperor of their Ching Dynasty, while rebel leader Li and his ragtag armies hastily looted and burned as much of the city as possible and then fled to the west. In his flight through the countryside, Li reverted to his former cruel methods of ruthlessly exacting supplies from the populace. Meanwhile, the Manchus sent Commander Wu to run down and wreak his vengeance on rebel Li. Before he could find him, however, Li had been abandoned by all his supporters and killed by disaffected peasant farmers.

Later the Manchus humored Wu by allowing him to rule over Szechuan and Yunnan provinces, and even gave Wu's son a sister of their boy-emperor in marriage. Eventually, Wu's pretentions to sovereignty irked the Manchus and they ordered him back to Peking, prompting Wu to stage a rebellion. The Manchus forced him to retreat into Yunnan, where he died of old age.

When news that Peking had fallen to the Manchus reached the secondary Ming capital of Nanking, court ministers and former followers of the notorious eunuch Wei Chung-hsien hastily proclaimed the local ruling prince as Ming emperor. It is said that this prince was chosen because he was weak-willed and could be easily dominated. During his short reign, his reputation as a tireless wencher caused parents in the entire area to try to marry their daughters off as fast as possible, as palace eunuchs scoured the area rounding up concubines for his harem. Ming annals say this prince was especially fond of subteen girls, some of whom died as victims to his unspeakable lust. Within just a few months, the Nanking government fell to the Manchu armies. The prince fled with his entourage, but was soon captured and murdered. From then on several princes throughout the south fought each other for the Ming throne as they fled from place to place, hotly pursued by the Manchus. One by one they were overcome.

In 1647 the last Ming pretender set himself up as Ming emperor Yung-li at a court at present-day Canton. When the Manchus took that city, they chased the fleeing Yung-li and his court to Kueilin. About this time, Portuguese Catholic priests from Macao intervened in behalf of the Mings, furnishing advice and cannon, mainly because a great number of Yung-li's imperial family and court had been converted to Christianity. Largely through the religious zeal of the palace chief eunuch, who had been christened Achilles Pang, a Jesuit missionary at court had succeeded in baptizing Yung-li's empress as Ann, her infant son, the heir, as Constantine, and the dowager empress as Helen or Elena. Fifty court ladies, forty eunuchs, and 140 nobles had been converted to Catholicism. If Yung-li could successfully regain the throne of all China, the Portuguese fathers thought, their ultimate dream of converting the whole Chinese populace to Catholicism might be realized.

Under eunuch Achilles Pang's urging, and with assistance from the fathers, Empress Dowager Helen wrote the pope in Rome, advising him that through her influence the emperor's mother, empress, and baby crown prince had been converted. Accompanying her letter, the eunuch Achilles wrote his own missive, advising the pope that, at sixty-two years of age he was commander of all Ming sea and land forces in two provinces, commander of the imperial guard with full powers over the commissariat and financial department, master of palace ceremonies, and guardian of the imperial seals. Though ostensibly these letters requested the pope to send many more Vatican emissaries and missionaries, between the lines it became clear that the Ming court's real need was for military and financial aid. However, the Catholic father who carried the letters to Rome was delayed there for two years by the pope's death, and succeeded in returning the Vatican's noncommittal answer to China only after the dowager had died.

In 1981, for the first time, the Vatican put these two letters on public display, along with other old documents from its secret archives. Dowager Empress Helen's letter, dated 1650, was written in delicate Chinese characters on pure silk, and was authenticated with the imperial red Ming seal of state.

By 1658 Yung-li's court had been driven into Yunnan, and the following year was chased across the southern border into Burma. In 1661 commander Wu San-kuei entered Burma, seized the Ming pretender, and turned him over to Manchu hands. He was brought back to Yunnan province and put to death by strangulation with a bow string. With him died all Ming Dynasty ambitions to regain the throne. Once again, China was to be ruled by aliens.

The Ming Dynasty was the last of three powerful long-lasting regimes—after the Han and Tang—to be fatally undermined by palace eunuchs. As has often been noted, all three dynasties were ruled by the Chinese themselves.

Notes

1. Albert Chan, *Glory and Fall of the Ming Dynasty.*
2. Ibid.
3. Wang Chia-yu, *Lives and Loves of Chinese Emperors.*
4. Albert Chan, *Glory and Fall of the Ming Dynasty.*
5. Ibid.
6. Ibid.
7. Ibid.
8. Ibid.
9. Albert Chan, *Glory and Fall of the Ming Dynasty.*
10. Ibid.
11. Ibid.
12. Charles O. Hucker, *The Censorial System of Ming China.*
13. Ibid.
14. Ibid.
15. Albert Chan, *Glory and Fall of the Ming Dynasty.*
16. Charles O. Hucker, *The Censorial System of Ming China.*
17. Ibid.
18. Ibid.
19. Ibid.
20. Albert Chan, *Glory and Fall of the Ming Dynasty.*
21. Ibid.
22. Wang Chia-yu, *Lives and Loves of Chinese Emperors.*
23. Albert Chan, *Glory and Fall of the Ming Dynasty.*

18

Eunuchs Under Alien Manchu Rule

EARLY CHING DYNASTY (A.D. 1644-1850)

Long before the vigorous, military-minded Tartar Manchus took Peking in 1644, they had established their own Chinese-style Ching Dynasty over Manchurian peoples, and were already putting into practice many Chinese court rituals. Indeed there was little to distinguish the Manchu conquerors from their Chinese subjects, except for their slightly elongated heads (produced during babyhood by having infants sleep only on their sides), and the menfolk's hairdos (their heads were clean-shaven except at the back of the crown, where the hair was allowed to grow long and hang down in a queue, that is, a single braided pigtail).

The first Manchu to rule from Peking, Emperor Shun Chih, came to the throne as a mere child under a strong regency of elders. As a way to win Chinese hearts, the Manchus made a conscientious effort to perpetuate Confucian culture, deliberately declaring themselves to be upholders of the Chinese tradition. This is part of the reason their reign in China lasted so long—268 years. They retained all the existing machinery and willing personnel of the Ming court, including many eunuchs. Chinese who chose to cooperate with the Manchus—and most Northerners readily did so—received special rewards: promotions for generals and bureaucrats, tax deductions for all others who entered government service. Those who resisted the new Manchu overlords received harsh and swift punishment, as did

Southerners in the lower Yangtze valley, where massive killings by Manchu troops have been described as the most atrocious in Chinese history.

As a mark of loyalty to the Ching regime, the Manchu overlords mandated that all subjects must shave their heads and wear the Manchu-style pigtail, a rule which was followed till the end of the dynasty. Inter-marriage between Chinese and Manchus was strictly forbidden. In the palace, the Manchu code was: "No Manchu eunuchs, no Chinese concubines"— for the Manchus, as the elite class, would never stoop to castration, nor to the corruption of their imperial bloodline with an heir born to a Chinese concubine.

From the very first, Manchu princes and regents, remembering how eunuchs had corrupted the Ming courts, looked upon the eunuch corps with distrust. They considered them a distasteful necessity. Regulations were again introduced forbidding any eunuch to wear the official button on their caps denoting rank above the fourth class. Eunuch activities and opportunities were harshly restricted. Manchu officials were given charge over the great variety of palace departments, including the eunuch household staff and all its duties.

By the time he reached the age of fifteen in 1651, Emperor Shun Chih had fallen under the sway of certain eunuchs who encouraged him to assume direct control of government. The assistance of his favorite eunuch, Wu Liang-fu, in overthrowing the powerful regents boosted the eunuchs' stock at court. Gradually, the young emperor found himself relying more and more upon eunuchs to help conduct internal palace affairs and even some state matters. Soon the eunuchs so controlled the young ruler's daily life that he could not escape their influence if he wanted to. Rumor had it that the eunuchs encouraged and led him into various vices and profligate activities to cause him to neglect his imperial duties.

In 1653 Shun Chih formally established thirteen palace offices headed up by eunuchs, some of them even in charge of issuing edicts and appointing officials. A Manchu bondservant now served as Manchu language tutor in the palace school for eunuchs. Although in 1655 Shun Chih had to warn the eunuchs to mend their corrupt ways—and three years later even had to reprimand eunuch Wu Liang-fu and his minions for stepping out of line—they continued to grow in numbers and influence. It is reported that, although Shun Chih was not fond of his first empress, it was the eunuchs who successfully encouraged him to degrade her.

Shortly after taking over the government, at a palace celebration, Shun Chih first noticed the wife of a young Manchu lord and immediately became passionately enamored by her beauty. Her hapless husband, on learning of the emperor's burning desire, committed suicide. Shun Chih had her brought into the palace and titled her Second Consort. His happiness knew no bounds for several years, and when she bore him a son he was ecstatic. Contemporaries noted that the royal couple was deeply in love, and when the consort and her baby suddenly died, the emperor's grief was terrifying to behold. Palace gossips suspected that the mother and child had been poisoned by the emperor's enemies. Shun Chih had thirty of her eunuchs and maids put to death and buried with her, and canonized her posthumously as empress. In his extreme bereavement, the emperor had to be forcibly prohibited from taking his own life.

From then on Emperor Shun Chih went into decline, subject to violent outbursts of temper, never to become an effective ruler. In 1659, when he learned of the siege of Nanking and declared his intention to go personally to the front lines of battle, he became so angered at the objections from his mother and wet nurse that he mutilated one of his thrones with a sword. He only quieted down under the admonitions of a favored European Catholic father and after news came that Nanking had been saved for the Manchus.

In his last years Shun Chih, suffering from poor physical and possibly mental health, turned to Buddhism, gradually becoming a religious fanatic under encouragement of his eunuchs. In 1657, on a hunting trip, eunuchs arranged the emperor's meeting with a charismatic monk who had once befriended the eunuchs. So charmed was the ruler by this priest that he frequently summoned him to the palace to lecture and perform Buddhist rites. Led to believe that in a previous incarnation he had himself been a monk, Shun Chih became a devout believer. From then on he associated much with Buddhist priests, persuading his empress, the dowager empress, and a number of palace eunuchs to become devotees of Chan Buddhism. He even once had his head completely shaved, with a view of entering the priesthood. When his empress died in 1660, he had elaborate and costly Buddhist ceremonies performed, with a monk lighting the pyre on which her body was cremated.

Early in 1661 the palace suddenly announced that Emperor Shun Chih had died of smallpox. Though he had previously designated his son as heir, with four Manchu nobles as regents, his mother and the regents now had the decree document destroyed. They issued a new will in the dead emperor's name wherein they had him blame himself for grave "errors," such as the unusual honors and extravagant funeral he had given his consort, his preference for Chinese officials over those of Manchu blood, and his restoration of eunuch-controlled offices in the palace.

Many believed that Shun Chih was deliberately murdered. Only five days before his death he had personally attended the tonsuring rituals of his favorite eunuch, Wu Liang-fu, in preparation for the eunuch's entrance into the Buddhist priesthood. Moreover, the minute the throne passed to the dead emperor's eight-year-old son, the new regents had eunuch Wu Liang-fu beheaded. Many eunuchs fell from grace at this time. Some were accused of misdeeds and executed, and some were merely dismissed. The inner-palace offices which Shun Chih had set up with eunuchs in charge were abolished, and once again Manchu banner men were appointed to head up offices controlling all eunuchs and palace servants.

After the weak and ineffectual reign of the first Manchu ruler in China, no one envisioned that his son, the child Emperor Kang Hsi, would develop into the one of the finest, strongest, most humane monarchs the empire was ever to know. When only thirteen years old, Kang Hsi took over the reins of government, threw out his detested regents, and to celebrate his accession, restored all lands unjustly seized by the Manchus to the rightful Chinese owners. In 1670, when only sixteen, he issued the famous "Sacred Edict" of sixteen simple maxims laying down rules for the moral conduct of his officials and subjects. These maxims came to be regarded with extravagant reverence. Kang Hsi's son and successor later decreed that the Sacred Edict should be read out to the public in every city and town in the empire on the first and fifteenth of each month.

In manhood, Kang Hsi became a noble, robust figure of above-average height. Nothing seemed to escape him, with his intensely bright and intelligent eyes, his prodigious memory, and his vast interest in everything about the empire, from the entire flora and fauna to the welfare and happiness of its multitudinous subjects. A hardy warrior himself, Kang Hsi often personally accompanied his armies on campaigns to regain the loyalty of tribute peoples who had drifted away. During his sixty-year reign, his armies overcame rebellious leaders in South China, reoccupied Taiwan, drove out encroaching Russians from the Manchu territory, and brought back recalcitrant Mongol and Turkestani peoples into the Chinese fold.

Kang Hsi was also an avid patron of Confucian education, the theater and arts, and the age-old examination system which brought learned men into his government. Under his personal supervision, huge and minutely detailed dictionaries and encyclopedia were produced. Though Kang Hsi urged his followers to retain their Manchu culture, it was under his wise, energetic, and sympathetic rule that the Manchus gradually assimilated Chinese culture.

While Kang Hsi relied unquestioningly on certain loyal personal eunuchs, he decreed that no eunuch should leave the capital. He also ruled that eunuchs caught in crimes should be punished more severely than ordinary men, for their very livelihood depended on their trustworthiness. "If too much grace is shown to inferiors," he said, "they become lazy and uppity and will be sure to stir up trouble. That is why I punished eunuch Chien Wen-tsai so strictly when he beat a commoner to death, saying my order of strangulation was not harsh enough. For eunuchs are basically *yin* (female) in nature—quite different from ordinary men. When weak with age, they babble like babies. Even my few eunuchs-of-the-Presence, with whom I might chatter and exchange family jokes, are never allowed to discuss political or government affairs. I have less than 500 eunuchs in all, as compared to the immense numbers kept by the Ming, and I keep them working at strictly menial jobs. I ignore their frowns and smiles, and make sure that they stay poor."[1]

He also ruled against foot-binding among Chinese females, but this rule failed so completely that within four years it had to be rescinded. Manchu women, however, were never allowed to have bound feet.

Kang Hsi was an avid writer, leaving copious memoirs that reveal the great man's character. He told his sons that he personally read all incoming palace memorials and wrote the condensations himself—"with the left hand if the right was paining too much." He also wrote all his own edicts, using the same ancient Chinese calligraphy in his old age that he learned as a boy from his eunuch tutors in the Peking palace, adding, "I also practice my Manchu script to keep it clear and rapid."

Kang Hsi told how he executed only one man for "treasonous writing"—a Chinese scholar who claimed that the late Ming pretenders should be properly listed as bona fide Ming emperors, and that the Manchus were imposing censorship to cover up evidence of their forceful conquest of Ming China. Though the Manchu Board of Punishment recommended that the scholar be sliced up to die slowly, that all his male relations over sixteen years of age be executed, and that all his female kin and children be enslaved to the state, Kang Hsi said, "I mercifully lowered his sentence to beheading and spared all his relatives." He further stated that in the early years of his reign, he learned many truths about the Ming Dynasty by carefully questioning Ming eunuchs, such as Yuan Peng-ching, who had served the Ming Dynasty but was now in Manchu employ. "Obviously," he wrote, "much information in Ming annals is incorrect." Kang Hsi was not one to be easily duped.

He even left advice on health and medicines, saying that while he usually gave steamed ginseng plasters, called "spring snow," to old folks with upset bowels, he had also personally tested out eunuch Ho Shang's prescription for decreasing the flow of dysentery. As for himself, he took every precaution to make both the physician and a eunuch sign each prescription analysis and taste each medicine before it was brought to him.

"When my personal eunuch Ku Wen-hsiang started the study of medicine, I warned him that it is better to do nothing than to learn common and vulgar medical practices," he wrote.[2] When a commoner once offered Kang Hsi a book said to contain the secrets of immortality, he threw the book back at the man, so little faith had he in Taoist magic aimed at attaining vigor and longevity.

As he was approaching old age, Kang Hsi reminded his family that one of the greatest Manchu taboos was against letting others support one by holding one up under the armpits. When his feet began swelling so painfully that even to touch them was an agony, he refused to let attendants support him except for a little help on each side. "We Manchus are placed over men and have people around to serve us," he said, "so we must bear our pains in silence. Otherwise what will eunuchs and the poor, who have no one to support them, do when they are old and ill?"[3]

He wrote at length about the "Chinese Rites Controversy" that had developed among factions of European Catholic priests over whether their Chinese converts should be allowed to call the Christian God "Heaven," and whether they should be allowed to worship their ancestors and Confucius by kneeling and making offerings.

Kang Hsi wrote: "I agree with the faction of Peking Catholic fathers who know that we honor Confucius as a sage, not a deity, and that our rituals to ancestors are an expression of love and filial remembrance—not intended to seek protection from their spirits. There is no idea that the soul of an ancestor dwells in his wooden ancestral tablet before which we bow and make offerings. When sacrifices are offered to Heaven, it is not the blue sky being addressed, but the lord and creator of all things. We venerate Confucius because of his doctrines and respect for virtue, his system of education, and his inculcation of love for superiors and ancestors.

"When I discovered on a southern tour in 1703 that there were Catholic missionaries wandering at will over China, I decreed that unless they signed a certificate agreeing with my views of Chinese rites, and agreed to stay for life in China, they had to leave the country. I also reiterated my 1669 edict that banned Westerners from preaching their Christian religion in the provinces.

"I've been told that the Western God fashioned a man with a human soul from the blood of a virgin called Mary; and that Jesus was born during the time of our Han Emperor Ai-Ti, who reigned from 8 B.C. to A.D. 1, and that he was killed on a cross for man's sins. People then held meetings in which slaves and masters, men and women mixed together and drank some holy substance. When I asked visiting fathers why their

God had not forgiven his son and kept him from dying on a cross, they tried to reply, but their answers were far from clear."[4]

Plainly Kang Hsi did not want his subjects converted to a religion which might obliterate the very heart of Chinese culture—Confucianism and its worship of Heaven and the Ancestors.

Kang Hsi's personal, informal letters to his most favored and trusted Chief Eunuch Ku Wen-hsiang, written during the spring of 1697 when he was off with his armies chasing the rebel Mongolian leader Galdan, reveal his personal solicitude for his family, consorts, and concubines left in the Forbidden City under the eunuch's care. During this prolonged military campaign, Kang Hsi ruled his empire from an army tent, with daily official runners bringing memorials and news from the palace, and returning with his edicts and messages. "The weather here is much colder than in Peking and I am really feeling it," he wrote his eunuch. "Some time ago the palace storeroom had two fur coats, one of wolf, one of desert fox. Have these coats lined, the sleeves with Yu satin, the bodies with Ling-ning silk. Send them along to me with the next batch of memorials. The coats mustn't be too tight—the lot you last sent were too small and very uncomfortable. You must be more careful of such things. When I left Peking the consort Te-fei was slightly ill. Is she better now? I hope that my sons who had the measles are all recovered and that the palaces are all clear of contamination. I myself am in fine health."

Again he wrote, "In the area where I now am, everyone from white-haired elders to babies in arms bows down to the ground before my horse, just as I experienced during my southern tour. I am happy in mind and well in body, as are all my retinue. Please pass this news along to ladies in the palace." Another time he wrote that he was especially enjoying one region's white noodles and added, "I know these are small details. I don't send them for outside transmittal, but just to let you people in the palace know of them. . . . Please offer up a box of white noodles which I'm sending in greeting to the consorts in the two palaces." After he had written in great detail of how to prepare delicious sun-dried muskmelon from another area, he told his Peking eunuch, "I know this is a trifling matter, but my heart is so far away from all of you—so don't laugh at me for this." Again he would send lists of undergarments and clothing needed by the female attendants in his traveling entourage, and sent special gifts for the empress dowager, consorts, and concubines according to specific lists he had carefully prepared. "The cucumbers you sent me are excellent—you must send more with each delivery of memorials—and also send me some radish and eggplant."

Finally he wrote his chief eunuch, "My great task is done. We have chased out the Mongolian enemy Galdan, he has committed suicide, and his followers have come back to our allegiance. We will be returning shortly, partly by land, partly by river transport. I can only say that my mind is expanded and my body at ease—and we're coming home!"[5] Kang Hsi's priceless letters, sealed in a box in the Manchu palace, were discovered by scholars after the 1911 fall of imperial rule.

Kang Hsi sired fifty-six children, but of his thirty-six sons, only twenty grew to manhood. All his sons were born to various of his 300 concubines except one, Yin-jeng, whose mother was an empress. She died giving birth. For this son and heir apparent, the emperor had great love and great expectations. But Yin-jeng turned out to be the greatest sorrow, disappointment, and shame of Kang Hsi's life. He grew up a pampered, spoiled prince, fawned over by the imperial family, eunuchs, and ladies of the palace. His doting father overlooked his youthful escapades and debaucheries, but when the prince reached manhood his excesses and blatant dissipation could no longer be excused.

In 1708, while on a journey, Emperor Kang Hsi, after learning of Yin-jeng's latest outrages, made his son kneel outside the royal palace tent before the entire imperial entourage to hear the reading of this edict: ". . . Yin-jeng rejects the virtues of his ancestors and disobeys my own orders. He is so dissolute, tyrannical, brutal and debauched, that it is hard even to speak of it. I've tolerated him for twenty years, but he has steadily grown worse, scorning and tyrannizing all at court. He has assembled a clique of ne'er-do-wells, he spies on my personal life, and once even slit the curtains of my tent to peek in on me at night. He intercepts and keeps tribute gifts sent to me, attacks princes and officials, and brutally beats them."[6] Sadly and angrily the emperor withdrew Yin-jeng's status of heir apparent, explaining that his son allowed "outside" women to come and go freely at his palace, and that he was buying up pretty little boys from the south through illegal agents and using them in unspeakable sexual orgies. But within a year Kang Hsi had a change of heart. Since Yin-jeng had been conducting himself in a somewhat more acceptable way, his father let himself be convinced that his son was not really mad, but had been acting so atrociously because he had been put under a malignant spell cast by a Lamaist monk hired by his own princely brothers. The guilty princes were punished, and Yin-jeng reinstated as heir.

By 1712, however, Kang Hsi found it necessary to report to the imperial clan that his heir's "madness" was back, and that the emperor could bear no more. Yin-jeng had been spying on people in the palace privies; spitting and swearing at his retinue, consorts, and eunuchs; and letting all kinds of depraved persons pass in and out of his gate. Heartbroken, Kang Hsi placed Yin-jeng in perpetual confinement and selected his fourth son, Yung Cheng, as heir.

Late in 1722 the aging emperor fell seriously ill from complications of a cold caught on a hunting trip. He retired to recuperate at his beloved summer palace northwest of Peking. Though on the winter solstice Yung Cheng had been deputized to represent him at the state sacrifices and was supposed to be at the Temple of Heaven, he instead showed up at his father's bedside. Within a short time, Yung Cheng emerged from the sickroom and announced to courtiers and attendants that Emperor Kang Hsi was dead, and was immediately pronounced the new emperor.

Unofficial chronicles strongly hint that Yung Cheng murdered his father, but the truth may never be known. We do know that the new emperor lost no time getting rid of all his brothers, five of whom died in jail. For official purposes, the great emperor Kang Hsi left the following valedictory edict to be read to his subjects: "I am now close to seventy and have been sixty-one years on the throne—this is all due to the quiet protection of Heaven and earth, and the ancestral spirits, it was not my meager virtue that did it. My fourth son has a noble character and profoundly resembles me. It is definite that he has the ability to inherit the empire. Let him succeed me on the throne and become emperor. When I die, announce to my people that they should be obedient to the rituals and wear mourning clothes for twenty-seven days."[7]

Yung Cheng, who became emperor in 1723, was a rather cold and colorless man, and lived to rule for only twelve years. He was competent, hardworking, and most careful of the public good, but a pale figure in comparison with his dynamic father. Only a few European Jesuit fathers remained in favor at Yung Cheng's court, tolerated because of their scientific knowledge and contributions, such as their knowledge about weapons and their work on the Board of Astronomy. By 1724 Yung Cheng had expelled almost all other Christian missionaries from the country, destroyed their churches, and relentlessly persecuted their Chinese converts.

The increase in national prosperity achieved during his father's long reign had produced an alarming rise in population. Now pressure and expansion of the Chinese populace into the hills and valleys inhabited by aborigine peoples in the southwest caused these tribes to rise up in rebellion. It took Yung Cheng many years and much expense to put down their guerrilla fighting. With this emperor's death in 1735, the throne passed to his twenty-four-year-old son, the well-known Chien Lung, whose sixty-year reign would bring the Manchu Dynasty to the peak of its power and prestige.

Though as a young prince Chien Lung had earned a reputation for reckless living, having carried on an extended illicit affair with his sister-in-law—their meetings at the summer palace arranged by his personal eunuch—he was to become one of the dynasty's greatest emperors. A strong military leader, intelligent administrator, and diplomat, he was also a keen classical scholar, an avid patron of literature, and an able poet, attributes greatly admired by his Chinese subjects.

Although Chien Lung employed several talented Catholic fathers at court and was personally friendly with several Jesuit portrait-painters and mathematicians, he nonetheless strictly forbade his subjects to embrace Christianity. As one father wrote, "He is a great prince who sees and does everything for himself. The older he grows the more favorable becomes his attitude toward Europeans. He and his nobles privately agree that our religion is good. If he forbids us to preach it in public, and does not allow our missionaries in the territories, we know it is purely for political reasons, and for fear that under the pretext of religion we are concealing some other devious plan. For the court is well aware of the conquests European countries have made in Asia [the British in India, Dutch in Indonesia] and are afraid lest something similar happen to China."[8]

Chien Lung completed the work of his revered grandfather, subduing Mongolia, Tibet, Burma, and even Nepal, beyond Tibet and the Himalayan mountains. In 1775, when his armies finally put down a prolonged uprising of the southern Miao aborigines, they left the tribal population decimated, carried their chieftains off to Peking, where they all perished under torture and their severed heads were exposed in the streets in cages. Manchu subjugation of the Miaos completed the conquest of China. By the end of Chien Lung's reign, the Chinese Empire again was the size it had been at the zenith of the Tang era. Thus, until he neared old age, Chien Lung remained in full command of his immensely laborious task as supreme autocrat over an empire of tremendous size.

When Manchu power reached its peak during Chien Lung's reign, the Forbidden City at the heart of Peking housed over 10,000 people: almost 100 in Chien Lung's immediate family, innumerable concubines, palace guardsmen, several thousand Chinese eunuchs, maids, sweepers, and gardeners. The tremendous Household Department was once again in the hands of eunuchs, who were classified into forty-eight grades and ranks, and most of whom were able to exact squeeze money for every activity performed. Eunuchs-of-the-Presence were highest in rank and had the greatest opportunity for the most lucrative squeeze practices. By this time the squeeze money system had become the accepted, normal means of getting things done in the palace.

Chien Lung's intrepid Grand Counselor Liu was noted for his vituperative memorials reporting the misconduct of officials high and low.

All officialdom dreaded Liu's poisonous pen, except a brazen chief eunuch who had become so overbearing that he fancied himself and his eunuchs above any condemnation from a grand counselor. One day this eunuch dared to halt the powerful Liu's carriage and insolently announce that, despite the grand counselor's power to report crimes of others, the eunuchs could laugh in his face, for he had no power over them since they never misconducted themselves. The grand counselor listened, remarked that he would take the matter up on the morrow, and went on his way.

Next day, saying nothing about the incident, Liu sent in a memorial warning that although eunuchs had been emasculated, it appeared that in many cases their sexual organs grew back to the extent where recastration was necessary. He pointed out (actually quite erroneously) that this had happened during the Ming, resulting in licentiousness between eunuchs and palace ladies, and that the Ming emperor, after an inspection of the eunuchs' privates, had found it necessary to recastrate many of them. Now, he said, to prevent such scandals from recurring, the entire eunuch corps should be at once inspected so those whose organs had even partially grown back might be "swept clean" once more. Alarmed, Emperor Chien Lung immediately issued orders that all eunuchs be examined and, if necessary, recastrated. Many eunuchs underwent a second operation at the hands of the eunuch clinic "knifers," and many of them died as a result. As the Chinese so expressively put it, they were "swept dead" instead of "swept clean." Those eunuchs who recovered, after severe suffering and shame, probably never knew that this setback for the eunuch corps was due entirely to the insolence of their own chief eunuch.

In 1774 Chien Lung had eunuch Kao Yun-tsung put on trial for having divulged to several high officials the emperor's private ratings of certain minor officials. In his confession, the eunuch revealed that a ranking official had helped extricate him from a lawsuit, and that he had also informed the same official about the emperor's private criticism of another bureaucrat. Emperor Chien Lung vehemently denounced the official involved for consorting with a eunuch, but allowed him to stay in office, while eunuch Kao Yun-tsung was put to death.

During imperial audiences, after a eunuch had announced each official's presence and led him to his appointed place, the eunuch promptly left the hall with an obvious show of subservience and reverent silence. If he failed to do so, or even lingered near the doors, Manchu law demanded that he be silenced forever by decapitation, so fearful was the throne that state secrets might be divulged.

Though Chien Lung was stern with his eunuchs, he was also concerned with their welfare, allowing them to build another eunuch temple, which they named after and dedicated to the worship of their patron deity, the self-castrated army general whom the Ming Dynasty had deified. At the same time, Chien Lung allowed the eunuchs to enclose an area for a second eunuch cemetery. The temple was also used as a recuperating place for sick eunuchs. When they reached age seventy, or were rendered unfit for duty by poor health, eunuchs were allowed to retire on a small pension, and those who so desired had the privilege of living in one of their temple compounds rent-free.

Most historians agree that while Chien Lung brought the Manchu Dynasty to its peak of power, towards the end of his long rule decline had already set in, and that his ostentatious court was but a magnificent facade hiding inner decay. When Lord Macartney came to China in 1793 representing the King of England at Chien Lung's court, he was not deceived by the outward display of grandeur. Later he astutely reported that China was like a great old ship now far gone toward decay and that it could never be rebuilt again on the same rotting bottom.

In a veritable architectural renaissance, Chien Lung continued his predecessor's extravagant spending to restore and perfect the splendid temples and palaces started under the Ming Dynasty. For his magnificent summer palace complex northwest of Peking, he employed French Catholic fathers to plan and lay out acres and acres of gardens, cut through with lakes and waterways spanned by lacy white marble bridges, the entire area studded with some 200 palaces and pleasure pavilions roofed with multi-colored glazed tiles.

In his last years, a rebellion erupted in Central China of the age-old White Lotus secret society, the leader claiming he was a descendant of the House of Ming. The rebellion heralded a century of disorder. To the six provinces where the rebellion spread, the throne sent its armies to conduct an inquisition of exceptional ferocity, in four months' time beheading over 20,000 rebels. The cost to the government ran into millions of taels, and the White Lotus rebels were not completely suppressed until into the next reign.

Perhaps Chien Lung's lavish extravagances reached their height in 1777 when his aged mother died and he decreed, "I hereby order that a *stupa* [a domed temple] be built of solid gold to contain the hair of Her Majesty the Empress Dowager, with an image of Amitabha Buddha enshrined within." When the treasuries could not produce enough gold, palaces and warehouses were scoured for gold utensils and ingots to be melted down. In the end, 700 taels of silver had to be added to make the *stupa* large enough to hold the Buddhist figurine and the gold casket containing the dowager's shorn locks. This approximately three-foot-tall creation is today on display at the Peking Palace Museum. Chien Lung also built the great Hall of Classics in the capital containing 3,000 stone tablets engraved with texts from China's ancient literature. Chien Lung himself often went there to expand his considerable knowledge of the Chinese classics.

Nobody knows for sure what possessed Chien Lung in his last years to almost completely turn the government over to the most corrupt scoundrel the dynasty was ever to produce. Some suggest that the emperor may have become senile by his sixty-fifth year, while most hint that he became sexually enamored of Ho Shen, a handsome young Manchu gate guard who charmed the aging monarch with his affable, self-possessed demeanor and exceedingly clever tongue. Chien Lung took Ho Shen into the palace as a close companion, and for twenty long years heaped upon him honors, titles, highest offices, and finally a long-coveted dukedom. Though he was intelligent and capable, Ho Shen's dominating trait was a voracious greed for wealth and power, which he proceeded to accumulate in vast amounts. Enjoying the complete, blind confidence and trust of the emperor, Ho Shen was able to cause the advancement or ruin of any official. No one dared refuse his demands. He placed his own henchmen in key positions and through them and other cowering officials managed to exact untold wealth from the masses, who were helpless in the face of the blatant corruption that flourished throughout the government under Ho Shen's aegis.

Perhaps the most sordid of Ho Shen's depravities occurred when impoverished people of Central and Western China, crushed by cruel exactions to meet his insatiable demands for taxes, were finally driven to revolt. Ho Shen and his crooked crony officials deliberately prolonged the campaign against these rebels for several years, while they pocketed the imperial funds that they falsely reported were going to meet military expenses, and ruthlessly continued to slaughter thousands of innocent noncombatants in order to report victories.

The Ching Dynasty's disintegration began during the time of Ho Shen's grip on the nation. While no one dared indict Ho Shen as long as his doting patron lived, when Chien Lung died the next ruler immediately had Ho Shen arrested for grand larceny, deprived of all his posts, and finally allowed to commit suicide. His amassed fortune and properties, estimated in value at 223 million silver taels, was confiscated by the imperial family.

From Chien Lung's reign onward, the Manchu nobility, forbidden by law to engage in commerce or any profession except government or military, were steadily losing the virility of their warrior ancestors, degenerating into a spendthrift aristocracy. Their main concern was extorting from the populace the money which their blatant extravagances so rapidly dissipated.

The Chinese scholar-gentry class had always owed its ranks and position to proficiency in knowledge of the ancient classics, and was neither expected nor encouraged to study practical sciences or economic concerns. Similarly, the scholarly class of the Manchus adopted the most conservative outlook, opposed to any new ideas in literature, politics, and philosophy. Industry, foreign trade, and commerce were regarded with disdain, and technical knowledge was for lowly craftsmen. As a result, the official and private world of the Manchu emperors, completely dominated by Confucian pedantry, was closed to all other knowledge. They refused to believe that anything valuable could possibly be learned from the Western barbarian merchants who were now making inroads along China's shores.

When Lord Macartney arrived from England on a mission seeking diplomatic relations with China and more ports for European traders, he was politely and humiliatingly dismissed. The Chinese court was unable to view the gifts he brought from his king to Emperor Chien Lung as anything other than tribute from "a small island nation at the end of the seas," whose representative had scandalously refused to kowtow before the Son of Heaven.

In return, the emperor's letter advised the king of England that while he certainly deserved some fine gifts for having taken the trouble to send a tributary emissary with presents from across such vast distances, the strange and costly items he had sent to China were of no interest to the emperor, for China already possessed her needs in all things and had no use for England's manufactures. He added that no foreign barbarian merchants would be allowed to come north to Peking from the one open port at Canton, and that any attempt to do so would bring most unfortunate results. "It behooves you, O King," he wrote, "to respect my sentiments and to display even greater devotion and loyalty in the future, so that by perpetual submission to the Chinese throne you may secure peace and prosperity for your country." Chien Lung signed the epistle saying, "Tremblingly obey and show no negligence! This is a special mandate!"[9] For the next century China would be humiliated again and again by European nations marching in to divide up the empire into their own spheres of influence.

In 1795, after he had ruled nearly sixty years, the aged Chien Lung abdicated in favor of his son, avowing that out of respect for his revered grandfather who had reigned for sixty years, no imperial Manchu descendant should rule longer. His son, Chia Ching, sat on the throne for three years before the old emperor died. Out of respect for his father, only then did Chia Ching actually take over as supreme monarch. This example of filial piety indicates how deeply Confucian principles and beliefs had become imbedded in the thinking of the Manchu ruling class, and how by this time the Manchus really had become "more Chinese than the Chinese themselves."

From this time on there was serious unrest in the empire. In 1803, as Emperor Chia Ching, carried in his imperial sedan chair, was about to reenter the palace gate, a strange man dashed at him and tried to assassinate him with a dagger. The assailant was overcome by guards and attendants. Later, he confessed that he was an unemployed cook. He had been driven mad by extreme poverty. Strange dreams and divinations had left him imagining that he was invulnerable and especially skilled in the martial arts. He was carted off to the execution ground and tied to a stake. His two sons were brought forth and made to kowtow before him, as an executioner cut slices of flesh from his body, limbs, and head. When the victim begged his torturers to end his life, the supervising official informed him that the emperor had decreed that the miscreant must be made to suffer as long as possible.

Much of Chia Ching's early reign went toward putting down the still raging White Lotus rebellion. Even after the revolt was quelled, secret semireligious societies among the populace remained active underground. Rebellions inspired by secret sects had always been early indications of misrule and the consequent general impoverishment of the masses, a warning which in this case the Manchus failed to recognize.

The autumn of 1813 saw the terrified Forbidden City under attack from some 100 members of yet another secret society whose fanatical leader had managed to win the allegiance and membership of seven eunuchs within the imperial palace. With eunuch ringleader Ling Te-tsai's guidance and assistance from his eunuch co-conspirators, the rebels stormed and scaled the palace gates to engage the guards, loyal eunuchs, and even two of Chia Ching's princely sons in bloody hand-to-hand combat. Carriages were even ordered for the consorts and concubines to flee the palace, before imperial troops arrived to finally overcome the outnumbered rebels and conspiring eunuchs. Days later, after all the guilty along with all their family members had been rounded up and sentenced to dismemberment, palace inhabitants remained so shaken that Chia Ching ordered his eunuchs to take herbal medicines especially prepared to relieve their "mental uneasiness" and drive away the evil spirits which had possessed some of their colleagues.

The emperor lost no time in decreeing that, from now on, no eunuch would be allowed outside the palace except for a limited number of hours, and only then in groups of three or four, so they could report each others' activities. One contemporary scholar wrote that the disgraceful attack on the palace fully exposed the laxity and corruption of the government, the stupidity of Manchu officialdom, the unpopularity of imperial rule, and the declining capacity of Ching Dynasty armies.

All in all, Chia Ching proved himself but a mediocre ruler, a worthless emperor exemplifying an increasing degeneracy and exhaustion in the imperial dynastic bloodline. His main interest in life was amassing wealth.

In 1816, when Lord Amherst arrived at Peking leading another diplomatic mission from England, he was unceremoniously dismissed back to the coast the same day even less diplomatically than his predecessor, Lord Macartney, had been treated. This may have been because Chia Ching's officials had assured him that Amherst would prostrate himself in the traditional kowtow before the emperor, and then when they learned that he had no intention of doing so, they sent him packing to save their own faces.

As China drifted along in intellectual stagnation and a petrified cultural tradition, the rising popular unrest at home and the disapproved materialistic progress of the European "foreign devils" only confirmed the Chinese ruling class in their belief that "Confucianism is for the Chinese what water is to fish"—a vital necessity.

In 1820, when Chia Ching died at the Jehol palace after being struck by lightning, his son was at once proclaimed Emperor Tao Kuang. Realizing the depleted state of national finances, this new ruler early embarked on a policy of frugality and reduction of palace extravagance. Reportedly the emperor himself sometimes wore old and patched garments. It was this close-fisted Emperor Tao Kuang who terminated the expensive practice of his forebears of spending summers at Jehol, accompanied by most of the court. He was content to reside in Peking, with occasional trips to the nearby summer palace. Alarmed at the terrible expense in putting down a fierce and costly three-year rebellion of the Muslims in Turkestan, he refrained from pursuing the war further west, and instead bribed the Muslims to accept peace.

Tao Kuang, himself a well-meaning, decent man, in 1827 was greatly saddened to learn that his third son had been hiding a eunuch wanted by the imperial household as a fugitive. It had long been noted that this prince's only interests were theatrical shows and music, and that he was far too familiar with eunuch actors in the court's theatrical bureau. The emperor was finally forced to issue an edict acknowledging that this son had never taken an interest in study or archery, that he loved to associate with "inferior persons," and that despite all Tao Kuang's efforts to reform him with special instruction and palace posts, his son had continued his unsavory, obviously homosexual relationships with eunuchs. Though the prince was degraded, he was reinstated a year later, only to continue keeping eunuch actors in his palace and grossly abusing his princely power by placing in confinement eunuchs and servants who dared displease him. For a while the prince complied with the demand of his mother, the empress dowager, that he release his imprisoned eunuch actor companions, but it was later learned that he had smuggled these eunuchs back into his home. Finally, in 1838, when the wife of one of his imprisoned retinue exposed the prince's debauched and illegal conduct to a censor, an immediate search of his premises by imperial orders disclosed the presence of over ninety prisoners in his palace. Many were simply released into freedom, but several attendants and eunuchs who had aided and abetted the prince's orgies were severely punished. After the scandal had cooled, the prince himself was only degraded one degree in rank.

By this time increasing corruption in the government had so emboldened palace eunuchs to lawlessness, that Tao Kuang found it necessary to decree that except when on purchasing commissions for the throne, eunuchs were forbidden to idle outside the Forbidden City walls or to attend Peking theaters and wine shops and that those who broke these rules would be punished without delay.

As late as 1838, Tao Kuang and his Manchu officials were threatening severe punishment for Chinese who practiced or allowed female foot-binding, though they met with little success. When one of Tao Kuang's Manchu concubines once costumed herself as a Chinese lady and tottered in on simulated bound feet to appear before her imperial master, he instantly ordered her away in disgrace, refusing ever to set eyes on her again.

In 1835 the Board of Revenue for the first time reported a Chinese population above 400 million. With no means to effectively increase the national income, such a population could survive only with a drastically lowered standard of living, which would in turn completely impoverish the legions of already poor. Nonetheless, some believe that Tao Kuang's reign might have peacefully regained her prosperity, had China been permitted to continue her accustomed isolation, undistracted by Western nations pushing and shoving their way into Chinese affairs.

The earlier Portuguese, Spanish, and Dutch merchants who had come to China only wanted to buy items of value at Chinese coastal markets, while the European Catholic fathers' principal goal was to win converts, from the imperial family on down to the populace. But now in the 1800s, the English were determined to open up the Chinese market in order to sell their manufactured goods to China's tremendous population, while at the same time Protestant missionaries converted the Chinese people to a creed that regarded much of China's traditional social system as repugnant. Not surprisingly, the Chinese government resisted.

Since China had little desire for British goods, whereas the British had a great yearning for Chinese tea and silk, England was not pleased with the resulting imbalance of trade with China, which was a drain on her treasuries. Though the Chinese throne had for a century been issuing edicts opposing the use and importation of opium, this was the product, the English discovered, most in demand by Chinese traders. By the 1820s, China's yearly consumption had risen to 4,000 chests of opium, most of which were transported on British freighters from their Indian colony. The British ships anchored off Chinese shores and sold the drug to Chinese smugglers who plied back and forth between ship and shore on small boats. Hundreds of Cantonese involved in the lucrative illegal opium business as middlemen, dealers, processors, and users gave the English suppliers their complete support—a situation not unlike that today by which drugs are brought into the United States.

In 1839 Emperor Tao Kuang sent an imperial commissioner to Canton to order that all opium in foreign hands be confiscated for destruction. This man managed to seize a great number of chests and dump them into the sea. Skirmishes between British and Chinese ships resulted, until finally in 1840 the English, angry and frustrated by decades of failed attempts to deal openly and amicably with the uncooperative and arrogant Chinese, arrived in a convoy of well-armed modern gunboats. China's ill-equipped army and her all but nonexistent navy were easily overcome. The British force sailed into Nanking and officially ended the war in 1842 by writing their own peace treaty, which demanded payment for the opium that had been confiscated and destroyed; the opening to foreign trade of Canton and four other "treaty ports"; and the establishment of a Crown Colony at Hong Kong. The defeated Chinese reluctantly had to agree to these terms, and were powerless to stop the opium trade.

Thus, Tao Kuang was the first, but by no means the last, Chinese ruler to be forced to suffer humiliation at European hands.

Notes

1. J. D. Spence, *Emperor of China.*
2. Ibid.
3. Ibid.
4. Ibid.
5. Ibid.
6. Ibid.
7. Ibid.
8. R. Grousset, *The Rise and Splendour of the Chinese Empire.*
9. D. Bloodworth, *The Chinese Looking Glass.*

19

The Last of the Powerful Eunuchs
THE COLLAPSE OF IMPERIAL RULE (A.D. 1851-1912)

The last half-century of imperial rule in China was colored throughout by an amazing little Manchu "lady of iron" known as Tzu Hsi, or the "Old Buddha," or just the Empress Dowager. Her career began in 1851 when, at sixteen, she was taken into the Peking palace as a low-ranking concubine to Manchu Emperor Hsien Feng. Very early she figured out that the surest road to the emperor's attention—or success in any endeavor— was through discreet bribes to the eunuchs, for, "thick as vermin" as they were in the palace, nothing escaped their eyes or ears. During most of her life, eunuchs would be her closest allies and constant companions, thereby gaining greater influence than in any previous Manchu reign.

The entire imperial family heaved a sigh of relief in 1856 when Tzu Hsi produced the first son to be sired by the emperor, an accomplishment which enhanced her status immeasurably. Since Hsien Feng had already taken an empress, Tzu Hsi was made highest ranking concubine and could look forward to being regent over her son, the heir apparent. Now her most outstanding endowments came to light: a charming but extremely forceful personality, an unquenchable ambition for power and riches, and a physical vitality that rarely failed her. Tzu Hsi later claimed that her intense interest and background in state affairs stemmed from these early years when her weak and ailing young husband allowed her to classify all his incoming memorials.

These were the times when the disastrous Taiping (Supreme Peace) Rebellion was brewing in the south, an upheaval that would rage on for the next fourteen years and shake the Ching Dynasty to its very foundations. The founder and leader of the Taiping sect was Hung Hsiu-chuan, a reputedly half-mad failed scholar who had received some little instruction and a translated portion of the Christian gospels from a fundamentalist American Baptist missionary in Canton. Before long, Hung was interpreting the "divine visions" he claimed he was having as proof that he was Jesus Christ's younger brother, destined to lead the Chinese people out of their misery into salvation and a decent livelihood. Hung preached his own muddled version of Christianity, set himself up as "Heavenly King," with converted leaders and generals under him called "Heavenly Princes," and gathered adherents by the thousands. By 1853 his competent armies had taken Nanking, where Hung set up court.

Though some claim that Hung was a crazed religious fanatic, he was wise enough to lay down rules that had wide appeal to his converts. No eunuchs were allowed in his palace; women were given equal rights with men; foot-binding, concubinage, and ancestor worship were outlawed, as was the Manchu pigtail. At first the Peking court sneered at the Taipings as "long-haired robbers," but when it became apparent that they were a dangerously subversive sect, imperial troops were sent against them, but with little success. Taiping armies spread into and took control of seven provinces, attacking and killing landlords, Confucianists, Buddhists, and Taoists, burning their splendid shrines to the ground. Though the Taipings left unharmed the European and American missionaries, merchants, and envoys—considering them brethren in Christianity—in the end it was the foreigners who volunteered weapons, leadership, and training for the Manchu army that finally put down the rebellion. During the two-year siege of Nanking during which Taiping leader Hung refused to surrender, 40,000 of his followers were killed. When Manchu troops finally stormed the city, they found that the starved inhabitants had been driven to cannibalism, and that Hung had committed suicide. During Hung's misguided "Christian" attempt at reform, twenty million Chinese lives were lost, and the empire was greatly weakened. The Western military aid given the Manchus did nothing to alleviate the Peking court's mistrust and hatred of the "foreign devils."

In the very midst of Hung's devastating rebellion, in an anomaly of history, British and French troops joined forces against Peking. Lord Elgin had arrived from England to ratify a treaty with China. But when Elgin sent an advance party overland from the coast to the capital, the party was seized and so brutally tortured by the Chinese that thirteen British and eight French died as a result, while the rest of the party was thrown into miserable, stinking prisons. After this atrocity, combined British and French armies marched forth to open the Peking city gates by threatening force. They occupied the capital, and in retaliation for the treatment of his advance party, Lord Elgin gave orders for the destruction of the beautiful imperial summer palace complex outside Peking, which had already been thoroughly looted of its priceless treasures by French and British troops and officers.

Lord Elgin found that on learning of his approach to Peking, the sickly emperor Hsien Feng, his empress Tzu Hsi and her four-year-old son and heir apparent, powerful officials, eunuchs, and palace maids had fled pell-mell for the old Manchu summer retreat in Jehol above the Great Wall, leaving the government in control of the emperor's brother. This sensible man, Prince Kung, saw the utter helplessness of China's position and concluded a treaty entirely advantageous to the foreigners, opening up more trading ports, giving all but diplomatic immunity to Christian missionaries and their Chinese converts, and agreeing to pay a stupendous indemnity for foreign lives lost and humiliations suffered. Only then did British and French armies withdraw from Peking.

During its year of exile in Jehol, the Manchu court was having problems of its own that had little to do with the Taiping Rebellion and the intrusion of foreigners. Possibly from the rigors of the arduous journey to the north—but more likely due to his continued debaucheries with women, wine, and drugs—the thirty-year-old Manchu Son of Heaven was slowly dying. Nobles whom Emperor Hsien Feng had already designated as regents over the child heir initiated plans to dispose of the empress and the heir's mother to insure their ability to maintain themselves in supreme power. But the indomitable Tzu Hsi was not to be disposed of, and arranged a coup of her own. When the emperor finally expired in Jehol and she learned through her eunuchs that it was safe to return to Peking, she contrived to arrive there ahead of the funeral procession. Quickly she sent out a long-trusted military confidant to arrest the plotting censors who were accompanying the imperial coffin. By this ploy, the mother of the heir apparent became Empress Dowager Tzu Hsi, while the quiet, unassuming empress of the dead emperor became Empress Dowager Tzu An. Together, as coregents over Tzu Hsi's little son—who became Emperor Tung Chih—the two women now officially controlled the Chinese empire, but it was Tzu Hsi who made herself the real power behind the throne.

A young eunuch by the name of An Te-hai, who had proven himself invaluable to Tzu Hsi as a loyal supporter and informer during the dangerous plot and coup in Jehol, now became her favorite agent and companion.

"Little An," as he was known, was handsome, suave, and an excellent singer and actor in the palace theatricals that all the court ladies loved. Tzu Hsi made the eunuch the influential head of the palace household and became so deeply devoted to him that he was allowed extraordinary privileges in the palace and in her private apartments. Palace tongues were set wagging, and some people doubted whether eunuch An had ever been properly castrated. Officials and courtiers writhed in resentment at Little An's daring arrogance and assumption of power.

In 1869 Empress Dowager Tzu Hsi, ignoring old Manchu prohibitions, allowed eunuch An Te-hai to head up a special mission to Nanking, ostensibly to check on silks and satins ordered by the palace, but probably more to satisfy her favorite's desire for a pleasurable outing. Chief Eunuch An sailed down the Grand Canal on two gorgeous imperial barges flying dragon and phoenix flags of royalty, followed by an entourage on several junks. He put on such a show of authority at stops along the way that awe-struck local officials met all his demands for goods and supplies, and even brought him tribute. When passing through Shantung, eunuch An hired local female musicians to come aboard, dressed himself up in dragon robes, celebrated his birthday in ostentatious style, and, some say, conducted such vicious orgies with local hired girls that one of them died as a result.

Infuriated, the governor of Shantung fired off to Peking a full report on the eunuch's illegal, outrageous conduct, the message arriving at a time when Tzu Hsi was out of the palace. The powerful Prince Kung quickly coerced the gentle coregent Dowager Tzu An into signing a decree ordering that the eunuch be executed at once. Eunuch An Te-hai was promptly beheaded by Shantung authorities, while most of his companions were strangled. When Tzu Hsi learned of her favorite's death, her deep shock and anger had to be carefully concealed, for there was no overlooking the fact that she had violated dynastic law in allowing the eunuch to leave Peking. She never forgot nor forgave this affront to her authority, which possibly was the beginning of a rupture between the two dowagers.

Another source of friction may have been that Tzu Hsi's little son, Emperor Tung Chih, seemed to prefer the soft-spoken Dowager Tzu An, who sympathized with his chaffing under his mother's stern demands for strict decorum and hours of dull and grueling tutoring each day. As he grew into his early teens, Tung Chih, balking at the confinement of the Forbidden City, found that the eunuchs in his personal retinue—who had been his only companions—were happy to introduce him to the pleasures and excitement of the city outside. Stealing out at night in disguise with favorite eunuchs, Tung Chih drank, caroused, smoked heavily, and ogled dancing and singing girls in Peking's houses of pleasure. Introduced to prettily painted transvestite and catamite actors at theaters and colorful street shows, by the time he was fifteen it appeared that the young emperor had inherited all his father's taste for bisexual debauchery.

When in 1872 Tung Chih reached the marriageable age of sixteen and was given control of the government, daughters of Manchu nobles and officials were summoned before him for his selection of a bride. An expert in Peking brothels with their harlots and forbidden Chinese girls with bound feet, he knew beauty when he saw it. He chose as his empress the lovely Alute, a well-bred daughter of a prominent Mongol official, and at the same time selected three other girls as concubines. The mild-mannered Dowager Tzu An approved his choice of consort, but his mother hated Alute from the very first, perhaps fearing the hold the intelligent girl would have over the emperor and her ability to one day supplant Tzu Hsi's authority. It is claimed that, despite Tung Chih's devotion to his new empress, Tzu Hsi did her utmost to keep them apart, even encouraging him to continue his profligate ways, leaving political affairs in her hands. When one of his most respected tutors pointed out to Tung Chih the evil reputation he was earning, and even named the eunuchs who were his drinking companions, the young emperor angrily cashiered him from all his posts.

Emperor Tung Chih, who evidently inherited his mother's fearsome temper, was again enraged when—after Tzu Hsi had conspired to have him rebuild the razed summer palace for her fortieth birthday celebration—he received a petition from his princely uncles begging him to call off the building project in view of grave national problems already draining the treasuries. At the same time they pleaded that he avoid the corrupting company of favorite eunuchs, more closely supervise the court and heed advice from elders, and watch his health and take exercise out of doors. He canceled the summer palace project, but in a fit of rage tried to degrade Prince Kung, while Tzu Hsi smoldered because her desires had been thwarted. Meanwhile, Tzu Hsi watched and waited for other furtive and more effective means to obtain the garden palace she coveted.

By this time Tung Chih's dissipations on the town were taking a toll on his health. Rumors flew that he had contracted a venereal disease, while the people, hearing of his poor condition, feared for his life when there occurred an evil conjunction of the sun and planets. In late 1874 the weakened young emperor was "visited by the heavenly flowers"—struck down by smallpox. From his sickbed, Tung Chih—no doubt aided by his mother—decreed that the two dowagers be reinstated as coregents to look after state affairs in his behalf during his illness. Though at one point he seemed to be improving, within a few months Tung Chih had a relapse and died. He was only nineteen and had been emperor for fourteen years, but he had actually ruled on his own less than two—and those under fear of his authoritarian mother.

One court official of the day in his memoirs accused Empress Dowager Tzu Hsi of having brought about her son's death. He claimed that Tzu Hsi, having been notified by eavesdropping eunuchs that the loving young Empress Alute was visiting her husband's sickbed, silently entered the room and overhead Alute saying she looked forward to his recovery, when he would be free of his mother's domination and interference. Tzu Hsi flew into a rage, rampaged about the room, seized the terrified girl by the hair and struck her, and loudly raved that by making love to the weakened emperor, Alute would cause his illness to worsen. Then she ordered the eunuchs to take the girl away and beat her in punishment. In his helplessness, Tung Chih reportedly suffered nervous paroxysms and his soaring temperature killed him.

On the day of her son's death, Tzu Hsi ordered imperial armies to surround the palace, then summoned the Grand Council, imperial clan, ministers, and tutors. She herself officiated from the Dragon Throne, while coregent Tzu An complacently sat at her side. Although the widowed young Empress Alute, now in deep mourning, might have been pregnant, Tzu Hsi shocked the whole court by announcing that her choice of heir and successor was her own three-year-old nephew, the son of her sister, wife of a brother of Tzu Hsi's late husband. Though this was in direct opposition to Manchu law of succession, she informed the court that she had legally adopted the nephew as her son, quelling fears that the deceased Emperor Tung Chih would have no one to conduct the imperial ancestral rights at his grave. By putting another child on the throne, Tzu Hsi also assured that supreme power would remain in her hands. It is said that when Prince Chun, the boy's father, heard that his son had been chosen to be emperor, and that he would now be a regent, he trembled, wept, and fell into a dead faint.

Taking no chances, Tzu Hsi demanded that the new little heir be brought to the palace that very night. Thin and in poor health, the child was snatched from his cradle in the hours before dawn, dressed up in tiny imperial yellow robes (suspiciously tailored in advance), and arrived squalling at the palace to be presented to his adoptive mother and made to kowtow before the later emperor's bier. In 1875 the boy was formally proclaimed Emperor Kuang Hsu. To silence any opposition, Tzu Hsi promised that as soon as Kuang Hsu completed his education under her direction and came of age, she would relinquish control of government—a convenient arrangement that would leave her in power for at least another dozen years.

Very soon after the death of the emperor, his young Empress Alute committed suicide, unable to face the desolate prospect of existence under the dominance and hatred of her mother-in-law. Most accounts say that Tzu Hsi deliberately goaded the girl into taking her own life. What is certain, at least, is that the girl's untimely death did not cause Tzu Hsi to weep a tear. A prominent censor wrote the throne soon thereafter to remind that Empress Alute, having committed *suttee* upon her husband's demise, should be given posthumous honors. Tzu Hsi quashed that idea in a hurry, acidly rebuking the censor for submitting a foolish memorial "based only on hearsay."

For the next forty years the well-known eunuch Li Lien-ying would be one of the most prominent figures at court, his heavy hand being felt in every palace intrigue and many affairs of state. In his early teens, the destitute Li had been apprenticed to a shoemaker, thereby earning the lifelong nickname of "Cobbler's Wax Li." On learning of the perquisites available to palace eunuchs, at age sixteen he presented himself for castration at the imperial eunuch clinic. Once taken into the palace as a eunuch—despite his tall, rugged physique and somewhat cruelly handsome face—Li suavely and craftily ingratiated himself with Empress Dowager Tzu Hsi, convincing her by word and deed of his absolute loyalty. She first made him a runner beside her sedan chair, then assigned him to the more intimate position of hairdresser in the ladies quarters.

Step by step eunuch Li worked his way up, assisting and protecting his mistress through a maze of palace jealousies and scandals, until she allowed him familiarities and companionship with her such as she never granted to anyone, not even her family members. It is reported that when Tzu Hsi once suffered a minor illness, eunuch Li cut flesh from his own thigh, ordered it cooked, and fed it to her as medicine—a cure mentioned in the ancient "Rules of Filial Piety," but rarely used except by the closest intimates. Palace gossips buzzed with shock when Tzu Hsi allowed eunuch Li to be seated next to her in the palace theater, and to speak openly to her without first receiving permission. It is said he shared her pleasure outings and sometimes her meals, and even was allowed to sit on the imperial throne chair on occasion. She made him chief of the eunuch corps and bestowed upon him the exalted rank of a second-grade official, flaunting dynastic law. For the rest of her long life, eunuch Li was her unquestioned favorite—a companion, advisor, agent, and, many suspected, her lover.

On eunuch Li Lien-ying's fortieth birthday, Tzu Hsi showered him with gold bullion, jades, and a robe embroidered with a dragon. He became immensely wealthy, as courtiers and officials—to impress the dowager and stay in her good graces—followed suit by loading him with valuable gifts beyond count. Li managed to extract his first big squeeze money from an official for whom he had wheedled a high ministerial post, and from then on officials everywhere looked up to him as "King of the Squeeze," even as they thronged about him for coveted invitations to his private mansion. It is known that the selling of one official post brought eunuch Li 320,000 silver taels. He often boasted that he held in his hands the making or breaking of thousands of men, and that he could defy the emperor himself. Under Tzu Hsi's protection and with her full knowledge, Li organized a system of douceurs levied on every high official in the empire, frequently sharing the proceeds with the dowager.

It was eunuch Li who gave Tzu Hsi the affectionate nickname of "Old Buddha," by which she was known among the Chinese populace and the foreign communities. It seems that during a widespread drought, Tzu Hsi, who was a devout Buddhist, prayed to Buddhist deities for three days, at the end of which rain miraculously fell in abundance. When Li then declared that she herself was a veritable Old Buddha, she was pleased, for in China to be old is to be venerated, to say nothing of her delight at being referred to as a deity. She loved to put on lavish palace entertainments, gorgeously costuming herself as the vastly popular Buddhist Goddess of Mercy, with eunuch Li beside her similarly got up as her guardian deity.

It was eunuch Li who widened the rift between the two dowagers. The usually placid Tzu An finally found it necessary to complain that the eunuch treated her with utmost arrogance, that he was disrespectful of her wishes, ignoring her authority to such an extent that she was mocked by her own subordinates. Tzu An also pointed out that Li was wrongfully allowing himself to be called Lord of Nine-thousand Years. Though the two ladies quarreled sharply over this matter, Tzu Hsi did nothing to curb her favorite's haughtiness. Later, possibly hoping to make peace, Tzu An came to the Old Buddha with an old, previously unknown decree that their mutual husband had given her privately before he died in Jehol. The old emperor had written that should Tzu Hsi ever overstep her position and threaten Tzu An, or become a danger to the state, she should be degraded and executed. Tzu Hsi read the missive and turned pale as death. When Tzu An good-naturedly tore up the decree and threw it into a fiery brazier—assuring her coregent that she need never worry about such a possibility—Tzu Hsi thanked her profusely.

Before long Tzu An received a box of her favorite pastries from the Old Buddha. Immediately after sampling a few of the sweets, Tzu An fell ill, and by evening she was dead, at age forty-five. Tzu Hsi was of course summoned at once, but by the time the grand councilors arrived to determine whether there had been any foul play, she had already had the corpse placed in a sealed coffin. An official report went out that Tzu An died of an unknown sudden illness. Once again, it was widely believed, as it is believed today, that Tzu Hsi had caused another palace death, this time by poisoning. Tzu Hsi herself always claimed that her coregent simply "choked on spit and died."

The year was 1881. With great enthusiasm, the middle-aged Tzu Hsi immediately took up her duties "behind the curtains" as sole regent to guide the empire for the boy-emperor. Very soon she removed Prince Kung from his offices, for fear of his powerful influence, but also to wreak vengeance on him for eunuch Little An's death. She replaced him with the boy-emperor's father, Prince Chun, who kept his post by complying with Tzu Hsi's every demand. In 1816, when Prince Chun was dispatched to inspect the imperial navy, the dowager sent along Li Lien-ying, evidently trusting the eunuch more than the prince. During this tour, a censor found it necessary to reprimand eunuch Li for blatant insolence, and to warn Prince Chun of the danger of allowing a eunuch so much power. Prince Chun, foreseeing Tzu Hsi's displeasure, meekly defended the miscreant eunuch—and said nothing when the dowager chose only to degrade the complaining censor.

Though Emperor Kuang Hsu was now of an age to assume independent rule, his father, Prince Chun, ingratiated himself with the Old Buddha by leading top-ranking officials in entreating her to continue on as regent. Immensely pleased, Tzu Hsi—after the expected sham show of reluctance—readily consented, saying she would keep control for a few more years "to instruct His Majesty in matters of state."

In 1888 Chief Eunuch Li, whose control of finances now extended far beyond the palace purse, devised an ingenious plan to complete construction of the ruined summer palace, a project upon which his mistress had firmly set her mind. Since there were insufficient monies for this elaborate scheme in the dwindling treasuries, eunuch Li helped Tzu Hsi divert funds allocated for the modernization and expansion of China's outmoded navy. Together they were able to ramrod Li's disastrous idea into effect, for neither Prince Chun nor the court officials were willing to thwart her desires. Although within the next five years the summer palace complex was developed into a veritable fairyland, China was soon to pay dearly for eunuch Li's folly. It is estimated that he defrauded the Board of the Navy of 30,000 taels.

In 1889, when Emperor Kuang Hsu became nineteen, the Old Buddha arranged—or forced—his marriage to her niece Lung Yu, a long-faced, flat-chested cousin of the emperor, who was three years his senior. At the same time, he acquired the lively young Pearl Concubine. It was she who won his heart. Kuang Hsu never cared for his empress—much to Tzu Hsi's resentment—but Lung Yu proved most useful to the dowager as the palace tattler, informing her of all goings-on of the emperor and his entire retinue. It is reported that when Lung Yu complained to her aunt that her husband Kuang Hsu was impotent, Tzu Hsi advised her to use a young eunuch, Hsiao Teh-chang, as a paramour. Whether or not this story is true, we do know that during these years several official memorials came to the throne denouncing the depraved morals and boundless extravagance of Dowager Empress Tzu Hsi's palace.

Finally, when construction of her summer palace was well underway—and there seemed to be no further excuse for her continuing in control—Tzu Hsi "abdicated" the throne to Kuang Hsu and went into "deep retirement." For several years she thoroughly enjoyed herself among the gardens, parks, and lakes of the summer palace, surrounded by her eunuchs and ladies-in-waiting, but she continued to demand that Emperor Kuang Hsu appear before her for regular audiences that kept her in close touch with the government. Even after "abdicating," Tzu Hsi retained the right to hire and fire officials of the two highest ranks, and to examine all state papers. During the three winter months, she moved her court back to the Forbidden City, where she and eunuch Li Lien-ying charged goodly sums for granting short audiences to officials. Thus, though she was now getting heavy-jowled and dumpy in body, she kept eunuch Li in constant attendance and remained by far the most powerful person in China.

Emperor Kuang Hsu, her adopted nephew, had never had a strong constitution and was to remain thin and small of stature. It is said he feared his domineering foster mother all his life as he had feared thunderstorms during childhood, and that his stutter was a result of Tzu Hsi's stern surveillance over every phase of his life. Unlike the dowager's real son, Kuang Hsu was an inquisitive student, and while quite young became fascinated with clocks, toys, and bicycles, which his eunuchs brought in from the markets for his entertainment. These items had been introduced by the foreign barbarians who were infiltrating China by the hundreds. As he grew older, Kuang Hsu remained especially close to his old tutor, who brought him translated books on Western sciences, law, and political philosophy in which he was very interested.

All this Kuang Hsu's Empress Lung Yu obediently reported to the dowager, whose envy and fear had been aroused by the emperor's Pearl Concubine, who shared her husband's interest in foreign learning. In 1894, when Tzu Hsi heard that the official she had recommended for a post had been passed over in favor of the Pearl Concubine's nominee, the Old Buddha was furious. She charged the concubine with accepting bribes from officials and ordered that she be stripped of her rank and title and beaten by the palace eunuchs. The emperor could do nothing to save his favorite from the bamboo rod, but she lived through the ordeal and was eventually reinstated.

Emperor Kuang Hsu's dreams of bringing China into the modern world were given a push in the direction of reality in 1895 when the nation suffered a colossal defeat in a war with Japan over the vassal state of Korea. Japan, armed with Western-style weapons and modern gunboats, all but annihilated the Chinese navy, which relied on the ships and weapons of an earlier era, and moreover, was deteriorated due to the embezzlement of its funds by eunuch Li Lien-ying to build the summer palace. This total defeat was by far the most appalling humiliation China had ever suffered at the hands of foreigners, for the Chinese had always despised the Japanese as "dwarf barbarians" who aped China's culture and had once even been a tribute-paying vassal. China had been brought to her knees. She was forced to sign a treaty deeding to Japan many of her possessions, including Taiwan, to relinquish her long suzerainty over Korea, and to pay an indemnity amounting to millions of taels. This mortifying treaty sharpened the greed of Western powers to carve out their spheres of influence on Chinese soil, as well as to vie with each other in negotiating crushing loans to bankrupt China, but it also thoroughly awakened young Chinese scholars to the nation's need for drastic change and reform.

Though Chief Eunuch Li Lien-ying and his eunuch followers were violently opposed to all thoughts of remodeling China's ancient way of government—fearing the eunuch system's perquisites and squeezes might be affected—one brave eunuch defied them all. Eunuch Kou Lien-tsai not only wrote a statement criticizing the empress dowager's policies, but handed it to her personally. Among other things, he urged her to dispense with the summer palace project, allowing increased spending on armaments to enable China to strike back at Japan. He also made the startling proposal that, since Emperor Kuang Hsu had produced no heir, the next emperor be chosen from among wise and forward-looking men of the empire. Apoplectic with rage, Tzu Hsi had eunuch Kou Lien-tsai immediately beheaded.

Within a few years many intellectuals came to the conclusion that the outmoded eunuch system was a main contributor to China's weakness and called for its abolition—for the first time in Chinese history, it is believed. One official based his argument on the fact that the strong foreign powers did not use eunuchs in their courts, whereas only weak countries such as Turkey kept the harems and eunuchs. One famous anti-eunuch memorial came from the Chinese Viceroy of Canton. He urged that, in view of the reduced number of imperial concubines in the Peking palace, eunuchs be replaced by female attendants, and claimed that the abolishment of the eunuch corps was the first and most vital step toward national reform. However, all these dissenting voices were silenced, or at least hushed, in the state-controlled Chinese press.

In 1898 Emperor Kuang Hsu, now twenty-six years old, backed by his old tutor and strongly influenced by scholars who fervently favored modernization, issued the first of his well known "Hundred Days Reforms"—for that is how long they lasted. The Old Buddha warily watched and waited, gathering about her diehard reactionaries who opposed any change which might affect their elite status and accustomed way of life. Eunuch Li Lien-ying, who especially feared the emperor's zeal for reform, became the foremost partisan and advisor of the frightened reactionaries, and acted as their go-between to urge the dowager to resume control. Yet Kuang Hsu—evidently for the first time in his life—persevered against Tzu Hsi and all opposition, saying, "The four barbarians [Japan, Russia, Germany, and England] are all invading us, gradually partitioning our country. China will soon perish—and that is the fault of those who prohibited China's advancement." He pointed out that "Westerners all pursue useful studies, while we Chinese pursue useless learning, and that is why we are in the present situation."[1] He decreed reforms modernizing the educational, civil examination, and judicial systems; introduced patents and copyrights to encourage inventors and writers; urged students and Manchu officials to travel abroad to expand their minds and to study professions; and advocated that assistance and encouragement be given the long-despised commercial, merchant, and trading classes. He decreed freedom of the press to allow journalists to publish their political views, whatever they may be, and Western-type training for China's armies.

The empress dowager, prodded by eunuch Li and the distraught reactionaries, summoned the emperor before her and warned him in no uncertain terms that it was she who placed him on the throne, and she would brook no further reforms that endangered loyal and venerable officials. Furthermore, she warned that if the young reform-minded scholars who wrote "filthy slander" about her policies and way of life ever came near the emperor again, it would be their last time. Then she had the emperor's faithful old tutor arrested and banished. Terrified, Kuang Hsu rushed to telegram his reformer-advisors, asking them to save him from the dowager's wrath. He made the mistake of also sending word to a powerful Chinese military official, Yuan Shih-kai, who had previously contributed funds toward the reform cause. But the turncoat Yuan Shih-kai—looking out for his own interests—betrayed Kuang Hsu by notifying the Old Buddha that the reformers were plotting to hold her prisoner until the "Hundred Days Reforms" could be implemented.

This news brought Tzu Hsi storming back from the summer palace. She gathered her legions of backers and ordered military troops into Peking. Shrieking with rage, she swept into the emperor's apartments and ordered palace guards to seize Emperor Kuang Hsu and take him as a prisoner to the Ocean Terrace pavilion on an island in one of the capital's imperial pleasure lakes. She had the drawbridge—the one escape route—drawn up and stationed soldiers to guard it. Then she threw out all Kuang Hsu's personal eunuchs and had fourteen of them beheaded. When the emperor's favorite Pearl Concubine pleaded to share his imprisonment, Tzu Hsi had her arrested and confined to her apartments. Only the skinny Empress Lung Yu, whom he didn't even like, was allowed to live with him, and from this time on, it is said, they even ceased speaking to one another. Then the feisty dowager issued an edict in Kuang Hsu's name decreeing that—since the emperor was dangerously ill—Tzu Hsi would assume the throne once more. Tzu Hsi had six of the main reform leaders who had influenced the emperor executed; the rest managed to flee from China— with a price on their heads. Then furiously Tzu Hsi abolished all the reform decrees.

The dowager charged her long-faithful Chief Eunuch Li Lien-ying with overseeing the emperor's prison pavilion, an assignment he took on with a vengeance. For the next ten years Tzu Hsi completely condoned the immoral eunuchs who introduced Kuang Hsu to all manner of unhealthy vices and licentious indulgences—excesses which furthered his poor health. When Tzu Hsi demanded periodically that the ailing emperor appear before her in audience, he was obliged to kneel, often for half an hour, at the inner palace gate awaiting summons from the vindictive Chief Eunuch Li. At each audience Kuang Hsu was compelled, like all palace officials, to pay a large squeeze to eunuch Li before admittance was granted.

As stories circulated that the emperor's health had worsened, and that eunuch Li was in charge of administering his medications, the British ambassador took it upon himself to subtly warn the empress dowager that if Kuang Hsu should suffer any foul play, she would have to answer to the British government. This affront must have galled Tzu Hsi, although by this time she was seeing the wisdom of playing up to foreign envoys and their wives, thrilling the ladies by inviting them to palace tea-parties at which the emperor was let out of prison and obliged to sit, meek and silent, behind and below her chair.

Nobody knows for sure exactly what prompted the so-called Boxer uprising which raged across North China in 1900 and finally brought the empire into war with the intruding foreign powers. A sect or movement of idle peasant youths went about practicing the old Chinese martial arts and exercises, sometimes going into frenzied religious trances and declaring themselves invulnerable to bullets or bodily harm. They called themselves the "Righteous Harmonious Fists." Western missionaries, whose numbers and activities had by this time greatly proliferated, called them "Boxers." Such semi-religious secret societies had often exploded into rebellion when misrule and natural disasters combined to reduce the peasantry to destitution, and in recent years North China had suffered a calamitous series of floods, droughts, and ruined harvests, leaving thousands homeless and near starvation.

Nobody knows for sure why thousands of these angry peasant youths soon unleashed their fury not toward the extravagant Manchu palace and corrupt, grasping ruling class but toward the white "foreign devils," especially the missionaries. There is evidence that the landed gentry and some local officials out in the countryside, who deeply resented foreign aggression and Christian evangelism, encouraged and backed the Boxers. It is known that Chinese people everywhere despised the missionaries' Chinese converts, calling them "rice Christians," who had sold their souls in return for food and lodging.

Grotesque rumors spread like wildfire that the missionaries plucked out the eyes of orphaned Chinese babies to brew strange Western medicines; that it was the missionaries, preaching their foreign creed, who had brought about the natural calamities; and that if all their heads were cut off, rain would fall. It was also believed that the foreigners had angered the local gods and spirits by disturbing graveyards and nature's order in tearing up land to build railroads, telegraph lines, and churches, and that the gods wanted them all beheaded. Soon the Boxer hordes in North China were brutally murdering entire missionary families and their Chinese converts by the hundreds, horribly mutilating their bodies, burning their compounds, churches, hospitals, orphanages, and schools, and destroying railway stations and telegraph facilities.

Before long it became clear that the empress dowager and her court were favoring the Boxers and deliberately allowing the carnage, despite repeated appeals from the foreign legations. By the spring of 1900, mobs of Boxers had started infiltrating Peking, now carrying posters which read, "Support the Ching Dynasty and destroy the Foreigners." Aroused to a fever pitch, they swarmed about the city roaring "Kill, kill, kill," indiscriminately killing, looting, and burning. Foreign ambassadors and missionaries and their families, along with nearly 3,000 Chinese converted Christians, and small legation guard units barricaded themselves in legation headquarters and the Catholic cathedral, and sent frantic messages to their home governments for troops to protect them. When Tzu Hsi ordered all foreigners out of China within a certain time, they were afraid to leave the barricade areas to go for fear of being slaughtered.

Word went out that Chief Eunuch Li, now wielding enormous power in the palace, had convinced Tzu Hsi to grant "head-money" rewards to Boxers and imperial soldiers for killing any foreigner they could get their hands on. She deployed imperial armies in concert with the Boxers and together they held the legation headquarters under siege for two months until troops of the Western powers finally arrived. When the foreign troops overpowered China's seacoast forts, and then occupied Peking itself, in a fury, the Old Buddha declared war on all the foreign powers, repeatedly declaring she would "sleep on the foreigners' skin and eat their flesh."[2]

During the siege, eunuch Li and many of his cohorts encouraged, backed, and aided the Boxers, some even going about the palace reciting Boxer slogans and wearing red Boxer sashes. For a long time eunuch Li actually had Tzu Hsi convinced that the Boxers possessed superhuman powers and were invulnerable to bullets, and that they could drive the foreigners out of China. A Manchu noble, Prince Tuan, placed himself at the head of the Boxers, working hand-in-hand with them and the strong anti-foreign element in the palace, and the Old Buddha herself donated thousands of bags of rice to feed the Boxers.

When Western allied forces were entering Peking, Tzu Hsi gathered up the prisoner emperor, his dour Empress Lung Yu, courtiers, attendants, and eunuchs in preparation to flee the capital. When the Pearl Concubine, who was to be left behind, dared to plead with the Old Buddha to allow Emperor Kuang Hsu to remain in Peking to help with peace negotiations— rather than have him flee in disgrace—Tzu Hsi furiously ordered eunuch Li and his subordinate eunuchs to throw the girl bodily down a palace well. There she was left to drown, as the emperor, his will completely broken, followed the court, bundled into ox carts, into exile several hundred miles to the west at Sian, the once-famous capital of the Tang Dynasty. (Ever after the murder of the Pearl Concubine, superstitious palace denizens claimed that in the dark of night they could hear her moaning from the depths of the well.)

Before departing the capital himself, eunuch Li Lien-ying managed to stash away in a secret area of his mansion his tremendous private fortune in jewels, artifacts, gold, and silver. For his mistress Tzu Hsi he also buried a wealth of her priceless imperial possessions in a remote corner of the palace. (A year later, when the court returned from Sian, the Old Buddha's treasures were recovered intact, for the foreign powers had agreed not to ransack the Forbidden City. But eunuch Li's entire cache had been discovered and confiscated by French troops. When Li learned it was one of his own eunuch subordinates who had sold the secret of his buried treasure to the French, he lost no time in getting Tzu Hsi's permission to have the traitor decapitated. Within a dozen years eunuch Li had more than recouped his loss through lucrative bribes and the sale of official positions and palace artifacts.)

Three days after the court's departure for Sian—which Tzu Hsi preferred to call a "journey of inspection"—when the party was well beyond the dangers of Peking, eunuch Li joined them. At first Tzu Hsi was incensed with him for giving her bad advice on the Boxers' invulnerability and for talking her into supporting them. But she soon forgave her favorite as he made himself invaluable in extorting donations, tribute, and supplies from the local populace on behalf of the throne, though pocketing his usual share. Gradually, some thousand Peking officials and nobles joined the fleeing party and set up court and an administration in Sian for the duration of the crisis.

When it was demonstrated to the Old Buddha that her eunuchs were mercilessly harassing the Sian countryside for plunder, she reluctantly had three of the offenders executed. The governor of Shensi was then placed in charge of palace accounts. He vastly reduced expenditures, stopped all squeeze practices by the eunuchs, and put them on modest salaries. Chief Eunuch Li, angered at this imposition, soon induced the dowager to dispense with the governor's services and reestablish himself in full charge.

During the court's year in Sian, vast quantities of tribute from the southern provinces were handled by eunuch Li, whose apartments were stacked with heaps of dragon robes, bolts of silk, jewels, and other valuables. Tribute bullion was divided up as follows: half to the empress dowager, a fifth to the eunuchs, and the balance to the military. In all, the tribute paid to the court in Sian amounted to over five million taels. Clever eunuchs even refused some of the tribute from Canton, causing Cantonese officials to fear that the Old Buddha might accuse them of having stolen this tribute. To avoid this possibility, they sent ever more valuable tribute. Another means of eunuch profit was to make large local purchases in the name of the dowager and then refuse to pay for them, knowing the merchants dared not complain.

It was left to the foreign allied occupational forces to restore law and order in Peking and surrounding areas, but before they did so, they, too, shamefully looted shops and homes. Officials whom Tzu Hsi had left in charge at the capital were forced to accept all the galling demands made by the foreign allies, and to sign a treaty for indemnities amounting to

450 million taels, payments of which would further bankrupt the nation.

No reckoning could be made of the vast number of Chinese who died in the Boxer uprising and the resultant one-sided war. As for the foreigners, among their dead were 247 missionaries, sixty-six members of diplomatic corps, and some 30,000 Chinese converts. This loss of lives and property did nothing to stem the voracious appetites of the foreigners in their race to partition China, nor did it dampen the evangelical zeal of Western missionaries, who continued to arrive in China in ever greater numbers.

In the fall of 1901, after astrologers had divined the most auspicious day for travel, Tzu Hsi—somehow having decided that the foreigners had forgiven her—set out with her court to return from Sian to Peking in a blaze of glory. Silk banners flew above the regiments, their weapons flashing in the sun, and they were followed by miles of carts and litters loaded with the spoils of over a year in exile. For the last legs of the journey, the Belgians and British offered the use of their rail cars, which Tzu Hsi accepted with relish. When the imperial entourage detrained in Peking, eunuch Li had Tzu Hsi carefully check over his itemized accounts of the carloads of treasure he had accumulated for her. Satisfied, she proceeded in a royal sedan chair through the palace gates. When she noticed a flock of foreign diplomatic families watching the splendid show from atop the city wall, she graced them with a little bow and smile, and in turn received their burst of applause.

Almost immediately, to placate foreign diplomats and the growing legions of reform-conscious Chinese—some of the latter even advocating revolutionary overthrow of the Ching Dynasty—Tzu Hsi decreed a great number of her own reforms, many of them duplicating those formerly decreed by the emperor, who was back in his lake prison. In 1906 she even announced that a Western-style constitution would be drawn up to be administered by the Manchu monarchy. Many doubted her sincerity. In any case, her edicts came too late to ever be implemented, too late to save imperial rule in China.

By 1907, at age seventy-two, Tzu Hsi suffered a slight stroke which left her with a facial tic, and the next year she was weakened from recurring bouts of dysentery. Meanwhile, the sickly Emperor Kuang Hsi, long-neglected in his prison retreat, took to his bed, reportedly overcome by a bewildering array of illnesses. One eminent Chinese physician who had visited him regularly—always with Tzu Hsi present, prohibiting him from touching or closely examining the sacred person of the Son of Heaven—wrote that three days before the emperor died he was writhing in agony from stomach cramps that, in the doctor's opinion, were the result of slow poisoning. Both Chinese and Western historians have had a field day trying to deduce who the culprit, if any, may have been. Was it Chief Eunuch Li Lien-ying, who knew his days were numbered should the emperor ever return to power? And did he act on his own or under the Old Buddha's direction? Or was it the traitorous Yuan Shih-kai, whom the emperor had openly avowed to behead for betraying him and his reform plans, and who was rumored to have paid 33,000 taels to eunuch caretakers for doing away with Kuang Hsu? Or was the emperor's death the result of his deep depression and many illnesses after ten years' imprisonment and suffering under Tzu Hsi's hatred and deliberate torments.

The day before Kuang Hsu died, Empress Dowager Tzu Hsi had roused herself from her sickbed to ordain that a third child emperor would next take the throne—the two-year-old Pu Yi, grandson of her sister and the old Prince Chun. She designated the child's father, the second Prince Chun, as regent, but specifically decreed that her unattractive niece, Empress Lung Yu, wife of the dying emperor, should be consulted and her advice followed. Possibly the Old Buddha made these hurried arrangements for the succession sensing that her own end—as well as that of the emperor—was near.

On the morning following Kuang Hsu's death, after Tzu Hsi had risen at dawn for a discussion with the grand council, and after a lunch of her favorite dish of crabapples and clotted cream, her dysentery returned. She fainted and had to be carried to her apartments. There, after being dressed in special "longevity" robes, she dictated her last edict to the nation, avowing that during her fifty years in power she had never been free of anxiety over calamities from within and aggressions from without that occurred in relentless succession.

Most histories say that in her last moments the old dowager paradoxically denounced the very imperial system that had made her the unchallenged ruler of China for half a century. Straightening her limbs and turning herself toward the south—the direction always faced by China's rulers—she spoke her last words: "Never again allow any woman to hold supreme power of state. It is against the house laws of our Ching Dynasty and should be strictly forbidden. Be careful not to permit eunuchs to meddle in government matters—the Ming Dynasty was brought to ruin by eunuchs, and its fate should be a warning to my people."[3]

The Old Buddha's corpse lay in state for nearly a year before astrologers announced the auspicious day of her burial. During this time, the faithful Chief Eunuch Li kept careful lists of all the invaluable gems and artifacts of solid gold and jade that poured into the palace as gifts to be buried with her. On the appointed day, the resplendent, miles-long funeral procession slowly issued forth from the Forbidden City, led and followed by officials and nobles in white mourning robes, priests and lamas in saffron, hundreds of eunuchs, cavalry with banners flying, and musical bands playing doleful tunes. Near the casket plodded the pitiful figure of eunuch Li Lien-ying, his huge frame sagging with grief and age, his face deeply lined and wet with tears. Tzu Hsi was interred in the imperial cemeteries at the Western Hills in the same ornate mausoleums as her master, former Emperor Hsien Feng, and her former co-consort Tzu An.

After three years on the throne, the boy Pu Yi's imperial government was overthrown by revolutionary Chinese forces in 1911, and the following year the new government demanded his abdication in favor of a Republic. The new government allowed Pu Yi to retain his title and the throne, but he had sovereignty only over the limits of the Forbidden City. The throne was granted an allowance of four million taels a year, which proved entirely inadequate to cover the enormous expense of palace upkeep, the demands of greedy and idle Manchu relatives, a thousand equally greedy eunuchs, and several hundred palace guards, cooks, and maidservants.

The new Republic of China didn't last long, for the nation soon disintegrated into devastating regional warlord struggles. By 1915 and for the next dozen years, generals, provincial governors, and landed gentry leaders and their armies fought one another for control of their territories or the entire empire.

Meanwhile, within the confines of the imperial palace the defunct Manchu court continued to bow and scrape before child emperor Pu Yi as though there was no doubt that the Ching Dynasty would soon return to power. Former Empress Lung Yu—now the ambitious empress dowager—announced to her favorite eunuchs and handmaidens that she intended to closely follow the Old Buddha's policies. The eunuchs all kowtowed before her, as their leader, Chang Yuan-fu, dutifully intoned, "Your Majesty's resolve will bring happiness to the empire and your unworthy servants as well."[4]

Lung Yu took control over five-year-old Pu Yi's education, carefully selecting eunuch tutors loyal to her, who would train him to recognize her authority rather than that of his father, the regent. For already she was leading certain palace inmates and officials in a faction opposing the regent and his adherents. At the same time, strife within the eunuch corps divided the eunuchs into two fiercely hostile camps: the followers of Tzu Hi's powerful old major domo, Li Lien-ying, and adherents of the arrogant young eunuch Chang Yuan-fu, favorite of Dowager Lung Yu. The court rapidly became a hotbed of scandals and abuses.

The histories have little more to say about eunuch Li Lien-Ying's career, except that when he died in 1912, authorities found that he was a multimillionaire. Much of his fortune had been invested in Peking money-lending agencies and pawnshops, which had done a tremendous business in artistic treasures secreted from the palaces. He was buried in a fine tomb at the eunuchs' cemetery outside Peking, and must have left lots of money to his relatives, because for years they came from some distance to his grave to leave offerings and pray for his departed soul.

After eunuch Li Lien-ying's death, eunuch Chang Yuan-fu came into his own as a power in the palace. When a renowned actor came to the palace to put on a theatrical performance and failed to pay the usual squeeze money to Chang, the eunuch convinced Empress Dowager Lung Yu to order the actor beaten with forty strokes of the whip "for failing to exert his best talent in her presence." Eunuch Chang also persuaded the dowager to sanction his expenditure of huge sums to completely refurbish one of the imperial palaces. No court official was allowed to supervise the contractor's work, estimates for which were drawn up by the eunuch in such a way that the builder could secretly complete construction of Chang's private residence as well.

In the next few years, eunuch Chang filled his elegant mansion with priceless curios filched from various imperial palaces or presented him by the doting dowager. It is said that in his later years eunuch Chang Yuan-fu lived like royalty in a veritable palace within the foreign legation compound. He owned racing horses that competed at the Peking racetrack built by the foreigners. It is also reported that he frequently beat his host of servants so inhumanely for the slightest infraction that, when one of them fled to the British police for protection and was promptly returned to his master, eunuch Chang had him beaten to death.

Through these years the boy-emperor Pu Yi sat on the defunct Manchu throne and grew into young manhood confined in an imperial palace filled with corruption and graft. Later, in his diaries, Pu Yi wrote, "Eunuchs waited on me when I dined, dressed, and slept; accompanied me on walks and at my lessons; told me stories and played with me. They never left my presence and were the main companions of my childhood, and were both my slaves and my earliest teachers."[5]

As a teenager, Pu Yi decreed that his personal chief eunuch, Chang Chien-ho, be elevated to the level of official second class, as had been Tzu Hsi's old powerful eunuch Li Lien-ying. Pu Yi wrote that eunuch Chang Chien-ho was his first tutor and personal companion, who entertained him at childish games at which the emperor was always allowed to win. He also wrote regretfully that he grew up falsely convinced by those around him that he was all-powerful, the Son of Heaven, above and beyond ordinary men. Thus he was pampered and spoiled, unpunished for fits of temper or cruelties to his eunuchs, whom he had severely punished for minor violations such as bringing him chicken pies when pork had been ordered. He enjoyed humiliating his underlings, once forcing a young eunuch to ride his English-made bicycle through the halls of the palace, laughing wildly when the eunuch weaved about in terror and finally crashed to the floor. In 1923 Pu Yi, at seventeen, devised a plan to flee from Peking. The attempt failed when one of his eunuchs—though he had been handsomely bribed to maintain secrecy—betrayed his imperial master by revealing the plan to the emperor's father.

Because the new Republican government was often unable to pay the yearly stipend promised to the Manchu court, Pu Yi and his courtiers found it necessary to sell some of the treasures in the imperial storerooms. Though elaborate inventories had been maintained, many items existed only on paper—probably they had been stolen. So, in 1923, great was Pu Yi's consternation and anger when he called for certain pieces from the inventories and found them missing. The thoroughly frightened eunuchs, to hide the scope of their widespread thievery, set the Palace of Established Happiness afire. Great quantities of irreplaceable antiques and works of art were ruined, including 2,500 gold images of Buddha and thousands of old Buddhist paintings. The great store of gold and silver ingots shown on the inventories—which should have survived the fire—had completely vanished.

Exasperated, Pu Yi told his father of his determination to abolish the ancient eunuch system. The thought of such drastic action threw the regent into a state of hysteria, but he finally had to give way to the emperor. For fear that if the eunuchs learned in advance of the plan, they might commence wholesale looting and burning, it was kept a close secret. When it was to be announced, under the watchful eyes of Republican soldiers, hundreds of eunuchs were assembled in a main palace courtyard. They stood in stunned silence as they heard of their dismissal. Then they were herded to the parade ground near Prospect Hill, where the people of Peking thoroughly enjoyed the spectacle of the "palace rats" seated in disconsolate groups awaiting their turn to be allowed back into the palace by twos and threes to collect their personal belongings and monies due them.

Only about fifty eunuchs were allowed to stay on in the palace. These were the chamberlains of three surviving old concubines of preceding emperors. Fat and spoiled by lives of luxurious idleness, the concubines pleaded that they could never manage without their eunuch servants. When one of these aged ladies died late the following year, her rapacious eunuch attendants took merciless advantage of her even in death by stealing all her possessions.

In 1924 Emperor Pu Yi was driven from the palace by a powerful warlord into the hands of the Japanese. The pitiful story of his life thereafter is too well known to be repeated here. He died as a common citizen in China in 1987.

In 1981 an American news correspondent in Peking, Michael Weisskopf, interviewed an eighty-year-old eunuch named Sun Yao-ting, one of the last three survivors of the eunuchs who had been dismissed in 1924 from the Forbidden City.[6] This eunuch had been castrated by his father at age ten—his destitute family was too poor to pay for the services of "little-knife Liu" who ran the court-sanctioned eunuch clinic outside the palace gates. Though he lost consciousness during the crude home surgery and could not walk for two months, he considered himself lucky to have been taken into the palace at age sixteen, for the waiting list of eunuchs was very long in those troubled times of 1916. Eunuch Sun Yao-ting was trained in court etiquette and became the favorite of emperor Pu Yi's teenage consort, romping about the palace entertaining her with games such as hide-and-seek.

After the eunuch system was abolished, life outside the palace was difficult for the dismissed eunuchs. They were taunted on the streets, and many were forced into beggary. Some were able to exist for the next twenty-five years in the eunuch's Green Dragon temple compound, though in dire poverty. In 1949, when the Communists seized power in China and nationalized the eunuchs' temple, the thirty surviving former palace eunuchs, including Sun Yao-ling, were given state jobs as maintenance workers or clerks, and lived privately in virtual seclusion.

Thus ended without fanfare the eunuch system that for 3,000 years had been such a potent and perilous element in Chinese imperial rule.

Notes

1. Marina Warner, *The Dragon Empress.*
2. Wm. J. Duiker, *Cultures in Collision: The Boxer Rebellion.*
3. N. J. Iröns, *The Last Emperor.*
4. Bland and Backhouse, *Annals and Memoirs of the Court in Peking.*
5. N. J. Iröns, *The Last Emperor.*
6. Michael Weisskopf, "Imperial Court Eunuch, Ward of State," *Houston Chronicle,* November 19, 1981.

APPENDIX

The Need for Eunuchs, How They Were Castrated, and Their Lifestyle

Throughout this book, little has been said about the way in which Chinese males were castrated for palace service. Almost nothing was written on the subject in Chinese histories. However, in the late 1800s a British official stationed in China, George Carter Stent, published a paper giving more information on this subject than was ever before generally known in the Western world.[1] Although his study of palace eunuchs was made late in imperial rule, the eunuchs' clinic which he describes is known to have existed in the preceding Ming Dynasty, and it is assumed that many of its methods were in use long before the Ming era.

In Stent's time there were only around 2,000 eunuchs employed in the Forbidden City, for the Manchu emperors had been determined to keep their numbers down. Another reason for the relatively reduced numbers of eunuchs may have been that during the previous fifty years, the Manchu Dynasty was ruled by a regent, Empress Dowager Tzu Hsi, for two successive little boy-emperors, which would have considerably lessened the need for concubines.

Besides the eunuchs in the imperial palace, the numerous princely sons and married princesses of Manchu rulers were allowed to keep thirty eunuchs each in their private establishments. Imperial nephews and younger unmarried princes had to make do with twenty eunuchs, and grandsons with ten. Sons born to lesser concubines could employ four to six eunuch servants. During Manchu times, the only other persons allowed to employ eunuchs were all the numerous descendants of the eight Manchu banner chieftains who had originally assisted in establishing the Ching Dynasty in the 1600s: they were allowed twenty eunuchs each. All these dignitaries were not only entitled to use eunuchs, but were compelled to do so, or lose their rank for failing to keep up the dignity of their Manchu station.

Every fifth year, each princely son was required to furnish the Manchu palace with eight young eunuchs who had been well trained, inspected for proper castration, and declared free of disease or uncleanliness in person. The palace paid 250 taels to the princes for purchasing and training each eunuch. Since this system did not nearly supply the numbers of eunuchs required by the palace, grown men could voluntarily have themselves castrated, but to be accepted for service at the palace, they had to find someone to vouch for their character, and they invariably ended up with menial jobs that did not necessitate entrance into the imperial ladies' apartments. Large numbers of young boys, purchased from their families, were castrated and drafted into the palace where they were especially favored by harem ladies as pets and companions.

All eunuchs were thought of as "pure," but those under ten years of age were termed "thoroughly pure." These were prized by palace ladies and given as much freedom and familiarity as if they were girls, and allowed to perform bedroom and bathroom duties of the most intimate nature. Boy eunuchs were supposedly free of any licentiousness, even in thought. As they grew older they were replaced by younger eunuchs and given duties outside the ladies' quarters.

Just outside the Forbidden City gate, but within the Imperial City, was a run-down building where several "knifers," who were recognized by the government as qualified to perform castrations, though they received no government salary, plied their trade. Theirs was a hereditary, family profession. They collected six taels for each surgery and nursing the eunuch through the initial stage of recovery.

When the surgery was about to take place, the candidate was placed on a low bed in a semireclining position, and asked once more if he would ever regret being castrated. If the answer was no, one man clasped him about the waist while two others separated his legs and held them firmly down to prevent any movement. Tight bandages were wound around the thighs and lower abdomen, the patient was given a bowl of "nerve-stunning" herbal tea, and his private parts were desensitized with baths of hot pepper water. Both penis and testicles were then swiftly cut off with a small curved knife as closely as possible to the body. A metal plug was immediately inserted into the urethra, and the entire wound covered with water-soaked paper and carefully bandaged. Immediately thereafter, the eunuch was made to walk about the room for two or three hours supported on each side by the "knifers" before he was allowed to lie down. He was not allowed to drink any liquid for three days, during which time he suffered great agony from thirst and extreme pain, and was unable to urinate. At the end of three days, the bandages were removed, the inserted plug pulled out, and hopefully the sufferer was able to obtain relief with a copious flow of urine, at which time he was congratulated and considered out of danger. If the surgery rendered the eunuch unable to urinate, the passages having grown closed, he was doomed to an agonizing death.

It is claimed that eunuchs rarely died from the crude surgery, only about two cases in a hundred proving fatal. This is not difficult to believe, for if the fatality rate had been high, it is unlikely that thousands of males would have chosen this means to try to improve their economic status.

When thoroughly recovered, usually in two or three months, and after perhaps a year of training in princely establishments, they were transferred to the imperial palace where they were again closely examined by old, experienced eunuchs to ascertain that they had been rendered completely sexless.

The severed parts, euphemistically called the *pao,* meaning the "precious," were preserved in a hermetically sealed vessel, and were highly valued by the eunuch. They were always placed on a high shelf to symbolize that the owner should rise to high rank. The eunuch also treasured his "precious" because, to be promoted to a higher grade, he was obliged to first display his emasculated parts and be reexamined by the chief eunuch. If his "precious" should be lost or stolen, at promotion time he had to buy one from the eunuch clinic, or he could borrow or rent one from another eunuch. It was also vital that the eunuch's organs be placed in his coffin at his death in the hope of hoodwinking the gods of the underworld into believing that he was a complete man: otherwise he was doomed to appear in the next world as a she-mule.

Besides the hundreds and sometimes thousands of eunuchs employed in household and harem duties, a few were "ordained" to become one of the eighteen Lamaist priests which the palace maintained expressly to attend to the spiritual welfare of the female inmates. Though often as not the chosen eunuchs could neither read nor write—and knew nothing about the craft of priesthood—they earned a double salary. Needless to say, vacancies among the eunuch lamas were filled without delay.

Another some 300 eunuchs were employed as actors and singers in the ever popular palace theatricals. Eunuch performers lived outside the palace in the Imperial City on small salaries, but were accustomed to receive gratuities from their imperial audiences for especially pleasing performances.

Eunuchs who ran away from the palace were invariably caught by special police and returned to the Forbidden City. First-time offenders were imprisoned for two months, given twenty blows of the bamboo or whip, and sent back to duty. Those who deserted a second time were put in a *cangue* for two months—a large wooden frame that clamped around the neck, preventing lying down or feeding oneself. Third-time defectors were banished to Manchuria for two-and-a-half years, as were eunuchs who were caught in thievery. If the stolen goods were valued by the emperor, however, the offender was beheaded at a special grounds about ten miles from Peking. Neglect of duty or laziness were punished by whippings. The chief eunuch summoned one eunuch from each of the forty-eight household departments to administer the whipping with bamboo rods. The culprit received 80 to 100 blows and was then sent to a doctor—also a eunuch—to have the wounds dressed. After three days, the offender was again flogged, in a punishment called "raising the scabs."

Eunuch salaries in the late 1800s usually ranged from two to four taels a month. Twelve taels was the highest pay allowed to eunuchs of any rank. In addition, each eunuch received a quantity of rice each month. Groups of eunuchs banded together to organize messes, each donating food as needed. The cooking was done in the palace kitchens. The eunuchs lived in small huts, called "menials' houses," attached to the sides of main buildings where their employers resided and where the eunuchs could be readily summoned. Each of the myriad of courtyards in the Forbidden City had a colony of eunuchs.

Palace eunuchs were allowed to worship in the temples, to burn incense, practice fasting, and donate money and offerings, but they were prohibited from ascending the altar of the main deity, as were all cripples, deformed persons, those lacking an eye, limb, or any other body part, and menstruating females.

Eunuchs were easily recognizable by their high falsetto voices (for which they were derisively called "crows"), as well as their want of beards, their cringing, hang-dog demeanor, and often their bloated appearance—though in old age they invariably became thin and deeply wrinkled, making them look like old women. Low-ranking eunuchs wore a long grey robe under a shorter dark blue coat, and had to wear their official hats and boots when on duty. In olden times, high-ranking palace eunuchs wore ornate robes of brilliantly embroidered colors.

Eunuchs had such a peculiar walk that they could easily be recognized at great distances. They characteristically leaned slightly forward, their legs close together, taking short, mincing steps, with the toes turned outward. Whether this odd walk was a physical necessity, or was imposed upon eunuchs as a rule of conduct to denote the eunuchs' station, is not known.

For a long time after castration, many young eunuchs wet their beds and themselves. No notice of this was taken for a time, but a long continuance of the problem resulted in severe floggings, which were continued until the habit was broken or outgrown. Thus, the Chinese spoke of them behind their backs as "stinking eunuchs," and claimed they could smell one a mile and a half away. A common expression used for a normal person who offended the nose was, "He's smelly as a eunuch." The most common and vulgar name for a eunuch was "Old Earl" or "Old Rooster," insulting terms that were never used to the eunuch's face. Eunuchs were so extremely sensitive to any reference to their deficiency, it is said, that such items as a spoutless teapot or a tailless dog were never mentioned in their presence.

Most of the eunuchs' leisure time was spent in gambling among themselves, their greatest source of enjoyment. It is said they were especially affectionate toward women and children, and loved pets, many of them keeping a puppy on which they lavished great affection. As late as the 1920s, one dismissed but fairly well-off eunuch was commonly seen ice-skating on Peking's outdoor rink, displaying miniature Chinese dogs that he sold to foreign ladies to make his living.

Note

1. G. C. Stent, "Chinese Eunuchs," in *Journal of the Royal Society,* North China Branch, no. XI, 1887.

Bibliography

Abbate, F. *Chinese Art*. N.p.: Peerage Books, n.d.

Anderson, Mary M. "The Quest for Immortality." *Echo of Things Chinese,* May 1974.

Balazs, Etienne. *Chinese Civilization and Bureaucracy*. Arthur F. Wright, ed. H. M. Wright, trans. New Haven, Conn.: Yale University Press, 1967.

Barondes, R. *China: Lore, Legend, and Lyrics*. New York: Philosophical Library, n.d.

Behr, Edward. *The Last Emperor*. New York: Bantam Books, 1987.

Bingham, Woodbridge. *Founding of the Tang Dynasty*. New York: Octagon Books, 1970.

Birch, Cyril, and Donald Keene, eds. *Anthology of Chinese Literature*. 2 vols. New York: Grove Press, 1972.

Backhouse, E. T., and J. O. Bland. *China Under the Empress Dowager*. London: Heinemann, 1910.

Bland, J. O., and E. T. Backhouse. *Annals and Memoirs of the Court in Peking*. New York: Houghton Mifflin, 1914.

Bloodworth, Dennis, ed. *The Chinese Looking Glass*. New York: Dell Publishing Co., 1980.

Bosse, Malcolm. *The Warlord*. Linda Grey, ed. New York: Bantam Books, 1984.

Cameron, Nigel. *Barbarians and Mandarins: Thirteen Centuries of Western Travelers in China*. China: University of Chicago Press, 1976.

Chan, Albert. *Glory and Fall of Ming Dynasty*. Norman, Okla.: University of Oklahoma Press, 1982.

Chandrasekhar, Sripati. *Red China: An Asian View*. New York: Praeger Publishers, 1961.

Chang Kwang-chih. *Shang Civilization*. New Haven, Conn.: Yale University Press, 1980.

Chesneaux, Jean. *Secret Societies in China in the Nineteenth and Twentieth Centuries*. Portsmouth, N.H.: Heinemann Educational Books, Inc., 1972.

"China." In *Encyclopedia Britannica*. Chicago: Encyclopedia Britannica, Inc., n.d.

Chou, Eric. *The Dragon and the Phoenix*. New York: Bantam Books, n.d.

Collins, John J. *Primitive Religion*. Totowa, N.J.: Rowman and Littlefield, 1978.

Coomaraswamy, Anada K. *Hinduism and Buddhism*. New York: Wisdom Library, 1943.

Couling, Samuel. *Encyclopedia Sinica*. 1917. Rpt. New York: Coronet Books, 1988.

Creel, Herrlee G. *The Birth of China*. New York: Frederick Ungar Publishers, 1954.

Crow, W. B. *Witchcraft, Magic, and Occultism*. N. Hollywood, Calif.: Wilshire Book Co., 1982.

Day, C. B. *Chinese Peasant Cults*. Taipei, Taiwan: Cheng Wen Publishing Co., 1969.

DeWoskin, Kenneth J., trans. *Doctors, Diviners, and Magicians of Ancient China*. New York: Columbia University Press, 1983.

Doolittle, J. *Social Life of the Chinese*. Taipei, Taiwan: Cheng Wen Publishing Co., 1966.

Duiker, William J. *Cultures in Collision*. Novato, Calif.: Presidio Press, 1978.

Dun, J. Li. *The Ageless Chinese: A History*. New York: Scribners, 1978.

———. *The Civilization of China: From the Formative Period to the Coming of the West*. New York: Scribners, 1975.

———. *Essence of Chinese Civilization*. New York: Van Nostrand Reinhold, 1967.

Durant, Will. *Age of Faith*. Story of Civilization Series. New York: Simon and Schuster, 1950.

———. *Our Oriental Heritage*. Story of Civilization Series. New York: Simon and Schuster, 1935.

Eberhard, Wolfram. *A History of China*. Berkeley, Calif.: University of California Press, 1977.

———, trans. *Folktales of China*. Chicago: University of Chicago Press, 1965.

Elegant, Robert. *Manchu*. New York: Fawcett Crest, 1980.

Er Si et al. *Inside Stories from the Forbidden City*. Zhao Shuhan and Er Si, trans. San Francisco, Calif.: China Books, 1986.

Fairbank, John K. et al. *The Cambridge History of China*. Vols. 10–13. New York: Cambridge University Press, 1980.

———. *Chinabound: A Fifty Year Memoir*. New York: Harper and Row, 1983.

———, ed. *Chinese Thought and Institutions*. Chicago: University of Chicago Press, 1967.

Ferm, Virgilius. *Encyclopedia of Religion*. 1945. Rpt. New York: Philosophical Library, 1976.

Fitzgerald, C. P. *China: A Short Cultural History*. New York: Praeger Publishers, 1985.

———. *History of China*. Boston: American Heritage Publishing, n.d.

Fitzgerald, C. P. *Southern Expansion of the Chinese People.* New York: Praeger Publishing, n.d.

Gernet, Jacques. *Ancient China.* Berkeley, Calif.: University of California Press, n.d.
———. *Daily Life in China on the Eve of the Mongol Invasion, 1250–1276.* Stanford, Calif.: Stanford University Press, 1962.
———. *A History of Chinese Civilization.* New York: Cambridge University Press, 1987.
Giles, H. A. *China and the Manchus.* New York: Cambridge University Press, 1987.
Goodrich, L. Carrington. *A Short History of the Chinese People.* New York: Harper and Row, 1982.
Granet, Marcel. *Chinese Civilization.* 1930. Rpt. New York: Alfred A. Knopf, 1974.
Grousset, Rene. *A History of the Chinese People.* P. Geuthner.
———. *The Rise and Splendour of the Chinese Empire.* Berkeley, Calif.: University of California Press, 1953.

Haldane, Charlotte. *The Last Emperor of China.* Constable, n.d.
———. *The Last Great Empress of China.* Constable, n.d.
Han Suyin. *The Birdless Summer.* London: Academy Chinese Publishers, 1985.
———. *The Crippled Tree.* London: Academy Chinese Publishers, 1985.
———. *Destination Chungking.* London: Academy Chinese Publishers, 1985.
———. *A Mortal Flower.* London: Academy Chinese Publishers, 1985.
Headland, I. T. *Court Life in China.* Old Tappan, N.J.: Fleming H. Revell Co., n.d.
Hedin, Sven. *Jehol, City of Emperors.* 1933. Rpt. New York: E. P. Dutton, 1981.
Heren, Louis. *China's Three Thousand Years.* New York: Collier's Books, 1973.
Hibbert, C. *The Dragon Wakes.* White Plains, N.Y.: Longman, n.d.
Hirth, Frederick. *Ancient History of China to the End of the Chou Dynasty.* New York: Columbia University Press, 1979.
Huang, Ray. *Ming Dynasty in Decline.* New Haven, Conn.: Yale University Press, 1981.
Hucker, Charles O. *The Censorial System of Ming China.* Stanford, Calif.: Stanford University Press, 1966.
———. *China's Imperial Past: An Introduction to Chinese History and Culture.* Stanford, Calif.: Stanford University Press, 1975.
———. *Chinese Government in Ming Times: Seven Studies.* New York: Columbia University Press, 1969.
Hughes, Robert. "When Britain Pushed Opium." *Asia Magazine,* Dec. 3, 1972.
Hummel, Arthur W., ed. *Eminent Chinese of the Ch'ing Period, 1644–1912.* 1944. Rpt. New York: Coronet Books, 1988.

Iröns, N. J. *The Last Emperor.* London: House of Fans, 1983.

Jing-shen Tao. *The Jurchen in Twelfth Century China: A Study of Sinicization.* Seattle, Wash.: University of Washington Press, 1977.

Jugel, Ulrike. *Politsche Funktion und Sociale Stellung Der Eunuchen Zur Spateren Hanzeit.* Weisbaden, West Germany: F. S. Verlog, 1976.

Lai, T. C. *Things Chinese.* London: Swindon Book Co., 1971.

———. *The Eight Immortals.* London: Swindon Book Co., 1972.

Langlois, John D., ed. *China Under Mongol Rule.* Princeton, N.J.: Princeton University Press, 1981.

Latourette, K. S. *The Chinese: Their History and Culture.* New York: Macmillan, 1960.

Lee, H. T. *The Story of Chinese Culture.* Taipei, Taiwan: H. T. Lee, 1964.

Legge, James. *The I Ching.* Second edition. Mineola, N.Y.: Dover Publications, 1899.

Levy, H. S. *Harem Favorites of an Illustrious Celestial.* Pasadena, Calif.: Oriental Book Store, 1957.

Li Ung Bing. *Outlines of Chinese History.* Taipei, Taiwan: Cheng Wen Publishing Co., 1926.

Loewe, Michael. *Imperial China.* New York: Praeger Publishers, n.d.

———. *Crisis and Conflict in Han China: Fourteen B.C. to A.D. Nine.* Winchester, Mass.: Allen and Unwin, 1975.

MacFarquhar, Roderick. *The Forbidden City.* New York: Newsweek Book Division, 1973.

Mackay, George L. *From Far Formosa: The Island, Its People and Missions.* Old Tappan, N.J.: Fleming H. Revell, 1972.

Mackerras, Colin, ed. and trans. *The Uighur Empire According to the T'ang Dynastic Histories: A Study in Sino-Uighur Relations, 744–840.* Columbia, S.C.: University of South Carolina Press, 1973.

Martin, Desmond. *The Rise of Chingis Khan.* Taipei, Taiwan: Rainbow Bridge Press, 1970.

Marton, Andrew. "Historic Vatican Documents Shown." *Houston Chronicle,* July 23, 1981.

Maspero, Henri. *China in Antiquity.* Frank A. Kierman, Jr., ed. Amherst, Mass.: University of Massachusetts Press, 1979.

Meskill, John, ed. *An Introduction to Chinese Civilization.* New York: Columbia University Press, 1973.

Mitamura, T. *Chinese Eunuchs.* Tokyo: Charles Tuttle, 1970.

Myers, Ramon H. *The Chinese Economy: Past and Present.* Belmont, Calif.: Wadsworth, 1980.

Parker, E. H. *A Thousand Years of Tartars.* New York: Barnes and Noble, n.d.

Parsons, James B. *Peasant Rebellions of the Late Ming Dynasty.* Tucson, Ariz.: University of Arizona Press, 1970.

Pearl, Cyril. *Morrison of Peking.* Topsfield, Mass.: Angus and Robertson, n.d.

Polo, Marco. *The Travels of Marco Polo.* Manuel Komroff, ed. New York: Liveright, 1953.

Rathbun, H. W. *Echoes of Chinese History.* Tokyo: Charles Tuttle, 1967.
Reischauer, E. O. *Ennin's Travels in Tang China.* New York: Ronald Press, 1955.
Reischauer, E. O., John K. Fairbank, et al. *East Asia: Tradition and Transformation.* Boston: Houghton Mifflin, 1977.
Rideout, J. K. "Rise of the Eunuchs During the Tang Dynasty." *Asia Minor,* New Series, Vol. I (1949–1950) and Vol. 3 (1952).

Schafer, E. H. *Ancient China.* Great Ages of Man Series. Alexandria, Va.: Time-Life Books, 1967.
Senzaki, Ngoyen, and Ruth Strout-McCandles. *Buddhism and Zen.* New York: Wisdom Library, 1987.
Shaw, Brian, and John Must. *China the Great Unknown.* New York: New American Library, 1971.
Smith, D. H. *Chinese Religions.* Orlando, Fla.: Holt, Rinehart and Winston, 1968.
Smith, Richard, J. *China's Cultural Heritage: The Ch'ing Dynasty, 1644–1912.* Boulder, Colo.: Westview Press, 1983.
Spence, Jonathan. *The Death of Woman Wang.* New York: Viking Press, 1978.
———. *Emperor of China: Self-Portrait of Kang-Hsi.* New York: Vintage Books, 1975.
Stent, G. C. "Chinese Eunuchs." *Journal of the Royal Society,* North China, no. XI, 1877.
Stuart, F. S. *Caravan for China.* New York: Book League of America, 1940.
Sun, E'Tu Zen. *Chinese Social History.* John DeFrances, trans. New York: Octagon Books, 1966.
Sung Yu, and R. Dickson. "Brush Strokes from Cathay." *Taiwan China Post,* July–Sept., 1973.

Topping, Audrey. "Tomb Yields Evidence of Culture and Cruelty." *New York Times,* June 25, 1981.
———. "China's Incredible Find." *National Geographic,* April 1978.
Towl, Diane. "The Golden Lotuses of China." *Echo of Things Chinese.* Dec. 1973.
Ts'Ao, Chan. *Dream of the Red Chamber.* Florence McHugh and Isabel McHugh, trans. 1958. Rpt. New York: Pantheon, 1975.
Tsien, T. H. *Written on Bamboo and Silk.* Chicago: University of Chicago Press, n.d.
Tucci, Giuseppe. *Tibet, Land of Snows.* Ann Arbor, Mich.: Stein and Day, 1973.
Tung-tsi, Ch'u. *Han Social Structure.* Jack L. Dull, ed. Seattle, Wash.: University of Washington Press, 1972.
Twitchett, Denis. *Cambridge History of China.* Vols. 3 and 7. New York: Cambridge University Press, 1974.

Van Gulik, Robert H. *Sexual Life in Ancient China.* 1961. Rpt. Atlantic Highlands, N.J.: Humanities Press, 1974.

Waddell, Austine. *Tibetan Buddhism with Its Mystic Cults, Symbolism and Mythology and Its Relation to Indian Buddhism.* Mineola, N.Y.: Dover Publications, 1972.

Waley, Arthur. *Life and Times of Po Chu-I.* Winchester, Mass.: Allen and Unwin, 1951.

———. *The Real Tripitaka.* Winchester, Mass.: Allen and Unwin, n.d.

Wang Chia-yu. *Lives and Loves of Chinese Emperors.* Taipei, Taiwan: Mei Ya Publishers, n.d.

Wang, Elizabeth Te-Chen. *Ladies of the Tang: Twenty-two Classical Chinese Stories.* Glendale, Calif.: Heritage Press, 1973.

Wang Gungwu. *Structure of Power in North China During the Five Dynasties.* Berkeley, Calif.: University of California Press, 1963.

Wang Zhongshu. *Han Civilization.* K. C. Chang et al., trans. New Haven, Conn.: Yale University Press, 1982.

Ware, J. R. *Alchemy, Medicine, Religion of China of A.D. 320: The Nei P'ien of Ko Hung (Pao-p'u tzu).* Mineola, N.Y.: Dover Publications, 1981.

Warner, Marina. *The Dragon Empress.* New York: Atheneum, 1986.

Watson, Burton, trans. *Courtier and Commoner in Ancient China: Selections from the History of Former Han by Pan Ku.* New York: Columbia University Press, 1974.

———. *Records of the Grand Historian of China.* 2 vols. New York: Columbia University Press, 1961.

Weisskopf, Michael. "Imperial Court Eunuch, Ward of State." *Houston Chronicle,* Nov. 19, 1981.

Werner, E. T. *Dictionary of Chinese Mythology.* 1932. Rpt. New York: Julian Press, 1976.

———. *Myths and Legends of China.* 1922. Rpt. Lincolnwood, Ill.: Harrap and Co., 1971.

Wieman, Earl. "The Empress Dowager of China." *Echo of Things Chinese.* Vol. 36.

Wilie, A. *Notes on Chinese Literature.* Taipei, Taiwan: Bookcase Shop, Ltd., rpt. of Shanghai edition, 1867.

Wilhelm, Richard. *History of Chinese Civilization.* London: G. G. Harrop, n.d.

Williams, R. T. "The Fabulous Eunuch." *Echo of Things Chinese.* April 1972.

Winn, Michael. "Following the Trail of Marco Polo." *Smithsonian,* April 1982.

Wright, Arthur F. *The Sui Dynasty: The Unification of China, A.D. 581-617.* New York: Alfred A. Knopf, 1978.